I0836674

AUSABLE CHASM ON THE AUSABLE RIVER.

THE

Military and Civil History

OF THE

COUNTY OF ESSEX, NEW YORK;

AND A

GENERAL SURVEY OF ITS PHYSICAL GEOGRAPHY, ITS MINES AND MINERALS, AND INDUSTRIAL PURSUITS,

EMBRACING

An Account of the Northern Wilderness;

AND ALSO THE

MILITARY ANNALS OF THE FORTRESSES OF CROWN POINT AND TICONDEROGA.

BY

WINSLOW C. WATSON.

ALBANY, N. Y.:
J. MUNSELL, STATE STREET.
1869.

TO THE

HONORABLE AUGUSTUS C. HAND.

ON A FORMER OCCASION WHEN I

Inscribed

YOUR NAME UPON A WORK, I WAS INFLUENCED

BY

CONSIDERATIONS OF RESPECT AND FRIENDSHIP.

IN ASKING

YOUR SANCTION TO THIS VOLUME,

I COMBINE WITH THESE SENTIMENTS A DESIRE TO EXPRESS MY

GRATEFUL ACKNOWLEDGMENTS

FOR THE COUNTENANCE AND AID BY WHICH MY LABORS HAVE BEEN SO EMINENTLY RELIEVED,

AND

FOR SUGGESTIONS TO WHICH SEVERAL IMPORTANT FEATURES OF THE WORK

ESSENTIALLY OWE THEIR EXISTENCE.

THE AUTHOR.

PREFACE.

In the year 1852, I received from the State Agricultural Society of New York, an appointment that required a complete and careful exploration of the county of Essex. In the discharge of that mission I visited nearly every school district in the county; made myself familiar with its natural history, its physical geography, and industrial pursuits, and collected the materials and traditions which form or illustrate its history. The result of these researches was published in the volume of the *Transactions* of 1852, as "The report on the survey of Essex county." That work suggested the present. The predominance, which the circumstances then required, of the agricultural aspect in the report, has been wholly abandoned in the following pages, while the historical sketch has been expanded into an elaborate and connected history of the region. In discussing a subject so affluent and interesting I have found it necessary to prescribe to myself a specific plan. I have attempted to present a minute and continuous account of events directly connected with the fortresses of Lake Champlain and of military operations more remote, of which they were the base; but in referring to movements, in which they were only for the time or incidentally the scene, my pen has been arrested, when the current of events has passed beyond the locality.

The publication of the documents collected in Europe by Mr. Brodhead, under the munificent auspices of the state, has opened fresh and delightful fields to the researches of the student of our colonial history. These rich mines of historic wealth would have remained almost inaccessible to the ordinary explorer, had not the amazing labor and persevering industry of Dr. E. B. O'Callaghan furnished the key that unlocks these hidden treasures, by his exact and perfect index to the massive folios. This invaluable work I have freely used.

I have experienced great and unexpected embarrassments in procuring materials for the account of the services by the troops of Essex county. Stimulated by the conviction, that the progress of a few years must obliterate much of the evidences of their heroic devotion, their toils and triumphs, I have labored with the utmost assiduity and zeal to collect memorials that might form at least a humble initiation of a movement commemorative of their patriotic services. In attempting to place an occasional wreath upon the graves of the gallant dead and to add a few leaves to the chaplets of the living, I have indulged in a labor of love. That some companies and regiments have been more fully noticed than others, should not be ascribed to any unjust or partial preference, but be imputed to the simple fact, that Essex was more largely represented in the former organization, or that my efforts to obtain information have been more successful in some cases than in others. I am conscious that the results of my labors are inadequate, and will prove, I fear, unsatisfactory to the gallant men, whose deeds and sufferings I have endeavored to describe. I have opened a path, which I trust will be pursued by more successful explorers.

In presenting, as far as my limited scope permits, a sketch of the physical geography and natural history of the county, I have not only noticed its native productions and animated nature, but have attempted to describe the remarkable topographical features and imposing scenery, that renders Essex one of the most attractive and interesting sections of the state.

To a notice of the ore beds and mineral wealth of the county, I have devoted a large portion of my volume. Many of the most important of these mines I have personally visited and explored.

I trust, that every reader will give to this portion of the work a careful consideration. The revelation to their minds of a mineral wealth, so vast but still in the infancy of its development, will excite astonishment and warrant a worthy exultation. The account of the industrial resources of the district will be read, I think, with interest and surprise.

I have reproduced in this volume extensively from my former works. Copious extracts from the latter have been recently appropriated by several authors without any acknowledgment I advert to this fact that I may be screened from the possible imputation hereafter, of having pirated myself upon such authors.

I have cited with care, as they occur, the numerous authorities I have used in the progress of the work. I mention, in the same connection with grateful acknowledgments, individuals to whom I am indebted for many acts of courtesy and laborious services in supplying me with valuable original matter which I have largely incorporated in my work.

W. C. W.

PORT KENT, *June*, 1869.

ERRATA.

Page 17, fourteenth line from top, *plumage* printed for *plumes.*
Page 50, seventh line from bottom, *Honiton* printed for *Horicon.*
Page 85, seventh line from top, *hundred* printed for *thousand.*

THE

HISTORY OF ESSEX COUNTY.

PART I.

MILITARY AND POLITICAL HISTORY.

CHAPTER I.

The Discovery.

The territory, now distinguished by the general designation of the valley of Lake Champlain was, for nearly a century, a debatable ground between the powers of France and England. Claimed by each under arbitrary charters or imaginary titles, overrun and subverted in turn by both, and permanently occupied by neither, it derived from the presence of their armies, little amelioration of its primitive savage aspect.

Earlier than this period, the same region seems to have been the frontier between tribes, or confederacies of tribes of aborigines, who waged a perpetual warfare of ferocious extermination. These circumstances, it is probable, had consigned it to desolation, and prevented the occupation of the country by a race which would have been allured to it by the strong attractions to the savage mind, created by the profusion of its game and fish. The possessions of the Indians were apparently most extended and permanent on the eastern shores of the lake. Few vestiges of their existence have been discovered upon its western borders. They appear, however, to have congregated in numerous villages along the lakes and rivers of the interior. The bold and lofty mountains which envelop that region, formed to them a bulwark against the assaults of their foes, while the forests and the streams yielded an abundant supply of their humble wants.

At an epoch nearly contemporaneous with the discovery of Canada by the French, the Roman energies and the extraordinary military prowess of the Mohawks appear to have borne their arms and established their dominion almost to the southern shores of the St. Lawrence. A tradition prevailed in this tribe, that the confederacy in which they always maintained a military supremacy, occupied at one period, the sites of both Montreal and Quebec. Subjugated nations acknowledged their domination from the Connecticut to the wildernesses of the Ohio, and the tribes bordering on the Gulf of Mexico trembled before the terrors of their arms.[1]

In the extraordinary native eloquence which is imputed to the aborigines, the Iroquois were preeminently conspicuous. They possessed an advanced intelligence, which conceived and formed wise and successful social institutions. Their progress in the simple arts that belonged to savage life was as distinguished as their martial science or political supremacy. This people asserted a sovereignty over northern New York, and to their persistent valor we are indebted for the boundary that now separates, in a long line, the domain of the state from the British provinces.[2]

The long and narrow tract of water, known to us as Lake Champlain, was doubtless the war path of the Huron and Iroquois, in their mutual hostile and sanguinary incursions. The mind may readily portray fleets of the Indian war canoes, caparisoned in the gorgeous trappings of barbaric pomp, bounding over the dark and still waters

---

[1] The French "taking advantage of the Indians being abroad as far as Cape Florida, at war, came down and burnt a castle of the Maquaes," etc.—*Governor Dongan's Report*, 1687.

[2] Bancroft.

of the lake, while the paddles kept tune to the cadence of their war songs; or gliding stealthily along the silent shores, upon their mission of rapine and blood. The Indian in reference doubtless to the fact that it afforded an avenue and facility to their reciprocal attacks, gave to the lake the impressive and appropriate name of *Caniadere guarante*, i. e. *The lake that is the gate of the country.*[1] An ally of the Hurons, Champlain, accompanied them in one of these incursions, and revealed to the civilized world the beautiful lake which has immortalized his own name.

France entered with ardor and enthusiasm into the great struggle of the age, the field of exploration upon the new continent. The zeal and enterprise of the fishermen of Normandy has already discovered and penetrated the gulf of St. Lawrence. Cartier, a French adventurer, entered in 1534, the mighty river of that name. The succeeding year, he guided to his new discovery, under the auspices of the royal government, a fleet, freighted with many of the young nobility of France, and blessed by the prayers and sanctions of the church. They departed in high hopes and with brilliant auguries to colonize this new France. Ascending the majestic stream, which was called *Hochelaga*, by the natives, but named from its mighty estuary, by Cartier, the St. Lawrence, they moored at what is now known as the Isle of Orleans. Cartier, from this point penetrated to the Indian town of Hochelaga, and to this he gave the name of Mont-Royal, the beautiful and opulent Montreal of modern times. In his progress up the St. Lawrence, he was greeted by the simple-minded and confiding natives with all the demonstrations of joy and festivity known to savage homage. Hochelaga was the chief town of a populous nation which occupied both banks of the river, and extended their possessions far below Quebec. From their dialect and insti-

---

[1] *Documentary History. Petaonbough,* signifying *a double pond or lake branching out into two,* is another aboriginal appellation, probably referring to its connection with Lake George.—*R. W. Livingston, Esq.*

tutions it has been inferred, that they were a branch of the Iroquois. The arrival of Cartier was celebrated by a multitude of the people, who poured forth from the palisades of their capital to meet him on the shore of the island, bearing the offerings of their joyousness and hospitality. Large openings in the forest had been formed by their rude toils, and here luxuriant crops of maize attested their industry and the fertility of the earth.

At Hochelaga, Cartier listened to the Indians' vague and shadowy tales of an unexplored region of lakes, of mountains and delightful plains. He ascended an eminence that arose from the centre of the island and from its summit, the first of civilized men, gazed upon the majestic and beautiful scenery that enraptured his vision. The broad stream, the islands that gemmed it, the cultivated fields of the Indians were before him, and far to the south beyond the glittering river, and the sea of forests that spread on every side, his eye rested on the mountains of Vermont and New York. The ensuing winter was passed by the adventurers at the Isle of Orleans amid intense sufferings from the rigors of the climate and the presence of disease.

Having taken possession of the country, with all the prescribed pomp and formulas of chivalry and religion, the colonization was abandoned and the expedition returned early in the season, to the mother country. On the previous voyage, Cartier had kidnapped and carried to France, two Indian youths, who now served him as guides in the exploration of the unknown Hochelaga. Emulating the infamy of the Spanish conquerors, when returning from his last voyage, he inveigled into his vessel Donnegana, the chieftain, who had proved a generous host and firm friend, and bore him with several of his nobles, into a hopeless captivity, in a strange land, and to death. This exploration ended thus inauspiciously, and the climate and country presenting to the children of sunny France, so few allurements, all schemes of further colonization seem to have slumbered, for several years. The Lord of

Roberval received in 1540 a commission from the French king, conferring on him an immense and almost illimitable territory, and which dignified him with the plenary powers of vice-royalty.

This parchment title and these titular functions overshadowed a vast region, and extended in every direction along the gulf and river St. Lawrence, comprehending in its wide domain the present limits of New England and Northern New York. The efforts, emanating from this authority, appear to have terminated without accomplishing any progress either in colonization or discovery.

During the half century succeeding the failure of Roberval, the subject of New France was unheeded amid the convulsions and conflicts of the religious wars by which the kingdom in that period was torn and agitated. In 1598, another abortive attempt, under governmental patronage, was made by De La Roche, to colonize the region of the St. Lawrence, by disgorging upon its shores the convicts from the dungeons and jails of France.

Private enterprise, unfolding the only just and secure basis of colonization of that region, by associating it with the fur trade, initiated the first successful effort. In 1600, Chauvin had obtained a comprehensive patent, which formed a monopoly of that trade. Repeated and prosperous voyages had been made, and settlements were about being formed, when the death of Chauvin dissolved the organization.

The year 1603 was signalized by the enterprise of Aymer De Chastes and a body of merchants of Rouen, who animated by this success organized a new company with similar purposes, which was rendered memorable by the introduction into the field of his future labors and glory, the founder of the new empire, and the leader who was preeminently great in the long series of brilliant men, that guided and moulded the destinities of new France. Samuel De Champlain was one of those rare and exceptional men who seem to stamp an impress of their own characters upon the age they illustrate and adorn. Champlain was a native of France, and of noble lineage. Peculiarly imbued with the impulsive and impetuous spirit of his country, animated by a bold and reckless courage, rejoicing in dangers and toils, his intuitive sagacity enabled him to surmount those obstacles that his intelligence and prescience could not anticipate and avoid. Enthusiastic, persevering and indefatigable in his purposes, he devoted all the powers of his active mind and the energies of his nature to the achievement of the great object of his life, the exploration of the wildernesses of the new world, and the creation in their recesses of a new empire to his country. De Soto discovered the Mississippi, but while he found an appropriate mausoleum beneath its dark waters, left no memorial of his name. Champlain, more fortunate, made his discovery a monument, which has perpetuated alike his services and his memory.

A rapid glance at the history of a man so remarkable for his intellectual and moral greatness, for his chivalrous exploits and the vastness of his services, and whose name is imperishably associated with the lake, that is alike the ornament and the commercial power of the district, the annals of which we propose to discuss, is appropriate, and should possess deep interest. His own abundant writings, with the memorials of his cotemporaries and associates, have rendered posterity familiar with events which impart an enduring and brilliant lustre to his name. Champlain was born at Brouage, a seaport situated on the Bay of Biscay. Addicted to an intercourse with the sea by the associations of his boyhood, near the most tempestuous waters of western Europe, he gratified his instincts by a connection at an early age with the royal marine of his native country. Although a catholic by birth and sentiment, he followed in the civil wars of France, the "banner of Navarre." When that cause had triumphed, he received a pension from the gratitude of his liberal but impoverished leader. Too active and ardent to indulge in the relaxations of peace, he conceived the design of a personal exploration of the colonial possessions of Spain, and to thus obtain a knowledge of their condition and resources, which was studiously veiled from the world by the jealous policy of that government. His scheme was sanctioned by the wise and sagacious head of the French administration. Through the influence of a relative in that service, Champlain secured the command of a ship in the Spanish West India fleet. This singular position, not perhaps in perfect accordance with modern conceptions of professional honor, was occupied two years, and when he returned to France his mind was stored with the most valuable information, and his journal, laded with the results of keen observation of the regions he had visited, was strangely illustrated by his uncultivated pencil. Champlain was unusually impressible by the spirit of the times, which delighted in the marvelous, and his work is singularly disfigured by representations of strange beasts, and accounts of miraculous events, and yet it is marked by his great ability, and by his eminently clear and comprehensive perceptions. He landed at Vera Cruz, penetrated to the city of Mexico, and visited Panama. His journal reveals the bold conception of a ship canal across the isthmus, by which, he says, "the voyage to the South sea might be shortened by more than fifteen hundred leagues." In this grasp of his investigating mind, Champlain anticipated by more than two centuries, the slowly moving projects of the present age.

Returning to the court of Henry, Champlain met De Chartes, who had been a comrade in battling against the league, and who, although crowned by years and honors, had just obtained from the government a patent empowering him to bear the cross, and to extend the power of France into the unexplored wilds of the new continent. Champlain, from his professional ability and great experience would be an invaluable associate, and invited by De Chartes, he promptly and zealously embarked in an enterprise, so peculiarly in conformity with his spirit, and which was destined to attach to his name an immortality.

The intrepid adventurers, embarking in two small shallops of twelve and fifteen tons burden, plunged into the Northern sea. Their voyage was prosperous, and after a surprizingly short passage, they entered the St. Lawrence and at once advanced to Hochelaga. There all was changed. The palisaded city that Cartier sixty-eight years before had visited, was gone, and in place of the dense population he described, Champlain only met a few wandering savages of another race and language. These Indians aroused the deepest interest in his investigating mind, as they delineated in a coarse diagram upon the vessel's deck, the regions along which the immense river flowed, and lakes from whence they traced its source. A new creation was unfolded to the vision of the explorer, and his fancy doubtless reveled in glowing anticipations of future discoveries and conquests, alike of the cross and the lilies of France. When Champlain returned to France, De Chastes, his protector, and the earnest patron of his enterprise, was dead; but the Sieur De Monts, a protestant gentleman of character and high position, was already maintaining his privileges, and preparing to pursue his colonial schemes. Under the broad shield of government patronage, De Monts had obtained an ample patent, conferring plenary commercial rights, with vice-regal powers, over a vast territory stretching its nominal dominion from near Philadelphia on the south, to the forty-sixth degree parallel on the north, with an indefinite expansion, both east and west. Here within its ample border, there was to prevail perfect freedom in religious immunities. The colony which De Monts undertook to guide to New France, was singularly jarring and incoherent in its elements. The gentleman and noble associated with the sweepings of the prisons and convict ships of France, while the disciple of Rome mingled with the followers of Calvin. Such incongruities disclosed strange scenes.[1]

---

[1] Champlain quaintly remarks in his journal: "I have seen our curè and the minister fall to with their fists on questions of faith. I cannot say

De Monts, in the assertion of his assumed sovereignty over this immense territory, made an effort to colonize Acadia, and occupied under this parchment title, a portion of Maine. Port Royal was founded by a companion of De Monts, and was the first European settlement permanently established north of St. Augustine. Champlain was associated with his accustomed prominence and efficiency, in all these enterprises, from 1604 to 1607. In that period he explored the shores of New England south to Cape Cod, which, from the white sand, he named Cape Blanc.[1] With an eye of science and observation, each of the harbors, streams, and estuaries of the coast was examined. He projected from this survey an accurate map and chart, "remaining," as he remarks, a second winter, "in order, with the help of God, to finish the chart of the coast which I had begun." This chart was subsequently published with his works, and is remarkable among the innumerable trophies of skill and industry exhibited by the French in their explorations upon the western continent.

At length, amid the changes and vicissitudes which marked the age, the prerogatives of De Monts were abrogated with the same readiness and ease with which they had been created. Champlain and Pourtraincourt, upon whom De Monts, in his decaying fortunes, had conferred what remained of his franchises, and acting under them, in 1606, made another voyage to New France in search of further discoveries, and with the design of forming a colony, based upon the novel idea of an agricultural settlement. They explored the New England coast still more widely, fought a battle with the natives, on the eastern shore of Cape Cod, wintered in unwonted comfort and luxuriance in their new settlement, and the next year

---

which had the more pluck, or which hit the harder; but I know the minister sometimes complained to the Sieur De Monts, that he had been beaten. I leave you to judge if it was a pleasant sight:

> "And prove their doctrines orthodox,
> By apostolic blows and knocks."

[1] Thoreau.

abandoning their project, returned to France. The tedium of the route was beguiled in the excitable and gay spirit of their country. They instituted the festive order of *de bon temps*, fraternized with their Indian neighbors, and rejoiced in general hilarity and abundance.

In the year 1608, five years after his advent upon the waters of St. Lawrence, Champlain embarked in a more energetic and systematic effort to form a permanent colony upon its banks. He embarked in a small vessel freighted with the elements of an earnest colonization, and bearing the germ of a new empire, accompanied by his former associate, Portgrave, in another vessel, laden with materials adapted to their projected fur trade. Advancing up the St. Lawrence, and examining its shores with a sagacious scrutiny, his judgment discerned, and his military science adopted a bold rocky promontory, at the confluence of the St. Charles with the St. Lawrence, as the site of the capital of that empire, which to his ardent and fertile imagination, was disclosed in the visions of the future, great, glorious, and prosperous. At once, laborers and artizans were actively employed in removing the forests, and preparing materials for the erection of dwellings and other structures. Soon the simple edifices arose, that asserted the presence of civilized man, and established his perpetual domination upon the mighty stream, whose fountains welled up more than eighteen hundred miles in the remote solitudes of the western wilds, and whose volume rolled to the ocean the tribute of more than a million of square miles.[1] Here Champlain erected fortifications formed of timber, for the safety of his infant settlement. A garden sprang up within its protecting walls, under the refined and graceful tastes of the cultivated pioneer. He was not exempt, however, from the usual cares and trials that attend the birth of remote and secluded colonies. A contemplated treachery that compassed his own death, he avenged by a prompt and stern retribution. In the succeeding September,

---

[1] Guyot.

Portgrave sailed for France, leaving Champlain to occupy Quebec with twenty-eight men, until his return in the spring with supplies and additional colonists. What were the occupations of Champlain through the dark and gloomy weeks of autumn, and in the winter rigors of an almost arctic climate? We can only surmise from our own conjectures, and the faint glimmerings of light his journal affords. He tells us, that he trapped foxes, and was amused in watching the futile efforts of the martins to seize the carcass of a dead dog he had suspended from a tree beyond their reach. But in fancy, we may discern him, with active zeal, employed in tracing and illustrating his journals, and wrapt in profound reveries, pondering on the hopes and projects of the future. The Indians gathered about his wooden ramparts; now, with a present supply, yielding to their insatiate habits of gluttony; and now, in the wasting pangs of famine. He doubtless heard their wild legends, and was amused and aroused by their stories of savage warfare with the Iroquois, their hereditary foes, whose far distant country, they described as a fair land, and delineated in their simple art, the lakes and streams which must be traversed to reach it.

Before the dissolving ice and bursting vegetation mitigated their sufferings and presaged the approach of spring, the scurvy, the fell scourge of every northern colony, had desolated the little band; and when Pontgrave's vessel appeared, only eight pale and emaciated survivors remained to rejoice in the relief it afforded. A consultation between the leaders decided, that Pontgrave should remain to guard the safety of Quebec, and that Champlain should pursue the project, which was the dream and purpose of every exploration of the age, and attempt the discovery of an avenue to the eastern world. This hope possibly inflamed the passions, which led him to accept the invitation of the Indians, to unite with them in a contemplated war party, which was intended to penetrate deeply into the regions, upon which his mind had expatiated during the weeks and months of his gloomy seclusion.

In May, 1609, he joined the camp of his savage allies, and while they looked in speechless wonder upon the strange apparition of a steel clad warrior, armed with weapons that discharged the lightning, he witnessed with scarcely less interest the war dances of the Indians, moving by the wild tones of their music, chanting their war songs and brandishing their stone-pointed tomahawks. He engaged at their council fire, attended their war feast, and mingled in all their barbaric rites. These mystic ceremonies performed, they proceeded upon their advance into a hostile and to him an unknown country. Champlain embarked in a small boat with eleven European companions and proceeded to the mouth of the modern Sorel, where the party was augmented by large numbers of savages from the upper lakes; but here dissension arose, and a great part of the Indian warriors returned to their homes. Champlain dismissed to Quebec all but two of his European followers. To these were added a force of sixty Indians, with a fleet of twenty-four canoes. A common or timid mind would have shrank from the appalling view of the future, abandoned by feeble allies, and left almost alone to the resources of his individual courage and unyielding energies, but he saw before him the beamings of glory and honor that awaited the revelation of a new region; he contemplated the rich country, the lakes, the islands, the streams that had been portrayed to his imagination, and he fearlessly and joyously entered upon his dubious mission. Champlain, as he did in all his explorations, gave to the world a minute and graphic account of this expedition, and so exact is his accuracy that the traveler may still trace his route and the scenes he describes. These productions are not alone interesting, as they portray the incidents of a singularly wild and romantic career; but they are of infinite value, as they illustrate savage life and exhibit their primitive habits and tactics when on the war path.

On the 2d of July, the party effected the transit of the Chambly rapids, and, having advanced some leagues up the river, prepared to encamp. A part of the savages, actively engaged in cutting down timber and peeling it to procure bark to cover their lodges, while others were felling large trees to form a temporary barricade. This, Champlain considered very formidable. The side of the encampment next to the river was not fortified, in order to facilitate retreat to the canoes, if necessary. The Indians dispatched three canoes in advance to reconnoitre, and, if nothing was discovered, to retire. Upon this exploration, they wholly depended for safety during the night." Against "this bad habit of theirs" Champlain expostulated, but with little effect upon a confirmed custom. They represented to him, that in war they were accustomed to divide their forces into three parts: one of which hunted to supply provisions; another always ready for battle marched in a compact body; and the other formed the vanguard and advanced in front to scout, and to ascertain the trail of a foe or friends. This they readily determined by certain marks, which the chiefs of the different nations interchanged, and which upon reciprocal notices were occasionally altered. The hunters never advance before the main body, but pursue their duties in the rear and in a direction where they do not expect the presence of an enemy. In this manner they proceed until they approach the enemy's country, when they advance "stealthily by night, all in a body except the scouts, and retire by day into picket forts where they repose." They make no noise nor "build a fire, except to smoke, and eat dried meal which they steep in water."

The second day, the party entered "the mouth of the lake," and saw "a number of beautiful islands filled with fine woods and prairies." "Game and wild animals, abounded on these islands. Passing onward, the lake in its widest expanse burst upon their view, in the beauty and grandeur of its verdant shores, and its emerald islands, embraced in its lofty and rugged mountain ramparts. Champlain describes the larger islands, and the rivers that "discharged into the lake surrounded by fine trees similar to those we have in Franee, with a quantity of vines,[1] "handsomer than I ever saw, and a great many chestnuts."

Referring to the exuberance of the fish in the lake, Champlain related some wild tales of his savage allies. "Continuing their route" on the west side of the lake, he says, "and contemplating the country, I saw very high mountains on the east side covered with snow," and he observed "others to the south not less high but without snow." The Indians informed him "that here were beautiful valleys and fields, fertile in corn, with an infinitude of other fruits, and that this country was inhabited by the Iroquois."[2]

They said, that the country they designed to attack was thickly settled; that to reach it they must pass by a waterfall, thence into another lake; from the head of which there was a transit to a river, which flowed towards the coast. The course of their projected campaign is thus intelligently unfolded to us. We discern a distinct description of their route, by the falls at Ticonderoga; the passage of Lake George, and the Hudson with its intervening transit; and the populous country of the Mohawks. Some village probably upon the banks of the Hudson was the point of their destination, and to become the scene of their ravages.

---

[1] The wild grape vine is yet a striking feature in the natural products of the Champlain valley, where it grows in great profusion, and often attains an immense magnitude, frequently embracing the loftiest trees in its treacherous and serpentine folds, and towering far above them, while its branches spread in every direction along the forest. I conjecture, that Champlain must have confounded the chestnut with the butternut tree, which occurs in abundance and of vast size in those localities. In a careful survey in 1852 of Essex county, I did not find a single chestnut tree growing in a native forest north of Ticonderoga.

[2] The presence of snow upon the mountains of Vermont, none of which exceeds five thousand feet in height, in July is incredible, and Champlain was probably deceived by an optical illusion produced by clouds or mist. I am inclined, however, to conjecture that the words "west" and "east" have been transposed. From the east side of the lake he might have seen the bold and naked peak of Whiteface from which that mountain derives its present name. It is situated in the town of Wilmington, Essex county, and stands out isolated and prominent, with its white summit a conspicuous object, which for many miles may be observed from the lake.

Whatever might have been their purpose, it was abruptly arrested by a hostile apparition, that suddenly crossed their path. Champlain with exquisite power vividly paints the scenes that followed: "At nightfall we embarked in our canoes, and as we advanced very softly and noiselessly, we encountered a war party of Iroquois, on the twenty-ninth of the month, about ten o'clock at night, at the point of a cape which juts into the lake on the west side.[1] They and we began to shout, seizing our arms. We withdrew to the water, and the Iroquois repaired on shore, arranged their canoes together and began to hew down trees with villainous axes, which they sometimes got in war, and others of stone, and fortified themselves very securely. Our party, likewise, kept their canoes one alongside of the other, tied to poles, so as not to run adrift, in order to fight altogether should need be. When in order, they sent two canoes to know if their enemies wished to fight, who answered that they desired nothing else, but that just then, there was not light to distinguish each other and that they would fight at sunrise. This was agreed to. Meanwhile on both sides the night was spent in dancing and singing, mingled with an infinitude of insults and other taunts; such as how little courage they had, how powerless their arms, and this they should experience to their ruin. Ours, likewise did not fail in repartee; telling them they should witness the effects of arms they had never before seen. After they had sung, danced and parliamented enough, the day broke. My companions and I were always concealed but in separate canoes of the savage Montagners.[2]

---

[1] I compress this narrative as far as possible, and hope to preserve the spirit of the text.

[2] This name was applied to all the St. Lawrence Indians, and was derived from a range of mountains extending north-westerly from near Quebec. *Dr. E. B. O'Callaghan's note on Champlain.* The term Iroquois, equivalent to the Five Nations, is used in the translations of Champlain's works to avoid confusion, but was of course unknown at the period of these events. The Mohawks were known as Maquaes by the Dutch, and Agnies by the Canadian Indians. The Iroquois designated themselves Aquanu Schioni, the United People.

"After being equipped with light armor, each took an arquebus and went ashore. I saw the enemy leave their barricade. They were about two hundred men, strong and robust, who were coming towards us with a gravity and assurance that greatly pleased me, led on by three chiefs. Ours were marching in similar order, who told me that those who bore the three lofty plumes were the chiefs, and that I must do all I could to kill them. I promised to do the best I could. The moment we landed, they began to run towards the enemy, who stood firm, and had not yet perceived my companion, who went into the bush with some savages. Ours commenced calling on me with a loud voice, opening way for and placing me at their head about twenty paces in advance, until I was about thirty paces from the enemy. The moment they saw me they halted, gazing at me and I at them. When I saw them preparing to shoot at us, I raised my arquebus and aiming directly at one of the three chiefs, two of them fell to the ground by this shot, and one of their companions received a wound of which he died afterwards. I had put four balls in my arquebus. Ours on witnessing a shot so favorable to them, set up such tremendous shouts, that thunder could not have been heard, and yet there was no lack of arrows on one side or the other. The Iroquois were greatly astonished at seeing two men killed so instantaneously, notwithstanding they were provided with arrow proof armor woven of cotton thread and wood; this frightened them very much.[1]

"Whilst I was reloading, one of my companions fired a shot, which so astonished them anew, seeing their chiefs slain, that they lost courage, took to flight, and

[1] The allusion to this armor presents an interesting and suggestive inquiry. We know of the product of no indigenous plant, which Champlain might have mistaken for cotton. He must have been familiar with that plant. The fact he mentions implies either the existence of a commercial intercourse between the natives of the north and south; or perhaps the Mohawks may have secured the cotton as a trophy in some of their southern incursions.

abandoned the field and their fort, hiding in the depth of the forest, whither pursuing them I killed some others. Our savages also killed several of them, and took ten or twelve prisoners. The rest carried off the wounded. Fifteen or sixteen of ours were wounded; these were promptly cured." These events are portrayed in language, so simple, clear and descriptive that we behold it almost as if the eye rested on the spectacle. We seem to hear the cool and chivalric postponement of the battle; the war songs and chants of triumph and defiance; we witness the skill and cunning of the Hurons, in disguising the presence of their potent allies; we see the marshaling of the hostile bands; the lofty forms of the Iroquois chiefs, decorated with their waving plumage and distinguished by their armor; their astonishment without blanching at the sudden appearance of the Europeans; the intrepid Frenchman advancing in front of the Hurons; the awe and consternation with which the Iroquois see the flash of the arquebus, hear the report and behold their chieftains slain as by the thunderbolt. The scene should demand the tribute of a more graceful art than the uncouth pencil of Champlain. "After having gained this victory they amused themselves plundering Indian corn and meal from the enemy, and also their arms, which they had thrown away the better to run. And having feasted, danced and sung we returned three hours afterwards with the prisoners."

Such was the first meeting of the Christian white man and the pagan savage upon the soil of New York, but its atrocities may be referred rather to the temper of the age than to any individual malignity of Champlain. This event enkindled a hatred towards the Frenchman in the heart of the Mohawks, that was unappeased by the streams of blood that for a century and a half flowed beneath the tomahawk and scalping knife. It is a singular coincidence, and may it not be regarded as significant of the presence and retribution of an overruling providence, that the first aboriginal blood shed by the Christian invader, and shed ruthlessly and

2

in wantonness, was on the soil which in another age, was destined to witness the sanguinary though fruitless conflicts of the mightiest powers of Christendom for the possession of the same territory; that both moistened with their choicest blood, and which neither was permitted permanently to enjoy?

Champlain places the site of this battle "in forty-three degrees and some minutes." Great precision could not have been secured under the circumstances, in his astronomical observations. The place was evidently in the vicinity of Ticonderoga.[1]

Champlain looking forth from the field of battle, upon the placid water that laved the spot, and probably exulting in the pride of even such a victory, thus baptized with innocent blood, named the lake, Champlain. His countrymen in succeeding years would have substituted the name of Mer des Iroquois, but the Anglo-Saxon and posterity averted the wrong—for the latter name was not known to the nomenclature of the Indian—and the lake still perpetuates the memory of its discoverer. On the retreat of this expedition, Champlain was constrained to witness one of those appalling scenes incident to Indian warfare, the torture of a prisoner. This terrific spectacle occurred, it is supposed, within the present limits of Willsboro'. The sufferings of the victim, inflicted in all the intensity and refinement of savage barbarity, which he in vain attempted to avert, were, in mercy, closed by the arquebus of Champlain.

A few weeks later, Hudson cautiously pursuing the tidal waters of the stream to which posterity has attached his name, penetrated to a point within less than one hundred miles of the advance of Champlain, but more than eleven

---

[1] I confidently assume this position, although a somewhat controverted point, from the distinct designation of the place upon Champlain's own map. I feel assured on this subject by several other considerations, which I deem conclusive. He probably saw the falls at Ticonderoga, in the pursuit which succeeded the victory. They had no motive in accordance with the plan of the campaign to have advanced south of that place by the lake.

years elapsed before the May-Flower approached the shores of New England.

The ensuing year, Champlain was again moving amid the voluptuous circles of Versailles, its animating spirit, thrilling and agitating the gay throng by the recital of the wonders of the new world and his own wild and strange adventures. Early in the spring, still under the auspices of De Monts who, although shorn of his vast prerogatives, persisted with unabated ardor in his colonial schemes, Champlain once more crossed the Atlantic. He ascended the St. Lawrence to an island near the mouth of the Richelieu, and while engaged in the orgies of an Indian feast and war dance connected with a solemn council, the approach of a band of Iroquois was announced. All rushed to the assault of the barricade of the foe. The contest was long and bloody, but victory was necessarily with the allies. In accordance with Indian custom this decisive success terminated the campaign, and closed to Champlain all immediate prospect of exploration and discovery. The opening season of 1611 saw Champlain again entering the St. Lawrence. He selected the position and marked out the foundations of Montreal; but fresh obstacles, interposed by the fickle and versatile Hurons, arrested his contemplated advance into the interior. While delayed by these impediments, Champlain, always delighting in peril and adventure, among the first of civilized men, descended the tremendous rapids of St. Louis, in a frail birchen canoe guided by an Indian pilot. But anarchy and ruin were darkly impending over the struggling colony; Henry, his firm and powerful protector, had fallen beneath the knife of Ravillac. Champlain hastened across the Atlantic, his enthusiasm enlisted the sympathy and interest of the nobility, and secured the appointment first of the Count De Soissons, and upon his death, that of the Prince De Condé as guardian and protector of New France, with all the prerogatives of vice-royalty. In 1612 Champlain returned to Quebec, clothed with the power and insignia of sovereignty, delegated to him by De Condé. Allured by wild tales of a vast northern sea beyond the head waters of the Ottawa, Champlain, the next year, with infinite peril and toil, ascended that gloomy and turbulent stream in a light Indian canoe; and there in the deep recesses of the forest, which have even now scarcely been approached by the arts of civilized industry, he dwelt in their wigwams, feasted and danced, harangued at the council fire, and erected the cross. Deceived and disappointed, he reluctantly abandoned the pursuit of the fabulous sea.

Montreal, fostered by the protection and policy of Champlain, was already a trading mart of importance and activity, where the French traders, bearing the products and gewgaws of other climes, assembled to meet the fleets of Indian canoes which descended the Ottawa and St. Lawrence, laded with the spoils of their widely expanded hunting grounds. The interposition of Condé had obtained the grant of a new concession from the government, which conferred on the association of merchants immense prerogatives, confirming the former patent and creating additional immunities, and, in 1615, Champlain, inspired by new ardor, and with an ambition stimulated afresh, embarked, once again, for the scene of his toils and hopes. At this time, equally zealous for the diffusion of the true faith, as he was energetic in promoting the temporal interests of the colony, he induced several Franciscan monks to accompany him. A formal council was held with the tribes gathered at Montreal, and while the Fathers were attempting to inculcate religious truths, Champlain was engaged in maturing schemes more consonant with savage passions. By this rude treaty he agreed to unite with the Indians residing upon the waters of the vast inland lakes, they dimly described, who, invincible in his alliance proposed to descend from their far distant land, like a destroying tempest upon the western tribes of the dreaded Iroquois. Champlain avers that he enlisted in this enterprise "to satisfy the desire I had of learning something about that country." Le Caron, one of the Franciscans, not less determined and intrepid than Champlain, offered alone to accompany the Hurons to their remote wigwams, and the humble missionary was the first European who gazed upon the wide waters of Lake Huron. Champlain, again encountering the perilous navigation of the Ottawa, and threading the long pathway of the Indians reached the Lake Nepissing, and from thence was guided by the Indians to the shores of a majestic sea, whose expanse of waters was alone bounded by the horizon. He contemplated it with wonder and delight, and named it the "Mer-douce," to which posterity, with more aptness, has given the name of Lake Huron. Champlain stood on the northern shores of Huron, a thousand miles from the Atlantic, five years before the foot of the puritan pilgrim rested on the rock at Plymouth. The provident savage hosts had constructed for his use a small cabin. Here Champlain found Le Caron, who had built an altar and erected the cross, and joined by the fourteen Frenchmen who had accompanied them, the mass was said and the Te Deum chanted in this humble temple, and we may conceive, with a solemnity and fervor, that does not always mark the worship of a groined Cathedral.

Amid a national jubilee the Huron warriors gathered from their scattered villages, and embarking their formidable bands in an immense flotilla of birch canoes, they skirted the eastern coast of the lake, bore their canoes over a transit into Lake Simcoe, descending the Trent river entered into the great lake of the Autonoronons, the modern Ontario. They traversed with singular temerity in vessels so frail, its broad waters, and concealing their canoes upon its southern shore, they advanced into the territory of the Autonoronons or Senecas. After marching several days, in which Champlain was revolted by exhibitions in varied and horrid forms of savage barbarity and habits of warfare, they arrived before the enemy's fort.[1] The garrison was

[1] Commentators on Champlain's journal are not harmonious in locating this scene. Some assume it to have been near Lake Onondaga, while others refer it to the vicinity of Canandaigua.

formed by the puissant Senecas, second only among the Iroquois to the Mohawks in power and martial prowess. The works were constructed with an intelligence and science, far superior to any evidences of skill that Champlain had witnessed among the aborigines. The village was enclosed by strong palisades of timbers, thirty feet high, interlocked with intervals of about six inches between, with galleries forming a parapet, defended by timbers "proof against the arquebuses." Gutters were led from a pond of water on one side, which afforded ample facilities for extinguishing fires that might be enkindled against the barricades.

The appearance of the iron clad strangers and the terrific discharge of their unknown weapons, astonished and startled, but excited no craven or panic fears in the dauntless Iroquois. Fighting with admirable valor, they retreated within their fortifications. Under the direction of Champlain, the Hurons constructed a tower higher than the walls with a protection against the arrows and stones of the Iroquois, which was "carried by two hundred of the strongest men and placed within a pike's length in front." On this "were posted four arquebusiers." An effort was made by the Hurons to burn the palisades, but the fire was promptly extinguished. "They went to the water and discharged in it such abundance, that rivers, it may be said, spouted from their gutters." The Senecas, although suffering severely from the arquebuses, fought with an undaunted courage, that extorted the admiration of Champlain, and far surpassed their savage foes in conduct, taunting them with cowardice in enlisting the white men in their quarrels. The science and tactics of Champlain were totally defeated by the perpetual improvidence and insubordination of his Indian allies. "This moved him," he says, "to use some pretty rude and angry words," but he generously remarks: "they are excusable, for they are not soldiers."

The discomfited and intractable Hurons, after a siege of several days, in spite of the expostulations of Champlain, determined to abandon the enterprise and retreat. He,

BATTLE BETWEEN CHAMPLAIN AND THE INDIANS OF WESTERN NEW YORK.

wounded by arrows in the knee and leg, was bound to the back of a vigorous savage, " like an infant in its swaddling clothes," and carried many leagues, until his impatience and suffering revolted.[1]

Although he denounces in bitterness and vexation the absence of discipline, obedience and system with the Indians, he warmly commends the skill they exhibited in effecting their retreat, " placing the wounded and old people in the centre, the warriors without breaking their lines march in front, on the wings and in the rear."

The winter that was approaching, the bold and indomitable pioneer passed in the gloomy lodge of a Huron chief, and in visiting the more remote tribes of the Algonquins; in the care of his wounds, in the reveries of his sleepless mind, and in communing with the savages on the themes which invigorated his energies and continually fired his imagination. But he who had braved death on so many battle-fields and amid the storms of the ocean, nearly lost his life from cold and exposure in the bleak forest of the Algonquins. Hunting on a dark day at the close of autumn without a compass, he lost his course, and wandered nearly three days bewildered in the masses of a trackless wood. When the frosts of winter had transformed the streams and morasses into icy avenues, Champlain again sought the villages of the Nipissings. He found the devout Le Caron in the same solitary wigwam, occupied in his missionary services, arranging a catechism and studying the Huron dialect. With the anchorite, Champlain spent several weeks, and then together, the soldier and the monk stimulated by the same brave and lofty spirit, but wielding far different weapons, visited in remote regions amid the wild recesses of nature tribes of savages before unknown to the Christian world.

Once more restored to active life and civilization, Champlain erected, in defiance of the grovelling cupidity of

---

[1] This is his language: " As soon as I could bear my weight I got out of this prison; or, to speak plainer, out of hell."

superiors, the castle of St. Louis. When the expense was grudged, "It was not best," he said, "to yield to the passions of men, they sway but for a season, it is duty to respect the future." Returning from one of his periodical visits to France in 1616, Champlain bore with him his wife, young and beautiful, whose charms seem to have melted the stoicism of the children of the forest into delighted admiration.

In 1628, he gloriously defended Quebec from an attack of the English, almost without arms or provisions, by the glory of his name and the energy of his courage, and only capitulated his famishing garrison when the last hope of relief had failed. But it was an abortive triumph to his conqueror. Peace soon gave Champlain his liberty, and restored Quebec to France.

Before and subsequent to these events, the checkered career of the explorer had been impressed by perpetual trials, perplexities and vicissitudes, with alternate depressions, and a return to power and position. Vanquishing by his inflexible perseverance and profound sagacity the hostilities of rivals and the evasions of a despotic government, he returned the last time in 1633, to the state his wisdom and zeal had created, invested by Richelieu with all his former prerogatives. Having suppressed the Indian excitement which had agitated his province, conciliated the jarring jealousies and angry feuds of mercenary traders and arbitrary officials, and amply ass erted and perfected the dominion of his sovereign over a vast region, Champlain died in 1635, and is commemorated in the annals of the country he served so ably and with such fidelity as "the father of New France."

Champlain has no peer, either in the brilliant lists of French or Anglo-Saxon discoverers of the age, in the magnitude of his services, the hardy daring of his exploits, in the courage and ability by which he achieved them or the capacious grasp of intellect that moulded the destinies

---

[1] Bancroft.

of half a continent. Twenty times he crossed the Atlantic[1] in tiny shallops from twelve to twenty tons, scarcely equal to an ordinary fishing boat, and with a celerity that is rarely surpassed in the voyages of the present day; he explored boundless forests, penetrated unknown lakes, overcame the turbulence of wild and strange rivers, associated with the savages in every form, encountered dangers and toils in it all their aspects, and gave to his country a domain far more magnificent in its proportions than the territories of the proudest kingdom of Europe. In an age reeking with venality, he never descended from his lofty pursuits to contend for sordid wealth or emolument. Nurtured in a licentious court, even when removed from the restraints of society, his piety and virtue attracted the wonder and excited the reverence of his savage associates. His justice and good faith created an unbounded ascendancy throughout the wide-spread Algonquin tribes, and in after years their love and veneration still lived undiminished for "the man with the iron breast."[2]

CHAPTER II.

Indian and Colonial Wars.

I am not aware that any evidence exists, that the environs of Lake Champlain witnessed the missionary labors of the Jesuits; but we can with difficulty believe, that a region so near and accessible, would have been unexplored by the deep devotion and ardent enthusiasm, which impelled them to bear the cross and to find their neophytes upon the remote shores of Lake Superior.

The policy inaugurated by Champlain and pursued as a cardinal principle by the vice-regal government, in form-

---

[1] Thoreau.

[2] For the materials of this chapter, in addition to the journals of Champlain and his cotemporaries, and the general historians, I am largely indebted to the facts compiled by Mr Parkman, and the views expressed in the glowing and nervous pages of Thoreau.

ing an intimate alliance with the Algonquins, although successful in its immediate object, the cherishing of the union and affections of the tribes of New France, in its results, excited the unyielding feuds and hostility of the formidable Mohawks, and entailed upon the French more than a century of fierce and bloody savage warfare. The western tribes of the Iroquois rarely yielded to the subjects of France, but the stern and implacable Mohawks, never. Between them and France occasional periods of peace or rather armed truces intervened, but at no time did there exist a cordial harmony, when "the hatchet was buried too deeply to be uncovered."

The French government, while it maintained the sovereignty of New France, wielded a powerful influence over all the aboriginal tribes, within its vast limits. The preponderance of England, even in the councils of the Iroquois, was often disputed by France, and rendered by her machinations, precarious and inefficient. The "chain of friendship," between France and the confederacies of the Hurons and Algonquins never was broken or became dim. The gay and joyous manners of the French won the heart of the savage. The solemn grandeur, and the imposing formulas and pomp of the catholic rituals, attracted his wonder and admiration and fascinated his senses, if they did not subdue his feelings. His appetites were pampered, and his wants supplied with a lavish prodigality, the result perhaps of governmental policy rather than that of Christian charity. To the mind of the Indian, these traits of the French were favorably contrasted with the cold, severe, and repulsive habits of the Englishman, with the unimposing forms of his religious rites, and with the close and parsimonious guard the British government held over its treasury and store houses.

The annals of Lake Champlain is a blood-stained recital of mutual atrocities. The feuds of the peoples of Europe and the malignant passions of European sovereigns, armed the colonies of England and the provinces of France, in conflicts where the ordinary ferocity of border warfare, was aggravated by the relentless atrocities of savage barbarism. Each power emulated the other, in the consummation of its schemes of blood and rapine. Hostile Indian tribes, panting for slaughter, were let loose along the whole frontier, upon feeble settlements, struggling amid the dense forest, with a rigorous climate and reluctant soil, for a precarious existence. Unprotected mothers, helpless infancy and decrepit age, were equally the victims of the torch, the tomahawk and scalping knife. Lake Champlain was the great pathway, equally accessible and useful to both parties, of these bloody and devastating forays. In the season of navigation, they glided over the placid waters of the lake, with ease and celerity, in the bark canoes of the Indians. The ice of winter afforded them a broad, crystal highway, with no obstruction of forest or mountain, of ravine or river. If deep and impassable snows rested upon its bosom, snow shoes were readily constructed, and secured and facilitated their march.

Although this system of reciprocal desolation impeded the progress of civilization in the territories of each power, and repelled from the frontier, bordering upon the lake, all agricultural and industrial occupations, both England and France asserted an exclusive right to the dominion of the territory. France based her claims of sovereignty upon the discovery of Acadia, and the gulf and river St. Lawrence, and subsequently upon the discoveries of Champlain. Before that event we have seen, she had conveyed to De Monts a parchment title to the entire region extending to the meridian of Philadelphia. The original charter of Virginia asserted the claim of England to the 45th parallel of latitude, while the other grants extended her sovereignty to the waters of the St. Lawrence. The ultimate acquisition of the title of Holland, by the cession of New Netherlands, fortified these pretensions, which England alleged were matured by the recognition in the treaty of Utrecht, of her paramount sovereignty over the possessions of the Iroquois, or as the

Iroquois assumed a broad and formal protectorate as a trust for their benefit and safety. Blood and treasures were profusely expended in the assertion of hostile claims, founded on these ideal assumptions to a rude and howling wilderness.[1] A long series of ferocious but indecisive wars prevailed between the French and the Iroquois, signalized by mutual woes and cruelties, and by alternations of victory and defeat. To avenge former sufferings as well as to arrest future incursions, the government of New France, in 1665, determined to attempt the destruction of the fastnesses of the Mohawks. The annals of war exhibit scarcely a parallel to the daring intrepidity, the exposure and suffering of that expedition.

The point of contemplated attack was distant almost three hundred miles, and to secure the more perfect secrecy, and an assurance of surprise, the season selected was the most rigorous of winter. "M. Courcelles, the governor of Canada, on the 29th of December, 1665, began his march with scarcely six hundred men, to seek out their inveterate enemies, the Mohawks." The snow that covered the ground, "although four feet deep, was hard frozen." The French were enabled, by the aid of the Indian snow shoes, to march rapidly along this surface. The use of horses was impossible, and it was equally impracticable for the troops, who consisted of about equal proportions of Indians and whites, to carry on an expedition so long and laborious, with their own supplies. "The

---

[1] The clause in the treaty of Utrecht, which bears upon this question and which excited for many years elaborate and angry diplomatic discussions is this: "The subjects of France inhabiting Canada and others, shall in future give no hindrance or molestation to the Five Nations or cantons of Indians, subject to the dominion of Great Britain, nor to the other natives of America who are in friendly alliance with them. In like manner, the subjects of Great Britain shall behave themselves peaceably towards the Americans who are the friends or subjects of France and they shall enjoy on both sides full liberty of resort for purposes of trade." The treaty secures to the Indians, equal freedom, "to resort to the colonies of either power for trade," and then continues, "but who are and who ought to be accounted subjects and friends of Britain and France is a matter to be accurately and distinctly settled by commissioners."— *Doc. Col. Hist.*, ix, 964.

governor caused slight sledges to be made in good numbers, laying provisions upon them, drew them over the snow with mastiff dogs." [1] Thus traversing Lake Champlain, they had at night, no covering but the clouds, the freshly fallen snow, or the boughs of the forest. Surmounting perils and toils like these, the French approached the Mohawk territory; but bewildered amid pathless snows, and exhausted and paralyzed by cold and hunger, they were only preserved from destruction by the active although ill-requited beneficence of a small Dutch settlement, standing on the outer verge of civilization. The potent influence and urgent intercessions of a prominent, although private citizen of Schenectady, averted from the suffering and defenseless Frenchmen, the vengeance of the exasperated Mohawks. It is rare that an individual, who, like Arent Van Corlear, moves quietly along in life without any prominence by official station, or brilliant deeds, secures the universal reverence of both friends and foes, while living, and to his name an honored place in history, by the pure force of probity and beneficence. Deeply loved by the Indians for his integrity and virtues, his influence over them was unbounded, and long after his death, they were accustomed, in their speeches and treaties, as the term of highest respect and reverence known to their hearts, to call the governor of New York — Corlear.[2] His benevolent zeal in the preservation of the forces of De Courcelles, was gratefully acknowledged by the colonial government, and De Tracy, the governor general, with expressions of the warmest regard, urged on him a visit to Quebec.[3] In the year 1667, Corlear accepted a courtesy so marked, and with the purpose of aiding in the negotiation of a peace between the French and Mohawks, accompanied by embassadors of the Iroquois, who, at his request, had received a safe conduct, commenced the long and perilous journey. While making the passage of Lake

---

[1] Relations of the march, etc., *Doc. Col. Hist.*, III, 118.

[2] *Idem*, III, 559, *et passim*. [3] *Idem*, III, 128, 152, *et passim*.

Champlain, "he was drowned by a sudden squall of wind, in crossing a great bay."[1] I have no hesitation in referring to Pereu or Willsboro' bay, in Essex county, as the scene of this catastrophe.[2] The lake, for many years afterwards, was known as Corlear's lake;[3] and localities and the scenes of events are frequently established in documents of the period, by references to the "place where Corlear was drowned."[4] It is an impressive and almost painful commentary upon the practice of the age, as I remarked upon an analogous instance in the life of Champlain, that the purity of Corlear did not shrink, while thus shielded by the mantle of an honored guest, from the very equivocal "promise to perfect the chart of the lake, with the French forts, and how it borders on the Maquais river."[5] We will not resist the emotions of a sad and tender sensibility, when we reflect that this noble and benignant man, on a mission of peace and conciliation, found a grave beneath the waters of Champlain, and within the borders of our own country.

A treaty of professed peace succeeded this event, but it seems to have formed no restraint upon the predatory spirit of either the Mohawks or the French. Two years had not elapsed, when a second expedition, guided by the venerable De Tracy himself, the governor general of New France, assembled at the Isle la Motte in Lake Champlain. Far more formidable than the preceding, it embraced one thousand two hundred combatants, borne by a fleet of three hundred bateaux and canoes, and strengthened by two pieces of artillery, which they transported to the remotest hamlets of the Iroquois.

---

[1] Relations of the march, etc., *Doc. Col. Hist.*, III, 156.

[2] No body of water which he could, in a usual course, have traversed on the lake, corresponds so strictly with this description. I am strongly fortified in my conjecture, by the statement of Dr. O'Callaghan, that an ancient map exists in the office of the surveyor general of the state, on which Pereu bay is named Corlear's bay.

[3] *Idem*, III, 554, 815. [4] *Idem*, 815, 817.

[5] Nichols to Corlear, Jan. 9, 1666, *idem*, 145.

Intimidated by the power of this armanent, the Mohawks abandoned their fortified villages, and "these barbarians were only seen on the mountains at a distance, uttering great cries and firing some random shots."[1] Having planted the cross, celebrated mass, and sung the Te Deum on the spot, "all that remained was to fire the palisades and cabins, and to destroy all the stores of Indian corn, beans, and other products of the country found there." The retreat of the French, from this abortive attempt, was deeply calamitous. Forts were erected at Sorel and Chambly to protect the province from the incursions of the Iroquois by the lake. The Mohawks, wily as powerful, were, by their habits and position, intangible; no blow could reach them. Suddenly bursting in 1689, with great force into Canada, they besieged and captured Montreal, and menaced the empire of New France with utter extinction. This movement averted a contemplated attack upon New York by Frontenac through Lake Champlain, and of a fleet by sea.

In the ensuing winter an event occurred, preeminent even in the atrocities of that warfare for its deliberate and ferocious cruelty. The people of Schenectady, that village whose Christian charity had saved the forces of De Courcelles from an appalling fate, reposed in a profound security. Although warned of impending danger, they had relied for protection upon the intense severity of the season, and an unprecedented depth of snow. A band of French and Hurons, conducted by ruthless partisans, precipitating themselves in a march of twenty-two days along the course of West Canada creek, fell[2] in a winter's midnight upon this doomed and undefended hamlet.[3] A common

---

[1] French report. [2] *Col. Hist.*, v, 656.

[3] This is opposed to the generally received idea that this road was along the line of Lake Champlain. A route by West Canada creek implies an avenue of communication between Canada and the Mohawk valley different from that afforded by the usual line traversed by the French, either from Oswego or by the way of Lake Champlain. The route mentioned possibly had a terminus on the St. Lawrence, near the mouth of the Black river. Writers constantly advert to the use of such an intermediate channel; but their attention does not seem to have been directed to its locality or

ruin involved the entire population. The blood of many mingled with the ashes of their dwellings. Some, half clad, fled to Albany amid the cold and snow, while others were borne into a hopeless captivity.

After perpetrating this massacre, the French made a rapid and disastrous retreat, pursued by the rigors of a destroying climate, and the vengeance of a fierce enemy.

Other sections of the English colonies were visited with similar and simultaneous assaults, tending only to aggravate national animosities, without attaining either military or

---

character. Sir John Johnson, it is stated, when he violated his parole and fled with the mass of his tenantry to Canada, consumed nineteen days, with great exposure and suffering, in traversing the wilderness by some interior line, known to him and the Indians. But no further light is thrown upon a question, which to my mind, is invested with much geographical and historical interest. I will venture the presumption, that, at this period more than one familiar route had been established through the vast primeval forests, which embrace the western confines of Essex county, which still exist essentially in their original gloom and solitudes. No other route would have been available, when both Oswego and Champlain, as often occurred, were in the occupation of a hostile power. The valleys of the streams which flow into the Mohawk and Hudson, and which almost mingle their waters with the affluents of the St. Lawrence, might have been ascended, and the lakes and rivers of the wilderness may have been used with great facility for a canoe navigation. A few trifling carrying places would have interposed only slight impediments, and when closed by the frosts of winter, these waters could still afford a most favorable route of communication. Other avenues through this wilderness were undoubtedly accessible, but my own observation has suggested one which I will trace. The upper valley of the Hudson may have been penetrated, until the line is reached of a small branch, which starting from the lakes in the vicinity of the Adirondac works, finds its way to the Hudson. Passing up the valley along which this stream gradually descends, the inaccessible range of mountains would be avoided. Thence traversing the Indian pass in nearly an imperceptible ascent, the plains of North Elba would be reached and these open upon the vast plateau of the wilderness, along which the Racket rolls a gentle current, adapted to the Indian canoe, to the St. Lawrence. This idea posssibly explains the origin of the modern name which has been assigned to the wonderful structures known to the natives as Otneyarh, the place of stony giants.

Gentlemen of great intelligence and careful observation have assured me that they have noticed evidences in the wilderness of other ancient pathways disclosed by still open tracks, the vestiges of rude bridges and the mouldering remains of coarsely hewn vehicles calculated for manual transportation.

political results. These inflictions awakened the colonies to the perception, that safety and protection depended on concerted action, and that they were strong alone in harmonious union. From such convictions, which at a later period were matured by the convention at Albany, emanated the first idea of an American congress. That body, constituted of delegates from Massachusetts, Connecticut and New York, assembled in 1690 at the city of New York. It was then resolved to combine their efforts for the subjugation of Canada. Massachusetts redeemed her engagement, to equip a fleet to assail the French possessions by sea. New York and Connecticut assumed the responsibility of effecting a descent, by a land force, upon Montreal and the forts upon the Sorel. An army was assembled at Lake George, and a flotilla of canoes, constructed for the purpose, wafted the army, powerful in numbers and appointments, down that lake to Ticonderoga. Transporting their armament to Champlain, they again embarked with high aspirations and in confidence of success. Some further progress was made, when suddenly a defective commissariat, with dissensions and divisions, constrained a retreat, and with it blasted every scheme of the projected attacks. The immense disbursements of the colonies in sustaining these extended efforts, exhausted their feeble resources, and left them almost powerless for the defense of their own frontier.

In this crisis, and during the year 1690, John Schuyler, a name distinguished by a long line of patriots and soldiers, organized a volunteer band of about one hundred and twenty "Christians and Indians," on a predatory incursion, into the French province. Traversing Lake Champlain and the Sorel, in silence and caution, he landed without detection in the vicinity of Chambly. Secreting his canoes and provisions, he penetrated, with a singular temerity and no less singular success, to La Prairie, amid numerous forces of the French, and far within the line of their fortresses. The merciless storm fell upon an unsuspecting rural population, engaged and rejoicing in their harvest. In the fell spirit that characterized these scenes, none were exempted from slaughter or captivity. The "scalps of four women folks," were among their trophies. Dwellings, barns, products of the field, "and everything else which would take fire," were remorselessly consigned to the flames.[1] The next year, Peter Schuyler, a controlling spirit in the colony, and who swayed an unlimited influence over the rude affections of the Mohawks, collecting three hundred whites and warriors of the tribe, daringly pursued the track of his brother, and assailed the same region. With great labor, Schuyler constructed bark canoes at White Hall, and Ticonderoga; some of which were of large dimensions equal to the transportation of twelve men. He traversed the lake slowly and with great caution, advancing, as he approached the object of his expedition, by night. Scouts, formed of whites and savages, were thrown cautiously in advance.[2]

"Resolving," he says, "to attack the fort at daybreak, went to prayers and marched." The firing of alarm guns at Chambly and La Prairie, announced that the French were aware of his approach and prepared to resist. De Collières, the governor of Montreal, had assembled a force of eight hundred men to oppose the advance of Schuyler. In the presence of an enemy so well prepared and formidable in numbers, he was compelled to retreat. This was achieved with great courage and ability, through a series of severe conflicts, continuing from La Prairie to their canoes, in which the French were repulsed with heavy losses. Enveloped by the enemy, Schuyler says: "I encouraged my men and told them, there was no other choice, fight or die they must, the enemy being between us and our canoes." Fight they gallantly did, and bursting through the hostile ranks, that in heavy masses enclosed them, regained their

[1] Schuyler's journals.

[2] The exceeding clearness of vision and watchful observation of the Indians illustrated by an entry in Schuyler's journal. "Our spies told us they saw somewhat like the striking of fire with a flint and steel in a canoe."

flotilla, and having inflicted much injury upon the inhabitants and crops, retraced their steps.[1]

Count Frontenac, impatient under the unyielding hostilities and perpetual ravages of the Mohawks, that no treaties could permanently suppress and no vigilance guard against, determined by a sudden and more efficient effort to extinguish their power in the citadels of their strength. He organized in the year 1689, a force of six hundred French and Indians, and secretly passing Lake Champlain upon the ice, and penetrating the forest burdened with deep snows, assaulted by a complete surprise, a race whose vigilance scarcely ever slumbered. Several of their villages were taken and burnt, and three hundred of the natives captured. But repulsed on a final attack by the unconquerable Mohawks, De Callières commenced a disastrous retreat, followed by the Indians with a merciless vengeance. Peter Schuyler, the ever firm and active friend of the Mohawks, with the militia of Albany, hastily gathered, joined in the pursuit. A violent snow storm and a narrow strip of ice which afforded a precarious passage over the Hudson, and was broken up as their rear crossed, saved the panic-stricken refugees, from the terrible inflictions of savage passions fiercely enkindled. So unexpected was the attack and sudden the pursuit, that the scanty supply of food was soon exhausted, and the savages literally fed upon the dead bodies of their enemies, while the fugitives to sustain life were compelled before they found relief in the borders of Canada, "to eat the leather of their shoes."

To the scope of more extended history belongs the narrative of efforts for the "conquest of New France," protracted for a period of two years from 1709, and extending in their field of operations along the entire frontier from Detroit to the Bay of Fondy, and embracing armaments, both by land and sea. Policy, as well as the exasperated passions of the colonies, aroused all their enthusiasm, and enlisted in support of the project, every energy and

---

[1] Peter Schuyler's journal. *Hist. Col.*, III, 800.

resource. This zeal was neutralized, or defeated by the apathy, the imbecility, or the negligence of the government of England. One provincial army, organized by the colonies for the attack of Montreal, was wasted by disease, while awaiting assistance and supplies from the mother country, which were never received. Another was disbanded when the inadequate naval expedition of England against the French possessions had been unsuccessful.

CHAPTER III.

The French Occupation.

The valley of Lake Champlain appears not to have been occupied until about 1731, either by France or England, with any permanent or tangible possession. France asserted no other than an ideal and constructive title. The claims of England, had, in the interval, been augmented by the cession of New Netherlands, which conveyed a tenure uniformly assumed by Holland, to reach the St. Lawrence, and by the fealty of the Iroquois, who had submitted to the sovereignty of the British monarch the entire environs of Champlain and the recognition of that title by France in the treaty of Utrecht.

The claims of the Iroquois, resting upon the rights of conquest, were necessarily vague and fluctuating, and after the ascendancy of the French interposed an arm of power between the Mohawks and Algonquins, the scope of these claims was repressed and in the early part of the eighteenth century scarcely embraced their original boundaries. Such boundaries, not only as they affected the foreign relations of the confederacy but as between the individual tribes, seem to have been accurately defined. Sir William Johnson, in a letter to the lords of trade, Nov. 13th, 1797, clearly and specifically describes the limits claimed by the

---

[1] *Col. Hist.*, VII, 572.

Iroquois as "original proprietors." Their limits on Lake Champlain were established by a remarkable landmark. "The hereditary domains of the Mohawks, he says, "extends from near Albany to the Little Falls (Oneija boundary), and all the country from thence eastward, &c., north to Rejiohne in Lake Champlain." In another letter Johnson refers to "Regiohne, a rock on the *east* side of said lake," as bounding the northward claim of the Iroquois.[1]

Few tourists traverse Lake Champlain, whose attention is not attracted and inquiries elicited, by the appearance of a dark and naked rock, ascending from the bosom of the waters, almost in the track of the steamer, as she approaches Burlington from the south. In almost the form of a perfect cone, the rock stands thirty feet above the surface, in solitary insulation. Its symmetry of contour is so perfectly maintained below the water line, that vessels may moor almost at its side. No vegetation softens or adorns its aspect, but it stands, gloomy, solitary and impressive. An aspect so remarkable was calculated to evoke the Indian love of the imposing and picturesque, and would have been a marked object in their hunting voyages and hostile expeditions. This is known as Rock Dunder, and I identify it with entire reliance as the Rock Rejiohne or Reggio of Indian annals. I arrive at this conclusion from various proofs, in addition to the views above presented. John Schuyler, in the journal of his expedition in 1691, writes, "advanced from the Crown point towards Reggio, thirty miles distant." Johnson twice refers to it. David Schuyler in a letter to the Earl of Bellomont, August 17, 1700, states "the French guards (sent out from Canada, &c.), met him in a canoe, within the bounds of this government, at the Otter creek eighteen miles, on this side of *Reggio, the great rock*, that is in Corlear lake." These distances were probably mere estimates, but singularly approximate to accuracy. I have consulted with intelligent mariners of the lake, who concur in the statement that no other rock exists in that

---

[1] *Col. Hist.*, III, 802.

section of the lake of a marked or peculiar character. The most conclusive evidence, however, is furnished by a French map of Lake Champlain "prepared about the year 1731, from divers memoirs," and copied into the *Documents relating to the Colonial History*, vol. IX, 1023. Between "the river Ouinouski" (Onion) and "river Aux Loutree" (Otter Creek), directly opposite the position of Rock Dunder there is inscribed on the map, and upon the eastern shore of the lake, the word "Reggio."

I am aware that one fact apparently militates against my theory. The Rock Reggio is described as the northern boundary of the monstrous Dellius grant, and that Rock Dunder does not conform to the seventy miles in length of that patent. Everything connected with that stupendous fraud it is conceded was undefined, inchoate and ambiguous, and I am not aware that the Dellius patent was ever practicably located by its pretended bounds. Modern writers and maps assume Split rock to be the Reggio referred to in that grant. In my judgment there exists insuperable objections to that assumption. Split rock is not strictly an isolated rock, but is a point of a promontory separated by attrition from the main land; is not on "*the east side*" of the lake, and does not conform in its position to the distances mentioned. John H. Lydius, the successor to Dellius, avers in an affidavit made 5th April, 1750, "that the land, as far as the Rock Rogeo belonged to the Mohawks, and is situated about ten leagues north of Crown point." This is very nearly the distance to Rock Dunder, while Split rock is scarcely eighteen miles from Crown point. Lydius continues, "neither hath he ever heard of any other rock called by the Indians Rogeo; Rogeo being a Mohawk word and the name of a Mohawk Indian who was drowned, as they say, in the lake near that rock long before the Christians came among them, from whence the Mohawks call both the rock and the lake, Rogeo." This catastrophe, probably of a distinguished brave, shrouded

---

[1] *Col. Hist.*, XI, 569.

the rock to the aboriginal superstition with an unusual awe and veneration. The rock was a conspicuous object visible in every direction far away upon the waters, and when it was recognized as a prominent landmark in the boundaries of powerful confederacies, it became a point of great interest and importance. The passage of a hostile canoe beyond its shadow might have constituted war. Fancy readily depicts fleets of canoes gathering around its base upon the placid bosom of the lake for conciliation and peace, and the council or sacrificial fire shedding its radiance widely over the waters.

The pretensions of France to the sovereignty of Lake Champlain and its shores, were not alone founded upon the discoveries of Cartier and Champlain, and the extent and distinctness of assumption from title based on such discoveries in subsequent grants, or concessions. France asserted other foundations of claim which were not without plausible pretenses of justice and right. The French diplomatists assumed, that Holland had never, in the exercise of its jurisdiction over the Iroquois, established claims to their territory paramount to the nominal possession of France; and justly asserted that England, in the conquest and cession of the New Netherlands acquired no other or higher title than had been enjoyed by Holland. The commissioners of France at London, in 1687, in a formal memorial, affirmed that all the Iroquois nations concluded, in 1665 and 1666, a solemn treaty with M. de Tracy, whereby they placed themselves under his majesty's (Louis XIV), protection, and declared themselves his subjects.[1] Formal treaties warranting this construction were executed by the western tribes of the confederacy, ratified and emblazoned by their distinctive symbols, but no symbol of the inflexible Mohawk is attached to the compact, although the Oneida embassadors appeared to have assumed to act for them.[2] The language of these treaties was in the illusory and ambiguous terms incident to all similar instruments, and

---

[1] *Hist. Doc.*, III, 507. [2] *Idem*, 122, 125.

subject to constant denial and evasion. These transactions were followed by immediate and perpetual hostilities. An insuperable obstacle to the language of such treaties being available in diplomacy, is established by the clear and obvious fact, that France exercised no powers or protectorate under their sanctions. Whatever may have been the inherent force of these instruments in effecting the right of the other tribes, no basis existed for the pretense, that they authorized any intrusion by France into the hereditary dominions of the Mohawks south of a boundary so distinct and apparently so well authenticated as the land-mark I have described.

The treaty of Ryswick, in 1698, declared that the belligerents should return their possessions as each occupied them at the commencement of hostilities. England forcibly alleged, that at the period contemplated by the treaty, the Iroquois, their allies, were in the occupation by conquest of Montreal and the shores of the St. Lawrence, and therefore entitled to retain possession of that territory. The French government seems to have recognized the theory, that the Iroquois were embraced in the provisions of that treaty.[1] Such were the jarring and complicated assumptions of European powers to the homes and dominion of the aborigines, where they had so recently exerted all the prerogatives of empire and of freedom. When France denied the claims of England and appealed to "the council fire at Onondaga," the stern savage orator replied: "We have ceded our lands to no one, we hold them of Heaven alone."[2] The verdict of common history has established the conclusion, that in the intrusion of France upon the domains of the Mohawks on Lake Champlain, at the sacrifice of so much blood and treasure, justice and the restraints and faith of treaties were subordinated to the lust of power and expediency.

Whilst neither power yielded its dominion to the other, each felt the extreme importance of securing the ascend-

---

[1] Louis XIV to Callières, 27th April, 1699, *Hist. Doc.*, IX, 598. [2] Bancroft.

ancy upon Lake Champlain. The command of that avenue shed over the colonies of the government which held it, a broad and ample protection. As clearly as facts can be adduced from the faint glimmerings of history or tradition, it appears probable that, in the early period of the eighteenth century, English occupation and improvement were gradually advancing toward the valley of Champlain; Crown point, then distinguished by its present name, was recognized in 1690, as a commanding and important position. The common council of Albany, instructing their scouting party in that year, directs them to proceed "to Crown point, where you shall remain and keep good watch by night and day." The fact appears also from the language of the purchase, by Dellius, that this purchase was ratified by a grant from Governor Fletcher in 1696. of a tract from the Mohawks, extending "more than twenty miles northward of Crown point."[1] His patent was so exorbitant in its claims, and comprehended so vast an extent of territory, that the colonial legislature, without hesitation, abrogated the grant, and thus exhibited an exercise over the region of one of the highest prerogatives of sovereignty.

The Crown point of history is a beautiful peninsula, forming a section of the present township of that name, which is distinguished for its agricultural fertility, and the rare and exceeding loveliness of the landscapes its varied scenery affords. The peninsula is formed by Bulwagga bay, a broad estuary on the west, and the lake upon the east, which at that point, abruptly changes its course nearly at right angles, and is compressed from a wide expanse into a narrow channel. A vast wilderness in 1731 extended on both sides of Lake Champlain, from the settlements on the Hudson to the Canadian hamlets, broken by rugged and impracticable mountains and ravines, and traversed by deep or rapid streams. No track penetrated it, except the path of the Indian. The lake, in its navigation, or by its ice,

---

[1] Point Le Caronne of the French.

afforded the only avenue of mutual invasion. The most unpracticed eye at once perceives that Canada could be the most efficiently shielded by the occupation of Crown point, that position forming the portals of the lake. Impressed, no doubt, by these considerations, the French vice-regal government, violating the sanctions of treaties, and the immunities of a profound peace, suddenly advanced through the lake, and seized by a military force, a promontory directly opposite Crown point, and immediately after, that position itself.

The site first occupied by the French is now called Chimney point, but they gave to it the more euphonious name of Point a la Chevelure. The poetical allusion it must have conveyed is lost to us.[1]

This action of France was the movement of no inconsiderate impulse, but the suggestion of a deliberate and matured policy. The scheme was distinctly urged in 1688 and never relinquished. Frontenac in 1693, was instructed to "build light vessels for the defense of the narrow defiles of the rivers and lakes on the route from Orange."[2] And in 1737, Beauharnois was directed to effect a survey of Lake Champlain with the purpose of introducing an armed sloop upon its waters.[3] The views of France, in reference to the importance of securing the control of Lake Champlain, were neither peculiar or unfounded. The secret councils of the colonial governments of England were constantly directed to the attainment of the same great object.[4] Lake Champlain was the most direct avenue of communication between the Hudson and Quebec. A military post, which commanded the lake, must necessarily control the large and lucrative fur trade that sought through its waters a transit between Chambly and Albany. It was the purpose of France to anticipate and defeat the

[1] It is frequently, but I think incorrectly stated, that this name was originally given to Crown point. All the old French maps corroborate my opinion.

[2] Louis XIV to Frontenac, *Hist., Doc.*, IX, 449. [3] *Idem.*, IX, 1059.

[4] Gov. Dongan, *Doc.*, III, 477; Bellomont, *id.*, 504; Lords of Trade, *id.*, 704.

designs of England for the occupation of Crown point.[1] The wise policy of the French government contemplated the formation of agricultural colonies beneath the shields of its military posts, and to thus secure the permanent defense and possession of the country.[2]

The instructions to Beauharnois directed that a simple stockaded fort should first be erected, " until a stronger one can be constructed."[3] Thirty men only formed the garrison of the incipient fortification. Beauharnois announces three years later to the government, that he is "preparing to complete" this feeble work. A position full of alarm and terror, and a constant "sharp thorn in the sides of Massachusetts and New York"[4] lingered thus for years in its slow and hesitating progress, continually exposed to be crushed with the sanction of England, by the military grasp of any single colony. In 1747, it appears to have attained only a slight advance in strength or proportions;[5] but in 1750, an emissary of Clinton thus describes its growth and commanding position and armament. "The fort is built of stone, the walls of considerable height and thickness, and has twenty pieces of cannon and swivels mounted on the ramparts and bastions. I observed the walls cracked from top to bottom in several places. At the entrance of the fort is a dry ditch eighteen feet square, and a draw-bridge. There is a subterranean passage to the lake. The citadel is a stout building eight feet square, four stories high, each turned with arches, mounts twenty pieces of cannon and swivels, the largest six-pounders. The walls of the citadel are about ten feet thick. At the entrance is a draw-bridge and ditch."[6] The writer of this report remarks a fact obvious to the most unmilitary eye, that the formation of the adjacent country rendered St. Frederick extremely vulnerable to assault by batteries.

Gov. Dongan, *Hist. Doc.*, III, 1023. [2] *Idem.*

[3] Louis XIV to Beauharnois and Hocquart, May 1731, *idem*, 1025.

[4] Delancy to Lords of Trade, *Doc.*, VI, 816.

[5] Johnson to Clinton, *Doc.*, VI, 389.

[6] Stoddart to Clinton, *Doc.*, VI, 582, abridged.

The protection of Canada from the inroads of the Iroquois was the ostensible reason and excuse for the erection of St. Frederic, assigned by France. Its real purpose, besides embracing the control of the lake, contemplated a still deeper policy. Occupying a position at the threshold of the English possessions, they could menace and impede their progress, and at any moment direct against their expanded and defenseless settlements, sudden and destructive assaults. Crown point was within the recognized possessions of the Iroquois, and by the treaty of Utrecht, their territory was guarantied to remain "inviolate by any occupation or encroachment of France." The governor of New York was at length aroused from his lethargy, by the indignant voice of Shirley of Massachusetts, to contemplate the arms of France and a commanding fortress far within the limits of his asserted jurisdiction. Massachusetts, always prompt and energetic in sustaining the national glory, and in redressing the wrongs of the colonies, offered to New York to unite at once with her, in an expostulation on the subject, with the French functionaries, and in the ultimate necessity, to unite their arms to repel the aggression.[1] The occupation of Crown point was only a link in the system, by which France was encircling the colonies of England by a cordon of fortresses. The colonies invoked in vain the attention of the home government, to these encroachments. In vain were protestations and memorials laid at the foot of the throne, urging that the safety and the colonial existence of New England and New York were endangered by the occupation of Crown point.

The earnest and imploring voice of the colonies fell on cold and deafened ears. To the vision of the British ministry, America was a wilderness, destitute of present fruition and promises of the future. Walpole, whose sagacity seemed to endow him almost with prophetic prescience in the affairs of Europe, could detect no germ of future empire

---

[1] Correspondence between Shirley and Clinton, *Hist. Doc.*,, VI, 419, 421, 423.

in the wilds of America. So even and indifferent had been the regard of the same government, to a subject of such momentous interest, to the colonies, and which had so deeply aroused their anxieties as the erection of the French fortresses on Lake Champlain, that the lords of trade, in December, 1738, confessed to Governor Clark ignorance of their location, and he in the succeeding year "pointed them out on a small map."[1] Not until 1789 did Waldegrave, the embassador to France, claim the attention of that government to the violation of the treaty of Utrecht, by the occupation of Crown point. The only response conceded to this expostulation was the denial of "all knowledge of the projected establishment," and the formal diplomatic assurance of instructions inquiring on the subject. Thus England slumbered, and the colonies toiled and murmured, while the formidable fortress of St. Frederick arose and secured to France the dominion of the lake.

Leading minds in the colonies were at that day suspicious that sinister and corrupt motives were influencing the British ministry, "who having reasons for keeping well with the court of France, the project" (of occupying the Ohio) "was not only dropped, but the French were encouraged to build the fort of Crown point upon the territory of New York."[2] Such was the denunciation of Spotswood of Virginia. England, by the ignoble treaty of Aix La Chapelle relinquished to France the fortress of Louisburg, subjugated by the treasures and blood of New England; but left to that power without a protest, the possession of Crown point. It was not until 1755, that the British government, with emphasis and decision, demanded from France the demolition of the fortress of St. Frederic. Diplomacy could not thus retrieve, after the hostile occupation of a quarter of a century, territory lost by imbecility or corruption.

---

[1] *Doc.*, VI, 139, 142. [2] Gov. Spotswood.—*Bancroft.*

Accumulated acts of neglect and injustice of the mother country, such as these, prepared and matured the colonies for independence. Had they been cherished by the guardian care of England, they might have rested upon her arm in effeminacy and dependence. Abandoned to the suggestions of their own policy, they were taught by these exigencies high and practical lessons of self-government. Compelled by a common danger, to mutual consultation and concerted action, they were admonished of the necessity and strength of a confederated union. Compelled to rely alone for protection and safety upon their own arms and energies, they were taught to resist aggression and to avenge injury. The deep fountains of their capacities were revealed to themselves, by the parsimonious policy of England, that constrained the colonies to resort to their domestic resources in their own protection and defense. Had Canada been a British province, New England and New York might have been exempt from the appalling scenes of carnage and suffering which are now impressed on their history; but the very exposures and dangers of their position, and the assaults and cruelties of a powerful and daring enemy, endowed them with lofty moral and physical courage; with endurance in suffering; with boldness and wisdom in council, and promptitude and decision in action. These are the elements of freedom.

Men, who literally tilled the earth with the musket at their sides, were ripening for any emergency and prepared to defend a heritage, endeared by their blood and sorrows, against every foe and any wrong. The career of the colonies, neglected, contemned and suffering, was to them a baptism of blood and sorrow, that consecrated a free and ennobled spirit, equal to any sacrifice or any conflict. The wars into which the colonies were forced by this policy of England, and the proximity of the French provinces, afforded the severe schools for their military education. The shores of Lake Champlain formed the nursery of future heroes of the revolution. The military spirit was here enkindled, that in after years blazed at Bunker hill, and Bennington, and Saratoga; and here, amid victory and defeat, the science and tactics of Europe were inculcated and diffused throughout the broad colonies. If Washington was taught on the banks of the Monongahela, to lead armies and to achieve independence for his country, Putnam and Stark, Pomeroy and Prescott, amid the forests and morasses of Horicon and Champlain, and beneath the walls of Ticonderoga, were formed to guide and conquer in the battles of freedom. Human wisdom, in her philosophy, may pause to contemplate such striking and singular coincidences, and to trace these causes to their momentous results; but the eye of faith will reverence them as the hidden workings of an overruling and beneficent Providence, who, in these events, was unfolding the elements and forming the agents of a mighty revolution, destined, not only to sever a kingdom, but to change the course of human events.

An ordinance of the king of France had authorized, as early as 1676, the issuing of grants of lands situated in Canada. In accordance with this power, and assuming the sovereignty of France over the valley of Lake Champlain, the government of Canada had caused a survey to be made of the lake and its contiguous territory, the year succeeding the erection of the works at Crown point. Many of the names of the headlands, islands and other topographical features of the lake, which are still perpetuated, are derived from that survey. In their descriptive force and beauty, they almost rival the euphony and appropriateness of the Indian nomenclature. A map and chart based upon that survey, was published at Montreal in 1748, and has not been surpassed by any subsequently made, in its scientific aspect or minuteness and accuracy. Extensive grants, under the ordinance of 1676, upon both sides of the lake, are delineated upon that map. A seigniory was granted to the Sieur Robart, the royal storekeeper at Montreal, in June, 1737. This grant, which seems to have been the only one issued for land within the limits of the county of Essex, embraced "three leagues in front by two leagues in depth, on the west side of Lake Champlain, taking, in going down, one league below the river Boquet, and in going up, two leagues and a half above said river.[1] These boundaries comprehend all of the present town of Essex and a large proportion of Willsboro'. The tract was soon after formally laid out and allotted by an official surveyor. We have no evidence that any permanent and actual occupation was formed under these grants. Kalm, who visited the region at an early period, asserts that few colonies, and these only in the vicinity of the fortresses, were formed by the French during their occupation.

The authority from whom I have already given extracts states that in 1750, "fourteen farms were occupied in the vicinity of Crown point, and great encouragement given by the king for that purpose," and "that other colonists were approaching."[2] The journal of Rogers contains repeated references to villages adjacent to Fort St. Frederic and situated upon both sides of the lake.

The devastation in 1745, of the settlement of Saratoga, by an Indian and French force, armed and organized at Crown point, and the deeper atrocities committed a few years later at Hoosick, by the same bands, while they increased the apprehensions of the colonies, excited to the highest intensity the desire and purpose of vengeance. This feeling could be best consummated in the destruction of St. Frederic. Whilst that fortress was occupied by a powerful and vigilant rival, the tenure of life and property in the adjacent English colonies, was esteemed so precarious and valueless, that the country north of the Mohawk, until the conquest of Amherst, was nearly depopulated.

A convention of the colonial governors had been held at Albany in 1747, but without yielding any fruits of practical utility. The increasing and more active aggressions of France, both in the Ohio valley and upon Lake Champlain, demanded a similar meeting in 1754, that was only mem-

---

[1] *Doc. History.* [2] *Doc. Hist.*, VI, 582.

orable for the adoption of a Plan of Union between the British colonies, inspired by Franklin, and which, although at the time futile, formed the prolific germ from whence in another generation sprung the American confederacy. It was on this occasion, that the venerable Hendrik, the great Mohawk chieftain, pronounced one of those thrilling and eloquent speeches that marked the nobler times of the Iroquois. It excited the wonder and admiration of those who listened, and commanded the highest encomiums where-ever it was read.[1] In burning words he contrasted the supineness and imbecility of England, with the energies of French policy. His hoary head and majestic bearing attached dignity and force to his utterances. "We," he exclaimed, "would have gone and taken Crown point, but you hindered us." He closed his philippic with this overwhelming rebuke: "Look at the French, they are men. They are fortifying everywhere. But you, and we are ashamed to say it, you are like women, bare and open without any fortifications."[2]

The admonitions of the provincial governments, and the cry of alarm and agitation that arose from every section of the colonies, at length aroused the English ministry to the duty of their protection, and the assertion of the honor of Britain. Between France and England a peace, under the solemnities of treaty, still existed. Four distinct expeditions were, however, organized, professedly to guard the colonial possessions of England; but prepared, at the propitious moment, to be hurled upon the strongholds of French power. In this combination an army, designed for the reduction of Crown point, was assembled at Albany, and confided to the command of William Johnson. The zeal and solicitude of New England, for the conquest of the fortresses upon Champlain, exasperated by the alarms and calamities of a quarter of a century, excited all the enthusiasm of her bold and energetic yeomanry. Every

---

[1] Dwight's Travels, *Gentleman's Magazine*, Shirley and Gov. Livingstone.
[2] *Stone's Johnson.*

requisition of the government was met amply and with promptitude. Levies from New York and New England constituted all the forces demanded.

France was not insensible to the gathering storm, which began to lower around her American empire, and prepared to meet and avert it.

CHAPTER IV.

Dieskau, 1755, 1757.

The bold and rocky cliffs which mark the confluence of the waters of Lake St. Sacrament with Lake Champlain, a position still more imposing than Crown point, and deeper within the domains of the Iroquois, had attracted the attention of the French engineers.[1] In the summer of 1755, De Quesne advised the construction of works at that point. "St. Frederic was threatening to fall on all sides."[2] The selection of the site and the construction of the fort, was confided to Lotbiniere, an engineer of the province. "A rock, which crowns all the environs, whose guns could command both the outlet and that leading to the Grand marais and Wood creek, "was selected as the appropriate ground for the projected fortification.[3] The original work, which a year later was in an unfinished

---

[1] Saint Sacrament, literally the Lake of the Blessed Sacrament, which name it obtained in 1646, from Father Jogues, because he passed through it on the festival of Corpus Christi.—*E. B. O'Callaghan, Doc.*, IX, 400. The common impression that the name of this lake was suggested by the singular purity of its water, is erroneous. By the aborigines, it was in one dialect called Canidere-Oit, or the tail of the lake, in reference to its relation to Lake Champlain.—*Spafford's Gazetteer*. By the Iroquois it was named Andiatarocte, "there the lake shuts itself."—*Relations*. Honiton, although redolent with beauty, seems to be a pure poetical fancy. The various names attached, as well to tribes as to places, in the difficult Indian language, often lead to confusion and error.

[2] Du Quesne to Vaudreuil.

[3] Vaudreuil, *Doc.*, X, 225. Modern engineers will ratify the complaint of Lotbiniere, that his salary was no more than six hundred francs.

state, "was a square fort with four bastions, and built of earth and timber.[1] Johnson, the same year, mentions Ticonderoga as an important, but unoccupied position.[2] Such was the inception of Fort Carillon, a fortress and a locality destined to a terrific preeminence in the future scenes of a sanguinary war.[3] At what period the massive stone battlements were constructed, which still reveal the former magnitude and strength of the fortress, by its grand and picturesque ruins, I cannot determine. At the approach of Abercrombie, in 1758, the French were energetically engaged in augmenting both the extent and strength of the works. Crown point, by its unfavorable position, and the decaying walls of St. Frederick, had fallen into a subordinate attitude, "as a second line of defense."[4]

When the court of St. Cloud was made aware of the departure of Braddock's formidable expedition, a powerful fleet was promptly dispatched from the French posts bearing six battalions of regular troops, designed to aid in the defense of the colonies. It bore also Vaudreuil, the governor general of new France, and with him came Baron de Dieskau as commander in chief of the colonial armies. Dieskau was a pupil of Saxe, trained from youth to age in the battle-fields of Europe, and skilled in the handling of drilled and veteran troops, ardent and aspiring, and stimulated by the desire of action and fame. Dieskau prepared without delay to open his American career by the capture of Oswego. Half of his forces were already advancing in accordance with that plan, and "the thing," he exclaims in his characteristic but imaginary conversation with Saxe in the Elysian fields,[5] "was inevitable," when Vaudreuil, alarmed by intelligence from St. Frederick, altered his design and hurried Dieskau, impatient and reluctant, to the defense of Lake Champlain. He hastened to Crown point with three thousand men, and

---

[1] *Doc.*, x, 414. [2] *Idem*, xi, 997.

[3] Carillon seems to bear the same signification as the Indian name, "the Onderoga," the original of Ticonderoga, noise-chimes, in allusion, doubtless, to the brawling waters.

[4] Montcalm. [5] *Doc.*, x, 340.

there learnt that Johnson was lying at Fort Edward and Lake St. Sacrament, slowly collecting his forces and preparing to advance.

Immediately upon his arrival in Virginia, Braddock convened a conference of the colonial governors at Alexandria to determine and harmonize a concerted action of the English colonies in a general attack on the French possessions. In consonance with the plan then decided upon, an army intended to move against the French works on Lake Champlain, was entrusted to the command of William Johnson, who had already achieved prominence in the colonial affairs of New York, by his estates, his commanding abilities, and by his efficient and zealous measure in organizing the militia of that province. Johnson was Irish by birth, and of ancient and respectable lineage. He emigrated to America in boyhood, and at an early age occupied a subordinate but highly responsible position as agent for the large landed property of his uncle, Sir Peter Warren, lying in the vicinity of the Mohawk river. Living in baronial magnificence among the Mohawks, his justice, magnanimity and generous habits imparted to him a potent influence over his aboriginal neighbors. He had never seen a field of battle, and had no knowledge of military affairs, only as he had derived it from the theory of books, or like his cotemporary Clive, he became a soldier from the intuitive perceptions of his own genius.

Most of the army which Johnson was to lead, had, in June, 1755, assembled in the vicinity of Albany. A large proportion of the troops were from New England, but the character of Johnson, and the influence of Shirley of Massachusetts, secured his appointment, and in its propriety there seems to have been a harmonious and loyal acquiescence.

The embarrassments and delays always incident to the organization of new levies, retarded the advance until the last week in August. Leaving a part of his troops at Fort Edward, and in an adjacent encampment for its protection, Johnson advanced with a force, including

Indians, of about thirty-four hundred men, to the foot of Lake St. Sacrament, of the French, and by him then first called Lake George, " not only in honor of his majesty, but to ascertain his undoubted dominion here."[1] He "found the country a mere wilderness, not one foot cleared."[2] Here he prepared ground " in a protected position for the camp of five thousand men," the number whose presence he was warranted in expecting. His army, fresh from the plough and the workshop, save a few who had been engaged at the siege of Louisburg, were novices in the arts and services of war. The provincials, clothed in the home-spun garments woven by wives and mothers, armed only with their own rifles and fowling pieces, without bayonets, but animated by the noblest impulses of patriotism and courage, and inspired by a fervid religious enthusiasm, which enkindled the faith that they were battling in defense of the altars of protestantism and for the subversion of idolatry. While the preparations were in active, but to their impatient ardor, slow progress, they were restive and impatient for the advance. On the sabbath, in obedience to their puritan habits, they assembled to unite in prayer and " to listen to the word," while their swarthy allies gravely hear the interpretation of a long sermon.[3] The native groves, the primitive temples of God, witness their worship.

Johnson, under the delusion of a singularly false security, neglected to erect even the slightest works for the protection of the army. His designs embraced the construction of a fort near the ground he occupied, in the view of ultimate security, and when the necessary bateaux were built he " proposed to proceed down the lake to an important pass called Ticonderoga, and there endeavor to take post until the rest of the forces join me, and thence march to the attack of Crown point. All of which I hope to be able to accomplish in three weeks."[4] But all these

---

[1] Johnson to Lords of Trade, *Doc.*, VI, 997. [2] *Idem.* [3] Bancroft.
[4] *Doc.*, VI, 999.

purposes were suddenly arrested by the startling and unexpected tidings, that a French army had landed at South bay, and rapidly advancing in his rear, was threatening to sever his communications with Fort Edward.

The written instructions of Vaudreuil to Dieskau were clear and positive, that he should advance from Crown point with his entire force, and that he should not attack the English entrenchments without a cautious recognition.[1] Each of these instructions was violated by Dieskau, but under circumstances that warranted him conducting a remote command, to exercise an individual judgment, which justified apparent disobedience. When disaster had clouded the fortunes of Dieskau, a complaint of this action was carried by Vandreuil with extreme bitterness to the throne.[2] With half his army, consisting of six hundred Canadians, six hundred Indians and three hundred regulars, Dieskau advanced, leaving the remainder to occupy Carillon, and to maintain a position known as the " two rocks," to cover his retreat in case of defeat.[3]

The motives which controlled the decision of Dieskau, he explains in the dialogue with Saxe. He intended a mere *coup de main*, and no regular investment or assault, and for that object he deemed his force adequate.[4] The close supply of provisions, the necessity of a rapid march through a wild and wooded country, and crossing deep streams, sometimes along a single log, rendered the use of a larger force impracticable. He had been informed by his spies, that Johnson lay in an unfortified camp at Lake George short of supplies, and that a body of nine hundred militia troops, which in a common professional spirit he despised,[5]

---

[1] *Doc.*, x, 325. [2] Vandreuil to Machault, *Doc.*, x, 318.

[3] These rocks, called the Pulpit and Narrows, stand on the junction of the towns of Dresden and Putnam.—*Fitche's Washington County*. Some discrepancy exists in the accounts of the relative proportions of Dieskau's forces, but none as to the aggregate.

[4] *Col. Doc.*, x, 341.

[5] They are such miserable soldiers that a single Indian would put ten of them to flight." — *Idem*.

were encamped near Fort Edward, and that this work was only protected by unfinished palisades. Upon this intelligence he formed the plan of his campaign. It was conceived with great ability, and in the instincts of bold enterprise, and its execution was attempted by the highest vigor and intrepidity. A brilliant success would have approved the scheme, had his army been composed of the drilled veterans he was accustomed to lead. But a just estimate of savage hordes and raw levies scarcely less intractable, did not enter into the contemplations of Dieskau, and in the anguish of wounds and defeat he bitterly exclaimed: "These then, are the troops which have been so much crowed up to me."[1]

On the fourth of September, 1755, Dieskau, in conformity with the designs he had adopted, proceeded up Wood creek, and, traversing the shallow waters of South bay, left one hundred and twenty men to guard his bateaux, and had advanced through the woods by three days' march, intending, on the morning of the fourth, to assail and defeat the militia before Fort Edward, and to capture the works; this accomplished he proposed to march rapidly against Johnson, cut off his communications, and to annihilate his army by a sudden and impetuous attack. But his guides, either bewildered in the mazes of the forest, or treacherous in their purpose, wandered from the proposed course, and when light appeared they were several miles on the road leading to the English camp. The Indians, who had become alarmed by the rumors of artillery on the fort, although not a single gun was mounted, refused to assail it or to cover an assault by the French, arguing with a singular casuistry, that the land it occupied belonged to England.[2] They professed a readiness to attack Johnson,[3] and while

---

[1] *Hist. Doc.*, x, 334. [2] *Idem*, 342.

[3] Johnson establishes in his letter to Sir Charles Hardy the wisdom of Dieskau's original plan: "Happily for us he complied [with the proposition of the Indians] for he would have found our troops separately encamped out of the works and no cannon there, and his victory would have probably been a very cheap one, and made way for another here." — *Hist. Doc.*, vi, 1014.

Dieskau was promptly changing his movements to gratify this caprice, he received intelligence that a large detachment was advancing from the lake on the road he occupied to relieve the fort.

Johnson, immediately, when informed of the advance of Dieskau, convened a council of his officers. The aged Hendrik participated in the consultation, and seems to have been its Nestor. When the march of a small body of troops was proposed, he remarked, in the laconic and sententious manner of his race: "If they are to fight they are too few, if they are to be killed, they are too many." And when it was suggested that the detachment should be divided into three bodies, he gathered three sticks from the ground: "Put these together," he said, "and you can't break them; take them up one by one and you may break them readily." Had the wise savage ever heard of the classic fable? Hendrik was the sage in council, the consummate orator, and on the war-path the bold and sagacious leader; and in the combination of those qualities, was the last of the noble Mohawks. He had visited England twice; was received with distinction at court, and was slightly educated. Immediately, before Colonel Williams began his march, Hendrik mounted a stage and harangued his people. His strong masculine voice, it was supposed, might be heard at the distance of half a mile. A spectator, who did not understand a word of his language, afterwards said, "that the animation of Hendrik, the fire of his eye, the force of his gestures, his emphasis, the inflexions of his voice and his whole manner affected him more deeply than any speech he had ever heard." [1]

It was decided by the council that Colonel Ephraim Williams, with a thousand provincials, supported by Hendrik and two hundred Mohawk warriors, should promptly march to relieve the fort. Williams, who a few days before, by a will executed at Albany, created the foundation of an institution, which a memorial of his love of science still preserves

---

[1] *Dwight's Travels.*

his name, was inspired by the earnest and heroic spirit of his province, was a gallant soldier, but untutored, except in trifling Indian warfare, by any military experience. He advanced precipitately, but with little soldierly circumspection. Hendrik, on horseback, led the van.

Meanwhile, the skill of the French commander had prepared for them a terrible reception. He placed his forces on the road he occupied, in a defile about three miles from Johnson's camp, arranging them in the form of a parallelogram, with front open, or as a *cul de sac.*[1] The Canadians were posted on the right, the Indians upon the left, and the regulars at the extremity, with strict orders to the two former, "not to move or to discharge a single gun, until the French had fired." The rock, the bushes and forest disguised the presence of an army, and Williams entered into this "valley of death" in the midst of an invisible foe. At this moment, when, to the practiced eye of Dieskau, the destruction of the whole detachment appeared inevitable, a part of the Iroquois arose from their hiding place, and, perceiving their Mohawk brethren in the English army, fired into the air, and thus revealed the ambush. These were Senecas, the western tribe of the confederacy, but domiciliated in Canada, whose fidelity, Dieskau, in his correspondence with Vaudreuil, had uniformly distrusted. This treachery, probably without premeditation, was stimulated by that strong fraternal affection, which united the different tribes of the confederacy in bonds firmer than their political union, and was a remarkable feature in the character of the Iroquois. Each canton might independently accept a subsidy from England or France, and would serve with fidelity and fight with courage against the adverse nation or in hostility to alien Indian tribes, but previous to the revolution were never—possibly some rare and brief exceptions may have occurred—brought into conflict with any other branch of the confederacy. In the war of independence,

---

[1] *Hist. Doc.*, x, 342, where he represents his formation by a diagram.

a part of the Oneidas received the war-belt from the American congress, and engaged in a sanguinary contest with their kindred tribes.

The friendly or treacherous warning came too late, to save the provincials and Mohawks from the fatal error of their leader. A crushing fire was poured upon them in front and from the right. Williams, who gallantly took position upon a rock—the same rock that is now the base of his own monument—at the first alarm, better to observe and direct the battle, early fell. Hendrik, nearly at the same moment, was also killed.[1] The provincials and Indians retreated in confusion, "doubled up," Dieskau wrote, "like a pack of cards, and fled pell-mell to their intrenchments."[2] They were soon rallied by Lt. Colonel Whiting, fought with great valor, and under cover of a party of three hundred men commanded by Colonel Cole, which had been opportunely detached by Johnson to their support, effected a retreat in good order to the camp.

Dieskau, bursting through the red tape instructions of Vaudreuil, and following the inspiration of the motto inscribed upon his crest: "Boldness wins," did not pause to reconnoitre, but leading the French and Canadians, rapidly pursued, hoping in the panic and confusion to enter with the fugitives, an unfortified camp; but again the Indians disappointed and deceived him. When they saw the semblance of an intrenchment, and "heard the roar of cannon, stopped short." He still advanced, but soon perceived the Canadians also "scattering right and left."[3]

Johnson, when he heard the noise of the battle, and knew by its approach that his troops were retreating, with admirable promptitude and energy, sent forth the reenforcement of Cole, and prepared for the impending conflict. The skilled woodsmen of New England rapidly felled trees, which, with the wagons and baggage formed a hasty

---

[1] A cotemporaneous account states that Hendrik fired the first shot in the battle.—Pownall to Lords of Trade, *Doc.*, VI, 1008.

[2] *Doc.*, X, 343. [3] *Idem*, 343.

and partial breastwork, while two or three cannons were hurried from the shore of the lake, where they had been placed ready for embarkation. The defection of the irregular troops compelled Dieskau to make a brief halt in front of the works,[1] which was a precious boon to the intrenching provincials. Then ensued, protracted through the horrors of more than four hours, the most severe and bloodiest fight the wilds of the new world had ever witnessed. Dieskau first assaulted with his regulars the centre, but, "thrown into disorder by the warm and constant fire of the artillery and colonial troops," was repulsed.[2] Then he assailed the left flank, and, in a last and desperate effort, hurled his wasted and bleeding veterans upon the extreme right, with the impetuosity and heroic daring that belonged to the troops of France. But this attack was also crushed by the overwhelming fire from the intrenchments. In their excited ardor, many of the provincials and Indians leaping over the frail breastworks, opposed the butts of their reversed guns to the glittering bayonets of the French, and completed with a great slaughter, their defeat.[3] The Canadians and Indians inflicted considerable loss upon the Americans from an adjacent morass, but were dispersed by a few shots thrown into their midst. And this was the extent of their services. However inherently brave, as was attested by many a bloody field, the habitans of Canada were reluctant and murmuring levies, forced into a war of conquest by a ruthless conscription, that swept, on the threshold of harvest, every able-bodied man from the district of Montreal, leaving their crops to be gathered by coerced labor, from other sections of the province.[4]

Dieskau appears not to have been adapted by temperament or manners, to conciliate the attachment or to command the confidence of his savage allies. Instead of indulging in familiar intercourse and yielding to their

---

[1] Johnson's official report. [2] Johnson's report. [3] Johnson, *idem*.
[4] Breard to Machault, *Doc.*, x, 309.

habits and peculiarities, he maintained with them — and equally with his subordinates and the Canadians — the stately German style of seclusion and exclusiveness. This course destroyed the influence and devotion, which could only be exerted over their rude and capricious nature, by controlling their impulses and affections. They could not comprehend the motive of Dieskau in his rapid attack on the entrenched camp, and asked delay, "that they might rest and care for their wounded." When he persisted, they exclaimed in amazement: "Father you have lost your reason, listen to us." [1]

Dieskau, thrice wounded and disabled, refused to be carried from the field by Montrueil, his subordinate, and "ordered him in the king's name to assume the command and make the best retreat he could." [2] Two Canadians came to his relief, "but one was killed outright," writes Dieskau, "falling across my legs to my great embarrassment." Bathed in blood and calmly supporting himself against a tree, while the tempest of bullets hurtled about him, he remained until the advance of the provincials, when he was again deliberately fired at by a refugee Frenchman.[3] The shot penetrating both hips, perforated an internal organ, and caused a wound, which. after twelve years of extreme suffering, terminated his life. But his mental anguish far exceeded any physical suffering. He was allowed by his king to languish a prisoner until the peace of 1763, neglected by his country and an object of unjust calumny and aspersion.[4]

Dieskau, when his name was known, was tenderly borne by the victors to the tent of Johnson, placed upon his bed and received the prompt aid of Johnson's own surgeon.

---

[1] *Hough's Pouchot*, I, 35, 47. [2] *Idem*, 343.

[3] "Leaping on me, he said in very good French, "Surrender." I said to him, "You rascal, why did you fire on me: you see a man lying on the ground bathed in blood, and you fire on him, eh?" He answered, "How did I know but you had a pistol? I prefer to kill the devil, than that the devil kill me."— *Doc.*, X, 343.

[4] Dieskau to Belle Isle.— *Doc.*, X, 806; *Idem*, 594.

Several Indians forced themselves into the tent and in passionate vehemence claimed the prisoner, that they might burn him to expiate the death of their chieftain. The determined attitude of Johnson and his great influence with the Mohawks, alone preserved Dieskau from this horrid doom.[1] Romance and sympathy still linger in the popular heart around the name of Dieskau. Able, valiant and generous, he fell, almost at the moment of victory, by the baseness and treachery of unworthy followers. He reached the St. Lawrence with high hopes and ardent ambition, when June had scarcely decorated its shores in the beauty and verdure of spring; but before the autumnal leaves had fallen, he was fatally stricken, defeated, and a captive.[2]

St. Pierre, the leader of the French Indians, and the defiant but chivalric negotiator with Washington on the banks of the Ohio two years before, fell on this bloody field. But the disasters of the French were not yet terminated. The army had scattered into fragments; and a party of about three hundred, stopping for a brief rest, were encountered by a body of provincials under McGinnis of New Hampshire and Folsom of New York, were again routed and flying in confusion, abandoned all their baggage and ammunition to the conquerors. This triumph cost the life of the gallant McGinnis.[3] The French at the moment of the assault had cast off the packs containing their supplies, and in the confusion of their hurried retreat did not recover them, and wandered two days in the woods and through morasses without food.[4]

The losses of the respective armies were nearly the same, each including several valuable officers, amounting to about four hundred and fifty of the French, and one hundred less of the English and Mohawks, while both could claim peculiar advantages from the results. The French had arrested the advance of the British armies, and for the sea-

---

[1] Dieskau, *Doc.*, x, 343. [2] Bancroft. [3] *Graham's Colonial History*, II, 200.
[4] Mortreuil to D'Argenson, *Doc.* x, 359.

son averted an attack upon the works on Lake Champlain. For Britain, a victory had been achieved, which, succeeding so soon the disasters of Braddock, thrilled the land with joy and exultation. In the mind of the provincials the prestige of invincibility, which had attached to science and discipline was gone forever, and the issue of this battle had its fruition by the influence it imparted in a future and a nobler contest for national independence and freedom. The narrative of this triumph will ever warm the heart of the American historian with interest and pride, for this was the first field on which the yeomanry of the colonies, led by their own citizens, met and vanquished the trained veterans of Europe.

Johnson, at an early stage of the conflict, was wounded, and left the field and the battle to be guided by the conduct and intrepidity of Lyman of Massachusetts. These and the fiery and persistent valor of the troops, won the victory. The Mohawks and the colonists were alike clamorous for the pursuit of the flying enemy; the one burning to avenge the death of their beloved sachem, and the other panting to crush a foe that so often had desolated their own borders with fire and blood. But the prudence, or timidity of Johnson who professed to fear a renewed attack with artillery, restrained their ardor, and the French secured an unmolested retreat to Carillon.[1] The voice of New England and the council of his officers urged the accomplishment of the original designs of the campaign, while the French army was demoralized by defeat, the works at Ticonderoga scarcely commenced and the walls of St. Frederick crumbling, but the Mohawks returned to their wigwams, and Johnson, irresolute and hesitating, lost the occasion, and wasted the season in the profitless labor of erecting Fort William Henry. The campaign was closed, and the army disbanded.[2] On another field, Johnson vindicated claims to high military talents; but here he seems to shrink from risking by the contingencies of war laurels already plucked,

---

[1] *Doc.*, x, 1013. [2] Bancroft and Graham.

and which he probably perceived in his visions, gilded with future honors and fortune. Johnson was magnanimous towards his fallen enemy, but unjust and ungenerous to his associates.[1] Ascribing to himself the glory of the great event, Lyman was not named in the official report, while a faint and cold commendatory notice was extended to a few of the subordinate officers. The services of Lyman, and the courage of the American citizens, who achieved the victory, received from England neither applause nor recognition, while Johnson was dignified by a baronetcy, made royal superintendent of Indian affairs with a grant by parliament of £5,000, wrung from the scanty pittance allowed the suffering colonies for the burdens they had in a generous patriotism self-imposed.

It was not until the summer succeeding these exciting events, that open and mutual declarations of war were proclaimed between France and England. The contest lanquished during the year 1756 upon the borders of Champlain. In that year, another force was organized for the attack of Crown point. As on the former occasion the colonies presented their required contingents, but delays, dissensions, the incapacity and indecision of the English commanders, again exhausted the season. Offensive operations were limited to the bold and romantic exploits of the American rangers and the partisan corps of France. Rogers, the gallant ranger, was particularly conspicuous in these wild and daring adventures. Sometimes stealing under the cover of night by the forts in canoes, he lay in ambush far down the lake, surprised and captured boats laded with supplies, which, unsuspicious of danger, were proceeding to relieve the garrisons. Frequently he approached the forts by land, and prowling about them with Indian skill and patience, until he ascertained the intelligence he was ordered to collect, he captured prisoners, shot down stragglers, burnt dwellings, and

[1] Dieskau to D'Argenson, *Doc.*, x, 318.

slaughtered cattle feeding around the works, and then defying pursuit, retreated in safety.[1]

In one of these bold incursions, which signalized the opening of the next year, Rogers and Stark had penetrated with a force of less than eighty men, to a point between the French fortresses, near the mouth of a stream, since known as Putnam's creek, and there, in ambush, awaited their victims. A party of French are passing in gay and joyous security on the ice toward Ticonderoga. Part are taken, the rest escape and alarm the garrison. The rangers attempt to retreat, pressing rapidly along the snow path, in Indian file, as was their custom, but on ascending the crest of a hill they receive the fire of an overwhelming force, posted with every advantage to receive them.[2] A fierce and bloody conflict ensued, protracted from near meridian until evening. The rangers retreating to a hill, are protected by the covert of the trees and there gallantly sustain the unequal conflict. Rogers, twice wounded, yields the command of the little band to Stark, who with infinite skill and courage, guides the battle, repulses the foe, with a loss far exceeding his entire force, and at night conducts a successful retreat to Lake George. Leaving there his wounded and exhausted companions, Stark, accompanied by only two volunteers, traverses on snow shoes, a distance of forty miles, and returns to them, with aid and supplies the second morning. This courageous band, reduced to forty-eight effective men, with their prisoners effected a retreat to Fort William Henry in safety. This incident, brilliant as it appears, is rivaled, if not

---

[1] *Rogers's Journal*, 16, 18, 20, 24. Rogers, on a later occasion, manifested that humor was blended with his daring. He killed fifteen beeves almost beneath the walls of Carillon, and to the horns of one attached a paper couched in these words: "I am obliged for the repose you have allowed me to take; I thank you for the fresh meat you have sent me. I shall take care of my prisoners; I request you to present my compliments to the Marquis De Montcalm. ROGERS, Commandant of the Independent Companies."—*Doc.*, x, 839.

[2] This battle is supposed to have occurred near the residence of M. B. Townsend, in Crown point.— *C. Fenton.*

eclipsed by a chivalric and daring exploit of the French. A detachment of fifteen hundred French and Canadians, led by Vaudreuil in the ensuing February, who traversed the ice and snows of Champlain and Lake George, a distance of more than one hundred miles, traveling upon snow shoes, "their provisions on sledges drawn by dogs, a bear skin for their couch," and "a simple veil" their only covering. Their errand was the surprise and capture of William Henry. But the garrison was wary and vigilant. The fort was defended with success, although the vessels and bateaux, with the store houses and huts of the rangers were consumed.

On the return of the French from this expedition they were exposed to an infliction, rare in the sufferings incident to war. The reflection of the bright March sun from the dazzling surface of the snow produced a partial although temporary blindness, in one-third of the party. So severe was this opthalmic attack, that those affected were obliged to be led by their companions.[1]

A bold and secret attack by English boats upon the outworks and flotilla at Ticonderoga, was, some months after, signally defeated with severe loss.

The northern colonies, still eager for the expulsion of the French from their borders, acceded to the requisition of Loudon, and assumed to raise four thousand troops for the campaign of 1757. These contingents, they supposed, were designed for the reduction of Crown point and Ticonderoga. Loudon, either from caprice or instability, suddenly announced the abandonment of that expedition, and his purpose of uniting his forces for the conquest of Louisburg. This futile and impracticable scheme left the frontier of the colonies open and unprotected. The vigilant and sagacious enemy, from their watch-towers, at Carillon, saw the error and prepared promptly to seize the advantage.

---

[1] *Garneau*, III, 88; *Pouchot*.

CHAPTER V.

Montcalm, 1756, 1757.

The Marquis de Montcalm was ordered to Canada as the successor of Dieskau. A nobleman of high birth, nurtured in camps from the age of fourteen, animated by spirit and genius in his profession, and guided by an uncommon grasp of views and perceptions in the political affairs of his country, he was calculated to act a distinguished role in the bloody drama then enacting in the new world. Montcalm had served with distinction in the wars of Italy, Germany, and Bohemia, and numerous wounds attested the severity of his services. He was a scholar deeply conversant with the classics of Greece and Rome. Repeated instances in the progress of events had illustrated how almost utterly valueless were the experience and science gained in the wars of Europe, in projecting or conducting a campaign in the wilds of America. The acute sagacity of Montcalm at once perceived this fact, and he promptly engaged in procuring "information of a country and a war, in which everything is different to what obtains in Europe."[1] Along the vast boundary line that divided the possessions of France and England, extending from Acadia to the Mississippi, an unbroken forest, often hundreds of miles in width, separated the occupied districts of the alien provinces. These forests had but slight assimilation to the poetical green woods of the old world, but disclosed only dark, tangled, dank and impervious tracts, penetrated alone by the trail of the Indian. On either side the bold and hardy pioneers were gradually, but constantly invading these solitudes. Their vigorous arms were slowly carving out spots, where the humble cabins were built upon the verge of this boundless forest. A perpetual warfare was waged between the savages, who regarded these wildernesses as their homes and their hunting grounds, and this vanguard

---

[1] *Doc.*, x, 400.

of civilization. The aborigines knew no other method of attack than the secret ambuscade, and surprise, and in actual fighting, the covert by each individual of a tree, a rock or a bush. The practices of civilized war, the concerted manœuvres of troops, or the mechanism that moved drilled battalions, were found in many a conflict with Indian warriors without efficiency, and powerless. The instincts of self-preservation compelled the settlers to adopt the method of savage arts, and they became expert pupils in this horrid warfare. With almost equal skill as their Indian teachers, they learned to form the ambush, to make the sudden attack, to thread the intricacies of the forest, to pursue the trail of a foe, and to disguise their own. The tomahawk was wielded by the backwoodsman with savage dexterity, and even the terrible offices of the scalping-knife were often familiar to his habits.[1] In these wars, mercy was seldom recognized, and a mutual extermination was their stimulating motive.

The exigencies of these circumstances and of the times, called into existence a novel organization of troops, little known to the military bureaux of Europe. The partisan corps of New France, and the American rangers and scouts, combined with most of the Indian characteristics some infusion of the discipline and subordination belonging to regular armies. These bodies, especially the French corps, united with a large savage element, were the most effective and active arm of forest warfare upon the borders of New England, and New York. These savages reached everywhere, overwhelming alike the hut of the frontier and the dwellings and hamlets, whose remoteness seemed to secure immunity from danger; flanking armies and fortresses, and suddenly striking a blow, far in the interior of the hostile territory, and retreating by the light of burning villages or the flames of solitary cabins with the scalps of childhood and age, of the soldier and woman, they would steal back silently to their lurk-

[1] *Hough's Pouchot*, 77.

ing places. Marin — the Molang of tradition and popular tales — was the prominent leader of the French expeditions, and by his brilliant qualities as a partisan, and by deeds of valor, often sanguinary, but sometimes redeemed by generous acts, he was a worthy, though formidable antagonist to Rogers and Putnam, the gallant chiefs of the American rangers. Marin was originally attached to the navy of France, but at an early age, allured by the romance and daring character of the border warfare of New France, he joined the irregular forces of the government, formed of Indians and Canadians.

The French, far more than the English, were successful in conducting military operations in association with their savage auxilliaries. More flexible in their own feelings, they were more yielding and tolerant towards the peculiar habits and temperament of the Indians. Coercion and reason were powerless with such allies. Capricious, and intractable, superstitious and fluctuating, they could only be moved by their affections and controlled by an apparent yielding to their humors and impulses. The Indians, in these border wars, were often the most valuable auxiliaries, and achieved victory upon more than one important field; but always unreliable, no safe calculations could be placed upon their services, their fidelity or constancy. Montcalm pronounced them inestimable as scouts and spies. The corps of Marin, so dreaded for its ubiquity, its bold exploits, and the desolation it inflicted upon the American settlements, was constituted chiefly of Indians. Scalps and prisoners commanded their price in market, and their comparative value was decided by the spirit of mercy or vengeance which happened to prevail in the council chamber.[1]

Montcalm arrived in May, 1756, at Quebec, and hastened without delay to the frontier, to acquire by personal inspection a knowledge of its conditions and capabilities

---

[1] Montcalm, in a postscript to D'Argenson, coolly adds: "Two canoes arriving while I write. They raise the dead cry. That wail announces that they have killed or captured eleven English."— *Doc.*, x, 422.

of defense. Fifteen busy days he occupied in their investigations. "Ambulances," he writes, "in a horrible condition; bread bad; the works at Carillon but little advanced; order to be introduced everywhere; recognizances of the passes to be made."[1] Recalled by Vaudreuil to Montreal, he "traveled night and day," and after one day given to consultation, repaired with the same rapid speed to Frontenac. Such zeal animated the ardor of Montcalm, and he desired to impart the same spirit to all branches of the service and administration. In August, he had organized an adequate force and armament, and advancing with a celerity that disguised his movements, he suddenly besieged Oswego, which, after a brief defense, capitulated. Abandoning his conquest, he left on its site only ruins and solitude.[2] In the autumn and winter succeeding, he was present at Carillon, and directed the events traced in the close of the last chapter. Marin, in July, 1757, was dispatched from Carillon, with a small body of Indians, to harass the English scouting parties. He surprised near Fort Edward, and attacked with success, two detachments, and retreated triumphantly in the face of a superior force, that pursued him. "He was unwilling," wrote Montcalm to Vaudreuil, "to amuse himself making prisoners; he brought in one, and thirty-two scalps."[3] Did this cold apathy presage the fearful scenes soon to occur at William Henry?

In the same summer, a party of three hundred and fifty provincials, under the command of Colonel Parker, in twenty-two bateaux, proceeding incautiously down Lake George, were surprised by a body of Ottawa Indians under Corbiere at Sabbath-day point. Only two boats and fifty men escaped the fatal ambush.[4] The next year when the British army stopped at the same place, they "beheld the melancholy remains of the command both in the water and on the land."[5]

---

[1] *Doc.*, x, 432. [2] *Bancroft.* [3] *Doc.*, x. 591. [4] *Idem,* 594. [5] *Idem,* 734.

Montcalm had directed all the powers of his genius and energies to the accomplishment of one great and desirable triumph. The fort at the head of Lake George, erected by Johnson, had been a perpetual object of alarm and anxiety to the government of Canada, and its conquest was a determined purpose, cherished in the colonial policy. The partial success of Vaudreuil, instead of repressing has prompted renewed effort. It was determined that the attempt should be repeated, with a force and efficiency, that must command success. In aid of this enterprise, all the savage tribes, controlled by the influence of France, were summoned. Their warriors gathered from the wilds of Lake Superior to the shores of Acadia, assembled around the fort at St. Johns. Montcalm, glowing with the triumph at Oswego, was there. By his success, his courage and endurance, he had conciliated their affection. He justly wrote "I have seized their manners and genius.[1]

He mingled in their war dance, and chanted their war songs, captivating their hearts by his largesses and kindness, and exciting their savage passions by visions of plunder and revenge. The warriors embarked in two hundred canoes, bearing the distinctive pennons of the various nations: the priests accompanied their neophytes, and while the war chants strangely blended with the hymn of the missionary, passed up Lake Champlain, to unite at Ticonderoga their rude forces with the legions of Montcalm. These had been rapidly assembled at Crown point and Carillon.

The transportation of two hundred and fifty bateaux and two hundred canoes across the portage between Lake Champlain and Lake George, a space of about three miles, "without the aid of oxen or horses" was a gigantic labor, achieved by "men's arms alone; entire brigades headed by their officers, relieved each other in the work."[2] The next day, when all the preliminaries had been arranged, Montcalm called together the chiefs of the tribes in coun-

---

[1] *Doc.*, x, 686. [2] *Idem*, 608.

cil. Upon the shore of the lake "they were placed in ranks settled by themselves." The domiciliated Iroquois, the most numerous of the bands, and "the former proprietors of the soil," assumed the office of hosts, and received the remote tribes with the rites due to strangers. To the Iroquois, Montcalm presented the "great belt of two thousand beads, to bind the Indians to each other and all to himself." When the tribes had been thus propitiated, he unfolded to them all the plans of the expedition.[1] These were satisfactory, and were adopted by a formal acquiescence. The insufficient supply of boats made it necessary for a part of the army to proceed by land. De Levis, with twenty-two hundred French and Canadians, escorted by six hundred Indians, starting two days in advance and leaving their baggage to be conveyed by water, undertook to traverse the rugged mountain track on the west side of the lake, which was scarcely practicable to the solitary hunter. On the 1st of August, the remainder of the forces embarked in bateaux. The artillery was transported upon pontoons, constructed by platforms resting on two boats, which were lashed together. The Christian Indians had employed the preceding days in the confessional, and devotion; but the pagan tribes from the upper lakes "were juggling, dreaming, and fancying that every delay portended misfortune." These tribes suspended "a full equipment to render the Manitou propitious." Montcalm, in a severe austerity, to which he cordially subjected himself, reduced the supplies of the army to absolute necessities.[2] He appropriated "a canvas awning to every two officers, of whatever grade." "A blanket and a bear skin," he said, "are the bed of a warrior in such an expedition."[3]

---

[1] These independent people, whose assistance is purely voluntary, must be consulted, and their opinions and caprices are often a law to us."—*Doc.*, x, 609.

[2] *Doc.*, x, 610. [3] *Idem,* 637, Montcalm's Circular.

The army was composed of about five thousand five hundred effective men, with an auxiliary force of sixteen hundred Indians.[1] On the second day, early in the morning, they saw three signal fires at Ganaouskè bay, that announced the arrival of De Levis, and the assurance of security in disembarkation. De Levis had encountered toils and obstacles, which were only surmounted by the perseverance of hardihood acquired from the habits and example of their Indian allies. The same evening Montcalm advanced towards the fort. During the night two English scout boats were discovered upon the lake, and pursued by the swift war canoes of the Indians. One of these boats was captured. Two only of the crew were saved, and the others massacred.[2] In the fight a distinguished warrior of the Nipissings was slain, and the next day the Indians consecrated to his funeral rites, in all the splendor and display of barbarian ceremonies.[3] The fort, garrisoned by five hundred men, commanded by a gallant veteran, Colonel Munroe, and supported by seventeen hundred troops in an intrenched camp adjacent, Montcalm was promptly and perfectly invested. De Levis occupied the right, the most exposed and important position, and held the road leading to Fort Edward; Boulemarque took position on the left resting upon the lake, and Montcalm held the centre.[4] Immediately before the investment, Webb, who lay at Fort Edward, fourteen miles distant, with four thousand men, had visited William Henry, escorted by Putnam and a body of rangers. Putnam descending the lake in a reconnaissance, discovered the approach of Montcalm, and at once returned, communicating the fact to Webb, and urging him to prepare to oppose

---

[1] *Doc.*, x, 625.

[2] The French account magnifies the crews into a hundred and fifty men, of whom "sixty or seventy were captured or drowned." The Indians attacked in their birch canoes, and by swimming "with guns and hatchets."—*Pouchot*, I, 86.

[3] *Bancroft.*

[4] *Doc.*, x, 601, 611. De Levis did not hold the left wing as stated by Bancroft.

the landing. Webb, enjoining secresy upon Putnam, hastily returned to Fort Edward. Johnson, on the day of Montcalm's departure from Carillon, received intelligence from Webb of the impending attack, and abandoning an Indian council in which he was engaged, collected the militia and Indians he was able to muster, and marched rapidly to Fort Edward, which he reached on the second day of the siege. The craven supineness of Webb was long deaf to the entreaties and expostulations of his subordinates to attempt the relief of the beleaguered fortress. He at length conceded to Johnson a reluctant permission to advance with the militia and rangers. But these generous designs were arrested, when they had scarcely proceeded three miles, by an imperative order from Webb to return.[1] Montcalm was apprised of the movements of Johnson, and with his accustomed promptness prepared to meet it.

The sole interest manifested by Webb for the heroic garrison, struggling in their hopeless position, was a chilling letter agitated by exaggerated fears, which he attempted to communicate to Monroe. In this letter, which was interrupted by Montcalm, but eagerly forwarded to Monroe, Webb advised, if "from the delays of the militia he should not have it in his power to give timely assistance," Monroe should obtain the best terms left in his power.[2] [2]For this letter see appendix A.] On the same fortunate day of this event, Montcalm received dispatches from France announcing "royal favors to his army and conferring upon himself "the red ribbon with the rank of commander in the order of St. Louis." The army was animated with a more ardent enthusiasm by this appreciation of the king, and the Indians "hastened to compliment the general at the distinction which the great Onontio[3] had just decorated

[1] *Thompson's Vermont ; Stone.* [2] *Pouchot,* II, 263.

[3] This term of respect was applied indiscriminately by the Indians to the king of France, the governor-general or other high officials. Its literal meaning is great mountain, an epithet originally applied to M. De Montmagny, governor of Canada, of whose name it is a translation. (O'Callaghan's note, *Doc.*, IX, 37).

him, as they knew how highly he esteemed it; that, as for themselves, they did not love or esteem him the more on that account, it was his person they loved, and not what he added to the exterior."[1] On the sixth day of the siege, Monroe, half his guns useless and his ammunition nearly exhausted, hung out a flag of truce. Terms the most liberal were extended to the garrison, either from a magnanimous respect for its gallant defense or dictated by an apprehension that Webb might arouse from his stupor and imbecility and assail the French rear.

It was stipulated by the first article of the capitulation, that the English troops should march out of the works "with their arms and other honors of war," and be escorted on the road to Fort Edward by a detachment of French troops and interpreters attached to the Indians.[2] In order to secure their performance of this capitulation, the Indians were made parties to it, and formally ratified its provisions.

The appalling event which followed the capitulation are involved in impenetrable mystery. They have been so distorted by passionate exaggerations and screened by such earnest and varied apologies and evasions, that they must ever remain among those problems in history, to which neither research nor speculations can afford any solution. This and many similar atrocities have been written upon the page of history, by unwise and unchristian policy, which added to the horrors of war by the introduction of fierce and savage barbarism into the conflicts between civilized nations. The distinct facts, which can be extracted from the confusion of conflicting statements and the angry passions of the times are nearly these. The night succeeding the capitulation had been spent by the Indians, in celebrating the victory with their customary orgies. Their minds were inflamed by the recital by the eastern tribes of real or imaginary wrongs recently inflicted by the English.[3] As the garrison was marching from the entrenchments early in the morning, the Indians in a menacing attitude

---

[1] *Doc.*, x, 613. [2] *Idem*, 617. [3] *Idem*, 616.

gathered about them and commencing their outrages by seizing the personal effects of the prisoners and brandishing the tomahawk and amusing themselves with the terror their savage pastimes excited among the English. Individual resistance was probably made to these indignities, and personal conflicts ensued. The Indians saw spoils, which as victors they thought belonged to themselves, eluding their grasp.[1] This idea combined with their inherent love of slaughter aroused their savage appetites. "The first blood that flowed inflamed all the ferocity of their nature, and for a while they recognized no regard to treaties or any restraints of power or influence. The panic-stricken Englishmen broke from their ranks, and, forgetting the weapons in their hands, fled in wild dismay pursued by the frenzied savages. At this moment Montcalm and other French officers rushed upon the scene baring their own breasts and interposing their arms for the protection of the prisoners and "by threats, prayers, caresses and conflicts with the chiefs, arrested the massacre."[2] "Kill me," cried Montcalm," but spare the English, who are under my protection." More than half the British troops, in fragmentary detachments succeeded in reaching Fort Edward; about thirty were slain; four hundred were rescued with their property and restored under the capitulation by Montcalm, and many others, at his solicitation, were ransomed from the Indians by Vaudreuil.[3] It is evident that the escort of French troops stipulated by the capitulation were not supplied until after the massacre.[4]

Montcalm and his apologists affirm in his vindication, that the English troops, in uncontrollable alarm, left the intrenchments at an earlier hour than had been agreed upon; that they had possessed, by the arms they carried, the means of resistance, but instead of this, scattered in ungovernable frenzy; that in disregard of the injunctions of the French, they gave intoxicating liquor to the Indians, in the hope of conciliating them; that Montcalm

---

[1] *Pouchot.* [2] *Doc.*, x, 637. [3] *Doc.* [4] *Idem.*

was powerless to control the hordes of peculiarly wild and ferocious savages who perpetrated the massacre, but had relied on the assurances of the chiefs, that they would maintain the treaty and prevent all discord; and that every effort was made by Montcalm and his subordinates, to arrest the violence, and by these exertions, an indiscriminate slaughter of the prisoners was averted.

These apologies are not fully sustained by the authenticated facts. Bourgainville, the aide and adviser of Montcalm, explicitly states in his official report, that he had destroyed "on the day of the surrender, all intoxicating liquors in the English works."[1] Montcalm, in his first summons to Monroe, avowed a distrust of an ability to control his savage allies. With that knowledge, he should have exerted the right and power of the victor, if the English, in their infatuation and terror, were rushing upon these appalling dangers, and arrested them by force, until an adequate protection was prepared. No motive of policy; no desire to propitiate the affections of the Indians, should have received the consideration of a moment, in restraining the exercise of his whole military force, for the preservation of his own fame, the honor of his country, and the sacred faith of a capitulation. One, who himself participated in the horrors of the scene, and stripped of his clothing, narrowly escaped the massacre, insists in a minute account of the occurrences, "that the French neglected, and even refused protection to the English," imploring their mercy and interposition.[2] British Indians, who were with the garrison, the French savages seized upon, without interference, and they perished in lingering and barbarous tortures.[3]

Calm history will always reject the impassioned tales, evolved from the exasperation and excitement of the times, of the complicity of Montcalm in a cold-blooded and premeditated slaughter of capitulated prisoners, and the wanton and barbarous cruelties imputed to him. Such

---

[1] *Doc.*, x, 615. [2] *Carver's Travels*, 204. [3] *Graham*, II, 268.

atrocities were utterly incompatible with his high character as a Christian noble, a gallant soldier and a refined scholar, whose sensibilities had been purified and elevated by communion with the poets and philosophers of antiquity. But it can never exonerate his fame from the imputation of criminal negligence and a reckless disregard to the safety of those confided to his honor and protection by the most solemn act known to warfare. A moral responsibility for the consequences rests upon those, who set in motion a power, which they know they have no ability to guide or control. The Indians, in their eager pursuit of plunder and scalps, violated many new made graves, and tore from the decaying corpses the dread trophies that commanded rewards. Several of these graves contained victims to the small-pox. The plunderers contracted the infection, and bore the fell scourge to their winter lodges in the far west. Its fearful desolation among the savages who knew no remedy, and in superstitious dread sought no relief, cannot be conceived. The noble tribe of the Pottawattomies was nearly extinguished by its ravages.[1]

The total demolition of William Henry, and the capture of an immense quantity of munitions and public stores were the rewards of this expedition. Montcalm's triumph was mingled with deep satisfaction, when he reported that this conquest had been achieved with the loss of only fifty-three of his own army. On the 15th of August, he abandoned a smoking ruin and bloody strand to silence and desolation. An ulterior object of the campaign contemplated the reduction of Fort Edward. Had Montcalm comprehended the imbecility and paralysis that had fallen upon the British councils, this result and possibly the destruction of Albany might have been accomplished. But the existence of facts so degrading, could scarcely enter into the calculations of his gallant spirit. The diminution of his forces an advance would have demanded, the limited extent of his supplies, and the urgent necessity imposed

[1] *Pouchot*, I, 91.

by an impending famine for the presence of the Canadians in their harvest fields, constrained Montcalm to be satisfied with the glory and success he had already achieved. Terror and alarm pervaded the English colonies. Webb sent his personal baggage to a place of security, and was preparing to fall back upon the highlands of the Hudson. Loudon, to defend the British possessions, had taken post upon Long Island. The English were expelled from the Ohio. Montcalm had established the domination of France throughout the valley of the St. Lawrence. A deep consternation and a cry of agony agitated New England. Britain and the colonies were alike stricken and humiliated.[1]

CHAPTER VI.

Ticonderoga, 1758.

The opening of the year 1758, was marked by an augmented activity and determination in the councils and operations of each of the belligerents. France and England, alike comprehended that the crisis was approaching which must decide their protracted struggle for the sovereignty of the North American continent. In that field, the vast disproportion in their material resources and military strength, became constantly more obvious and decisive. Much of the soil of Canada, for more than one season, had been abandoned or only partially tilled, and the scanty harvest insufficiently gathered, while a large proportion of the peasantry, who should have cultivated the earth and gathered the crops, had been drawn into the field by the exigencies of the war. An unpropitious season in 1757, caused a failure of the harvest, and especially that of wheat, which was the chief reliance of both the people and the army. For more than six months in the year, nature formed an impenetrable barrier to the naviga-

---

[1] *Bancroft.*

tion of the St. Lawrence. British ships thronged the track of the ocean between France and her colonies, rendering the transmission of supplies and troops precarious and nearly impracticable. A scarcity that nearly reached destitution, already prevailed in Canada.[1] In February, 1758, Montcalm addressing the French minister writes: "the article of provisions makes me tremble."[2]

The population of Canada was estimated by Montcalm at only eighty-two thousand, and from these he computed he might rely upon about seven thousand men in the field at one time. This force was augmented by nearly four thousand regular troops. With this strength and with such resources, he was required to confront an army of fifty thousand men, subject to the orders of Abercrombie,[3] and sustained by a rich and prosperous population in the British colonies of a million and a half, enjoying a constant and commodious intercourse with England. These embarrassments were aggravated by other annoyances and difficulties, that galled the high, incorruptible spirit of Montcalm, and fettered his energies. An universal scheme of venality and peculation pervaded every branch of the colonial government. The king was defrauded, and public measures paralyzed; the people were oppressed, and the army, both officers and men, suffering and impoverished. Huge fortunes awarded the corrupt and debauched officials.[1] A bitter animosity, inflamed by perpetual charges and

---

[1] Vaudreuil states that in the late expeditions of the autumn of 1757, the troops were chiefly dependent for support upon the uncertain toils of the hunters.—*Doc.*, x, 701. The citizens received a daily supply of one-fourth of a pound of bread, and this scanty ration was reduced to two ounces.—*Montcalm*, 448. Doreil writes: "many persons have died of hunger. *Idem* 898. [2] *Idem*, 686.

[3] Hildreth.

[4] *Doc.*, x, 960, 963. At the termination of the war, these frauds were investigated in France judicially. Vandreuil was acquitted. Bigot, the intendant, Varin, the commissary at Montreal, Breard, the comptroller of the navy, were convicted and banished. Pean, the instrument of these iniquities, by the influence of his wife, the mistress of Bigot (*Pouchot*), and the Madame Pompadour of Canada, was mulct in the sum of 600,000 livres.—O'Callaghan, *Doc.*, x, 1126.

mutual recriminations, disturbed the relations between Vaudreuil and Montcalm. The one imputed to the governor-general gross ignorance in military affairs, duplicity, and disingenuousness in the exertion of power, and practices that trammelled and embarrassed his operations.[1] Vaudreuil complained of the arrogance of Montcalm, his jealousies and the assumption of authority not warranted by his position.[2]

In every age and in all countries, commanders, operating in a remote field of action, have often experienced the paralyzing influence produced by the instructions and the intrusive councils of men, who are necessarily ignorant of concurring events and often without a competent knowledge of military affairs. Generals have felt this malign influence, and history has recognized and recorded it as the aulic council policy in war. Genius and spirit have often commanded success in ascending beyond or bursting through these restraints. Montcalm was not exempt from this blind and arbitary intrusion into his measures. While tracing the military character of Boulamarque, Montcalm portrays with equal force both the nature and effect of this system when he says: Boulamarque "follows too literally orders issued eighty leagues distant, by a general who knows not how to speak of war." [3]

These favorable circumstances, which were calculated to impart such preponderance to England in American affairs, were to a certain extent counterbalanced by advantages peculiar to France.

The British provinces were independent in their government by their chartered organization, and widely separated in geographical position. These incidents often produced conflicts of interest, collision in sentiments, and acrimonious jealousies. An absence of that harmony, so essential to successful action, was not unfrequently apparent in their councils. The population of Canada was concentrated and accessible, and all the measures and resources of the colony

---

[1] *Doc.*, x, 786, 800, 778, 812. [2] *Idem*, 885, 781. [3] *Idem*, 491.

were, in theory, controlled by a single mind, which could decide and act, while the English governments were contending or advising. French policy and intrigues excited a perpetual alarm or hostility against England among the Indian tribes, that lay along the borders of her colonies from Acadia to the Spanish possessions, and hung like a dark and threatening cloud upon their horizon, which might at any moment burst upon their settlement in tempests of fire and blood. This sagacious policy of France, which to such an extent fettered the strength of the English colonies, cannot be understood without a comprehension of the dread inspired at that time by the horrors of an Indian war. The people of Canada, although continually revolted by the supercilious and arbitrary deportment of the French, which was limited to no grade, sustained the conflict with a zeal and devotion never surpassed by any race in any age of the world.[1] The great amount of Canadian levies which joined the French armies, so totally in excess of the proportion usually supplied by an equal population, may be referred to a cause, which possibly exerted some influence in stimulating the great apparent ardor. The feudal system, as it existed in France in the seventeenth century, was transplanted into Canada at its colonization. The seigniories in the province were held under the feudal tenure, which included military service. The sovereign prerogative under this system was empowered to call out the seigneurs, and the tenants holding under them were subject to their military orders in obedience to the call. This fact partially explains the extraordinary aspects exhibited by the virtual conscriptions of this epoch. Montcalm, in one of his letters presenting an estimate of the Canadian force he might calculate on, uses the feudal terms *ban* and *arriere-ban*.

But we must ascribe to the immense superiority in character and intellectual qualities of the men who guided the civil and military affairs of the province, the prominent

---

[1] *Doc.*, x, 463, 585.

agency by which the preeminence of France was so long sustained on the continent and by which the impending ruin of its empire was so long averted. Britain sent to her colonies effete generals, bankrupt nobles, and debauched parasites of the court. France selected her functionaries from the wisest, noblest and best of her people, and therefore her colonial interests were usually directed with wisdom and sagacity. England and America were raised from their humiliation and despondency by the potent genius and splendid combinations of Pitt. His ardent appeals to the patriotism of the colonies, although enforced by no coercion of power, aroused and enlisted their whole energies in support of that gigantic scheme, which contemplated a widely extended attack on all the colonial dominions of France. The irregular warfare between the rangers and partisans and the savage auxiliaries of both nations, crowded into the spring and early summer deeds of brilliant courage achieved in scenes of romance and excitement. In March, Rogers left Fort Edward with one hundred and eighty men under orders to make a reconnaissance in the vicinity of Ticonderoga. He marched upon the ice, until he approached the French outposts, when to disguise their presence, the party plunged into the dense forest, traversing the deep snow through thickets and over broken ground upon snow shoes. Having nearly reached the foot of the lake, they encountered a body of about one hundred Indians and Canadians. These they attacked and dispersed. Pursuing in the confidence of victory, the rangers were suddenly confronted by a largely superior force, which had used their advanced guard to allure the English into an ambush. To retreat was impossible, and a desperate conflict ensued. The rangers scattered into small parties, fought independently with their wonted ardor, but were defeated, and almost the whole detachment slaughtered.[1] Many submitted to

---

[1] Near the scene of this battle is Rogers' slide. The marvelous escape, imputed to him by tradition, must have occurred after this reverse, but I

capitulation, but were slain under circumstances of peculiar atrocity. Rogers, with a small number escaped, but one hundred and forty-four scalps, with two *living letters*, the designation the Indians gave to prisoners whom they saved for intelligence, were the horrid trophies they bore to Montcalm.[1] This was one of the most novel and remarkable conflicts that impressed their strange wildness upon these forest campaigns. It was fought in a dense wood, amid overhanging rocks, upon the declivities of mountains, and on the surface of snow lying four feet deep.[2] The reports on neither side refer to a fact too common to require remark, but the circumstances to my mind imply that both parties were in the battle and fought upon snow shoes.[3]

Another strange episode is said to have imparted additional romance to the campaign of 1758. Putnam, employed in protecting the communications of the English army from the movements of the French partisans, occupied a commanding position with a body of rangers, which, on the eventful night was reduced to thirty-five, below Whitehall, at a point where the lake forms a sharp angle, that is now known as Fiddler's elbow. High ledges of rocks on each side compress the water into a narrow passage. Upon the cliff on the east side, he erected a stone breastwork, which was disguised by arranging pine boughs in such a manner as to present the appearance of a natural growth. Here, he lay four long summer days with the patience and perseverance he had learnt from his savage associates. On the evening of the fourth, his vigilant scout announced the approach of a flotilla. Soon it was discerned gliding stealthily along,

---

regard the whole story to be a myth. I notice no reference to the incident in Rogers's journal, and he is known not to have been diffident in commemorating his own exploits.

[1] *Doc.*, x, 703; *Rogers*, 82; *Pouchot*, I, 199. [2] *Rogers's Journal.*

[3] Locomotion in the depth of snow described would have been impracticable without some artificial aid. The two officers who escaped, and after wandering several days found refuge at Carillon, state explicitly that they fled from the battle on snow shoes. (*Rogers*, 92, 93).

but the effulgence of a full moon revealed every movement. The leading boats had passed the parapet, when the gun of a ranger grating upon the rock produced a slight sound, but sufficient to reach the watchful ear of the foe. They hesitated, and for a moment the boats clustered together, and were about retreating, when the rangers poured upon them a deadly fire. Volley succeeded to volley, in rapid succession. The French returned the fire, but their bullets flattened innoxiously upon the rocks. They attempted to land and gain the rear of Putnam, but were repulsed by the gallant Durkee, with twelve men. The day began to dawn, and his ammunition all expended, Putnam abandoned his fortress, and retreated, bearing with him two wounded men, his only loss. This position is still known as Put's rock. Afterwards, when a prisoner in Canada, he learnt from Marin, that he, with five hundred men, was the antagonist in that romantic encounter, and that the French lost one-half of the force engaged. Perhaps an allowance should be made for a degree of exaggeration, from the courtesy of the brave Frenchman or the credulity of the hearer.

The capture of the fortress on Lake Champlain, and that achieved a descent upon Montreal, were the prominent and most vital objects embraced in the schemes of Pitt. In consonance with this design, an army was gradually assembled in the early summer of 1758, at the head of Lake George. This army, the most magnificent by the number and character of his troops, and the extent and perfection of its appointments, that had ever appeared in the campaigns of the western continent, was intrusted to the command of James Abercrombie. Neither the antecedents of this commander, nor any native ability, justified his selection to a position which would exact the highest efforts of skill and energy. Abercombie was a creature of the court; but Pitt, in the selection of Lord Howe, sought to supply those qualities, in which his superior was so fatally deficient. Howe, elevated to the rank of brigadier-general, was the controlling spirit of the enterprise. Before the arrival of Abercrombie at the camp, the zeal and precaution of Howe had obtained, by the agency of Rogers, a plan of the French works at Carillon, with surveys of the vicinity, and recognizances of the immediate districts.

At the dawn of the beautiful morning on the 5th of July, the whole army, amounting to about sixteen hundred men, including six thousand three hundred and thirty-seven regulars, embarked in nine hundred bateaux, and one hundred and thirty-five whale boats. The artillery was mounted on rafts.[1] The flotilla descended the lake in imposing and splendid order. The rangers, and light infantry were in front, the regulars occupying the centre, and the provincials on either wing.[2] Modern times had witnessed no parallel to this impressive and gorgeous spectacle. We are even now impressed with a degree of awe, as we contemplate the dark, gloomy frame-work of mountain scenery that encloses Lake George in its narrow bed, and by the silence and solitude that rests upon its waters. When the fleet of Abercombie ruffled the placid surface of the romantic lake, the primeval stillness and seclusion of nature were undisturbed along its rugged shores and all its territory, by the habitations of civilized man. The brilliant spectacle moved amid the scene, almost like the illusions of fancy. Amid the clangor of martial music, the glittering of burnished arms, the gleaming of bright scarlet, the fluttering of parti colored plaids, mingled with the woodman's uniform, and the humbler tints of the homespun garments of the provincials, and their banners floating in the breeze, the flotilla glides rapidly forward, exhilarated by the inspirations of heroic daring, and the confidence of victory. We may fancy the hearts of the gallant Highlanders turning back to other days, as the strains of the bagpipes were returned in a thousand echoes from the mountains, recalled the scenes and the joys of their Scottish homes.

---

[1] Abercrombie to Pitt, *Doc.*, x, 725. [2] *Rogers's Journal*, 111.

Towards evening the expedition reached Sabbath-day point, and landed there to rest and refresh. At ten o'clock in the night it again cautiously advanced, Howe, in a whale boat leading the van. Early in the morning of the 6th, a landing was effected without opposition, on the west side of the lake in a little cove still known as Howe's landing. The night before, Howe, reposing on the same bear skin with Stark, discussed in an anxious and investigating spirit, the nature of the defenses at Carillon, and the future movements of the army.[1] Equal in age, alike daring and intrepid, the one a descendant of royalty, and the other an humble pioneer of New Hampshire, they were united by a kindred spirit and warm, mutual esteem. De Boulamarque was stationed with three regiments at the foot of the lake, to observe, and if possible resist the landing of the English army. On its approach, in overwhelming numbers, he burnt his camp with its materials, and effecting a retreat, rejoined Montcalm, to aid in constructing the entrenchment. De Trèpesée, who had been detached with a body of three hundred and fifty men, was constrained to pursue a circuitous route through a heavy forest, was bewildered in its intricacies, and after an exhausting march of twelve hours, while essaying to ford at a rapid, intercepted an English column involved in a similar confusion.[2]

Boulamarque, on his retreat, had very judiciously burnt both the bridges that crossed the outlet of Lake George, and thus obliged Abercombie to advance through a pathless wood on the west side of the stream, who, leaving at the burnt camp his artillery, baggage and supplies, immediately marched towards the French works. The English were arranged in four columns, the regulars in the centre, and the provincials on the flanks; "but the woods being very thick," and the ground uneven and "impassable for a large body of men in any regularity,[3] and the guides unskillful,"

---

[1] *Sparks's Life of Stark.* [2] *Doc.*, x, 726; *Montcalm*, 758; *Pouchot*, I, 111.
[3] Abercrombie to Pitt, *Doc.*, x, 625.

the columns became intermingled and broken. Lord Howe marched at the head of a centre column, which, disordered and obstructed by the tangled underwood and intricate forest, was wandering in confusion when it encountered the fugitive detachment of Trèpesée. An irregular skirmish ensued. The French troops, inferior in numbers, surprised, and worn, and exhausted by their laborious march, fought with desperate valor. Lord Howe fell at the first fire.[1] The regulars, strangers to this mode of forest warfare, appalled by the death of Howe, and intimidated, as a British historian alleges, by the Indian war whoop, faltered and broke, but were gallantly sustained by the provincials.[2] The brave Trèpesée was mortally wounded, and almost the entire detachment either slain or captured, with an insignificant loss to the English. If the British army narrowly escaped by this panic a renewal of the bloody scenes on the Monongahela, it is equally probable, if Howe had lived, and a rapid and vigorous advance been made after the annihilation of Trèpesée's party, that the imperfect entrenchments of the French might have been entered and captured in the disorder and alarm of the moment.[3] But the bugle of Abercrombie sounded the retreat, and the opportunity was lost.

The death of Howe paralyzed the army. With him expired its spirit, its confidence, and hope. All afterwards was prompted by imbecility, indecision and folly. Generous and kind, gifted and accomplished, instinct with genius and heroism, Howe died deeply lamented. The next day a single barge retraced the track of the flotilla bearing the body of the young hero, who but yesterday had led its brilliant pageant. Philip Schuyler, then just entering upon his distinguished career, escorted the remains with all the tenderness and reverence due the illustrious dead. The

---

[1] *Doc.*, x, 738, 726.

[2] *Graham*, II, 279. *Doc.*, x, 726, 725. A few Indians were with Trèpesée. *Doc.*, x, 735.

[3] *Doc.*, x, 735; *Graham*, II, 279.

body was conveyed to Albany and buried in St. Peter's Episcopal Church, which stood in the middle of State street. His obsequies were performed with every pomp of military display and all the solemnities of religious rituals. An heraldic insignia marked the location of the grave. Forty-four years had elapsed, and in the progress of improvement, that edifice was demolished and the grave of Howe exposed. A double coffin was revealed. The outer one, which was made of white pine, was nearly decayed; but the other, formed of heavy mahogany, was almost entire. In a few spots it was wasted, and the pressure of the earth had forced some soil into the interior. When the lid was uncovered, the remains appeared clothed in a rich silk damask cerement, in which they were enshrouded on his interment. The teeth were bright and perfect, the hair stiffened by the dressing of the period, the queue entire, the ribbon and double brace apparently new and jet black. All, on exposure, shrunk into dust, and the relics of the high bred and gallant peer were conveyed by vulgar hands to the common charnel house and mingled with the promiscuous dead.[1] The character and services of Howe received the most generous tribute of respect and eulogium from the French. Massachusetts, in gratitude and reverence, erected a monument to his memory in Westminster Abbey.[2]

---

[1] Montcalm's dispatch.—*Pouchot.*

[2] I am indebted, in part, to a published letter of Mrs. Cochrane for the fact of the interment of Howe in St. Peter's, and to the manuscript of Elkanah Watson for the circumstances of the exhumation. The tradition that Howe, as an example to his troops, caused his hair to be cut short, has cast some doubt on the accuracy of the statement in the text. Pouchot alludes to the same fact, and says the hair was left "two fingers breadth long." (*Pouchot,* I, 110). In my judgment, if the story is correct, it does not conflict with the account in the manuscript. It was the fashion of the age to wear the hair in long locks or ringlets. This habit had probably been introduced into the army, and Howe desired to correct it. No motive of cleanliness, which was doubtless the prominent object with Howe, made the excision of the queue necessary. Short hair, rather than long, would have exacted careful dressing for a funeral preparation. The manuscript states that the identity of the grave was established not only by the coat of arms which surmounted it, but also by the recollection of Henry Cuyler, a half pay British officer, who was at the time a highly respected resident of Greenbush.

TICONDEROGA AND ITS DEPENDENCIES, AUGUST, 1776.

From a plan drawn by Col. John Trumbull.

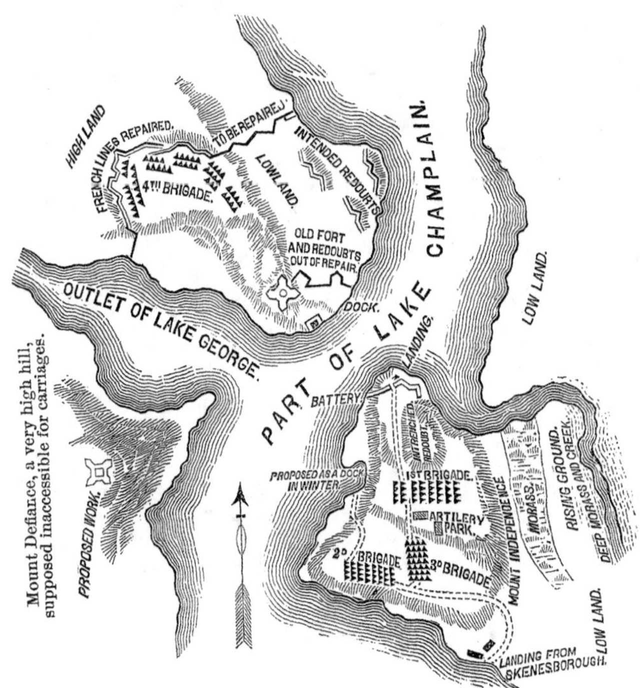

On the morning of the 7th, Abercrombie added to the depression of the troops by withdrawing the whole army to the protection of the works erected at the landing. About noon of that day Bradstreet took possession of the sawmills, at the falls, which were two miles distant from the fort. He rebuilt the bridges, and in the evening the army again advanced and occupied this position.[1] These vacillations and delays of Abercrombie afforded to his alert and energetic adversary the precious hours he needed for the perfection of his defenses.

The promontory held by Montcalm was a narrow and elevated peninsula, washed on three sides by deep waters, with its base on the western and only accessible side. On the north of this base the access was obstructed by a wet meadow, and on the southern extremity it was rendered impracticable to the advance of an army by a steep slope, extending from the hill to the outlet. The summit between these points was rounded and sinuous with ledges and elevations at intervals.[2] Here and about half a mile in advance of the fort, Montcalm traced the line of his projected entrenchment. It followed the sinuosities of the land, the sections of the works reciprocally flanking each other.[3] The entrenchment, which was about an eighth of a league in length, was constructed by Dupont Le Roy an accomplished engineer. "It was formed by falling trunks of trees one upon the other and others felled in front, their branches cut and sharpened produced the effect of a *chevaux de frize*.[4] All of the 7th the French army toiled with unremitting vigor upon the lines, with flags flying along the works, and exhilarated by the inspiration of music, the officers participating in the labor. The parapet arose to the height of eight to ten feet along its whole course. The abatis was about one hundred yards in width.

---

[1] Abercrombie to Pitt, *Doc.*, x, 726. [2] *Pouchot*, I, 114; *Doc.*, x, 739, 742.
[3] *Idem.* [4] Montcalm's report, *Doc.*, x, 739.

De Levis, who had organized an expedition against the Mohawk valley, was recalled by Vaudreuil to meet the perils which were menacing Ticonderoga. Hurrying onward with all celerity that oars and sail could give, his four hundred veterans reached the scene of danger on the night of the 7th, diffusing joy and hope by the announcement of the approach of De Levis, who arrived at five o'clock on the morning of thememorable eighth, accompanied by the brilliant De Senezergues, who, second in command on the plains of Abraham, died there with Montcalm.[1] Nearly at the same hour of De Levis's arrival, Johnson with three or four hundred Mohawks joined the English camp. That the design of evacuating Ticonderoga, which was imputed to Montcalm as a grave fault by Vaudreuil, was entertained by him, may be assumed from other and less prejudiced evidences.[2]

He compared his insignificant force with the overwhelming array of Abercrombie, and saw how easily Carillon might be made untenable. At an earlier day Dupont Le Roy, the chief engineer, had written to the government in emphatic condemnation of the works, and had declared that to capture the fort "I would only require six mortars and two cannon."[3] It is asserted that Montcalm did not decide to make an earnest defense until the morning of the attack.[4]

That purpose of retreating persisted in, would have eclipsed his own great glory. Its consequences would not only have embraced the loss of Ticonderoga and the capture of St. Frederick, but the surrender or disorganization of the French army. The means he possessed of escape by water were totally inadequate to the transportation of his troops and munitions. Pathless forests, lofty and dislocated

---

[1] *Doc.*, x, 794; *Pouchot*, I, 108.

[2] Vaudreuil to De Massiac, *Doc.*, x, 781; Dain to Belle Isle, *Idem*, 814; *Pouchot*, I, 115.

[3] *Doc.* x, 720, Memoir in cipher. This language has been imputed by Mr Bancroft and those who have followed him, to Montcalm, but I find nothing of the kind in his correspondence with the government.

[4] *Pouchot*, I, 110.

mountain ranges, and deep rivers interposed an insuperable barrier to the retreat of an organized army by land.

As far as the limited time permitted, all was prepared along the French lines for the imminent crisis. Montcalm held at Ticonderoga on that day three thousand and six hundred men, and of these, four hundred and fifty were Canadians and troops of the marine.[1] A few Indians only were present. The number of fighting men actually behind the trenches amounted to two thousand nine hundred and ninety-two.[2] At daybreak, the troops were summoned to the lines by the *generàle*. To each was assigned his post, and then the whole army returned to labor upon the entrenchment and abatis.[3] The meadow on the extreme right, with a slight abatis in front, was occupied by the Canadians and irregular troops. The battery of four guns, which was designed to flank this point, was not completed until the morning after the assault. The guns of the fort commanded this opening, as well as the slope on the extreme left. De Levis, on the right, defended the line with three regiments; Montcalm was in the centre with two battalions and pickets, and De Boulamarque occupied with an equal force the left. The precipitous declivity that extended to the outlet was guarded by two companies. Behind each battalion was stationed a company of grenadiers in reserve. The men, still laboring on the works, were ordered to repair to their respective stations, on the discharge of an alarm gun, and at "the moment and signal prescribed, all the troops were under arms and at their posts," just as the van of the British columns appeared.[4]

Abercrombie had been impressed by the advices he received, with the conviction that large reenforcements were approaching Montcalm. Influenced by the report of Clarke, his engineer, who had reconnoitered the French lines from the opposite side of the river, he decided to order an im-

---

[1] These were irregular troops. [2] *Doc.*, x, 739; *Pouchot*, I, 114.
[3] *Idem.* [4] *Doc.*, x, 740, Montcalm's report.

mediate attack, without waiting for his powerful artillery. The English engineer, familiar only with the formal and scientific works of Europe, was doubtless deceived by the peculiar construction of the intrenchment, but the practiced eye of Stark, who knew the strength of the rude parapet of Johnson in 1755, detected formidable lines where Clarke discovered only a frail defense.[1] With a fatuity common to the European leaders in America, Stark's opinion was rejected.

The advance exhibited a grand and imposing military spectacle. The army was formed in three lines. The first was composed of the rangers, bateau men, and light infantry; next the provincials marched with wide spaces between the regiments; and behind these openings, the regulars were formed in columns. The New Jersey and Connecticut levies formed the rear guard. Johnson, with his Indians, occupied Mount Defiance, then known as Sugar-loaf hill, an elevation across the river, near and south of the fort, but, with the exception of an occasional shot, were mere spectators of the conflict. The regulars advancing through the openings with a firm, quick, and steady tread, their bayonets fixed, rushed upon the French lines, along an open space in front of the felled trees. But when they reached the abatis and became entangled in it, all order and regularity were broken. The heroic veterans, struggling individually to surmount these impediments, fought with a valor never surpassed, but against all hope. Two columns charged the right, another assailed the centre, and a fourth was hurled upon the left. They could not advance beyond the terrible abatis, and would not retreat. Even the instincts of nature were dominated by the force of discipline. The British soldier knew no law but obedience. No command came to them to retreat, while the destruction, by the deadly fire of the French musketry, and the howitzers planted at intervals along the line, was terrific. Some of the Highlanders

---

[1] *Pouchot,* I, 116.

fell almost on the entrenchment. The French, protected by their works, were little exposed. "They were invisible," only "a small bit of their caps was to be seen," while they swept down the English by an unbroken storm of fire.[1] The fire of the provincials and marksmen, interspersed between the columns of regulars, was more effective.[2] The moment of greatest peril to the French occurred late in the afternoon, when two of the British columns, by a concerted movement, concentrated an attack upon an angle on the left of the right defense of the French line, and nearly wrested the victory from inexorable fortune. But De Levis, who was temporarily relieved by the pressure upon his right, promptly supported the endangered point, and Montcalm, whose eagle eye watched every change of the battle, rushed to the rescue with a body of the reserve, and this last cast for victory was lost.[3]

Early in the engagement, Abercrombie directed two rafts, mounted with two guns each, to descend the outlet for the purpose of enfilading the French lines, but they were with ease repulsed by the guns of the fort, and the fire of the two companies stationed to defend the extreme left. Frequent, bold and successful sorties were made during the assault by pickets and grenadiers, aided by the Canadians and marine troops from the opening on the right, in which the flank of the attacking column was assailed and prisoners captured.

While these sanguinary scenes were in progress, Abercrombie was reposing in inglorious security at the saw mills; but Montcalm, casting off his coat in that sunny afternoon,[4] was everywhere present meeting every peril; animating his troops by voice and example, ministering to all their wants, and imparting the fervor of his own heroic spirit. On the first assault, the military eye detected the

---

[1] *Doc.*, x, 736.

[2] Montcalm speaks of their murderous fire, *Doc.*, x, 740. "Their fire greatly incommoded those in the entrenchments."—*Pouchot*, I, 116.

[3] *Doc.*, x, 740, 743. [4] *Bancroft.*

utter hopelessness of the enterprise. The attack commenced shortly after meridian, and five long hours had rolled on amid this carnage and desperation, and still the British troops maintained the conflict with determined but unavailing constancy. No order came to stop the ruthless slaughter. The hour of six had arrived, and the devoted columns continued to assail first the right and then the left of the impregnable entrenchment, but at seven the retreat was accomplished.[1] Some loss was inflicted upon the British troops, caused by their firing on each other in the common disorder and excitement. At length regiment after regiment, without any general orders, or concert, retired to the camp; the provincials covering the retreat.[2]

Then ensued that strange and inscrutable phenomenon, which is sometimes exhibited among troops the bravest and most reliable, when an electric influence pervades the masses, communicating an universal and irresistible panic. These veterans, whose steadiness and valor received the generous homage of their victorious foes, and whose country, even amid her grief and humiliation, exulted in their heroism and sacrifices, fled in wild terror and confusion, rushing to the boats in a precipitancy that threatened a general ruin. The firmness and efforts of Bradstreet alone averted fresh and dishonorable catastrophies, which their antecedents could not redeem.[3]

The exhaustion and paucity of the French army, the darkness of the night, the impossibility of traversing the woods without Indian guides, and the entrenchments which the English had erected along their route, restrained pursuit.[4] When De Levis, at break of day on the 10th, followed the track of Abercrombie, he found only the vestiges of a stricken and routed army; the wounded and supplies abandoned, clothing scattered along the woods, with

---

[1] Montcalm, *Doc.*, x, 740. [2] *Pennsylvania Archives.*

[3] It was fortunate we were not pursued in our retreat, we should certainly have lost 2,000 more men.— *Idem.*

[4] Montcalm's report.

the charred remains of boats and pontoons.[1] Before that hour arrived, Abercrombie had fled "in the extremest terror and consternation" and secured a dishonored safety by interposing the length of Lake George between his army and its dreaded conqueror. No pen inscribed for the research of posterity any account of the ignominious flight, so singularly contrasting with the splendor of the advance. The night that closed on a day, among the most glorious that ever beamed upon the arms of France, was spent by Montcalm in the deepest solicitude for the morrow. His troops were under arms or laboriously perfecting their incomplete works, preparing for the anticipated renewal of the assault. Although the English still exceeded the French forces fourfold, with their artillery ready for action, Abercrombie abandoned the campaign.[2] Bradstreet soon after, with a detachment of the same troops, measureably restored their confidence, and vindicated the fame of England by the siege and conquest of Frontenac. Abercrombie admitted the loss of about two thousand men, but the French assumed it to be far heavier, and stated their own to be less than five hundred, but Boulamarque severely and Bougainville slightly were included among the wounded.[3]

The arrival of the younger Vaudreuil on the 12th with three thousand Canadians, followed by six hundred Indians on the 13th, furnished some apparent basis for the apprehension of Abercrombie that reenforcements to Montcalm were approaching, by which he professed to justify his

---

[1] We found in the mud on the road to the falls five hundred pairs of shoes with buckles.—*Pouchot*, I, 121. The soldiers returned loaded with plunder and an immense quantity of shoes with buckles.—*Doc.*, x, 725, 741.

[2] The French asserted that he entrenched on the ruins of William Henry, and removed the guns to Albany for security, retaining all his artillery.—*Doc.*, x. 819; *Bancroft.*

[3] A singular incident occurred during the progress of this remarkable battle. A captain of the Royal Roussillon in bravado, tied a red handkerchief to a gun, and waved it in a sort of defiance towards the English. The English column opposite, supposed it indicated a purpose on the part of the French to surrender. Under this impression, holding their guns horizontally above their heads, they ran toward the entrenchment, crying quar-

precipitate attack on the French works.[1] Abercrombie lingered in imbecile indecision at Fort George, while Montcalm was felt at every point, where his ardor and activity could deliver a blow. Eight days after the repulse at Ticonderoga, a band of five hundred partisans, lurking in the woods near the half way brook between Lake George and Fort Edward, surprised an English detachment and secured forty scalps.[2] A few days after, another party attacked a wagon train on the same ground, loaded with provisions and merchandise. Forty carts, two hundred oxen, the contents of the convoy, one hundred and sixteen scalps and eighty-four prisoners were the fruits of the bold enterprise.[3] Rogers and Putnam with a detachment of seven hundred troops pursued without success the active partisans. Engaged in this pursuit, with the purpose of suppressing similar movements, they descended Lake George, traversed the rude mountainous district to Woodneck, and were returning to Fort Edward. Montcalm was apprised of their march, and dispatched Marin with about the same number of partisans, to follow and intercept the English. Both parties were near Fort Ann, wandering in a dense forest each ignorant of the vicinity of the enemy they were vigilantly pursuing. Rogers, forgetting his

---

ter. The French, ignorant of the circumstances, on their part, believing the English desired to surrender, mounted the works to receive them and ceased firing. The English, under this mutual mistake, had nearly entered the lines, when Pouchot, who witnessed the scene, and perceiving the consequence which would result from their doing this, promptly gave the word to his troops to fire. They did so, with most deadly effect upon the exposed ranks of the English. This is Pouchot's own account of a somewhat ambiguous transaction. He adds, "they have since charged us with using an unpardonable deceit.—*Pouchot*, I, 114.

[1] This is the statement of Pouchot (vol. I, 122). Other accounts reduce the number of the Canadians to three hundred—*Doc.*, x, 745. This fact with the assertion of Rogers that the assault was commenced "before the general intended by an accidental fire from a New York regiment on the left wing," (*Journal*, 115), is the only extenuation of Abercrombie that can ever be adduced.

[2] *Pouchot*, I, 123 ; *Rogers*, 117.

[3] *Rogers*, 117 ; *Doc.*, x, 818 ; *Pouchot*, I. 123.

usual prudence, indulged in firing at a mark with a British officer. Marin heard "the report of three shots" while hesitating as to his course, but the shots revealed the position of the rangers, and, selecting an appropriate spot, he formed an effective ambush.[1] The English, unsuspicious of danger, were threading the woods in Indian file; Rogers in advance, D'Ell in the centre, and Putnam in the rear. They marched directly into the trap that had been so skillfully prepared. Suddenly, the forest resounded with the fearful war whoop, and a terrific fire was hailed upon them from every side. The English, familiar with such scenes, promptly rallied, and a sanguinary conflict followed. Then occurred those thrilling incidents, whose story has agitated for more than a century, thousands of young hearts.

Putnam and a few others, in the surprise and confusion, were cut off from the main body. The men were slain, and Putnam captured and securely bound to a tree. As the changes of the battle surged around him, he was placed at times between the fire of the contending parties and his garments torn by the shots, alike of friend and foe. While in this helpless condition, a young Indian approached and amused himself with the strange pastime of hurling his tomahawk at the prisoner, practicing how near he could approach, without striking the mark. A still more savage Canadian presented his gun at Putnam's breast, but it missed fire. He then indulged his fierce passions by inflicting upon the prisoner several severe wounds with the butt of the weapon. When the French were repulsed and commenced their retreat, his Indian captor released Putnam and extended to him that mysterious tenderness and care with which the Indians treat their victims destined to the torture. The savages encamped at night, and then the strange motive that actuated this kindness was revealed. Putnam, stripped of his clothing, was again tied to a sapling; dried faggots were piled about him; the torch applied, and while the smoke and crackling flames began

[1] *Doc.*, x, 511.

to ascend, the thoughts of the brave ranger dwelt upon his happy home and prattling children. When the agony of death in this frightful form was almost passed, the generous Marin, who had learnt of his peril, rushed to the spot, and bursting through the circle of shouting savages, scattered the firebrands and rescued the victim. In the ensuing autumn Putnam was exchanged, and returned to new fields of glory, but to none of such appalling horror.[1]

CHAPTER VII.

The Conquest, 1759.

The campaign of 1759 opened under gloomy and portentous auguries for the future of New France. The dearth of provision had become intensified into the startling horrors of an absolute famine. The province was nearly exhausted of all the domestic animals. Life in a great degree was sustained, both in the army and among the citizens, only by the consumption of horseflesh. In 1758, these animals had been purchased by the government in large numbers, and their flesh sold to the famishing poor at a trifling cost, and distributed in rations to the troops.[2] The habitans relinquished, either from coercion or cupidity, their ordinary food to the use of the army, and for "two months before the harvest" of 1759 depended for sustenance upon the spontaneous products of the earth and forests. At rare intervals, an adventurous ship, eluding the British squadrons, might increase the scanty supplies of the province by a small pittance, but all regular and reliable succor by this channel was interrupted. Every department in the province revealed evidences, that could not be mistaken, of destitution and decay.

---

[1] On the breaking out of the war of independence Rogers adhered to the government, was subjected to confiscation and outlawry, went to England and there published his journal.

[2] *Doc.*, x, 704, 837; *Pouchot*, I, 135.

Almost every man, that the debilitated population of Canada could yield, was wrested from the fields to replenish the military ranks. "We want provisions; we want powder; and France should send ten thousand men to preserve the colony." Such was the portentous appeal to the home government.[1] But that government was unable to transport a single regiment with a rational hope that it would escape the British ships that thronged the ocean and the gulf. For three years of fierce trials, but resplendent in personal and national glory, Montcalm, by his own genius and energy, had maintained the unequal and desperate contest. But Doreil exclaims, in a letter to Belle Isle, "Miracles cannot always be expected, Canada is lost if peace is not made this winter."[2] In the spring of 1759, Montcalm, in anguish of spirit, writes to the same minister: "If the war continues, Canada will belong to England, perhaps this campaign or the next."[3]

The general venality to which we have referred continually increased, and was a deep cancer that had eaten into the vitals of colonial strength, and was an active cause of its hopeless and irremedial decay. Jealous asperities, and deepening alienations, prevailed between the native French and the Canadians, that marred the harmony and concert all essential to their successful cooperation. The French disparaged the military character of the provincials, burlesqued their pretensions, and scoffed at the pride of the Canadian noblesse.[4] The Canadians were revolted by the hauteur and insolence of the French officials, and indignantly repelled their arrogant assumptions of superiority.[5]

---

[1] *Doc.*, x, 926. [2] Dorcil to Belle Isle *Doc.*, x, 829.

[3] Montcalm to Belle Isle, *Doc.*, x, 960. In the same letter he utters this emphatic language: "If there be peace the colony is lost unless the entire government is changed;" and, with stinging inunendo, quotes Mirabeau, "that those should be disgraced who return from colonies with wealth, and those rewarded who return with the staff and scrip with which they went forth."

[4] *Doc.*, x, 419, 460, 1043; *Pouchot*, I, 37. [5] *Doc.*, x, 78, 419; *Pouchot*, I, 95.

Vaudreuil was of noble descent, but a Canadian by birth, and however deficient he may have been in the attainments of military science, his whole career develops the eminent qualities of his mind, in a native vigor and resources. He was unhappily surrounded by relatives and retainers, and his enemies ascribed to him a nepotism and colonial sympathy, to which were subordinated the higher claims of individuals and paramount public interests.[1] These suspicions and animosities, if they did not originate it, were fostered by the feuds that disturbed the intercourse between Vaudreuil and Montcalm. The latter pretended no disguise of the contemptuous view in which he held the military capacity of Vaudreuil, and with extreme bitterness denounced his incompetent interference, his injustice and want of magnanimity. We cannot fail to detect in the utterances and measures of Vaudreuil, jealousy of the overshadowing martial fame of Montcalm, and often an ungenerous purpose of escaping responsibilities and attempting to grasp the glory that belonged to the deeds of others.

The accusations which Vaudreuil industriously carried to the throne, imputed to Montcalm, insubordination, a haughty neglect of instructions, denunciations of officials, an indiscriminate jealousy, a want of adaptation by temperaments and habits to the command in Canada, and an arbitrary and stern deportment that offended the pride and repelled the services of the Indians and provincials.[2] Whether imaginary or just, the causes of these dissensions, their existence exerted a baneful influence upon the measures of the war. Perhaps the spirit that tends to the disparagement of all irregular troops, common to the professional soldiers, many have tinged the estimate by Montcalm of the provincial levies. The Canadians possibly were deficient in the formula of the parade, or the efficiency of the drill, but in their native qualities, no braver race ever stood upon the battle-field. These ani-

---

[1] *Doc.*, x, 859. [2] *Idem,* 791, 782, 780, 444, 789.

mosities formed a deep line of demarkation, which may be traced in the colonial affairs between the friends and advocates of Montcalm and the partisans of Vaudreuil. The savage tribes, although their professed fealty was undisturbed, no longer gathered about the French camps in numbers that oppressed the commissariat. As an element of strength to the armies of France, they were now unreliable. Perhaps, with the native sagacity that sometimes marked the policy of the Indians, they detected the ascending fortunes of England. Vaudreuil ascribed this defection to the "petulance and impatience" of Montcalm. The presence of a large body of warriors at Ticonderoga had been assured to Montcalm, and he felt the profound conviction, that with their aid as guides through the forest on the night of the assault and the effect of their appearance and fearful whooping in inflaming the panic of the English, a defeat so overwhelming must have been inflicted on Abercrombie, that he would have fled with the mere fragments of an army, leaving to the French a more crowning and decisive victory. Exasperated at these consequences of their delays, when at length they did join him, Montcalm rebuked them with a stern and injudicious, however just, severity. The chiefs carried their complaints to Vaudreuil, and he with an active assiduity communicated them to Versailles.[1] The proud and independent freemen of the woods were doubtless revolted by this violence and a large part returned to their lodges.

While these clouds were gathering about the falling empire of New France, Britain was collecting all her energies for the impending conflict, with a renewed vigor and enthusiasm, inspired by the zeal and spirit of Pitt. The fortress of Louisburg had scarcely fallen, when Amherst, learning of the fatal issue of Abercrombie's campaign, with an unwonted ardor, not waiting for orders,

---

[1] When the chiefs proposed "to go on the road to Fort Edward," Montcalm told them "to go to the d—l." A young chief came back quite furious saying Montcalm had turned him out of doors.—*Doc.*, x, 805.

immediately embarked four or five regiments, and hastened to Boston. He commenced at once a march through the forest towards Lake George, which he, in person, reached in October. In the preceding month, Abercrombie had been recalled, and Amherst appointed the commander-in-chief of the forces in North America.[1] In November, 1758, he assumed the command, and Abercrombie returned to England; evaded censure; was gladdened by promotion, and lived to vote as a member of parliament for the taxation of a country, which his imbecility might have lost, and which was always the object of his malignant aspersions.[2]

Amherst, without any claim to brilliancy or genius, was calculated to command success by the excellence of his judgment, his prudent circumspection, and persevering firmness. His character and policy had secured to him the respect and confidence of the colonies. His measures were not stimulated by the arrogance of Braddock, nor trammelled by the feebleness and indecision of Abercrombie, nor dishonored by the pusillanimity of Webb.

When the exactions for the campaign of seventeen hundred and fifty-nine were known to the colonies, they were appalled by the magnitude of the burdens that were contemplated. Under the assurance that the campaign of the last year should be the final effort, they had yielded their appropriations to it with unbounded fervor and enthusiasm. But they had seen their blood and treasures lavished, without securing any adequate results. The voluntary contributions and public taxation had consumed their resources, while the population was almost exhausted of its available strength by the constantly recurring demands of the protracted war.[3] Although reeling under these debilities, every colony north of Maryland, stimulated by the ardor of Pitt and wielded by his influence, with an abiding reliance on the integrity and skill of Amherst, freely yielded to

---

[1] *Doc.*, VII, 345. [2] *Bancroft*; O'Callaghan, *Doc.*, VII, 345.
[3] *Minot. Grahame.*

his fresh requisition, their wealth and their sons. On the twentieth of June, Amherst took up a position near the ruins of William Henry. Although his entire army, consisting of about eleven thousand effective men, formed in about equal proportions of regulars and provincials, did not assemble until the twenty-first of July. On that day another gorgeous and imposing procession in four columns moved down the quiet lake. A landing was effected without opposition on the eastern shore nearly opposite to Howe's cove. In the combinations of this campaign the British ministry designed to direct a blow at the heart of New France by an attack upon Quebec from the gulf with a powerful army led by Wolfe, while Amherst should cooperate by advancing with a still more formidable force along the Champlain frontier.

Montcalm, oppressed by the annoyances and impediments we have noticed, and despondent from his wasting estate and absence from a dependent family, had reiterated demands for his recall. This request was endorsed and pressed with extreme sincerity by Vandreuil.[1] But France felt that his great intellect alone sustained the tottering fabric of her colonial power. Instead of an acquiescence, the ominous despatch arrived from Versailles: "You must not expect to receive any military reenforcements; we will convey all the provisions and ammunition possible; the rest depends on your wisdom and courage and the bravery of your troops."[2] All the martial ardor of Montcalm was enflamed, and his patriotic devotion enlisted. He resolved to fall beneath the ruins of the colony. To a kinsman in France he wrote: "There are situations where nothing remains for a general but to die with honor. * * * * My thoughts are wholly for France, and will be even in the grave, if in the grave anything remains for us."[3]

---

[1] *Doc.*, x, 758, 769, 783.

[2] Belle Isle to Montcalm, February 19th, 1759, *Doc.*, x, 943.

[3] Private letter of Montcalm, see Appendix.

Montcalm, collecting his scattered battalions, and summoning to his standard all the population of the province able to bear arms, repaired to Quebec to oppose the operations of Wolfe. With a feeble force of twenty-three hundred men, Boulamarque remained in charge of the fortresses upon the lake, to confront Amherst and to retard his progress, while resistance would not endanger the safety of his troops. He proposed to assail the English in their advance through the woods; but the Indians, most useful under such circumstances, defeated the scheme by refusing to cooperate. He left a garrison of four hundred men at Ticonderoga, with orders to maintain the position, until the investment was completed, then to blow up the fort and fall back upon Crown point. Amherst effected the investment of the fort on the 23d; but on the evening of the 26th, a heavy explosion announced the evacuation of Ticonderoga, and that the domination of France had ceased. Amherst immediately occupied the abandoned fortification.

This conquest, the desire and labor of so many years, was at length achieved almost without the effusion of blood. Townsend, the adjutant-general of Amherst, a young officer of high promise and in many qualities the counterpart of Howe, was killed, while reconnoitering the fort, by a cannon ball. His death, and the loss of about eighty men, were the sacrifices by which this important conquest was secured. Exact, cautious and fettered by the prescribed forms of military progress, Amherst consumed two weeks in the guarded and anxious scrutiny by his spies and scouts, before he ventured to advance upon Crown point. He found it abandoned and desolate. Boulamarque had retreated with his army and munition, to fortify the Isle aux Noix. Amherst, as soon as the occupation of Crown point was safely accomplished, commenced the preparations for erecting a new fortress near the site of St. Frederic, but on a scale of increased magnitude and strength. Unnecessary at that time, and rendered wholly useless by the conquest of Canada, he left the work unfinished after the expenditure of more than ten millions of dollars. The most conspicuous ruins at Crown point visited with such deep interest by the tourist and antiquarian are the remains of this fort.[1]

Amherst, with great assiduity and vigor, prepared means to secure a naval preponderance upon the lake. While he awaited the building of a flotilla at Ticonderoga, two measures were accomplished by his orders, unconnected with each other and infinitely dissimilar in their character and results. The first was the construction of a military road from Crown point to Charlestown, or Number Four on the Connecticut river, which, traversing the entire width of Vermont, rendered a large and valuable territory accessible to civilization and improvement. The remains of this work may still be traced.[2]

The other contemplated the destruction of the Indian village of St. Francis, situated on the river of that name, about midway between Montreal and Quebec. Their frequent and active incursions and the relentless atrocities that made this band of the Abenakis conspicuous in a horrid warfare, had rendered them the terror of New England, and objects of peculiar vengeance.

On the 13th of September, Rogers, with great secrecy, and a careful concealment of his design, left Crown point on this perilous service. His party consisted of one hundred and forty-two effective men. Descending the lake with the utmost caution and vigilance, in the hope of escaping the observation of the French, on the tenth day from his departure, he reached the foot of Missisqui bay. Here the boats were concealed, with provisions to supply the party on its return, and leaving two trusty Indians to secretly watch them, Rogers proceeded on his expedition. The second day after, the Indians overtook him, with the alarming intelligence, that the boats had been discovered and removed by the French, and that a detachment of about two hundred were in rapid pursuit. Notwithstanding the disguise and caution of Rogers, Boulamarque, perfectly advised of all his movements, had fol-

---

[1] *Doc.*, x, 670. [2] *Goodhue's Shoreham.*

lowed his track, seized the boats, and lay in ambush, expecting the return of the English.[1] But Rogers's shrewdness could not thus be entrapped. Hesitating for a moment, the decision of the bold ranger was formed. Dispatching Lieutenant McMullin and eight men, who were to penetrate the pathless wilderness to Crown point, with a request to Amherst, to send the necessary supplies to meet the party at the Cohase intervales, a point sixty miles north of Number Four, the extreme northern post of the English on the Connecticut, Rogers determined to prosecute the original design.

Nine days his march continued, wading through unbroken swamps and morasses; sleeping upon hammocks elevated above the water, by boughs cut from the trees, and fording deep streams. On the evening of the twenty-second day of his expedition, the party approached their unsuspecting victims. Rogers and two of his officers reconnoitered the village, and found it abandoned to revelry and dancing. Amherst, in his instructions to Rogers, had given expression, rare in that age of savage cruelty, to the voice of mercy and humanity. "Take your revenge on the warriors; but remember," he said, "it is my orders that no women or children are killed or hurt." Just as the day was dawning, the troops "on the right, centre, and left," burst upon the slumbering villagers. The surprise was complete and few escaped. "We killed," reports Rogers, "two hundred Indians,"[2] and took twenty of their women and children prisoners. He dismissed all but five of the latter prisoners, whom he retained, and released five English captives. The light revealed the horrid spectacle of more than six hundred scalps, of both sexes and of every age, chiefly English, floating like dread pennons from the lodge poles and cabins of the savages. When the rangers looked upon

[1] *Doc.*, x, 1042.

[2] The term Indians was often used to designate warriors, and we may hope it was so in this instance; but Pouchot states that the warriors were absent.—Vol. I, 223.

these symbols of Indian barbarity, they might, with truth, have felt, that they were not only instruments of vengeance, but ministers of justice. The village was consumed, and many of the Indians, who had sought a refuge in the cellars and lofts, were burnt to death. Captain Ogden, of the rangers, was severely wounded, six others slightly, and one Indian of the party killed. Loading the men with all the plunder and corn they were able to carry, Rogers immediately commenced a retreat in the direction of the Connecticut. He was pursued by a body of Indians, and repeatedly attacked, with the loss of a few prisoners. At length he turned upon his pursuers, and dealt them a punishment so severe, as to arrest further open assaults, but they hung upon his rear with a deadly tenacity; and when the detachment separated into small bodies, which policy Rogers was constrained to adopt, on the eighth day of the march, in order more readily to procure subsistence, they attacked and killed or captured many of the party.[1]

The different bodies toiling in intense labor and suffering, marching over steep rocky mountains, and traversing rivers and deep morasses, were sustained, amid fatigue and hunger, by the confident hope of finding relief and repose at the place designated by Rogers. They reached it, and found the brands, enkindled by the party which was to convey them supplies, still smouldering; but no friends, no food. McMullen, penetrating the vast forest a hundred miles in extent, arrived at Crown point on the ninth day of his march. Amherst, with no delay, had directed a lieutenant Stephens to convey the requisite supplies to the appointed rendezvous, and to remain while a hope existed of the return of Rogers. He reached the place with ample provisions, but fearing the approach of the Indians, continued only two days at his post and abandoned it, as after-

[1] The Indians massacred some forty, and carried off ten prisoners to their village, where some of them fell victims to the fury of the Indian women, notwithstanding the efforts made by the Canadians to save them." *Doc.*, x, 1042

wards appeared, but two hours before the arrival of Rogers. He heard the signal guns fired to recall him, but believing them to indicate the presence of Indians, his flight was precipitated.

Leaving his exhausted and famishing comrades with the assurance that in ten days they should be relieved, to procure "what wretched subsistence they could in a barren wilderness," Rogers, accompanied by Ogden, a ranger, and an Indian youth, undertook to descend the river upon a raft in pursuit of aid. Rogers does not intimate his motive for carrying with him the Indian, but we may form a fearful conjecture. The first raft was lost among the rapids; destitute of implements, they could only construct another, with trees felled and reduced to the appropriate length by burning. The fort at Number Four was reached by an inflexible determination, and a canoe with supplies immediately despatched, which arrived at Cohase on the day designated by Rogers. He returned to Crown point on the 1st December, and when the scattered parties were reassembled, he reported the loss after the detachment retreated from the ruins of the St. Francis village, of three officers and forty-six privates.[1]

On the eleventh of October, Captain Loring of the navy, to whom the work was confided, had succeeded by the most energetic efforts in completing the construction of a sloop carrying sixteen guns, a brigantine and radeau mounted with six cannon of large calibre. Amherst embarked his army in a vast flotilla of bateaux, and, escorted by these vessels, proceeded on his long procrastinated expedition. The next day he encountered one of those severe autumnal gales, which often at that season sweep over the lake.[2] Twelve of the boats were foundered, and the remainder sought shelter under the western shore of the lake. Amherst probably advanced while struggling with these adverse circumstances to the vicinity of Valcour

---

[1] *Rogers's Journal*, 144, 159. [2] *Pouchot*, I, 146; II, 66.

island, and there on the mainland formed an encampment.[1] Loring, with the sloop and brigantine, continued on his course, and compelled the French to destroy two of their vessels in a bay on the north-east angles of Valcour; a third was sunk, and one only, the schooner, escaped, and sought shelter under the guns of the Isle aux Noix.[2]

Experience or inquiry might have suggested to Amherst, that these periodical gales on the lake are always limited in their duration, and usually succeeded by a term of serene and genial weather. But ever controlled by an extreme of prudence and caution, he returned to Crown point after an absence of ten days, relinquishing the combinations his movements were intended to promote, and abandoning Wolfe to work out the fortunes of his army by his own unbounded energies and genius.

It is not my province to pursue the course of events on the banks of the St. Lawrence, but a brief space devoted to the last scenes in the life of one who has occupied so wide a space in our narrative, can need no apology. On the 24th of August, 1759, Montcalm, as if in the cool tracings of history, instead of the speculations of prophetic prescience, wrote: "The capture of Quebec must be the work of a *coup de main*. The English are masters of the river. They have but to effect a descent on the bank on which this city,[3] without fortification and without defense,

---

[1] I adopt this conclusion from the language of an English writer of the period, and from the popular traditions of the region. Those are still living who recollect an opening on the Pine bluffs, south of the Au Sable river and directly upon the boundary line between Clinton and Essex counties, which, in the early part of the century, was known as Amherst's encampment. It exhibited vestiges of extensive field-works the habitual caution of Amherst would have led him to erect, and also remains of tar manufactories, formed in the primitive method of the pioneers. It is a singular coincidence, that the tar and pitch used in the equipment of McDonough's fleet, more than fifty years afterwards, were made on the same ground and by a similar process.—*Alvin Colvin, Esq.*

[2] *Doc.*, VII, 405; X, 1042; *Pouchot.*

[3] Montcalm must here speak comparatively and refer to the inadequacy of the works which surrounded Quebec. A reference to this remarkable and deeply interesting document will be found in Appendix B.

is situated, and they are at once in condition to offer me battle which I cannot refuse, and which I ought not to be permitted to gain. In fine, Mr. Wolfe, if he understands his business, has but to receive my first fire, to rush rapidly upon my army, to discharge his volley at close quarters, and my Canadians without discipline, deaf to the call of the drum and the trumpet, and thrown into disorder by this assault, will be unable to recover their ranks. They have no bayonets to meet those of their enemy; nothing remains for them but flight, and I am routed irretrievably."

Three weeks later, Wolfe, pursuing the instincts of a congenial spirit, had fulfilled the presages of Montcalm, and stood with his army upon the plains of Abraham. Prophecy became history, and Montcalm, routed as he had predicted, was borne back to Quebec with a fatal wound, rejoicing "that he should not live to witness its fall." Confiding to his subordinate the honor of France, and commending the companions of his misfortunes and glory to the clemency of a generous foe, he exclaims: "As for me, I shall spend the night with God."[1] Montcalm survived his illustrious rival only a few hours, and at his own request was buried in a pit excavated by a shell in exploding; "A meet tomb for a warrior, who died on the field of honor."[2]

Rashness and precipitancy have been imputed to Montcalm in the campaign before Quebec, and with a degree apparently of justice. Why did he hasten the attack before the aid he had summoned could arrive? The motives that

---

[1] *Bancroft. Pouchot.*

[2] I dissent with much hesitation from the suggested doubts of an eminent authority, in reference to the grave of Montcalm. (O'Callaghan's note, *Doc.* x, 400). I accept the statement not alone on the authority of the *Biographie Universelle,* but on the strength of the commemorative painting of his death, dictated by his officers (*Pouchot,* I, 217), but more especially on the language of the majestic epitaph of the French Academy of Inscription: "Deposited his mortal remains in a grave which a falling bomb in exploding had excavated." For this epitaph and the elegant and feeling correspondence between Bougainville and Pitt on the subject, see Appendix B.

influenced his action are buried in his grave. Montreuil, a veteran and experienced soldier, asserts that delay would have enabled Wolfe to entrench upon a hill, and thus render his position impregnable.[1] Bishop De Pontbriand, who participated in these events, sustains the same views, and says "that Montcalm deigned to avail himself of the first impulses of his troops." He adds a fact, which if it existed, manifests the highest wisdom and skill in the measures adopted by Montcalm: "had he delayed an hour the enemy would have been reenforced by three thousand men and eight pieces of cannon.[2] Bougainville, who had ascended the river with two thousand select men, to watch the operations of Wolfe, was instantly, on the landing of the English army, ordered to return. Did the rapid conception enter into the sagacious mind of Montcalm, that Bougainville should return while the battle raged, and falling upon the the rear of Wolfe annihilate his forces; and success, in bold and consummate strategy, like this, would have emblazoned with the brightest radiance the martial fame of Montcalm. Obloquy and detraction did not pause at the glorious grave of Montcalm. He was charged not merely with recklessness and presumption, but the base offense was imputed to him, of sacrificing his own life and the realm of New France to a groveling jealousy of Vaudreuil.[3] These calumnies have never satisfactorily explained why Vaudreuil, lying within a mile and a half of the scene of action, with fifteen hundred men, did not advance with greater celerity, assume the command warranted by his rank, and direct the operations of the army. The advance of Wolfe could not have been veiled from his knowledge.[4]

A want of enterprise has been singularly ascribed to Montcalm, not only by his detractors of that age, but a

---

[1] *Doc.*, x, 1014. [2] An impartial opinion etc., *Doc.*, x, 1061.

[3] *Doc.*, x, 1034, 1043; *Garneau*, II, 327.

[4] Bancroft says that "messenger after messenger was dispatched to Vaudreuil to come up;" I know not on what authority. No official document I think discloses the fact, and the *Relations*, etc., explicitly denies it.— *Doc.*, x, 1061.

modern Canadian writer indulges in the same strictures.[1] The marvellous exploits, achieved with means so inadequate, should dispel all these imputations. And it should be remembered that wise enterprise is always tempered by prudence and discretion. Vaudreuil, after the capitulation of 1760, went back to France, and he, in turn, was marked by adverse fortune, and an object of injustice and persecution. The friends of Montcalm, it is said, pursued and oppressed him with a vindictive animosity; but he was in life able to secure the vindication of his honor and integrity.

The repose that rested upon the shores of Champlain, was interrupted by no event of public interest, until the campaign of the next year. The attention of Amherst was devoted to the extension and improvement of the works at Ticonderoga, and the erection, as we have already noticed, of a magnificent fortress on Crown point.

The remains of these works, now crumbling ruins, still attest their original splendor and strength. They are now guarded and preserved by private taste and intelligence, from the vandal outrages which were rapidly destroying them. We may cherish the hope, that the most extensive and imposing ruins in America, redolent with the brightest historical associations, and becoming shrouded in the venerableness of antiquity, will be perpetuated to excite the admiration and to attract the pilgrimage of future ages. These fields of glory are now tilled in the peaceful pursuits of husbandry. In the vicinity of Ticonderoga, balls, muskets, swords, and numerous other relics of war, are constantly revealed. At one period, the line of the fatal abatis might almost be traced by these dumb but significant memorials of the spot where the harvest of death had been the most exuberant.

The course of the circumvallations and trenches, singularly complex and interlaced, may readily be distinguished. Part of the battlements rising above the rocky cliff are

---

[1] *Doc.*, x, 1043; *Garneau*, xi, 327.

almost entire. The line of the ramparts is still traced; the ruins of a portion of the barracks remain, although private cupidity has removed much of the brick and stone of the buildings. The bakery is in a state of good preservation. At Crown point the ruin is still better preserved, although here the deep interest that entrances at Ticonderoga, is less profound and exciting. The mounds of Fort St. Frederic are yet perceptible, although fallen and dilapidated. The oven, the covered way, and magazine, are easily distingished. The fort erected by Amherst, might even now be restored. The form of the vast quadrangular barracks, which enclosed the esplanade, may still be distinguished, although one side has been totally demolished, and another partially removed. They formed, until the desecration was arrested by the present proprietors, quarries that supplied building material to a wide region. Two of these barracks remain in partial preservation, one a hundred and ninety-two feet and the other two hundred and sixteen feet in length. The walls yet stand, and although roofless, without floors, and the beams charred and blackened, they are in more perfect condition than any other part of either ruin. The inner walls bear the soldiers' idle scribblings of more than a century ago. Each room contains a broad and lofty fireplace. The garrison well, almost one hundred feet deep, remains. The direction of the covered way, conducting to the lake, although occasionally fallen in, may readily be discerned.

How changed the scene, since the chivalry of France and England, and the savage warriors from Acadia to the precincts of Hudson's bay, were marshaled on these shores. Last autumn, standing on a lofty eminence on the southern limits of Essex county, I gazed far along the bold banks and tranquil bosom of Lake George. The view was as lovely as in the age of Montcalm and Howe; but not a sound broke the deep stillness of nature, not a form interrupted its solitude. When I stood amid the ruins of Crown point, cattle were ruminating in its bastion, and a solitary robin twittered among the branches of a tree, whose roots were interlaced among the rocks of the ramparts. I saw sheep feeding upon the walls of Fort Carillon, and plucked wild grapes from a vine clustering upon the ruins of its magazine.

CHAPTER VIII.

The Colonization, 1760 – 1775.

While Amherst procrastinated his movements, the last convulsive, but nearly successful struggle for a prolonged dominion, was made by De Levis, in the attempted recapture of Quebec. The battle of Sillery, contiguous to the plains of Abraham, had been fought, where the brave but presumptuous and incompetent Murray experienced a defeat as severe in its losses and complete in the route, as that which proved fatal to Montcalm. But circumstances were not equally propitious to the French for the consummation of the victory.[1] Amherst reserved to himself the command of the largest column of the British armies, which in accordance with the plan of the campaign of 1760, consisted of ten thousand men and was designed to approach Montreal by Oswego and the line of the St. Lawrence. Proceeding with a slow caution, that the enfeebled condition of the French forces did not exact, and incurring to his army great and unnecessary toil, and sweeping away as he advanced all the remains of hostile power along these waters, he appeared early in September before the walls of Montreal.

Haviland was in charge of the troops which remained at the fortresses on Lake Champlain. While delaying for the progress of Amherst's operations, several bold and successful incursions were made from this point, against the settlement of Canada, by Rogers, in connection with

---

[1] The battle of Sillery was fought near the Cote d'Abraham; this, with the celebrated Plains of Abraham, was called after one Abraham Martin, who owned a farm in the immediate vicinity.— O'Callaghan, *Doc.*, x, 1801.

the naval force, which now held the control of the lake. On the 16th of August, 1760, the last brilliant martial procession of the war departed from Crown point. Bearing about three thousand regulars and provincials, under the command of Colonel Haviland, it moved down the lake in a long line of bateaux, under the convoy of four armed vessels, with an equal number of radeaux, each of which bore a heavy armament. Richard Montgomery, who had already attracted the attention and won the applause of Wolfe, at Louisburg, accompanied this expedition, as adjutant of the Seventeenth regiment of foot.[1]

Haviland effected a descent near the Isle aux Noix, without opposition, and at once erected batteries opposite the fort upon the main land. Bougainville, who occupied the works with sixteen hundred men, had strengthened his position by anchoring a fleet of small vessels on his flank. These were vigorously attacked and soon dispersed or captured. The rangers swam out to one, tomahawk in hand, boarded and seized her.[2] Weakened by this loss, Bougainville, on the night of the 29th, abandoned his position. The forts at St. John's and Chambly were evacuated at the same time, the garrisons retreating slowly towards Montreal. By a skillful execution of happily concerted movements, Haviland appeared before Montreal on the 7th of September, the day after the arrival and junction of Amherst and Murray. Murray had ascended the river from Quebec, driving before him the remnants of the French army, occupying the country and imposing the oath of allegiance upon the people.[3]

In this last stronghold of New France, Vandreuil, its last governor-general, had gathered the gallant relics of his wasted army, and with an intrepid front, made the most prudent and skillful disposition for a final conflict.[4] As the blood in the process of dissolution recedes from the extremities and collects about the heart, so all the Cana-

---

[1] *Rogers*, 133; *Armstrong's Life of Montgomery*. [2] *Rogers*, 191.
[3] *Graham*. [4] *Idem;* De Levis, *Doc.*, x, 1125.

dian power of France had gathered around the only remaining citadel of its strength. All the chivalry of France that still survived on the soil of Canada, had assembled here, animated by a zeal and ardor that almost defied destiny. There was De Levis, second alone to Montcalm in renown and services; there was Boulamarque, the target of every battle-field; and Montrueil the successor of Dieskau at Lake George; and Bougainville, the pupil and friend of Montcalm, and to become illustrious as the first French circumnavigator of the globe. "If we do not save the country," wrote De Levis to Belle Isle, "we will sustain the honor of the king's arms."[1] But the contest was hopelessly unequal, and on the 8th of September, Vandreuil proposed terms of capitulation which were soon adjusted by Amherst in a spirit of humane magnanimity, and the sceptre of New France was yielded to England.

By the treaty of Paris the next year, the province of Canada was formally ceded to Great Britain. England, in wild exultation, rejoiced over this conquest, which added the domain of almost half a continent to her realm, as "the most important that ever the British army had achieved."[2] But the far-seeing and comprehensive mind of Choiseul, discerned in it the germ of the dismemberment of the British empire.[3] The keen forecast of Montcalm, three weeks before his fatal field, found consolation in contemplating the same view. In the letter from which I have quoted in another page, he writes: "I shall console myself to some extent for my defeat and for the loss of our colony by the profound conviction which I entertain, that this defeat will one day become of greater value to my country than a victory, and that the victor here will find his grave, in his very victory." He then proceeds to trace with a master's hand, the consequences which will be entailed on England by the annexation of Canada, from its influences upon the attitude of the British colonies.[4]

---

[1] *Doc.*, x, 1103. [2] *Smollet.* [3] *Bancroft.* [4] See Appendix B.

The inference derived from the subsequent aspect of the country, and the silence of documents and history on the subject is strong, if not conclusive, that the actual occupation of the Champlain valley by the French, for practical and agricultural purposes, although they maintained their military ascendancy for more than a fourth of a century, did not extend far beyond the protection of their fortresses.

The extent and character of these early settlements is a question of strong interest, as well in the illustration it affords of the history of the region, as in the antiquarian researches it demands. Whatever may have been the number or situation of the French occupants, they appear to have receded before the approach of the victorious arms of Amherst, and probably accompanied the retreat of the French forces. The most decisive evidence remains of the presence, at some former period, of a considerable and civilized community in the vicinity of Crown point. The vestiges of their occupation which still exist, indicate a people who knew the comforts and amenities of life, and possessed numbers and means to secure their enjoyment. The allusions of ancient manuscripts corroborate the traditions preserved in the reminiscences of aged persons, that a population, ranging in the estimate from fifteen hundred to three thousand persons, were gathered around the fortress of St. Frederic. A very important traffic, it is known, existed between the French and English possessions, as early as 1700, and that Lake Champlain was the medium of the intercourse. Several years anterior to that period, Crown point, it will be recollected, was referred to, as a prominent landmark, in the public instructions of the municipal authorities of Albany. May it not have been, previous to the French occupation, an important mart of this commerce? We think the conclusion is warranted, that Crown point was probably, at an early period, a trading post, at which the merchandise of the French and English colonies were interchanged, and where the Indians congregated from widely extended hunting grounds to traffic their peltries.

We have already briefly sketched the peninsular position of Crown point—one side resting on Bulwagga bay, and the other washed by the waters of the lake. When we last witnessed it the clearest evidences remained of the ground, for many rods along the margin of the bay, having been graded and formed into an artificial slope, inclining to the water. Ruins of enclosures are still visible. The fragments of a former wall, in one instance, distinctly mark its course. Trees which have sprung up, along the line of the wall, have supported and preserved spaces of it almost entire. This enclosure, embracing an area of about two acres, was evidently a fruit yard or garden. Fruit trees were flourishing in it within the recollection of the present owner.

An avenue seems to have swept in a wide curvature along the margin of the lake in front of the enclosure, and approached a landing place, adapted to the craft which at that time navigated its waters. Still more distinct and palpable indications are exhibited parallel to this avenue, upon the crest of a slight eminence, of the former residence of a dense and prosperous population. A street may be traced, reaching a long distance towards the mainland, raised and covered with broken stone not unlike the Macadam roads of the present day. The ruins of cellars, many of which are excavated from the solid rock, line this street on each side. The compact arrangement of these cellars and the narrowness of the avenue, present a striking analogy to the antiquated villages in Canada, founded by the French, and leave little doubt that their origin was the same. No vestige of this by-gone age so thrilled upon my feelings and excited my imagination, as the remnant of the sidewalk along this street. It is formed of flagging similar to that now in use in our cities. The stones are smooth and worn, and remain in the position they were left by the generation who once thronged them in the busy scenes of life. We were assured by the occupant of the ground, that he has displaced many continuous rods of this pavement, in the course of his agricultural operations, which were in perfect preservation. These and equally marked indications, extend over a wide space about the fort along the shores of the lake. Two large cemeteries, one near the garrison grounds and the other three miles south, attest that the living, in numerous assemblies, once animated these scenes. The worthy occupant of the former, remarked, without seeming conscious that he was yielding to the dictate of a refined sentiment, that he had felt constrained in particular spots to arrest the plow, because it so fearfully exposed the relics of the dead.

Still another touching testimony remains that man, in an advanced stage of society, has left his foot-prints on these scenes, to indicate his former presence. Asparagus, other hardy plants and shrubs, usually cherished by the hand of human culture, still flourish, wild and uncared for, upon these fields. The settlers, who occupied the territory after the revolution, found, in an area of about four miles from the fort, not a tree or a bush to obstruct the view over the beautiful and wide champaign, that had been once highly cultivated. Now, a heavy forest covers half the tract. Rogers, in describing one of his predatory excursions, speaks of luxuriant crops waving upon these fields, and on another occasion, he alludes to his firing, in a sudden foray, the village itself. He mentions also "settlements on the east side of the lake, one of which was two miles from the fort, and refers to the presence of "three hundred men chiefly inhabitants of the adjacent villages." This number, it may be computed, would represent a population from one thousand to twelve hundred. In a previous page I have referred to the occupation of the adjacent country by actual settlers. No reasonable doubt exists, that large tracts of land lying between the works at Crown point and Ticonderoga were cleared and cultivated long previous to the permanent colonization of the English, and probably at the epoch of the French occupation. The heavy forests which now stand in various localities in this district exhibit conclusive evidence that they are of second growth. Kalm, the Swedish traveler, saw about the fort in 1749, "a considerable settlement," and "pleasant cultivated gardens," and "a neat church within the ramparts." Persons recently deceased, whose recollection extended to a period beyond the revolution, recalled Crown point when its business operations were conducted in several stores. A circumstance occurring at a later period, which we shall introduce, with its evidences, in a subsequent part of this narrative, that seems to have contemplated Crown point as a capital of a projected province, is strongly suggestive of its central position and political importance. A solitary farm house now occupies the peninsula of Crown point.

Soon after the cession to England by the treaty of 1763, of the French possessions, embracing the claims of France to the environs of Lake Champlain, the attention of the colonial government of New York was directed to the importance of establishing a town at Crown point. Gov. Moore in 1768 pressed the subject with great urgency upon the ministry. He represented that the measure would be attended "with great advantages to the province and the service of his majesty," and advises that "the lots in the town should be granted on the easiest terms," and "that their presence would contribute to the rapid settlement of the entire region." He also encloses "the plan of the town made by Adolphus Benzel.[1] A memorial addressed to the New York legislature in 1775, contains the names of thirty-eight males, described as residents of the district of Ticonderoga and Crown point. We may infer from this fact the presence, at that period, of a population of some hundreds.

Although Canada continued in the military occupation of the armies of England, the clouds and uncertainties,

---

[1] *Doc.*, VIII, 140. Benzel was a Swede, emigrated to America and joined the army in 1752. In 1770 he was appointed "inspector of the royal woods and forests and unappropriated lands on the Champlain, with a large salary for that period. Nathan Beaman, the youthful guide of Allen, informed Mr. O. F. Sheldon, that about the year 1775, he rowed a party from Vermont, of some festive occasion, to Crown point, and mentioned seeing on the table of Benzel, silver-ware and other evidences of wealth and luxury. Benzel obtained the grant of the military reserves at Crown point.—*Doc.*, VIII, 488.

which shrouded her future policy in reference to the permanent acquisition of the country, retarded the settlement of the environs of Lake Champlain by American emigrants. The officers and soldiers, of both the regular and provincial line, in their repeated campaigns, had become familiar with the region, and appreciated its beauty and fertility. The teeming west was still the domain of the savage. The impediments to colonization referred to were dispelled, when, by the treaty of 1763, Canada, Acadia and Cape Breton, were ceded to England.

A proclamation made October 7, 1763, by the king of Great Britain, authorized the colonial governors to issue grants of land to be located in any colony as the grantee preferred. The reduced officers and men, who had served in the Canadian campaigns, were especially to be regarded in the issuing of these grants. The holders were empowered, by the terms of their grants, to make locations upon any unappropriated lands. This revolution, in the attitude of the country, communicated a new impulse to its affairs, and opened its portals widely to immigration. The decade succeeding the year 1765, exhibited vast progress in its improvement and cultivation. Numerous patents were granted, and the locations made under them, came frequently into collision with grants issued during the French intrusion. Stimulated by the value of the lands, immensely enhanced by these events, many grants, utterly fictitious, were asserted, and others revived that had been abrogated by the French government, or forfeited by a failure in the performance of their conditions. Others derived from France, were preserved by actual tenure, and had been recognized by the government of Great Britain. Many of these classes were also violated by location of grants issued in pursuance of the ordinance of 1763. No grants, in addition to those already mentioned, appear to have been issued by the French authorities, to any portion of Essex county, except one of November 15, 1758, which comprehended a large part of the territory, which now constitutes the towns of Crown point and Ticonderoga. The adjustment of the conflicting rights of the patentees, under these adverse grants of the French and English authorities, was extremely difficult and embarrassing. A proper sense of justice induced a suspension by the government, in 1768, in the issuing of all patents of lands northward of Crown point, which were claimed under any French grants.[1]

These collisions again threw a cloud over the progress and prosperity of the country. Many of the French claims were ultimately repudiated by England, on account of forfeitures through the neglect of the conditions upon which they were dependent; others were compromised by grants to the claimants of land in Canada of an equivalent value.[2] England exhibited towards the claimants of these seigniories great tenderness and liberality, in not assuming the obvious position, that the French held the shores of Lake Champlain alone by an usurped occupation, which could neither create nor convey any rights. These questions agitated and disturbed the colonies for several years, and led in the home government to anxious and protracted discussions.

The multiplicity and extent of the grants, issued under the ordinance of 1763, the existence of these conflicting claims, and the repugnance of many of the patentees to the occupation themselves of their land, combined to depress their value and throw them into market.

William Gilliland, a native of Ireland, was, at that period, a merchant, residing in the city of New York. Endowed with great force of character and enterprise, and possessing expanded and sagacious views, he became conspicuous in the early settlement of Clinton and Essex counties, and held, for many years, a controlling ascendancy in the affairs of that region. Patents of rich and

---

[1] *Doc.*, VIII, 115. In the year 1809, the validity of these ancient French grants was adjudicated upon by the supreme court of New York, with a result adverse to the claim of title under them.—*Johnson's Reports*, IV, 163.

[2] *Doc.*, VIII, 577.

extensive manors had been, anterior to this time, granted in the southern sections of the province. Actuated by the desire of forming to himself a similar estate, the mind of Mr. Gilliland was attracted to the valley of Champlain, then surrounded by the circumstances to which allusion has been made. He employed, with this view, competent agents to explore the west shores of the lake. The larger proportion of the territory upon the eastern side, had already been granted and appropriated. He decided upon the result of this survey, to locate his proposed domain near the Boquet river, expanding southerly along the borders of the lake towards Split rock.

The remarkable beauty and fertility of the tract still vindicate the wisdom and tact of his selection. His first location was a section of two thousand acres, under a grant to James Field. This was situated immediately south of the Boquet,[1] and is now designated as Field's patent. Mr. Gilliland subsequently purchased seven additional claims, which embraced in the aggregate more than fifteen thousand acres of land. The territory he comprehended and located under these grants, commencing a half mile south of the river, extended to Judd's patent, which seems to have been previously surveyed, near Split rock, presenting on the shore of the lake a line of about six miles, and spreading three or four miles into the interior. The purchase of these rights was effected in 1764, and the grants issued and the land surveyed the ensuing year. Impressed by the natural predilections of an European to manorial institutions, his policy seems to have designed the creation of an estate in fee in himself, with subordinate estates to a tenantry held at annual leases. The consummation of a

---

[1] The origin of the name of this river is uncertain. Tradition says it was thus named by Mr. Gilliland, from the profusion of flowers on its banks. It is also supposed to have been derived from Gen. Boquet, an English officer of considerable distinction. An ingenious friend has suggested that it may have been derived from the French word *baquet*, trough, a term peculiarly descriptive of the form of the river, between the falls and its debouch into the lake.

scheme of this character, applied to a wild and uncultivated region, demanded an exercise of extreme skill and sagacity.

The inducements presented by Gilliland to immigration, were conceived in the most liberal and enlarged spirit. His arrangements for organizing the proposed colony manifested every regard for its comfort and success. He seems to have secured a body of intelligent and industrious emigrants, formed principally of mechanics and laborers, and adapted to endure the toil and privation of a pioneer life. Amply provided with implements, tools, provisions, and all other requisites, he left New York with his colony on the 10th of May, 1765, and occupied ten days in the voyage from that city to Albany. Deciding, at this place, to convey a part of the immigrants and the material by water, to Fort Edward, he was compelled to purchase bateaux at Schenectady, and to transport them overland to Albany. In the laborious toil of eight days, contending with the strong current and dangerous rapids of the Hudson, he reached Fort Edward in safety. A part of the train had proceeded by land, driving with them a herd of forty-one head of neat cattle, destined for the future use of the colony. The oxen were employed in the transportation of the boats and effects to Lake George. Three days were exhausted in this operation, when the little fleet was again launched, and wafted by sails to Ticonderoga. Two days more of transportation by land, brought them to the waters of Lake Champlain. One bateau was freighted with lumber at Ticonderoga, supplied by saw mills which were erected during the French occupation. Again embarking, they arrived on the shores of the Boquet on the 8th day of June, having occupied in their journey thirty days of arduous and incessant labor.

After the interval of two days, devoted to rest and preliminary arrangement, they proceeded up the river to the point of their ultimate destination, and formed their encampment upon an island at the base of the falls, which, from that circumstance, still bears the name of Camp island.

With promptness and energy operations were at once commenced. A road was opened to the falls, and by the 15th of that month ground had been cleared, timber prepared, and a house, forty-four feet by twenty-two, partly erected. This edifice was probably the first dwelling built by civilized man, on the western shore of Champlain, between Crown point and Canada. The cattle had been driven to Crown point, and there made to swim the narrow passage. Proceeding to a point opposite to Split rock, they were ferried over, and from thence driven through the woods to Gilliland's settlement. A part of them were confined and fed upon the leaves of the trees, but the largest portion were turned loose to the unlimited range of the forest.

The first great necessity secured, by the erection of a dwelling, the colonists prepared for general improvement. The forest was opened, the vicinity explored, timber prepared for a saw-mill, which was erected in the autumn, at the lower part of the falls, and supplied with power by a wing dam, which was projected into the current, turning the water into a flume that conducted it to the mill.

Game was abundant in the woods; the most delicious salmon thronged the stream, that at most laved their threshold, and the beaver meadows yielded them sufficient hay for the approaching winter.[1] The spontaneous products of a bounteous land were thus within the reach of their industry and energies. Meanwhile, as these efforts were in progress, Mr. Gilliland had visited Quebec, and returned laded with all the other necessaries to secure the comfort and safety of his people.

---

[1] Another resort to procure a supply of fodder was of infinite value to the first settlers, and is still not unimportant to the inhabitants of the country. This was the marshes, created by the spring overflowings of the low alluvials upon the shores of the lake. The hay cut upon these marshes is very inferior to that cured from cultivated grasses, or even the product of the beaver meadows. The growth upon the natural meadows is usually a coarse and harsh grass, intermingled with rushes, brakes and ferns. On more elevated ground, a better quality of hay is produced.

"During his absence he had examined the region with a vigilant eye, upon both shores of the lake; had ascended the navigable streams, sounded their depths, and explored their banks. Twelve grants had now been located by Mr. Gilliland. Eight of these were situated within the present towns of Essex and Willsboro'; two at Westport, and two at Salmon river, now in Clinton county. A tier of lots, intended for farms, was surveyed and numbered in this year (1765), ranging along the shore of the lake, from the mouth of the Boquet to Judd's patent. Many of these lots were immediately selected by the settlers, but on account of the advanced season were not occupied until the succeeding spring." The settlement upon the Boquet was named Milltown. Mr. Gilliland, in November, left it, with his other interests upon Lake Champlain, in charge of a kinsman, whom he dignified with the European title of steward. He passed the winter himself in New York, engaged in preparations for the removal of his family to his new estate. The cattle which had been turned out upon their arrival, were recovered with great difficulty in the autumn, and in a condition almost as wild as the native denizens of the forests. The first winter of these pioneers in the wilds of New York, was passed without suffering or remarkable incident. Their time was occupied in attending the cattle, cutting and drawing saw-logs to the mill, and in the preparation of timber for the construction of their buildings. In January, 1766, their hay was drawn upon the ice, from a beaver meadow, two miles south-west from Split rock (now Whallon's bay), to Milltown.

At the approach of spring, all the efforts of the settlers were enlisted in constructing their dwellings, and making other improvements upon their newly acquired farms. The first house upon these lots is supposed to have been erected for Robert McAuley, April 14th, 1766, on the north bank of Bachelor's creek. Others rapidly succeeded, until the whole space between the Boquet and Split rock was studded by the neat cabins of the settlers.

During the spring, the provisions of the colony began to fail, but their wants were promptly supplied from the stores of the garrison at Crown point.

In June, Mr. Gilliland returned with his family, and bearing supplies for another year. "His journey had been difficult and disastrous. In passing the rapids of the Hudson, near Stillwater, one of the bateaux had capsized, precipitating part of his family into the rushing torrent. One of his daughters was lost. They resumed their voyage in fearful forebodings, sometimes drawing their boats on land, and again launching them upon the water. Worn with grief and toil, they arrived at length at Milltown, and were soon settled in their wilderness home on the banks of the Boquet."[1]

By a royal ordinance of October 7th, 1763, the parallel of forty-five degrees north latitude had been established as the boundary between New York and the province of Quebec. This ideal line, was, however, indefinite and controverted. In September, 1767, Governor Moore, of New York, and Carlton, of Quebec, caused the line to be fixed by careful astronomical observations. The same observations established the latitude of Crown point at forty-four degrees one minute twenty seconds. On this occasion, the munificent hospitalities of Milltown were extended to the royal commissioners and their suite.

The return of the proprietor had infused a fresh spirit, and imparted a new and vigorous impulse to the little commonwealth. The colony continued to advance in improvement and prosperity. The saw-mill was in successful operation, supplying all the demand for lumber. A smithery had been erected. Various seeds had been sown to supply culinary vegetables. The government, political as well as moral, of the community, was in the exclusive guidance and control of the proprietor. Its administration seems to have been eminently patriarchal. The appointment of justice of peace, which had been

---

[1] *O. F. Sheldon.*

conferred on Mr. Gilliland, in his primitive jurisdiction, endowed him with a plenitude of powers, that essentially embraced all the functions of counsellor, judge, and chancellor. The ample limits of Albany county, at that period, embraced the whole region of northern New York.

During the winter of 1767, Gilliland made an accurate and minute survey upon the ice of the lake shore, along the entire front of his locations, and named the prominent topographical features. In the same season the first horse introduced into the settlement, was brought out upon the ice, for Mr. Gilliland, from Canada.

William McAuley, a relative, and one of the prominent and most efficient coadjutors of Gilliland, occupied as a farm, the site of the present beautiful village of Essex. James Gilliland, a brother of the proprietor, and in after years a distinguished officer in the American army, settled on a lot on the north bank of the Boquet. This stream, at the time of Gilliland's colonization of its shores, and for a subsequent period of several years, was a conspicuous landmark in the country.

The site and the water-power of the village of Port Henry was granted in 1766, to Benjamin Porter, a miller. It is supposed a milling establishment was erected by him and abandoned or destroyed before or during the revolution. When tranquillity was restored after that event, he returned to the scene, and in connection with a Robert Lewis, of Albany, rebuilt the mills. The ruins of these structures existed until a recent date.

No prominent event distinguished the annals of these settlements for several years. Their agricultural and industrial improvement continued to advance, the colony gradually increased in population, flourishing mills were erected, and other conveniences and refinements of civilized life were introduced. Schools were early established. The position of the first school-house is still pointed out. Occasional religious services were enjoyed. I cannot ascertain the existence, in the early epoch of the settlement, of the stated administration of religious ordinances, although a clergyman, named George Henry, accompanied Mr. Gilliland with the first body of emigrants.

Albany county was divided in 1772, and the northern section, embracing both sides of Lake Champlain, was organized into a new county, which received the name of Charlotte.

An event occurred in 1775, which forcibly illustrates the tendency at that time of public sentiment to democratic institutions, and exhibits its bias towards the doctrines of self-government. This settlement, it has been stated, was in the ideal limits of Charlotte county, but it possessed no tangible and practical political or social organization. It was too remote to be reached by the protecting arm of government, and too unimportant to receive any specific legislative action. The presence and ascendancy of some civil or political power were demanded, in the changed condition and increased population of the colony, by their common interests, and for their mutual protection and safety. Under these circumstances they convened on the 17th of March, 1775,[1] by common approbation, an assembly of the colonists, and constituted themselves in effect, into a pure democracy. At this popular convention it was determined to institute for many practical purposes a local government. A system of police and social regulations was matured, formally adopted, and ratified by the individual signatures of the citizens. It was made imperative upon all, and each was pledged to abide by its provisions "by every tie of honor and honesty."[2] In contemplating in its humble aspect this singular and most interesting incident, the mind instinctively reverts to the cabin of the

[1] They were chiefly Irish, and St. Patrick's festival was no doubt designedly adopted for the occasion.

[2] But ten years had elapsed since the arrival of Gilliland with his colony, and still only two signatures are attached to this document of all those who accompanied him as original settlers. And thus it is almost uniformly in the history of our country. The pioneer opens the wilderness, and levels the highway for the advance of civilization; but as its march approaches, he recedes and passes onward to new scenes of toil and to incur fresh privations.—*Pioneer History of Champlain Valley.*

May-Flower, where a similar scene was enacted, under the guidance of the same spirit and resting upon the same eternal principles. The officers of the association, thus constituted, comprised a moderator, two superintendents of roads and bridges, three appraisers of damages, and a town clerk. William Gilliland was elected the first moderator, and Jotham Gardner the town clerk. The first act of this primitive organization was an ordinance, authorizing the construction of a bridge, by a tax to be levied and paid in labor, assessed on the basis of property.

A project is believed to have been agitated at this period, which, in its success, would have formed a prominent feature in the annals of this colony, and been an event of grave interest and importance in the political history of the country. A scheme, in which Gilliland and the elder Skeene, of a family which attained subsequent revolutionary notoriety, were the prominent agitators, was discussed and essentially matured, which contemplated the organization of a new province. Its imagined limits were to extend from the St. Lawrence to the Connecticut, resting at the north on the Canada boundary and with an undefined line at the south. In this project Skeene was to receive the appointment of governor of the contemplated province, and Crown point was to be constituted the capital.

I have yielded my own convictions of the reality of this scheme, not alone upon the traditions on the subject, and the assurances of those who profess to have seen and possessed documents which elucidated the whole subject, but upon other forcible considerations.[1] Amherst, it was

[1] Mr. Gilliland, the younger, who, at the commencement of the revolution, was a schoolboy of fourteen, and died in Plattsburgh, in the year 1847, assured Mr. Sheldon that this project was a frequent and familiar theme of conversation by his father. That he had often himself read the correspondence between his father and Skeene, on the subject. and that he had the letters of Skeene still in his possession. Mr. G., who was a gentleman of great intelligence, engaged to find and submit them to Mr. Sheldon, but he died before the time fixed for the purpose arrived. With the permission and aid of the Messrs. Gilliland, his sons, who reside at Salmon river, on a part of the original estate, I have carefully examined the family papers, but can discover no trace of this document.

asserted by Colden, contemplated the erection of a separate government at Crown point, immediately after its reduction.[1]

The aspect at that epoch of the controversy, relative to the New Hampshire grants, rendered such an occurrence exceedingly probable. Cotemporary annals appear to recognize the existence of some project of an analogous character and purpose.[2] Skeene, it is known, at this period, visited England on some important political mission, and was on his return to America on the verge of the revolution, bearing, as he alleged, the appointment of governor of Crown point and Ticonderoga.[3] In this designation of the limits and title of his government, is it not probable that he merely referred to these fortresses as prominent points embraced within his jurisdiction? Crown point, it is asserted, was the designed capital of the projected province. This idea strengthens at once the opinion I have attempted to enforce, of the prominence and importance of Crown point at that period, and attaches form and coherence to the existence of this scheme. Skeene was then possessed of a large landed estate, not only at Skeenesboro', but elsewhere in the environs of Lake Champlain. He held a tract in Essex county, still designated Skeene's patent.

The theory, that the erection of a new province was contemplated at this period, seems to receive a degree of strength from the proceedings of a convention held at Westminster, Vermont, in April, 1775, which resolved to petition the royal government " that they might be taken out of so oppressive a jurisdiction [that of New York], and either annexed to some other government or erected and incorporated into a new one." The commissioners of Vermont, in their appeal to congress in 1779, refer to the same measure, and affirm their probable ability to prove the creation of this new province, and that Governor

---

[1] *Doc.*, VII, 558; Skeene to Pownall, *Doc.*, VII, 515.

[2] *Williams's History of Vermont. Haskins's do.*

[3] *Skeene's Letter to Hawley*, March 16, 1775.

Skeene had been appointed to preside over the same. "By the accomplishment of this design might have involved the most momentous and sinister political results, at that peculiar epoch, when the vehement contest between New York and Vermont had acquired its deepest rancor and excitement. It is not probable, had that event occurred, whatever may have been the political consequences, that Northern New York would now exhibit a vast expanse of uncultivated and primeval wilderness.

An occurrence of deep import suddenly dissolved all these visions of political plans and speculations, and for years arrested the progress of this miniature republic, and dispersed widely its population. A blow was struck, within the present limits of Essex county, which vibrated not only through the wide colonies, but was felt within the palace walls of St. James.

CHAPTER IX.

The Revolution, 1775–1776.

Haldimand, the commandant of Crown point and Ticonderoga, announced to the British government, in 1773, that the fort at Crown point was "entirely destroyed," and that at Ticonderoga, in a "ruinous condition," and "that both could not cover fifty men in winter." The appeal to arms, which had sounded from the plains of Lexington, in April, 1775, seems to have suggested simultaneously to patriotic individuals in various sections of the colonies the idea of seizing these important fortresses, while in their dilapidated and exposed condition. Members of the provincial legislature of Connecticut, embracing the names of David Wooster and Silas Deane, and with its secret connivance, but without any public recognition by that body, raised a fund to effect this object, and appointed a private committee to proceed to the scene, and to pursue measures calculated to secure the execution of the plan.

It was known that a large number of cannon, with an immense amount of every military munition, had been accumulated at these posts. The seizure of these materials would supply a deficiency severely felt in the American army, already assembled before Boston. This motive, the obvious policy of occupying the stronghold which commanded the communications of Lake Champlain and the desire of achieving a decided success, which would tend to strengthen and animate the popular enthusiasm, stimulated this movement. Edward Mott and Noah Phelps, who were embraced in this committee, and were intrusted by the projectors of this daring scheme with the arrangements for its execution, proceeded with a small body of men, raised in Connecticut, to Berkshire county, Massachusetts. At Pittsfield, Colonel Easton and John Brown embarked with ardor in the enterprise. The expedition numbered about forty volunteers when it reached Bennington, and here the zealous spirit and powerful influence of Ethan Allen was enlisted.

On the 7th of May, 1775, an intrepid band of two hundred and seventy men, all of whom but forty-six were Green mountain boys, had collected at Castleton, and were devoted to this bold design. While they were organizing for the advance, Benedict Arnold, bearing a commission from the committee of safety in Massachusetts — but dated the 3d of May, the day on which the expedition reached Bennington — and clothed with plenary powers to accomplish the same purpose, appeared upon the scene, and claiming precedence in the command of the expedition. The contest which ensued, and which threatened to prove fatal to the enterprise, was terminated by the troops refusing to march unless under the guidance of Allen, their tried and cherished leader. Arnold was constrained to yield, and joined the force as aid to the commander. Noah Phelps, a name that national gratitude should commemorate, assuming the garb and deportment of a settler, boldly entered the fort at Ticonderoga, and with the pretence of seeking a barber, wandered unsuspected about the works, and thus obtained complete knowledge of their condition and the strength of the garrison.

Captain Herrick had been ordered to proceed to Skeenesboro', and having captured the younger Skeene, with the materials collected at that place to join Allen at Ticonderoga; Douglas was sent to Panton, to secure all the boats that could be discovered and return to Shoreham. Upon his success chiefly depended the means of transporting the troops. Instructions were communicated to Remember Baker, always the active and unfaltering coadjutor of Allen to cooperate from his position at Otter creek. Major Beach had been dispatched to Rutland and the adjacent towns in order to gather volunteers, and accomplished on foot, tradition asserts, a circuit of sixty miles in twenty-four hours.[1] When the agents of Connecticut reached Sheffield, they communicated with the Albany committee on the subject of their expedition, by messengers; but that body refused to interfere, without instructions from the New York committee, which although applied to, appear to have given no response.[2] The force under Allen advanced in profound secrecy and silence to the eastern shore of the lake, in the town of Shoreham.[3]

Sentinels and pickets were placed on every avenue by which intelligence of the movement might be communicated to Ticonderoga. The party lay in concealment nearly a whole day and night, in what is now known as Hand's cove, a short distance north of Larrabee's point. They were disappointed in crossing immediately as was

---

[1] *Goodhue's Shoreham.* [2] *Hall's Vermont.*

[3] A number of the inhabitants of Shoreham engaged in the enterprise, and from them and local tradition, the Rev. Josiah T. Goodhue, long the pastor of the Congregational church in that town, has collected and preserved many incidents connected with the capture of Ticonderoga of great interest and value. In the frequent discrepancies which obscure the history of this event, I have deferred to him as the most credible and authentic authority. I am indebted to Hon. A. C. Hand, a native of Shoreham, for a knowledge of Mr Goodhue's work, and for several important facts.

intended, by the delay in the arrival of the necessary boats. A large oared boat owned by Skeene, which was lying at anchor in the lake near Crown point, was seized by a stratagem; Douglass brought a scow from Orwell, and with these and a few small boats which they had secured in the vicinity, Allen determined to attempt the passage. Eighty-three men were embarked in the night of the 10th, at Hand's point, and landed beneath the protection of a cluster of willows on Willow's point, about one mile north of the fort. The dawn began to appear, and as immediate action could alone command success, it was decided to advance to the assault without awaiting the return of the boats with the remainder of the party. A patriotic farmer of Shoreham had supplied Allen with a guide in the person of his son, an active and intelligent lad of fifteen, who had gained a perfect knowledge of the works, in his pastimes among the boys connected with the garrison.

Allen, when the little band were formed, addressed them in a low and earnest voice, but in the rude and forcible eloquence by which he was wont at all times to control his associates. He spoke of their antecedents; of their widely extended reputation for valor which had led to their selection to accomplish an important undertaking: he represented the desperate attempt as only adapted to the bravest of men; that he purposed to conduct them through the gate; that they must that morning quit their pretensions to heroism or in a few minutes capture the fortress; he would urge no one to follow him contrary to his own will, but, he exclaimed, "you that will undertake voluntarily, poise your firelock." Instantly every musket was elevated. Again, the harmony of the expedition was imperiled in the renewed assertion by Arnold, of a claim to precedence in leading the assault. It was, at length, arranged that the two leaders should advance together, Allen on the right, guided by young Nathan Beaman, the Shoreham boy; with Allen and Arnold at the head, the column marched rapidly and in silence to the sallyport.

The sentinel stationed there snapped his gun against the breast of Allen, and retreated through the covered way, closely followed by the Americans, who, uttering a terrific shout, formed upon the parade in two lines, each facing the barracks. The garrison were awakened from their sleep by the wild clamor, and Captain De La Place, suddenly aroused, burst from his quarters in his night apparel, to be confronted on the corridor by Allen; and in reply to the summons to surrender, asked by what authority it was demanded. Allen thundered forth the immortal response, in words then strange and ominous, but now engraven in our national annals: "In the name of the Great Jehovah and the Continental congress." The fortress, the garrison, and the vast munitions were won without the effusion of a single drop of blood. A part of these trophies was forty-eight prisoners, one hundred and twenty-four pieces of cannon, a number of mortars and howitzers, a large amount of ammunition of every kind, and extensive and invaluable materials for ship building.

Warner, who had succeeded in crossing with the rear detachment, arrived at the fort soon after the surrender. He was, without delay, dispatched with a hundred men to seize Crown point. A heavy wind prevented the immediate movement, but the next day he was able to advance; captured without resistance the fort and its small garrison of twelve men with its entire armament. Herrick had been equally successful, and soon after joined Allen, having captured the works at the head of the lake, and Skeene with all his forces, and made the yet more important acquisition of several boats and a schooner, which had been used as a regular trader between Skeenesboro' and St. Johns. The triumphant success of this most skillfully concerted measure was completed, when Baker arrived with two dispatch boats sent from Crown point with intelligence of the capture of Ticonderoga, which he had intercepted and taken on his passage from Otter creek. The military material secured at Crown point largely enhanced the spoils of Ticonderoga. Amos Callander was immediately detached with a small party to the fort at the head of Lake George. This design was effected by him without difficulty, and he soon after conducted all the prisoners, amounting to fifty-two, to Hartford, Connecticut.[1]

The intelligence of this great and extraordinary event was received by the people in astonishment, and with transports of enthusiastic joy. The day after the capture of Ticonderoga, John Brown bore to Albany a letter from Allen, communicating the fact of its surrender and expressing an apprehension, that an attempt might be made for its recovery, and asking for assistance by reenforcements and supplies. Again the committee faltered and hesitated, and wrote to New York. That committee then also refused to act, and forwarded the dispatches to the congress in Philadelphia. Meanwhile, Brown, untiring in his zeal, had also reached that city, and was called before Congress to give an account of the exciting transactions at Ticonderoga. That body received his intelligence with the highest secret exultation, but in the reserve due to a deliberative assembly, and in the undefined posture of affairs, hesitated to assume a distinct responsibility for the act, and adopted a formal resolution, recommending the committees of New York and Albany to "immediately cause the cannon and stores to be removed from Ticonderoga to the south end of Lake George," and indirectly advised a "strong post to be established at that place." It also recommended "that an exact inventory of them should be taken, in order that they might be safely returned when the restoration of the former harmony between Great Britain and the colonies, so ardently wished for by the latter, should render it prudent and consistent with the overruling law of self-preservation." In tumultuary times, men responsible for the exercise of power are seldom abreast of popular sentiment. The post proposed to be strengthened on Lake George might afford partial protection to Albany, but would leave the people on the grants, who

[1] *Goodhue's Shoreham.*

had achieved the aggression, exposed, unshielded to the royal vengeance. Allen, with earnest indignation, remonstrated against the project. Connecticut and Massachusetts gave utterance to equally emphatic protests, and the execution of the purpose was happily abandoned.[1]

The character of the men who led in the achievement of an exploit, that exhibits more the similitude of romance than the cooler form of reality, proves that the scheme was wisely and carefully concerted, and that any design deliberately adopted by them, would have been accomplished, if within the scope of human power or courage. Each, in his own station, became eminent in the progress of the revolution. Seth Warner, in the affections and confidence of their fearless associates, was scarcely second to Allen, and conspicuous in every field on which he moved, his military science and capacity was superior. Herrick was the efficient coadjutor of Stark at Bennington; Easton was gallantly distinguished in the army of Montgomery; Baker died before St. Johns in the same service; and Brown, after a glorious career of high distinction, fell at Stone Arabia.

A few months later an extreme public necessity was disclosed, that could only be relieved by the fruits of this conquest, and destined to prove its infinite importance. Washington had closely beleaguered Boston, but the progress of the siege was retarded by the want of appropriate cannon. Henry Knox, the youthful bookseller of Boston, the future chief of artillery in the American army, whose science was to excite the surprise and admiration of engineers trained in the schools of Europe, had chiefly constructed these works before Boston, by an almost intuitive genius. With equal energy and skill, in the depth of the winter of 1776, he traversed a wilderness of two hundred miles; collected numerous teams of oxen, and with a long train of sleds, transported fifty heavy guns from Ticonderoga to the camp of Washington.

---

[1] *Hall's Vermont.*

This unwonted procession was welcomed by an enthusiastic ovation, amid the joy and shouts of the patriot army.[1]

Arnold renewed his pretension to the supreme command after the reduction of the fortresses, with his accustomed arrogance and dictatorial spirit. The troops rejected these assumptions, and the Connecticut committee interposing, conferred upon Allen, by a formal instrument, temporary powers as commandant of the army and forts. Arnold yielded to necessity, and acquiesced in a measure which was ultimately approved by Massachusetts.

A small armed vessel was lying at this time in the Sorel river, near St. Johns. Her possession would secure to the Americans the entire naval force upon the lake, and they determined to effect her seizure before an alarm should be excited. Fifty men engaged by Arnold in Massachusetts, and over whom he exercised undoubted authority, arrived oppportunely at Ticonderoga. With these men, he manned the schooner captured at Skeensboro', and on the fifth day after the surrender of the fort, sailed for St. Johns. Allen, with another party of one hundred and fifty men, accompanied him in bateaux. The wind was propitious to the zeal and ambition of Arnold, and outsailing the flotilla of boats, he arrived within thirty miles of his destination, when a calm prevented further progress, but promptly embarking thirty-five men in two boats, he pursued his design, surprised and captured the fort at St. Johns, with a sergeant's guard of twelve men, and seized the schooner, her crew, and two small brass guns. Apprized of the near approach of a large detachment of troops, he deemed it prudent to retreat, bearing with him his prize and provisions, and four boats loaded with stores. Five other bateaux he destroyed. On his return he met Allen hastening onward to participate in the perils and glory of the enterprise. Although Arnold represented to him the cause of his own retreat, Allen

---

[1]*John Adams's Diary.*

persisted in advancing, but the presence of a superior British force with artillery, which had anticipated his arrival, compelled him to reembark.

History, in forming its judgment of the character and the services of the men who achieved these perilous and daring exploits, should regard the fact, that they acted under the authority of no legitimate and recognized government, but from the impulses of individual enterprise and patriotism; that their acts constituted rebellion, and that a failure would have entailed upon them the retributions visited upon treason and outlawry. By a singular coincidence, the congress that determined to raise an army to assert the civil immunities of the colonies, assembled on the very day that beamed upon the capture of these fortresses. The reduction of Ticonderoga and Crown point, opened to the colonies the gates of Canada.

The prescience of Allen's mind, and his practical sagacity, comprehended at a glance the magnitude of the consequences which might result from the measure, and which he saw within the grasp of congress. In urging with the warmest importunity and with irresistible reasoning, an immediate attack on Canada, he foreshadowed a policy, which then rejected, was afterwards adopted, when the auspicious moment had passed. In a communication to congress on June 7th, he utters this vigorous and emphatic language: "I would lay my life on it, that with fifteen hundred men I could take Montreal."

Ethan Allen stands out in bold prominence and originality among the extraordinary men, whose high attributes of mind and character were evolved from the crucible of the times. His own age, under the prejudices of controversy, was too prone to regard him as a rude and ferocious adventurer, inflamed by the mere animal impulse of courage, but without the intellectual qualities to guide and elevate their purposes. The intellect that could attain and preserve a mastery over the minds and hearts of such a race as the "men of the Green mountains," and wield that "fierce democracie" to his purpose, possessed no ordinary powers. At Castleton, when Arnold asserted the command, every man shouldered his musket, and prepared to return to his home; but with Allen, their leader, they knew no doubt; they had no fear. It was no common mind that enabled him, with kindred spirits on one hand, to repress what they considered the aggressions of New York; and, on the other, by his keen diplomacy to arrest the progress of the British arms. Whatever judgment posterity may form of the ambiguous events in his subsequent career, no one will doubt the energy of his character, or distrust his love of liberty and loyalty to his own peculiar people. Why should not the magnanimity and patriotism of New York erect a monument on the cliffs of Ticonderoga, that would consecrate his name, and be a perpetual memorial of his great exploits?

In June, Allen relinquished the command of the posts on Champlain, to Colonel Benjamin Hinman, who occupied them with a thousand levies from Connecticut. Arnold, still persisting in his assumptions, claimed the command, but the controversy was terminated by Massachusetts discharging him summarily from her service.[1]

Congress long deliberated on the policy of invading Canada, hesitating between the adoption of a measure, the immediate expediency of which was obvious, and an apprehension of its effect upon the mind of the American people; and the influence an act, so marked and aggressive in its character, might exert upon the sentiments of their advocates in England. Circumstances were auspicious. A large part of the royal troops had been withdrawn from the province to strengthen the army in Boston; a few feeble garrisons alone occupied the forts and prominent towns. Although the yoke that England had imposed upon the Canadian people had been gentle in its pressure, it was that of an hereditary enemy, and the friends of the contemplated measures urged, that if sustained by an

[1] *Hall's Vermont.*

adequate force the masses would throw off the hated domination. In addition to this view, it was believed that England was in no condition to supply immediate reenforcements in that direction, while the brevity of the season in these northern seas would early suspend navigation.

When at length the purpose had been decided upon, an army of three thousand men was concentrating with all possible celerity at Ticonderoga from the provinces of New England and New York. General Schuyler held the chief command, with Richard Montgomery and David Wooster as subordinates, who were appointed brigadier-generals. Sir Guy Carleton, the governor-general of Canada, soon became apprised of these preparations, and with characteristic energy determined to arrest the advance of the patriot army, by creating a naval force competent to maintain the control of the lake. Montgomery resolved to advance with the small body of troops which had already assembled, and by the vigor and activity of his measures to defeat the designs of Carleton. With this purpose, he rapidly descended the lake and seized the position at the Isle aux Noix, which commanded the entrance of the Sorel river. He was soon after joined by Schuyler, and united with him in issuing an earnest and conciliatory appeal to the Canadians, assuring them of the fraternal sympathies of the American people, and exhorting them to aid in the emancipation of Canada from British power. The direct effect of this proclamation was favorable to the American interest, as it confirmed the provincial population in their neutral attitude. Carleton had been defeated in his efforts to enlist the masses in any aggressive movements. He had appealed to the bishop of Quebec, to issue a fiat, to be read in the churches, exhorting the people to take arms in support of the government. This dignitary revolted from the service, as unworthy his pastoral character, and contrary to the canons of his church. A few subordinate ecclesiastics, with consciences more ductile, and the noblesse, whose interests had been essentially protected by the Quebec act, exerted themselves with great zeal to overcome this popular feeling, but with little definite success. The indefatigable efforts of Carleton embraced other expedients. By the influence of large bounties, and the assurances of peculiar privileges and immunities in the affairs of the colony, he succeeded in gathering a few recruits, who were enrolled as the corps of the Royal Highland Emigrants.

The royal agents effected more favorable results by their overtures to the savage tribes. In July, Guy Johnson, the intendent of Indian affairs, arrived at Montreal, accompanied by a large band of Iroquois chiefs and warriors, and among them Brant, the Mohawk chieftain. A solemn council was held, and these representatives of the powerful confederacy swore in their barbarian forms fealty to England, pledging its support to the cause of the king against the insurgent colonies. Thus originated the employment of the Indian in this contest, and to this action may be traced the ruthless scenes of blood and rapine that marked the progress of the war.[1] The American commanders conceived a demonstration against the fort at St. Johns expedient, in order to secure an impressive effect to the proclamation which had been issued. They advanced from the island with only one thousand effective men, and repulsed on their march a spirited attack by the Indians. A slight breastwork was erected near the fort, but without the power of assailing works, which were found to be quite formidable. Schuyler determined to fall back with the view of protecting his original position. By the erection of a *cheveau de frize* in the Sorel river, he effectually obstructed all access to the lake, by the vessels which Carleton was actively employed in constructing at St. Johns. Schuyler was recalled to Albany by public affairs, and while detained there was attacked by a severe and protracted sickness, that prevented his return to the army. The command of the expedition devolved on General

[1] *Stone's Life of Brant.*

Montgomery, and it could have been confided to no more competent or illustrious leader.

Montgomery was a native of Ireland, and born to high social position. His mind, endowed by eminent native qualities, was adorned by culture, refined by habits, and elevated and expanded by military experience. He served under Wolfe at Louisburg with much distinction, was promoted and attached to the army of Amherst, in which he acted as adjutant of the 17th Regiment of foot. He accompanied his regiment to the West Indies, and retired from the army with the rank of captain in 1772. Soon after his resignation, he married a daughter of Robert R. Livingstone, and, settling upon the banks of the Hudson, devoted himself to the pursuits of peace. Here, in 1775, he was dwelling in elegant repose, surrounded by all the refined blandishments of society and the joys of domestic felicity. His adopted country summoned him from these happy scenes, demanding, in her impending struggle, the influence of his character and the aid of his genius and acquirements. He freely consecrated all to the cause of liberty and independence.

The early arrival of reenforcements and artillery enabled Montgomery to pursue aggressive measures, and he again advanced and formed the regular investment of St. Johns. That fortress, situated on the Sorel, was now considered the key to Canada. It was occupied by a garrison of seven hundred men commanded by Major Preston, and its strong works were impregnable to the ordnance of Montgomery, who was alike deficient in guns and ammunition. Fortunately, the fort at Chambly, a short distance below, upon the same river, was held by a small body of troops and guarded without prudence or vigilance. Montgomery promptly resolved to avail himself of these circumstances, and a party led by majors Livingstone and Brown, descended the river in silence and in the obscurity of a dark night, attacked and captured the fort after a feeble defense. This successful enterprise relieved the great embarrassment of Montgomery, and furnished him with several heavy pieces of cannon, a hundred and twenty-four barrels of powder, and a large quantity of stores and provisions. The colors captured at the fort were transmitted to congress, with imposing forms, as the first testimonials of success.

A more favorable disposition towards the Americans was disclosed among the Canadians, and large numbers joined the army, bringing with them supplies and ammunition. With a view of fostering this spirit, by intercourse with the people and an exhibition of strength, as well as to procure supplies, Montgomery caused detachments of his troops to traverse the country in various directions. Allen and Brown, at the head of two of these parties, having approached Montreal, hastily concerted an attack on the island. The conception of crossing a wide and turbulent river, in the presence of a superior and vigilant enemy, was bold and extravagant; but heroic daring was the spirit of the times. Allen, securing boats at Longueil, crossed the river at night with one hundred men, many of whom were Canadians. Brown, who it was intended should cross above the river, and cooperate by a diversion with the other party, was unable to effect his part of the plan. Allen was thus left to meet the united strength of the garrison, and was assailed by an overwhelming force of regulars, Canadians, and savages. He made a gallant resistance, but was compelled to surrender with his entire party. Carleton, departing from the generous clemency that adorned his character, refused to recognize Allen as a prisoner of war, but, loaded with chains, he was transported to England, and subjected on the passage to every barbarous indignity. In that country, he was transferred with capricious tyranny from one jail to another, and from prison castles to convict ships; continually pursued by the same unrelenting persecution, but powerless to shake the stern devotion of his republican zeal. After an imprisonment of almost three years, he was exchanged and received by a grateful country, with every demonstration of respect and interest. Allen had been superseded in the command of the Vermont troops by

Warner, and in his connection with the army of Montgomery, held no distinct or formal official position.

Carleton, elated by this success, determined, in conjunction with Colonel McLean, who was stationed with the corps of Royal Emigrants at the mouth of the Sorel, to effect the relief of the garrison at St. Johns. With a force of one thousand men, consisting principally of Canadians and Indians, he undertook to effect the passage of the river from Montreal to Longueil. Warner, however, in anticipation of the movement, had occupied the eastern bank, lying in concealment at Longueil with three hundred of the Green mountain boys, and fortifying his position by a few small pieces of artillery judiciously planted. As Carleton approached the shore, he was received by a sweeping shower of grape and musketry. His raw troops, unaccustomed to an ordeal so unexpected and severe, were at once repulsed and fled back precipitately to the island. McLean retreated to his former position, and having learnt by a letter, from Arnold to Schuyler, which had been intrusted to an Indian runner, and fell into the hands of McLean through treachery or accident, the astounding intelligence that an American army was descending the valley of the Chaudiere with the design of seizing Quebec, hastened with all the force he was able to collect to occupy that place. Montgomery immediately secured the possession of the important post evacuated by McLean, and by the erection of a commanding work at the junction of the Sorel with the St. Lawrence, sustained by floating batteries, obstructed the navigation of both streams. This energetic proceeding totally isolated Montreal, and the forts upon the upper waters of the river and lakes, from all communication with Quebec and the ocean.

Preston, having been apprised by Montgomery of these adverse circumstances, surrendered St. Johns, with its garrison, its armament of fifty guns, eight hundred stands of arms, and a large amount of munitions. This most valuable conquest being accomplished, Montgomery, without any delay, marched upon Montreal, and offering that city the most liberal and humane terms; it capitulated without making any defense. Carleton, anticipating the arrival of Montgomery, relinquished the command of Montreal to Prescott, and repaired to the fleet, which he had assembled below the city. Its descent was, however, obstructed by the works that had been erected at the mouth of the Sorel, and which had already inflicted on the fleet a severe repulse. The capture of the governor-general, an event that would have been almost decisive of the war in Canada, appeared inevitable, but he effected an escape in disguise, floating by the American batteries in a boat with muffled oars, and under the protection of a dark night. Prescott, who subsequently attained such notoriety in his second capture on Rhode Island, on the thirteenth of November, surrendered the fleet and a large part of the garrison of Montreal which had sought refuge on the vessels, with many persons of both civil and military prominence.

Montgomery, throughout the campaign, had been tried and oppressed by the character of the troops over whom he held a nominal command. Inspired by the loftiest heroism and enthusiasm, the army was composed of recruits without experience, hastily levied with only a brief term of enlistment. At home they had been accustomed to a social equality with their officers in the same pacific pursuits and the unlimited exercise of opinion and the freedom of consultation. They carried these habits into camp, and asserted there the same privileges. The restraints and rules of obedience, usual to military service, were but slightly recognized. The native eloquence of their leader, his conciliatory spirit and wise deportment, strengthened by the high respect felt for his character and attainments, enabled Montgomery to mould this inchoate mass into the appearance of an army; but the period was too limited to impart the discipline and efficiency of which materials so intelligent and brave were susceptible. In addition to these embarrassments, the army imperfectly clothed already suffered from the rigors of the climate and all the evil consequences of the mistaken policy of short enlistments began to be disclosed. A large part of the troops were even then entitled to their discharges, and the expiration of the term of many others was rapidly approaching.

Montgomery distributed to the soldiers warm clothing, and by the most earnest importunities, and addresses to their soldierly spirit and patriotism, endeavored to prevail on them to remain until the close of a campaign which had opened with such brilliant presages. All these appeals were in the main unsuccessful. Montgomery had been educated in a strict school of military subordination, and his spirit was galled and depressed by this laxity of discipline, and of the bonds that held together an army, upon the conduct of which depended his own success and fame, but over which he saw that he could exert little controlling power. An enthusiastic devotion to the cause to which he had pledged his service, alone restrained an immediate abandonment of the command; but he announced to congress a fixed determination to resign, whenever the pending operations were terminated.

While these events were transpiring on the St. Lawrence, one of the most remarkable adventures of the age was in progress in another quarter. Washington, in the camp before Boston, had conceived the idea of a measure, so daring and terrible, that its execution seemed scarcely within the compass of human endurance. It was one of those conceptions, that occasionally burst through the Fabian policy, which circumstances imposed upon him, and proved that inherent impulses would have prompted him to measures of bold enterprise and vigorous action. He resolved to dispatch a body of one thousand men under the command of Arnold, who should proceed up the Kennebec river, and, surmounting the hideous wilderness where its fountains mingled with the waters of the St. Lawrence, and which had never been traversed save by the Indians and the mountaineer, should descend by the Chaudiere to Quebec. With a supreme knowledge of Canadian affairs, Washington wisely conceived, that wholly unsuspicious of danger from this direction all the available troops would be withdrawn by Carleton from the lower St. Lawrence to oppose Montgomery, that Quebec would be unguarded, and that the citizens, favorably disposed to the American occupation, would, with joy, capitulate. This plan would have been crowned by complete success, had not untoward delays been created by the insuperable obstacles that nature interposed. It is not within the range of our narrative to trace the details of this marvelous exploit, beyond its connection with the operations of Montgomery.

About the middle of September, Arnold commenced his wild and adventurous march, and did not reach the banks of the St. Lawrence until the 9th of November, more than three weeks later than the day designated in the original design. No band of heroes have ever surmounted equal perils and suffering with firmer constancy and resolution. Thirty-two days they were buried in this desolation of forests and mountains, of rivers, morasses and lakes. Their progress had been protracted by the most formidable impediments, struggling amid gloomy solitudes, cheered by no human countenance, and without a single aspect of civilization. When thirty miles from the first Canadian cabin, the last remnant of provision was exhausted. The pet dogs of the officers, which had lovingly followed their masters through these perils, had been eaten, with food still more loathsome and repulsive.[1] When at length the expedition reached the settlements far up on the Chaudiere, it was received with cordiality and kindness, and the wants of the famishing troops relieved to the utmost extent permitted by the limited resources of the people. Here Arnold was constrained to indulge his army in a brief repose, while he awaited the gathering of the scattered detachments and dispersed the forcible and conciliatory proclamation of Washington. Colonel Enos, who conducted the rear division, consisting of one-third of the army, after reaching the sources of the

---

[1] *Sparks's Life of Arnold.*

Kennebec, was compelled to return by an utter destitution of subsistence for his troops.

When this array of unknown men, burst into their seclusion from the pathless wilderness, the simple minded habitans looked upon them in wonder, mingled with awe. It almost seemed to them

> As if the yawning hills to heaven,
> A subterranean host had given.

Rumor spread with wild exaggeration, the report of the numbers of the invaders. They were represented as terrible in their powers of body, invincible in courage and cased in iron. These intrepid adventurers stood upon the shore of the St. Lawrence. Quebec, the prize that was to have rewarded all their toils and suffering, was in view, but beyond their grasp.

The letter which had been intercepted by McLean, communicated to him the designs of Arnold. The alertness that secured the presence of the former at Quebec, and the vigor of his measures, saved the city from capitulation. Vigilant and experienced, he adopted every expedient to insure its safety. All the boats he could seize were removed from the eastern shore of the river; sailors to man the batteries were drawn from the ships in the harbor, and the defenses of the city generally were reorganized and strengthened. Had Arnold been able to effect the immediate passage of the St. Lawrence when he reached its shores, he would have found a universal consternation prevailing, Quebec undefended, and the people disposed to yield to him the possession of the city. The precautions of McLean frustrated this measure, the original plan of the campaign. The prevalence of an impetuous storm and the delay incident to the collection of means of transportation caused a detention of four days. Having succeeded in procuring thirty or forty frail birch canoes, by the assistance of the Canadians, Arnold crossed the river with five hundred men on the night of the 13th, although the Lizard frigate and a sloop were lying in front of the city, for the purpose of intercepting them, and their guard boats were continually patrolling the stream. The little flotilla had made three passages, and as the last party landed, the discovery of the movement by one of these, made it unsafe to attempt the crossing of the rear division amounting to one hundred and fifty men, who remained in the occupation of Point Levi. Arnold ascended the precipitous cliffs that Wolfe had rendered memorable, and stood when the day dawned, with his little band on the plains of Abraham. The hope of seizing the city by a surprise was disappointed. The guard boat had communicated information of the crossing by the Americans; the city was alarmed, and McLean alert and prepared to meet an attack.

An assault of a fortified city, guarded by a garrison of eighteen hundred men with his small party, almost without ammunition, destitute of artillery and a large part of their guns rendered useless by the exposure of their march, Arnold saw would be a hopeless and a desperate sacrifice. The next day, with his usual audacity, he sent a flag summoning the city to surrender, but it was fired upon without permitting an approach to the walls. He occupied, during three days, lines in front of the place, and attempted by various devices to excite a cooperative movement by partisans within the works. These demonstrations secured no favorable results, and learning that a sortie by the garrison was contemplated, while a body of two hundred troops, which had escaped from Montreal was approaching his rear, Arnold decided to fall back to Point au Tremble, twenty miles above, and there to await a junction with Montgomery.[1]

[1] Much discrepancy will be discovered in the language of historians in reference to these events. Marshall states that Arnold crossed on the 14th, that McLean did not arrive at Quebec before Arnold reached the eastern shore of the St. Lawrence; that the guard boat neglected to impart intelligence of the crossing, that no apprehension existed of an attack, and had Arnold been aware of these facts he might have marched through St. John's gate into the city, unopposed. Botta affirms that a council of naval officers refused to allow the sailors to land in support of the garrison.

Arnold with deep chagrin, saw the vessel that conveyed Carleton to Quebec safely descending the river and to learn that on his arrival at Point au Tremble, that Carleton had landed there only an hour or two before.

The troops, whose period of service had terminated, resisted every appeal to their patriotism and duty urged by Montgomery, to induce them to remain, and by their persistent determination to assert their legal rights nearly dissolved his army. After leaving feeble garrisons to maintain his different conquests, he joined Arnold on the 1st of December with a detachment of three hundred men. But he brought an ample supply of woolen apparel to clothe the suffering army of Arnold.

On the 5th of December, the combined forces, forming an aggregate of less than a thousand men, again appeared before Quebec and renewed the siege. A battery of six small guns was erected. The frozen ground resisted all efforts to use it for that purpose, and Montgomery resorted to the novel expedient of substituting snow for earth, in the construction of the work, which, saturated with water and hardened by frost, acquired almost the consistency and firmness of marble. The guns, mounted on the battery, proved too light for effective service. Montgomery renewed the formal summons to surrender, but his flag was again fired upon and repelled. This unusual action was intended to interdict communication between the besiegers and citizens. At first a strong favorable disposition existed among the people towards the republican interests, but this feeling had been much modified by the policy of Carleton, and the alarm excited by an apprehension of the probable consequence to the town of a hostile occupation.

Darkness and gloom were gathering around the enterprise, but the inflexible spirit of the leaders, sustained by the enthusiasm of the army, could be subdued by no common obstacles. The sufferings of the troops in their exposed condition from the severity of the weather, and the unremitting toil and fatigue to which they were subjected, transcended all that had been imagined of distress and hardship. These calamitous circumstances were intensely aggravated by the appearance of the small-pox in the camp. This fell pestilence, then the most dreaded scourge to armies, raged with peculiar virulence and fatality, and pursued the troops with an unmitigated severity until their final return to Ticonderoga.

Montgomery knew that the loftiest expectations had been inspired by the early successes of the campaign, and the confidence in his genius and skill. A brilliant enterprise, which should shed around a failure a blaze of glory, would prove less disastrous in its influence upon this popular enthusiasm, than an inglorious retreat without an effort. His own fame, and the reputation of the army demanded a great effort, and he resolved to risk a general assault upon the city. A council of war approved the design, and the army, which it was necessary to consult, after the disaffection of a part of Arnold's command, had been surmounted by the influence of Morgan, embraced it with extreme ardor. An assault, although in the highest degree perilous and doubtful, was far from desperate. The very magnitude of the work, occupied by a feeble garrison, was an element of weakness. The Canadian levies were known to be disaffected, and the citizens without zeal towards the government. Audacity often wins where judgment hesitates and calculation fails.

The plan ultimately adopted by Montgomery, contemplated two demonstrations against the upper town, by detachments chiefly composed of Canadian recruits and led by Livingstone and Brown, while the real attack should be made upon the lower town by Montgomery and Arnold, assailing it at opposite points. The combined movements commenced at four o'clock in the morning of the 31st day of December, 1775. A driving snow storm, impelled by a fierce north-east gale, enveloped the scene in profound obscurity. Each commander at the head of the forlorn hope, led his own column. The vigilance of Carleton was unslumbering; the batteries were armed, the guns charged with grape and canister ready to offer the assailants a fearful reception. Yet, so skillfully had the measures of Montgomery been conducted, that Carleton knew not from what direction to expect the impending blow.[1] The Americans advanced with caution and in silence, slowly groping their way, amid darkness and the tempest. Montgomery assumed to himself the dangerous duty of leading the column, which was intended to make the assault by a narrow and obscure pathway that passed between the base of Cape Diamond, a lofty and inaccessible precipice and the river St. Lawrence. This defile was defended by a strong block-house with palisades extending from the cliffs to the river. A picket had been constructed a short distance in advance, which was occupied by a few Canadian soldiers. At the approach of the assailing party, this guard fled in alarm and disorder, firing a harmless volley, and communicated their panic to the troops at the block-house, who also precipitately abandoned their post.

The advance of the Americans was impeded by an immense and nearly insurmountable barrier of ice, which at this point had been formed by the surging tide and where the drifting snow had accumulated. The troops, able only to advance in single file or individually, were slowly and with excessive difficulty surmounting these obstacles, while Montgomery was aiding with his own hands in removing the palisades. He halted sufficiently to be joined by about two hundred of his followers, and boldly advancing, shouted: "Men of New York, you will not fear to follow where your general leads." At this moment a single cannonier, tradition states a drunken sailor,[2] returned to the battery, and, seizing an unextinguished match, discharged one of the pieces. The storm of grape swept along the narrow passage with frightful destruction. Every man in the advance, except a Canadian guide and Aaron Burr, a youth of nineteen who had joined Arnold as a volunteer, was stricken down.[3] Montgomery, pierced by a ball through the head, and both legs lacerated by

---

[1] *Carleton's letter.* [2] *Silliman's Journal.* [3] *Palmer's Champlain.*

another, fell dying into the arms of Burr. Cheeseman and McPherson, the aids of Montgomery, both fell at the side of their commander. That single explosion was fatal to the enterprise. The fall of their leader crushed the spirit of the troops. Colonel Campbell, who succeeded to the command of the column on the fall of Montgomery, hastily retired and abandoned the assault without further effort.

The operations of Livingstone and Brown were defeated by the furious tempest, and they necessarily failed in effecting the diversion contemplated by the plan of attack. Arnold, marching promptly at the concerted signal, approached in silence along the St. Charles, moving through St. Roques street toward the Saut au Matelots. At this point a battery of two twelve-pounders had been constructed. This barrier could only be approached by a path which, at that time, obstructed by an enormous mass of snow and ice, afforded only a deep and narrow passage of the breadth of a single track. The difficult defile might be raked by the guns of the battery and swept by the musketry from the walls and pickets of the garrison; but it furnished the only avenue by which the Americans could advance to the assault. Arnold rushed along this terrible gorge at the head of Lamb's Artillery Company, with a single field-piece mounted upon a sled. It became impossible to move the gun through the pass, and it served only to obstruct the path and to impede the passage of the troops. The main body closely followed the artillery, preceded by Morgan's riflemen. An alarm was soon sounded, and a severe fire of grape and musketry opened upon the assailants. As Arnold, leading with the most daring intrepidity, approached the battery, he was prostrated, by a ball that shattered his leg, and borne from the field. Morgan, the future victor at the Cowpens, succeeded to the command and assailed the battery with irresistible impetuosity. Receiving the fire of one gun almost at its mouth, and while his riflemen fired upon the defenders through the embrasures, the barricade was scaled by ladders carried on the shoulders of his men. The battery and the guns, with most of the guards, were captured. Morgan was the second man who crossed the barricade. His gallant sergeant, Charles Porterfield of Virginia, afterwards a lieutenant-colonel and slain at Camden, was the first.

Notwithstanding this success, the situation of Morgan was in the highest degree critical. He was alone with his own company, and a few bold individuals who had pressed to the front; all the efforts of Lamb to advance his gun were ineffectual. Morgan had no guides, was ignorant of the formation of the city, and without intelligence of the cooperative movements. The soldiers were oppressed by the cold; icicles covered their clothes; they were bewildered by the intense darkness and the raging of the storm. A temporary pause was necessary, and Morgan returned to the barrier. Here he succeeded, with the active aid of Colonel Green and Major Bigelow and Meigs, in assembling a body of about two hundred men. When the appearance of light revealed the aspect of affairs, the spirit and confidence of the troops were reanimated, and with a united voice, they called on Morgan to lead against the second battery, which was near, but disguised by an angle of the street. Morgan, placing himself at their head, and animating them by his voice, pealing above the howling of the tempest and the din of battle, rapidly advanced. Passing the angle, he was confronted by a body of troops, commanded by Captain Anderson, who called on him to surrender. Morgan instantly shot him dead, and the Americans rushing onward planted their ladders against the barricade, under a galling fire as well from the windows of the adjacent houses, as from the works. A sanguinary conflict ensued, and a few of the most resolute of Morgan's little band mounted the ladders, but when they reached the top of the parapet, an obstacle was revealed calculated to appall the stoutest heart. Two lines of British troops stood on the opposite side; the butts of their muskets resting upon the ground and the bayonets pointed to the summit of the barricade, formed an impenetrable abatis of steel. Part of the Americans retreated into the stone houses which lined the narrow street, securing shelter both from the elements and the furious fire to which they had been exposed, while from the window they were able to assail the enemy. One circumstance which was peculiarly depressing, greatly impaired the efficiency of the riflemen. Although the precaution had been observed of binding a handkerchief about the lock of each gun, not one in ten had been effectually protected from the storm, and was fit for service.

The failure of the assault upon the other parts of the town empowered Carleton to hurl the whole force of the garrison against this single column. Dearborn, who held with a company in reserve the entrance of the gorge at the St. Roche gate, had been already surprised and compelled to surrender, and that avenue of retreat was therefore in possession of the enemy. Morgan, with the concurrence of the officers who survived, determined to burst through every obstruction, and to effect an escape; but when the attempt was made to collect the troops and animate them to the effort, overwhelmed by the cold, oppressed by a conviction of their desperate situation, and intimidated by the deadly fire to which they had been exposed in the street, they shrunk from the undertaking, and the bold proposition was abandoned. Compelled to relinquish this purpose, Morgan determined to maintain his position in the faint hope of receiving succor from the other detachments. Attacked, however, by a foe whose strength was increasing every moment, in front and rear, and by a still more destructive fire from the windows, Morgan, after contending for several hours with the utmost skill and gallantry against all these adverse circumstances, was at length constrained to capitulate. Thus disastrously terminated a daring and energetic enterprise, in which the Americans lost, including sixty killed and wounded, about four hundred men. The valor and ability of the defense exhibited by Carleton were not more conspicuous than the generous humanity of the conqueror. The prisoners were treated with kindness; the wounded cared for in the hospitals, and the dead interred.

The body of Montgomery, lying in a guard house with thirteen corpses of his brave followers, which had been exhumed from the snowdrift that had formed to them a common sepulchre, was recognized by an American officer and consigned to the care of an old companion in arms, and was reverently buried near the ramparts of the city. The loss of his great military talent and acquirements, and the influence of his social and intellectual eminence was irreparable. The death of Montgomery was deplored not only by his own countrymen, but in every clime where the love of liberty was cherished. Even in the British parliament, the loftiest eloquence pronounced his eulogium, and Barrè, and Burke, and Fox, ascribed to his deeds and character the exalted virtues which adorn the names of the noblest heroes and patriots of antiquity. Lord North, while denouncing the course of Montgomery, and reprehending these tributes to his worth, pointed and enforced the panegyric, when he exclaimed in the language of the poet:

> Curse his virtues, for they have undone his country.

It was a fit and beatiuful coincidence that this youthful hero, for he had not attained his fortieth year, the pupil of Wolfe, a disciple of the glory and spirit of Montcalm, should have fallen on this consecrated ground.[1]

The body of Montgomery reposed for almost half a century in the grave where it had been deposited by a generous enemy; but in the year 1818, the executive of New York claimed the sacred deposit for removal to the state of Montgomery's adoption, and the governor-general of Canada gracefully acceded to the request. The remains of Montgomery were borne through the country, accompanied by every exhibition of love and reverence. A single day they lay in state, in the rotunda of the Capitol at Albany, and thousands of a grateful posterity visited

---

[1] *Botta's Graham.*

them, rendering the homage of gratitude and veneration. His final obsequies were performed in New York in all the imposing solemnities of civil and military rites. His relics were buried in a grave near the monument erected at an early period, by congress, to his memory, in St Paul's church-yard.

He left no children to bear the heritage of his glorious name, but his widow survived to an extreme old age, an object of respect and interest as the relict of Montgomery.

CHAPTER X.

The Retreat from Canada.

Arnold succeeded to the command upon the death of Montgomery, and was compelled by the exigencies with which he was surrounded to convert the siege into a blockade. In the judicious policy of Carleton he was left undisturbed, although inflicting severe suffering upon the town and garrison. The troops had become insubordinate, the Canadian people disappointed and harassed, and stimulated by the potent influence of the rural priests, who refused the last consolations of religion to those who adhered to the Americans, had assumed a hostile attitude, while the American army was oppressed by disease and exposure. M. Beaujeu, an influential and intrepid Canadian, had organized a hostile corps; but this, by a sudden and vigorous attack of Arnold, were broken up and dispersed. At length, baffled in various attempts to effect a surprise of the city, Arnold erected batteries and assaulted the city and shipping by shells and hot shot; but all their efforts were defeated by the skill and prudence of Carleton.

On the 1st of May, Arnold was superseded by the arrival of General Thomas, who assumed the command. Arnold, always impracticable in a subordinate position, was early involved in dissensions with his superior, and severe injury affording the pretext, he was transferred from the active duties of the field to the command at Montreal. In that position so favorable to the exercise of his worst passions, he revealed the cupidity and rapaciousness, which in after years, and on another stage deformed and debauched his whole character.

My limits restrain me from tracing the narrative of the republican army in its retreat. Its extreme necessities, its endurance from the fell scourge that pursued it, the inefficiency that demoralized its strength and its inadequacy to resist a more powerful enemy, have afforded thrilling pages to general history.

On the fifth of May, the hesitating councils of the American general were decided by the arrival of three British ships, the precursors of a large fleet, which with infinite peril and hardihood had braved the tempests of the gulf, and, pressing up the river amid storms of snow and vast ice fields, had effected the passage far earlier than usual. The reenforcements and supplies they conveyed were immediately landed. The retreat of the American army was at once commenced, and with a precipitation that constrained the abandonment of most of its sick and wounded, and all its military stores. At Sorell, Thomas died of the prevailing epidemic, and was succeeded by General Sullivan, who conducted the movements of the retreating army with a consummate ability that evoked the highest encomium of the country and the formal recognition of congress.

The treatment by Carleton, of the sick and wounded Americans, who, wandering from the line of march, had been concealed and cherished by the characteristic charities and kindness of the Canadian people was signalized by an exalted clemency and generous benignity. Wise policy may have suggested these beneficent acts, but it were unjust to withhold the recognition of deeds of mercy so habitual, and not to concede that they may have had their inspiration in purer and more exalted emotions.

The calamities which marked this retreat were deeply intensified by a repulse at Three Rivers, and the sanguinary catastrophe at the Cedars. After these reverses, Sullivan pressed his retreat to the Isle aux Noix, slowly and defiantly receding before Burgoyne, while Arnold was narrowly escaping by extreme energy and promptitude, another column directed upon Montreal to intercept his escape.

Sullivan dismantled the works he had occupied, and burnt or destroyed every craft that he did not remove in the conveyance of his own army and stores. The sick and wounded were first transported to Crown point, and were immediately followed by the troops. The suffering of the former was scarcely paralleled by the endurance and distress of any scenes of that war, so replete with sacrifices and hardships. They were necessarily placed in open and leaky boats, drenched continually with water and exposed to the burning rays of the summer's sun, with no food but raw and rancid pork and hard biscuit.[1]

While at St. Johns, Arnold caused the frame of a vessel on the stocks at that place to be taken to pieces, carefully numbered and marked, and transported to Crown point. He superintended, with indefatigable vigor and activity, the embarkation of the army on its retreat to Isle aux Noix. Colonel Warner, with the Vermont regiment, formed the rear, and collecting most of the sick and wounded, effected a safe retreat, rejoining the army some days after the main body had arrived at Ticonderoga. The operations of war are always in their result preeminently influenced by fortune and accident. The American campaigns in Canada singularly illustrate this maxim. An elegant and philosophical historian with great force remarks, that although the direct results contemplated in the invasion of Canada were not achieved, the measure exerted a powerful influence upon the issue of the war, by compelling England to adopt the policy of dividing her armies in isolated attacks, when their united strength

---

[1] *Palmer's Champlain.*

11

would have been irresistible, and probably subversive of the republican cause.[1]

The Canadians, whose overt adherence to the invaders compromised their relations with the British government, were pursued with a severe retribution. Large numbers followed the American army in its retreat; those who remained were hunted down with a stern severity; many were tried and convicted of *rebellion*, and several, immediately after the repulse at Quebec, were executed.[2] Soon after the termination of the war of independence, the state of New York devoted a large and valuable tract of land in the county of Clinton, designated the Canadian and Nova Scotia refugee tract, for the relief and indemnification of these sufferers; but a large proportion of the grant was either not accepted or forfeited by the grantees, or lost by obstacles interposed by corrupt and designing speculators.[3] When the retreating army reached Crown point, its muster roll indicated a force of five thousand men, but more than half of the number were prostrated by disease, and chiefly by the terrible scourge, that desolated it like the sword of the destroying angel. The troops remained at that post ten days, and during that time, most of them were lying in the agony of their suffering, with no protection from the rain and storms, except open huts or frail coverings, formed by pine bowers, and destitute of almost every comfort and even the most common necessaries due to the sick and dying. The dead and the dying were exposed together, without any discrimination, in all these wretched receptacles of woe and charnel houses of death. In this brief period in the pause of its retreat, three hundred new-made graves arose as sad memorials of the sacrifices of this devoted army. Happily the judicious prescience of Sullivan had spread an ample shield of protection between its helpnessness and the assaults of the foe.

---

[1] *Boat.* [2] Tryon to Earl of Dartmouth, *Doc.*, VIII, 663.

[3] *Land Papers*, Secretary of State's Office, vol. XLVII, 126–172.

When the British commander arrived upon the waters of Champlain, he found farther pursuit imperatively arrested, until a new fleet and fresh means of transportation could be organized. The important and decisive struggle now arose to secure the naval supremacy upon the lake. To attain this object Carleton directed all his energies and resources. He caused six vessels of a large class, which had been constructed in England, to be taken apart below the Chambly rapids, conveyed in pieces to St. Johns, and there rebuilt with the utmost celerity. Bateaux, with incredible labor, were made to ascend the rapids, and boats and transports of various dimensions were constructed in the navigable waters of the Sorel. By such vigorous measures, Carleton succeeded in creating a fleet of thirty-one vessels, ranging in their armament from one to eighteen guns, and on the 1st of October was prepared to appear upon the lake. This formidable fleet was navigated by seven hundred veteran seamen, and armed in addition by an efficient corps of artillery.

Congress had been equally alert and energetic, but with means totally inadequate to the magnitude of the issue. The timber required for the construction of a fleet was yet standing in the forest, and was to be cut, prepared, and conveyed by human labor to the shipyards at Ticonderoga and Crown point. The material for its equipment must be transported a long distance over roads, nearly impracticable. The ship carpenters, who must construct the vessels, were occupied by urgent duties in the yards upon the sea coast. Amid all these adverse circumstances, the indomitable energies of Arnold formed and equipped a squadron of fifteen vessels, bearing an aggregate battery of fifty-five guns, and armed by three hundred and fifty gallant and determined men, who had, however, little or no experience in naval affairs. The great exigency invoked courage and sacrifices; and, notwithstanding this vast disparity of strength, Arnold decided boldly to throw himself across the path of the advancing enemy.

While the belligerents were thus sedulously laboring at the opposite extremities of the lake to attain the momentous design that prompted each, Arnold cruised with a few small vessels in undisputed ascendancy upon its waters. For a short space we will pause in the narrative of public events and recur to the domestic history of the colony on the Boquet. Amid the eventful scenes which surrounded it, the settlement had not escaped the tempests which were raging along the lake. Mr. Gilliland early espoused the patriotic cause, and in concert with men of congenial sentiments, a military organization, embracing both sides of the lake, had been formed immediately after the capture of Ticonderoga. His zeal and activity marked him as a victim to be pursued by the special vengeance of the government. He enjoyed, with a few other patriots, the high distinction of being by name proscribed and outlawed. A proclamation was issued by the governor of Canada in June succeeding the surrender of the Champlain fortresses, offering a reward of five hundred dollars for the arrest and rendition of Gilliland to the government. The allurements of this reward overcame the patriotism and fidelity of some of his tenants, who engaged in unsuccessful attempts to seize and convey him to Canada. Abortive efforts were made to seduce his household slaves into schemes for his betrayal. Various other attempts were made to effect his capture, and the most formidable one was nearly accomplished, by a sheriff of Tryon county, who penetrated into the settlement "with four tories and three savages." With great adroitness, Gilliland not only escaped the peril, but succeeded in effecting the surprise "and capture of the whole party with all their arms, and sent them prisoners to Crown point."

Gilliland, with his family, withdrew to the vicinity of Crown point, but returned, with part of his tenants, to secure their harvests, and to remove and secrete their property. Ponderous articles were buried or sunk in the lake. Many families, homeless and destitute, embracing Carleton's offers of amnesty, joined the British forces, and in a few cases, adopted the interests of England. Much valuable property, thus secreted, was, by the agency of these loyalists, exposed to the British officials, and seized and confiscated. Earlier than these final disasters, strange and unexpected trials gathered about the path of Gilliland, accumulating additional cares and anxieties. The perils and exigencies of the times demanded the most active vigilance, and often subjected the patriotic to unjust suspicions and unworthy surveillance. Although the patriotism of Gilliland had been the most zealous, and manifested by such efficient services, he was not exempt from the consequences of these jealousies. The acts of the tenants, whose defection we have noticed, and over whom he was supposed to exercise an absolute control, reflected upon him suspicion. Formal charges were preferred against him by Colonel Hartley, in July,[1] but these imputations seem to have been satisfactorily explained.[2]

This difficulty could scarcely have been composed, when an incident transpired that involved far more serious and enduring consequences. While Arnold was cruising on the lake, as we have already mentioned, the soldiers and sailors, attached to the fleet, were permitted to land at the plantations of Gilliland, and in the "most impudent and licentious manner," committed destructive ravages upon his own, and the crops and property of his tenants. These acts, Gilliland evidently believed, were perpetrated with Arnold's complicity, and yet on the 1st of September, he addressed to Arnold a letter on the subject, clothed with the most courteous and respectful language. He earnestly complained of the depredations, and submitted a statement of the crops and property that had been seized and conveyed away.[3] The amount was not only in itself considerable, but at the time and under the circumstances, the losses could not be retrieved. A month elapsed, and Arnold had returned no response, while it seems the outrages were

---

[1] *American Archives*, 5th series, I, 564. [2] *Idem*. [3] *Idem*, II, 102.

continued. Gilliland, always impetuous and resolute, and revolting at injustice, appealed to General Gates. The letter of Gilliland was then communicated to the commander-in-chief, accompanied with charges by Arnold against Gilliland, of disloyalty and fraud upon the government. The frivolous and malignant character of these charges are apparent from the documents themselves.[1] Gilliland, in his remarkable memorial to congress, alleges, "that Arnold sent a party of soldiers to tear your memorialist from his property, dignifying him with an officer for a commander, whose rank was so high as a sergeant, with private orders not to allow him to remove any of his property." In this manner Gilliland was conducted a prisoner to head-quarters, but no evidence exists that further proceedings were prosecuted on these charges against him, and from the letter from Gates to Arnold, it appears that he was dismissed.[2]

In another part of the same memorial which was addressed to Congress in 1777, Gilliland bursts into a magnificent and scourging invective of Arnold, which, if it were the only memorial we possess of the moral and intellectual qualities of Gilliland, would stamp him a man of extraordinary character. Arnold, when this denunciation was uttered, was in the zenith of his fame and influence, yet Gilliland boldly proclaimed before the highest tribunal of the nation his rapacity and perversion of power, and almost animated by the spirit of prophecy delineates his character with a fearless and unfaltering hand as striking as is the eloquence and vehemence of his language. He exclaims after glancing at his own services and losses and describing his arrest: "Gen. Arnold is your servant; all the power and authority he has is derived from you and that has enabled him to commit the acts of tyranny and outrage upon your memorial-

---

[1] *American Archives*, II, 592. All the documents bearing on this affair are collected in *The Pioneer History of the Champlain Valley*, pages 56 to 68, where the subject is fully examined and discussed.

[2] *Idem*, II, 847.

st and others, whose complaints have been laid before you. [t is not in mine, but it is in your power to bring him to ustice. Bursting with pride and intoxicated with power :o which he ought to have been a stranger, but which he has had the art to obtain from you, he tyrannizes when he can. If :emerity, if rashness, imprudence, and error can recommend nim to you, he is allowed to be amply supplied with these qualities, and many people think, they ought to recommend nim in a peculiar manner to Lord North, who, in gratitude 'or his having done more injury to the American cause :han all the ministerial troops have the power of doing, ought to reward him with a generous pension."

Carleton had been employed during this short period of repose, with extraordinary energy in constructing a fleet and organizing a powerful land force. The forts at St. Johns and Isle aux Noix were repaired and strengthened, and an army of seven thousand veteran troops, assembled at those points, was ready to advance against the colonies, the moment the ascendancy on the lake should be secured. Towards the middle of October, Carleton left his station with a fleet, which at that epoch, would have been esteemed respectable and even formidable in European seas. It consisted of the Inflexible, mounting eighteen guns; the Maria of fourteen guns; Carleton of twelve guns; heavy radeau; several gondolas and twenty gun-boats and long-boats armed in the efficient manner we have described. The naval supervision was confided to Captain Pringle, an officer attached to the royal navy and of great experience. Carleton accompanied the fleet, and controlled and guided its operations. Arnold, who had occupied with a part of his fleet a position at the lower extremity of the lake, retired on the approach of Carleton, and sought and moored his vessels in a secluded cove on the western shore of Valcour island, situated between the mouths of the Saranac and Au Sable rivers. The fleet collected at this place included the sloop Enterprise, mounting ten guns; the schooners Royal Savage, twelve guns, and Revenge, eight guns; three galleys, carrying each eight guns; and eight gondolas, each mounting eight guns. The fleet consisted of fifteen vessels bearing an armament of eighty-four guns. The disparity between the two fleets in the number of guns and weight of metal was very decided, but less unfavorable to the Americans than the materials that formed the respective crews. While the British vessels were manned by veteran seamen and gunners, the crews of Arnold were wholly raw and unpracticed, many of them drafts from the regiment at Ticonderoga, and "few of them had ever been wet with salt water."[1] But the motley crews of Arnold had been drilled during the short period of their naval service, at the guns and in other duties, with the utmost care and assiduity, and were animated by the loftiest heroism.

The position selected by Arnold afforded almost a perfect concealment to his fleet, from the observation of vessels passing up the lake by the usual track, which was through the centre of the lake, and east of Valcour. We are left to mere conjecture, as to the motives of Arnold, which prompted this manœuvre. Possibly, he may have designed, when the British vessels had passed up the lake in an illusory pursuit of the American fleet, to strike some audacious blow in their rear, suggested by his bold and fertile mind. The cove in which the American vessels were lying, was directly opposite the dwelling of a settler named Hays, situated on the mainland. With this family, Arnold had formed intimate relations, and arranged with them to present a signal when they discerned the approach of the enemy. Pringle, on the 11th of October, had advanced beyond Valcour to the south, before he became aware of the position of Arnold. His course was immediately changed, in order to reach the American fleet; but the purpose was frustrated by the direction of the wind. The British gun-boats, however, soon after supported by the Carleton, were able to approach so near as to commence an attack. Arnold meanwhile had arranged his vessels in a line across the narrow

---

[1] *Arnold to Gates.*

strait between Valcour to the mainland. The Royal Savage, with three galleys, advanced in front of the American lines, and was engaged for some time in a sharp conflict with a part of the enemy's fleet. The schooner was severely crippled, and in attempting to fall back, grounded upon a point of land near the south end of Valcour, was abandoned by her crew, and during the night burnt by the British. The papers and wardrobe of Arnold were lost on board of this vessel.[1]

The engagement immediately involved the whole American fleet, and commencing a little after meridian was maintained more than four hours with unfaltering ardor and resolution. Arnold was on board the galley Congress, and fought with his characteristic impetuosity, pointing almost every gun himself, and inspiring the conduct of the crew by his example and voice. Waterbury, in the galley Washington, and Wigglesworth on board the Trumbull, emulated the spirit of Arnold. Waterbury, at the close of the action, was the only officer on the Washington capable of duty, and most of the other vessels suffered with equal severity. The gondola, Philadelphia, sank soon after the engagement. A body of Indians was landed on the island, and maintained a constant but ineffective fire upon the American vessels. Another body of the savages lay in ambush on the mainland prepared to seize any of the crews of Arnold's fleet, who might attempt to escape.

The damages inflicted upon the British vessels engaged were also extremely heavy. Two gondolas were sunk, and another blown up in the engagement, with the loss,

---

[1] This circumstance has proved the prolific source of popular speculation in reference to the contents of the vessel. Forgetting the extreme poverty of the Continental congress at that epoch, innumerable attempts have been made to secure the treasures she was supposed to have been freighted with. Efforts have been made to raise the wreck, and skillful divers have examined her cabin and hold. She was scarcely submerged eight feet in low water, and was distinctly visible. "During the prevalence of remarkably low water in the summer of 1868, Captain George Conn anchored his vessel above the wreck and with grappling irons succeeded in wrenching several large pieces of oak plank from its sides. The wood is as black as ebony

as Arnold reported, of sixty men.[1] Pringle, having been disappointed in his efforts to bring his larger vessels into the action, at 5 o'clock P. M., withdrew those engaged, and formed a close line beyond the range of the American guns, stretching from Garden island towards the western shore of the lake. It was his intention to renew the attack in the morning.[2]

Although no body of men have ever exhibited in any naval battle higher traits of zeal and resolution, it was evident to the American officers that resistance to the united strength of the British fleet would be hopeless and unavailing. Arnold adopted the prompt and daring determination to attempt an escape, and to seek protection beneath the guns of Crown point. As soon as the darkness secured concealment to the movement, the American fleet commenced its perilous operation. The Trumbull led, followed by the other vessels in a single line. Each vessel carried at her stern a light, to guide the one that followed her. The fleet, silently and unmolested, passed around the north end of Valcour and early in the morning reached Schuyler's island, a distance of nine miles. At this place, the shattered condition of the vessels compelled Arnold to lay to and repair. Two of the gondolas were here abandoned and sunk. With the remnant of the fleet he again sailed in the hope of reaching Crown point, but the wind had veered into the south, and baffled his design.

---

and almost as heavy.—*Plattsburgh Republican.* It is represented, that the bottom of the lake in the vicinity is strewn with balls and bullets, the latter white and glistening by the attrition of the sand. Many interesting relics, among them a bursted cannon, have been raised and preserved from this wreck.

[1] Arnold to Schuyler, Oct. 15th.

[2] This picturesque island lies about one-fourth of a mile south of Valcour, and in the legends of the lake is an object of considerable interest. It is circular in form, with steep rocky shores, which, it is represented, renders it inaccessible except at one point. It embraces half an acre of land, and tradition asserts that its name is derived from the fact that it was cultivated first by the French and afterwards by the English officers stationed upon the lake, as a garden. Until recently, it is stated by those who have visited the spot, that garden-beds and other artificial arrangement might readily be traced on the surface.

The first dawn of light revealed the escape of the American fleet to the vigilant foe, and an instant pursuit ensued. A naked and solitary rock, standing in the midst of the lake, immediately east of Valcour, and then shrouded in the mist of an autumnal morning, it is the general received tradition, was mistaken for an American vessel, and a cannonade directed against it. The rocky islet is still known as Carleton's prize. While the progress of Arnold was retarded by a light and contrary wind, a breeze from the north-east which was first felt by the British, aided in the pursuit, by their fresh ships, of the disabled American fleet. The Washington, more shattered than any other of the fleet, was overtaken near Split rock, and, after receiving a few broadsides, surrendered. Four vessels, including a gondola, escaped in safety to Crown point. One galley was blown up by her commander. A single gondola, beside the Washington, was the only trophy secured by the enemy. After the capture of the Washington by the Maria and Inflexible, those ships aided the Carleton in a combined attack upon Arnold's vessel, the galley Congress. He maintained during a running fight of four hours a spirited contest, enveloped by this irresistible superiority of force, and when he could no longer hope for success or escape, with sails and hull of the galley torn and shattered, he ran her, accompanied by four gondolas, ashore on the beach at Panton, Vermont. The crews he ordered to wade or swim to the shore and armed with muskets arrest the approach of the enemy's small boats, while he remained upon the galley the last man, and until the conflagration had advanced too far to be extinguished. The flags were not lowered, but were consumed and the whole flotilla wrapped in flames.[1] Their charred and blackened wrecks remained upon the beach at Panton,[2] monuments of his gallantry and patriotism, long after other deeds had con-

---

[1] *Sparks's Life of Arnold.*

[2] The remains of these wrecks are still visible, and within a few years interesting relics have been recovered. I have in my own possession, bullets which were taken from them.

signed the name of Arnold to ignominy. Arnold, when he had witnessed the successful destruction of the vessels, led their crews rapidly through the wilderness to Crown point, and by the activity of his movement escaped an Indian force, which was pursuing him.

The killed and wounded of the Americans in both engagements, were about ninety, and the loss of the British, including those involved in the explosion, was nearly the same. The conduct of Arnold and his subordinates, alike in fighting and manœuvering the fleet, and the unsurpassed bravery of the crews, extorted the highest admiration of their conquerors, and although their heroism had been unavailing, aroused the warmest enthusiasm and exultation of their countrymen. Carleton, after securing the victory, manifested his wonted clemency and conciliation. The wounded Americans received the most tender care of his own surgeons; to the prisoners he expressed the warmest encomiums upon their intrepidity, with regrets that it was expended in an evil and desperate cause; he relieved their wants and dismissed them on parole. This humane and politic deportment impressed and won the regard and gratitude of these men to an extent that rendered their communications with the army unsafe, and without being permittted to land at the forts, they were at once sent into the interior.[1]

The British forces, immediately after the success of the fleet, had opened the pathway of the lake, commenced

---

[1] I think the version I have given in the text, although not in accordance with the common impression, is warranted by the facts as they appear in documents, and which were corroborated by the information I have personally derived from those who were familiar with the occurrences of that era. Mr. Palmer, in his *History of Lake Champlain*, adopts the same view. The circumstances connected with the Hays family were communicated to me by Mrs. Elmore, a daughter of Mr. Hays, who has deceased within a few years at a venerable age. She was an infant in her mother's arms at the time of the engagement. The signal mentioned according to the tradition in her family, was a sheet displayed from a window. While the battle raged, Mrs. Hays carrying her infant, went to a spring in a ravine near the lake, which was then mantled by a dense thicket. To her unutterable

their advance. General Gates, who was in the immediate command of the American troops in that department, had augmented, by every expedient, the strength and efficiency of the works at Ticonderoga. The army embraced from eight to ten thousand men. On the approach of Carleton, Crown point was evacuated by the small detachment by which it had been occupied, and the British general, on the 14th of October, took possession of that important post without opposition. He remained in the occupation of the fort, which he diligently fortified, as well as the works at Chimney point, until the 3d of November. The interval was employed in either feigned or real preparation for the attack of Ticonderoga. Cautious and thorough examination revealed so great strength in the lines and fort, and such perfect arrangement to meet an assault, that Carleton was constrained to abandon the design, and retired into Canada for winter quarters. This decision was eminently judicious. The precautions of Washington had caused all the cattle and horses, which might afford food or means of transportation, to be removed from the reach of the enemy; Carleton felt that the vicinity of a formidable American army, animated by extreme ardor, would be eminently hazardous to his exposed and isolated position, while the interrupted or suspended navigation during the winter would virtually cut off all intercourse with Canada. Upon such considerations he adopted the policy of retreating, which subjected him to severe and unjust strictures. When the approach of Carleton was

---

surprise and terror, she found herself in the midst of a large body of Indians hideous by their war paint and savage costume, and armed with guns and tomahawks. The mother, agitated and alarmed at her helpless condition, and frantically clasping the child to her breast, wept bitterly. An aged chief, she judged from his appearance, approached, and unable to communicate consolation or an assurance of safety by language, manifested his purpose of protecting her by gently and in a soothing manner wiping away her tears with the skirt of his shirt. Neither the mother nor child was molested. The motive of the ambush was doubtless that assigned in the text; but I infer from this account, that no attack on the fleet was made by the Indians from the mainland.

apprehended, Gates had made an earnest appeal, through Colonel Warner, to Vermont for support in both men and provisions. This appeal was responded to with great promptness and efficiency. Flour and grain were immediately transmitted, while, with equal alacrity, two regiments marched to reenforce Ticonderoga. When Carleton retreated, these troops were discharged, with warm acknowledgments for their "spirit and alertness" by Gates, in an official document addressed to their commanders.

CHAPTER XI.

The Invasion, 1777-1782.

The energies of England had been occupied more than a year in the organization of a large and perfectly equipped army in Canada, with the design of hurling an irresistible force upon the insurgent colonies. Burgoyne, who had attained a high European reputation, succeeded Carleton in the command of this army. The wise and generous qualities of the latter had suggested measures, not in accordance with the policy of the administration. The corps destined to this service were assembled at St. Johns and Isle aux Noix, and consisted of various British and German regiments, aggregating more than seven thousand effective troops, besides Canadian irregulars and the hordes of savages, that had been summoned and were expected to join the British standard. A magnificent park of artillery and an ample supply of munitions augmented its efficiency. The officers who led this array under the commander-in-chief, were skillful and experienced, and vast expectations had been formed of the results of the expedition. The Hessians, a general term applied to all the German mercenaries, were at first objects of extreme terror and solicitude to the American people. Clothed in uncommon vestures, speaking a harsh and strange language, with manners rude and severe, rumor imputed to them a character the most ferocious and cruel. But grown familiar with these new enemies, the people overcame this dread, and regarding them as the hirelings of tyranny purchased of German despots, to trample down American liberty, they animated hatred and excited disgust, while their presence tended to stimulate enthusiasm and to confirm every purpose of resistance. Generals Phillips, Frazer, Powell and Hamilton commanded the British troops, and Riedesel and Specht the German auxiliaries. Early in June, 1777, this brilliant army moved from St. Johns in boats, and arrived on the banks of the Boquet and took position at the deserted settlement of Gilliland, which had been designated by Burgoyne as the place of junction with his Indian allies. He paused here ten days, which were employed in a reconnaissance of Ticonderoga in reorganizing his forces and in drilling the boatmen on the estuary of the river in the evolutions incident to their duties upon the waters of the lake, and possibly in the visions of hope upon those of the Hudson.[1]

On the 21st, Burgoyne held his celebrated treaty with the Indian tribes. The summons of the Brilish commander, was responded to in far greater numbers, than he had either expected or desired. A redoubt which had been erected on an eminence below the village and impending over the river was signalized by this picturesque and impressive spectacle. The operations of agriculture have now obliterated all vestiges of this work, although until recently its lines could be distinctly traced. These hordes were addressed by Burgoyne in a speech intended professedly to restrain their ferocity, but calculated by its influence to inflame their savage passions. A war chief of the Iroquois replied with equal vehemence, pledging the tribes to a zealous warfare against the foes of England. A feast was held, a war dance celebrated, and the merciless savages were let loose upon the colonies.

---

[1] *O. F. Sheldon's Manuscript.*

The speech of Burgoyne at the Boquet and his subsequent proclamation from Putnam's creek, which was regarded as an exposition of the actual purpose of this Indian treaty, aroused a wide attention. The formal and recognized employment of the savages, and the direction of the tomahawk and scalping knife against a people, kindred in language, in religion and civilization, revolted the moral sentiment of the Christian world, and evoked the severest denunciations in the British parliament. No measure, not even the subsidizing of the Hessian, so fully harmonized the popular heart of America and precipitated with such perfect union, the infuriated yeomanry of New England upon the British entrenchments at Saratoga and Bennington. Burgoyne, as the instrument of this ruthless warfare, was in America the object of universal detestation.

Forgetting the character of his auditors, Burgoyne, in well chosen and sonorous periods, expatiated on mercy and forbearance; explained the nice distinctions between enemies in the field, and the unarmed and inoffensive citizen; and between political friends and armed foes; but at the same time stimulated the ardor and activity of his savage allies, in the prosecution of a sanguinary warfare. He severely denounced the practice of cruelty against any class; offered rewards for prisoners, and sternly forbade the taking of scalps from the living, or even the dying, but by a strange infatuation, allowed them to be torn from the dead on the field of battle. As if the subtle Indians would hesitate to bring the prisoner, the wounded and dying, within the scope of this provision. Could these admonitions of mercy follow the fierce savage raging amid an hostile people; or would these metaphysical distinctions be regarded in the heat and tumult of the battle? Subsequent events revealed the fallacy of these humane professions, and the proclamation of the 29th of June, exhibits in its barbarous and bloody threats of Indian atrocities, the insincerity of the admonitions, and the convictions of Burgoyne of the futility of the restraints he professed to impose, and the hollowness of the Indian assurances of obedience. While the arrogance and inflated grandiloquence of this manifesto amused the intelligence and disgusted the taste of the colonists, it aroused an unconquerable hostility to England, that was never extinguished. Europe was everywhere shocked by its monstrous spirit, and afterwards, when arraigned at the tribunal of popular sentiment, in England, for the dishonor it had attached to the British name, Burgoyne was able to offer no other apology or extenuation, than that its language was intended only for intimidation and effect.

The command of the northern department of the republican army was held by General Schuyler, while the direct charge of Ticonderoga and the works of defense connected with that fortress were confided to Arthur St. Clair, a major-general in the service of congress, an officer of great experience and marked ability, but singularly unfortunate in his military enterprises. These fortifications, while they should be maintained by the Americans, formed an insuperable barrier to the progress of Burgoyne. The infinite importance of preserving them was felt by the congress, but unhappily its resources were inadequate to the exigency of the occasion. The extent and magnitude of these works demanded a garrison of ten thousand effective men with sufficient armament and supplies for their appropriate occupation, and yet when the British army appeared at Crown point, Schuyler had succeeded with all the energies and efforts he was able to exert, in collecting a force in the whole department of only five thousand troops, of which about three thousandwere scattered through ths defenses entrusted to St. Clair. One-third of this feeble force was composed of militia imperfectly equipped and armed, and nearly destitute of bayonets to their insufficient muskets.

In another page we have already described the peninsula at Ticonderoga; but twenty years had produced important changes in the arrangement of the works, their capacity and extent. The old French lines, which were so success-

12

fully defended by Montcalm, had been strengthened by additional erections and by a block-house. The landing at Lake George, and the saw mills, where new works had been constructed, were occupied by feeble detachments. A small fort erected on Mt. Hope, a commanding eminence in this vicinity, guarded the left of the American lines. The new works, the most effective and upon which the Americans placed the greatest reliance, were erected on Mt. Independence, a high circular hill situated on the eastern shore of the lake and directly opposite Fort Carillon. On the summit of this elevation, a star fort had been constructed, enclosing a large square barrack. This fort was heavily fortified and well supplied with artillery. The base of the hill and its precipitous sides, were carefully entrenched and lined with artillery. The distance between Ticonderoga and Mt. Independence was about fifteen hundred yards. These two positions were connected by a floating bridge, which had been erected by enormous labor and expenditure. The structure was supported by twenty-two sunken piers of immense size, and placed at intervals. These spaces were filled with separate floats, each about fifty feet long and twelve feet wide. The whole was firmly united by heavy chains which were closely rivetted. To protect this work, which was of the last importance to the safety of the whole position, from the attacks of the enemy's naval force, a boom, formed of enormous timbers, connected by chains and bolts of immense size, was constructed on the northern or lake side of the bridge.[1]

Another point still, had engaged the attention of the American engineers. This was Mt. Defiance, which rises to an altitude of seven hundred and fifty feet, and forms a bold, rocky promontory at the confluence of Lake Champlain and the outlet of Lake George, and is laved by both waters. This eminence is about one thousand

---

[1] Thompson, in the *History of Vermont*, states, that this bridge, when Burgoyne approached, was in an unfinished condition.

and four hundred yards distant from Ticonderoga and separated from Mt. Independence by fifteen hundred yards, and by its position and greater height commanded both works. The imagined impregnability of these works would at once fail, in the event of this eminence being occupied by a hostile battery. St. Clair had been apprized of this momentous fact by the examination of the preceding year. Pont Le Roy, the engineer of Montcalm, evidently referred to it in the epigrammatic utterance I have quoted; and we cannot doubt, that the possession of Ticonderoga during more than eighteen years, had disclosed the military value of this position to the British commanders. But St. Clair was destitute of the resources necessary for holding and fortifying the place, and of averting the impending danger. His feeble garrison was insufficient for the occupation of the more prominent and exposed lines. He was constrained to rely upon the hope for the same impunity the fortress had formerly enjoyed from an attack in that direction. Conscious of his weakness he could alone in maintaining the fortresses have contemplated creating a delay, which would secure an infinite advantage to the republican cause, or of a successful resistance to an active assault, that he might have anticipated from the impetuosity and presumption of Burgoyne.

A fatuity seems to have rested upon the American councils, in the affairs of the Champlain frontier. A singular ignorance prevailed, in reference to the strength and movements of Burgoyne, inconsistent with the most common military skill and prudence. The people, the government and the commanders, were alike impressed by the conviction, that the menaced invasion by the waters of Champlain, was a mere pretext to disguise other operations, and that no competent force for the purpose had been organized in Canada. When its reality was demonstrated, by the actual appearance of the British army, little preparation had been made to oppose its advance. On the 25th of June, St. Clair communicated to Schuyler the perilous circumstances by which he was surrounded, and reiterates, as he asserts, his views of the inadequacy of his resources and the fatal consequences which would result from a regular siege or blockade of the works. This letter, three days later, was transmitted to Washington by Schuyler, accompanied by the representations of his own utter inability either to support St. Clair or resist a prompt advance by Burgoyne. The obvious and transparent error, which involved so many disastrous consequences, and for which all, who exerted a controlling influence upon the measure, were in common, responsible, was the delay that occurred in the evacuations of Ticonderoga and its dependencies. Had that movement been executed when its necessity was first apparent, it might have been conducted with a leisure and circumspection, that would have secured the removal of the munitions and artillery, and the safety of the army, without demoralization. St. Clair, in a letter to congress, alleges, that his instructions gave him no discretion in reference to the abandonment of the work, except from the presence of a last and imperious necessity.[1]

While the American affairs were involved in these strange delusions, and paralyzed by this inaction and hesitancy, Burgoyne had occupied Crown point, and with extraordinary promptitude and vigor marched upon Ticonderoga. On the 1st July he advanced in three columns. The left wing under Riedesel proceeded along the eastern shore of the lake, which here, deep and narrow, exhibits the proportions and appearance of a river. He advanced to East creek, a small stream, which, spreading out in the form of an estuary as it enters the lake, washes the northern base of Mt. Independence. Burgoyne himself embarked with the centre column in bateaux, and convoyed by two ships slowly ascended the lake. Phillips, with the right wing, moved upon the western side, and the next day extended his flank, threatening the outposts of St. Clair. The parties which held the landing and Mt. Hope were ordered after destroying the public property, and burning the mills,

---

[1] *Marshall.*

to fall back into the American lines. The British general immediately seized this important post, and by its occupation commanded a portion of the remaining works and effectively severed St. Clair's communication with Lake George.[1] St. Clair resisted these operations by a heavy cannonade directed against the several positions of the enemy. While actively occupied in enveloping the American works by a cordon of posts, Burgoyne caused a careful reconnaissance to be made of Mt. Defiance. The result corroborated the opinion of the American engineer, submitted the last year, and announced that the ascent was not only practicable, but that the brief space of a single day was sufficient for the construction of an available road for artillery to the summit. The fourth was devoted by Burgoyne to the landing of his battering train, and the concentration of his munitions and supplies. On the same day, the proposed ascent of Mt. Defiance was effected with a success only equaled by the ardor and toil exerted in its execution, and on the morning of the 8th, a battery had been erected, and eight pieces of heavy artillery mounted, and ready to open a plunging and insupportable fire upon the doomed garrison.

St. Clair witnessed these operations without any power to arrest them or avert their consequences, and yielded to the perfect conviction that neither Ticonderoga nor Mt. Independence was longer tenable. The difficulties of his perilous situation were enhanced by the fact, that only a single link now remained to accomplish the investment of the entire works, and to secure the control of the water communication with Skeensboro'. Riedesel was about closing that space, by stretching his forces from the position he occupied on East creek, around Mt. Independence to the waters of the narrow lake south of that post. Op-

---

[1] Mount Hope is situated near the Lower Falls, on the outlet of Lake George. It is a steep and rocky eminence, and tradition asserts, received its name from Phillips, when he seized it in this campaign. Vestiges of military works are still visible upon it, and also the ruins of a log bridge, built on the occasion.

pressed by this gloomy aspect of his affairs, the American commander convened a military council, which with perfect harmony and without hesitation, concurred in the opinion, that the works could not be maintained, and that an immediate evacuation was necessary. The same night this resolution was executed. The sick, the hospital and other stores, and all the guns, munitions and provisions, which under the pressure of the circumstances could be moved, were embarked in two hundred boats, which, guarded by about six hundred men under Colonel Long, and convoyed by five armed galleys, proceeded to Skeenesboro'. The lights in the camp were all extinguished, and caution and profound silence enjoined. Prudence demanded that during the day no unusual movement in the forts should reveal to the enemy, who watched their proceedings from the summit of Mt. Defiance, the contemplated design. The short time allowed for the execution of the measure and the obscurity of the night, necessarily created some degree of haste and confusion; but the retreat was conducted with such skill and celerity that, although the moon was shining brightly, it escaped the observation of the British sentinels. St Clair, with the leading column, crossed the bridge at 2 o'clock in the morning, and was closely followed by Francis with the rear of the army. No suspicion of the enemy had yet been excited, and every circumstance indicated the most favorable results. But at the moment, when these appearances were thus auspicious, a house on Mt. Independence, occupied by General de Fermoy, was discovered to be on fire. The flames spread widely, and casting a bright illumination over the scene, revealed all the movements of the retreating army. The British camp was instantly aroused, and the drum and trumpet sounded the alarm through all its sections. The abandoned works were immediately occupied, and a fire opened upon the rear of the Americans. Frazer led a strong detachment at once across the bridge which St. Clair had not had time to disturb, and commenced a rapid and vigorous pursuit. He was immediately followed by Riedesel with his German corps. With indefatigable activity and vigor, Burgoyne, by the labor of a few hours, skillfully directed, removed the boom and bridge — stupendous fabrics, that had exacted a vast expenditure of money and material and the unremitting toil of months. Early on the morning of the 6th, these obstacles upon which the Americans had relied in perfect confidence, were obliterated, or sufficiently displaced to allow the passage of two ships and several gunboats, which with the utmost ardor and celerity pursued the American flotilla. The latter had reached its destination in safety, and while the troops were indulging in rest and in fancied security after the excessive labor and fatigue of the retreat, their repose was suddenly broken by the guns of Burgoyne, in an attack at the wharves of the galleys and boats. The overwhelming force of the English rendered resistance impossible, and having burnt or destroyed the military works, the mills and the bateaux with three of the galleys, two had been captured by Burgoyne, Long hastily retreated in the direction of Fort Ann. By this prompt and rapid movement he eluded a British force of three regiments, which, pursuing the track of Dieskau, had landed at the foot of South bay, and advanced with great celerity to the Fort Edward road for the purpose of intercepting the retreat. While Burgoyne achieved these signal successes, St Clair was pursuing a forced, and to some extent disorderly, march, towards Castleton, which he reached during the night after the evacuation.

Three regiments, under Warner, Francis and Hale, which constituted the rear division of the American army, paused at Hubbardton, in order to reorganize and to collect the stragglers, who had fallen out of the line on the precipitate retreat. This force occupied a favorable position, and it was decided to await an attack. The pursuit of Frazer had been eager and unremitting. That night he lay on his arms near the American position, and early on the morning of the 7th, without hesitating for the arrival of Riedesel, which was momentarily expected, advanced with ardor to the attack of the American lines. The command of Frazer embraced eight hundred and fifty veteran regulars. The opposing force consisted of about thirteen hundred men, but a large proportion of these were militia; and the inequality in numbers was speedily removed by the retreat of Colonel Hale's regiment. This command was composed mainly of the sick and convalescent incapable of field service, and Hale, therefore, after a brief though warm skirmish with the British advance, continued his retreat towards Castleton, but he was intercepted by a British column, and himself and nearly the entire regiment were taken prisoners.[1]

A long and sanguinary engagement ensued, which was conducted with skill, and fought with the highest spirit and resolution. The battle of Hubbardton has not acquired the prominence in American history or the consideration from the country, due to the valor and sacrifices by which it was signalized. At one period of its changing aspect, when the British line recoiled in disorder before the impetuosity of the American charge, victory seemed assured to the republican arms; but Frazer soon restored his ranks

[1] Colonel Nathan Hale commanded one of the battalions raised in 1776 by New Hampshire. Some modern writers, each adopting the statements contained in the narrative of Ethan Allen, without apparently having examined the subject, have imputed to Colonel Hale misconduct in this battle, and asserted that his command was surrendered without resistance. These charges, it is alleged, inflict unjust censure upon a brave soldier and patriotic citizen. Gordon, Williams, and other subordinate writers reflect the views of Allen, but Marshall, the most authentic, by the sources from which he received his facts, of any historian of the period: Botta, Steadman and other authors, both American and English, are silent on the subject, and ascribe blame to no one. The charge that Hale "surrendered without striking a blow" is discountenanced, at least, by the simple account, bearing upon its face the impress of truth, of one who was present in the engagement—was wounded and taken prisoner. The author, who was attached to Carr's company in Hale's battalion states that early in the morning of the 7th, while the troops were preparing their breakfast, under marching orders, the enemy suddenly appeared in line. The American troops were ordered to "lay down their packs and be ready for action." The firing immediately commenced, and a sharp skirmish occurred. The

and the appearance immediately after of the Germans upon the field decided the contest, and the Americans dispersed in every direction. Colonel Francis fell gallantly at the head of his regiment. The aggregate American loss in this warmly contested action was about three hundred, and that of the British one hundred and eighty-three. Warner, with his wonted decision and intrepidty, reassembled his troops at Manchester, and led them to unite with Schuyler at Fort Edward. Severe censure has been attached to St. Clair, that lying only six miles from the field of battle with his detachment, he had not returned to the support of Warner and Francis. His apologists allege, that he made the most earnest efforts to do so, but that the troops who were principally composed of militia regiments, refused to march to their aid.

The capture of Ticonderoga was a deep calamity to the republican cause. The trophies announced by Burgoyne to his government, embraced one hundred and twenty-eight pieces of artillery; all the boats and armed vessels in the harbors, and the provision stores and munitions. The great flag of the garrison was also abandoned in the confusion of the retreat, and fell into the enemy's hands. The intelligence of this event was received in England by

---

republicans sought the cover of trees, but "were a few in number in comparison with the enemy." While discharging his musket, in that position, the author was wounded, and captured, when the battalion retreated.—*Narrative of Ebenezer Fletcher*. Belknap, a contemporary, in his *History of New Hampshire*, states, that "Colonel Hale's battalion was ordered to cover the rear of the invalids," and the next morning was attacked by the advance of the enemy. Barstow, in his history, says, in allusion to this event, "a sharp skirmish ensued, in which Major Titcomb (of Hale's battalion) was wounded." These authorities seem to disprove one serious point of the strictures. Colonel Hale claimed from Washington the right of being exchanged, that he might vindicate his conduct before a military tribunal, but he died, while still a prisoner, before this desire could be gratified.

The memory of Colonel Hale is entitled to the consideration due to other facts. At the commencement of the revolution, he was in easy pecuniary circumstances. After the battle of Lexington, he raised a company of minute men, at his own expense, and by patriotic sacrifices like this, when he died in the vigor of manhood, he left his family in comparative poverty.

the partisans of the ministry with the most rapturous exultation, and confidently accepted as a propitious augury of the final issue of the contest. At no period of the revolution did any other disaster press upon the popular heart in America, with a more chilling and despondent influence. Surprise and astonishment mingled with rage and grief. The imputations of imbecility, negligence, and incompetency, did not reach the expression of public sentiment, but hostile and malignant tongues gave free utterance to the terms, baseness and treachery. Even the serene and just mind of Washington was disturbed. St. Clair was suspended, and Schuyler superseded in the command of the northern army, at the moment when success and glory were about becoming the fruition of his wise, skillful, and patriotic measures. But time dispersed the clouds that for a period shadowed the fame of these able and devoted patriots, and a mature investigation of the facts, afforded them an ample and decisive vindication.

Phillips, as soon as the means of transportation could be organized on Lake George, advanced with his division to Fort George and established at that post and also at the foot of the lake, depots of supplies, and the proximate base of the army. At Fort George, he found only dismantled and naked walls. Schuyler, in the judicious but stern policy by which he had rendered savage nature still more hideous, and created in the front of the foe a waste and desolation, had either destroyed or removed every material that might impart comfort or facilities to the invader. This narrative must relinquish to general history the recital of the future progress and history of Burgoyne, and that great culminating victory, which was not only decisive of his career, but decisive also of the great contest of England with her rebellious colonies.

While Burgoyne was urging a slow progress as he gradually surmounted the vast obstacles, which the sagacity of Schuyler had interposed, Lincoln was engaged in collecting and organizing a body of four thousand militia at

Manchester, Vermont. The flank of the British army by this movement was seriously menaced. A portion of these troops, it was decided, should be used in a bold and important operation, which was intended to sever the communications of Burgoyne, and if possible to seize his base at Ticonderoga. Colonel Johnson, with a party of about five hundred men, was detached by Lincoln against Skeenesboro' and Fort Edward, but with the special object of covering the retreat of the two other detachments led by Brown and Woodbury. Colonel Brown, with a party of rangers of nearly the same strength, was instructed to proceed to the landing on Lake George, to rescue American prisoners confined there, and having accomplished this object to act on the suggestions of his own judgment. He crossed Lake Champlain at the narrows above Ticonderoga, and marching all night conducted alone by the signals emitted at short intervals by his guides, hoots, in imitation of the owl, he traversed the rugged mountain range that separates the two lakes, and toiling in the darkness, amid precipices and chasms, a distance of fourteen miles, just as the day was breaking, burst upon the enemy at the foot of the lake, by a complete surprise. He captured without resistance nearly three hundred British troops, the works at Mount Hope and at the landing, and seized two hundred bateaux, an armed sloop and a number of gun-boats, which had been transported from Lake Champlain with severe toil, and were stationed here to protect the carrying place. In addition to these successes he accomplished the primary object of the expedition by liberating one hundred American prisoners. Captain Ebenezer Allen had been detached with a small and resolute band by Brown to assail the works on Mount Defiance. Scaling cautiously and in silence the precipitous acclivities of the mountain, so steep in one place that the assailants were able only to ascend by climbing over the shoulders of each other, they reached the summit and captured the battery without the discharge of a single weapon. Colonel Johnson, with a detachment of about an equal number, arrived early the next morning and joined Brown before Ticonderoga.[1] The united forces immediately invested the fortress and summoned General Powell, the commander of the garrison, to surrender. He returned a defiant answer, and after an ineffectual cannonade of four days with ordnance too feeble to make an impression upon the works, the attack was abandoned. At the landing Brown embarked forces in the captured boats, and ascended Lake George with the design of seizing Diamond island, where Burgoyne had deposited an immense quantity of stores and munitions.

Upon the surrender of Burgoyne, the small garrison at Ticonderoga dismantled and evacuated the works, and, embarking in a few open boats, sought refuge and security by a silent and stealthy flight down the lake. This inglorious retreat of the relics of a great host presented an impressive contrast to the ostentatious array, that a few weeks before had traversed the same waters, bearing, as if in a triumphant procession, a vaunting leader and an army inflamed by the confidence of approaching victory. These fugitives, however, did not wholly escape the vigilant eye of the Americans. Near where the village of Essex now stands they were intercepted by Ebenezer Allen. He cut off and captured several of the rear boats, seized fifty prisoners and a large amount of military stores, baggage, horses and cattle. Among the spoils, he captured a negro slave with an infant child. "Being conscientious in the sight of God that it is not right to keep slaves," these he declared "to be forever free," and caused a certificate of their freedom to be recorded in the town clerk's office at Bennington, where it still exists.[2]

Refugee tories and other irregulars, more ruthless than their savage allies, fugitives from the fate that was impending over the British army, passed through in their flight the deserted settlement on the Boquet. Carleton and

---

[1] Several authorities assign the command of the third detachment to Colonel Warner. I follow the statement of Marshall.

[2] Butler's discourse on Ebenezer Allen, *Hall's Vermont*.

Burgoyne had been merciful in their visitations. The rapacity of Arnold and the exactions of the government had spared the dwellings and structures of the settlers; but these gleaners in devastation left only ashes and desolation in their track. Tradition asserts, that they consigned to the flames every edifice from Split rock to the Boquet in a wanton and merciless destruction.[1] In November, 1778, a large British force, and several armed vessels advanced to Ticonderoga, and inflicted a general devastation upon the property on both sides of the lake, that had escaped former ravages.

In the spring of 1780, Sir John Johnson organized at Ticonderoga a band of about five hundred men, composed of regulars, a party of his own corps of Royal Greens and two hundred tories and Indians, and proceeded on an errand, which, in its spirit and purposes, presented one of the most revolting scenes of this fratricidal war. Penetrating the rude wilderness of mountains, forests and waters, which spreads westward from Lake George, he reached and ascended the valley of the Sacondaga. This route compelled him to cross a site, which his father in happier days was accustomed often to visit in pursuit of relaxation and rural pastimes. Recollections of youthful joys must have welled up in the memory of the invader, when he recalled the incidents of former years, associated with the Fish house. An outlawed fugitive, a dishonored soldier, who had violated his parole, he broke the quiet and secluded repose of the scene, in a mission of vengeance and blood. These memories could not have softened his vindictive passions, for he passed onward, unchanged in his fierce designs to descend at midnight upon his native valley in a whirlwind of rapine and flame. Near the baronial halls of his father, the motley band was divided into two detachments, that the work of destruction might be more thorough and wide spread. The inhabitants were slumbering in perfect security, ignorant and unsuspicious of danger.

---

[1] *Sheldon's Manuscript.*

A common and indiscriminate ruin involved all who had adhered to the republican cause. Neither the former friends nor aged associates of his father, nor the companions of his own boyhood were exempt from the universal desolation. There was nothing left in a wide track along the beautiful valley of the Mohawk, where yesterday stood the abodes of plenty,

But a mass of ashes slaked with blood.

The professed object of this pitiless incursion was the recovery of a mass of valuable plate, which a faithful slave had assisted to bury in 1776. With silent and unwavering fidelity he had watched over the deposit, although in the confiscation of the Johnson estate he had been sold to another master. The plate was recovered, and distributed in the knapsacks of forty different soldiers. By this means it was all safely conveyed into Canada. An alarm had been immediately sounded, and the local militia, under Coloner Harper, beginning to assemble, Sir John made a rapid retreat. He bore with him what plunder he was able to convey, and forty prisoners; and reaching his bateaux at Crown point returned to Canada in safety, successfully evading the pursuit of Governor Clinton aided by detachments from the New Hampshire grants.

Major Carleton, in the autumn of the same year, proceeded from St. Johns with a formidable fleet, conveying more than one thousand men. He advanced secretly and undiscovered, and on the 10th and 11th of October, with a trifling loss, captured Fort Ann and Fort George. He completely devastated the country along his line of march; but the marked exemption of the territory of Vermont from these ravages were calculated to excite jealousy and apprehension. This unimportant expedition terminated these hostile incursions of the enemy beyond the fortresses of Champlain.

At this epoch was initiated the enigmatical and extraordinary relations, which subsisted for several years between the British authorities in Canada and the government of

Vermont. The people of the New Hampshire grants had formally declared their independence in 1777, and under the name of Vermont had assumed the attitude and prerogatives of a sovereign state. Any discussion of the character of these relations, a subject that has so nearly baffled all distinct and satisfactory explanation, is foreign to our purpose, except as the events were interwoven with the military history of Ticonderoga. A glance at the peculiar posture of Vermont in her domestic and public affairs is necessary, in order to approach a just appreciation of the ambiguous policy of her leaders at this juncture. A difference of opinion even yet exists in legal minds, in reference to the legitimacy of the claims of New York upon the New Hampshire grants. Whatever may have been the strength or validity of these claims, it is certain that a deep and bitter hostility towards New York was the all pervading feeling of the heroic and independent people who occupied the territory in dispute. This sentiment was stimulated by the sincere conviction, that these claims were unjust, and that Vermont had endured great wrong from the grasping injustice and oppression of her more powerful neighbor. To evade the real or imaginary evils which were impending from this source, and to escape the political absorption which they believed was contemplated by New York, was the inexorable determination of the remarkable body of men, who at that period guarded the policy of Vermont. With them, the purpose was paramount to every other consideration. The devotion of these leaders, in common with all the population of the grants, to the cause of American independence, through all the early vicissitudes of the contest, had been active and ardent. They now indignantly cherished the belief, that their efforts and sacrifices would not yield to them an equal participation in the common blessings which might be secured by the successful issue of the conflict; that congress had turned a deaf ear to their importunate demands for a recognition of an independent position and political immunities; that they were threatened with dismemberment by the pretensions of other states, and standing alone between these states and an exasperated enemy, they were abandoned, to meet single-handed, the dangers and sufferings of a hostile invasion. The overruling law of self-preservation, the astute statesmen of Vermont alleged, justified and even demanded a resort to extraordinary measures, and such as would be warranted by no common emergencies. Their apologists now aver that these men designed, by shrewd diplomacy, to shield the state from the overwhelming assaults of the British army lying upon its borders, and at the same time to secure an ultimate protection from the aggressions of New York. At this time in the light of later disclosures the position will scarcely be controverted, that it was their fixed and deliberate purpose if the exigency arose of deciding in the choice of two great evils, to return to a colonial dependence, fortified "by safe and honorable terms" rather than submit to the power of New York.[1] The same determination was avowed by Governor Chittenden in 1781, in his official correspondence with Washington.[2]

At the opening of the year 1780, the political leaders of Vermont were occupying this strange and anomalous position. In March, Beverly Robinson of New York addressed a letter to Ethan Allen, which was delivered to him at Arlington in the following July by a British soldier disguised in the garb of an American farmer. Allen received and read the letter, and without causing the agent to be arrested, returned an ambiguous verbal answer. Robinson, in this communication, which was couched in the most specious terms, appealed to the known prejudices of Vermont, attempted to influence the popular passions, and to prompt Allen to aid in the subversion of American independence. This document Allen submitted to Governor Chittenden and a small circle of confidential friends. They all concurred in the opinion that no answer should be returned. Robinson not having received a reply in

---

[1] *Ira Allen's Political History of Vermont,* London, 1798.
[2] *Ramsey's Washington.*

February, 1781, wrote Allen again, enclosing a copy of the previous communication. The second letter was still more bold and distinct in its language, and the seductive allurements to Vermont and to Allen personally it presented. After an interval of almost a year from the reception of the first letter, Allen transmitted both instruments to congress. He communicated at the same time to that body, an elaborate vindication of the course of Vermont, urging the acknowledgment of her political existence, and announcing an unalterable and resolute determination to assert her independence. He closed his communication in characteristic energy, with these remarkable words: "and rather than fail, I will retire with the hardy Green Mountain boys, into the desolate caverns of the mountains and wage war with human nature at large." Vermont, in the hour of trial, was not without the influence in congress of earnest and powerful friends. Roger Sherman gave indirectly his countenance to the proceedings of which New York complained, and afterwards with great zeal vindicated the claims of Vermont to political recognition, and Elbridge Gerry pronounced, that "Vermont had a perfect right to her independence."[1]

During the summer of 1780, Sir Frederick Haldimand with a large force, resumed the occupation of Ticonderoga. This movement, at that time mysterious and without any apparent motive, was afterwards known to have been dictated by the desire of fostering the negotiations with Vermont. He proposed to Ethan Allen, who then commanded the troops in Vermont, that hostilities should be suspended pending an arrangement for the exchange of certain prisoners. After some actual or pretended hesitation, Allen finally decided to accept the proposition, and that a temporary armistice, embracing that part of New York, claimed by Vermont and extending westward to the Hudson, should be established. Ira Allen, a subtle and sagacious politician, and Joseph Fay, were appointed commissioners

[1] *Life of Gouverneur Morris.*

for Vermont with the professed object of effecting the contemplated exchange of prisoners. While this ostensible negotiation was openly pursued, but with singular procrastination, the commissioners were actively engaged with secret emissaries of England in consummating the preliminaries of an arrangement of far higher import. Overtures were submitted by the British agents for the independent organization of the Vermont government, under the royal protection.

These proposals were received by the representatives of Vermont with attention, and, although with no committal in reference to any ulterior action, in a manner that cherished the expectations of the English officials.[1] Under the same pretext of exchanging prisoners, Ira Allen, in the ensuing spring, proceeded to the Isle aux Noix, and again the momentous negotiation was resumed. The fact which has been already mentioned should not be disregarded, that during all this period, and to the termination of the war, Vermont was left by congress without protection or defense, and abandoned to oppose with her single strength alone, a British army of ten thousand troops, that continually menaced her frontier. In response to the propositions of the British agents, that the armistice should continue; that the Vermont leaders should gradually prepare the popular sentiment for a return to their allegiance; that Vermont should be clothed with high and peculiar privileges, and that those who might aid in the consummation of this scheme should be approved and rewarded by the most ample royal munificence. Allen conceded the perilous position of Vermont, and admitted that her people had been remiss in the prosecution of the war, from the fear that success might subject them to the government of New York, a result far more deplorable in their view, than the subjugation of the United States by England. While conceding this, he avowed that the hour for action had not arrived.[2] These

---

[1] *Thompson's Vermont.* [2] *Stone,* II, 199; *Thompson,* 63.

interviews were extended through a period of seventeen days; and Allen, with an exquisite adroitness, without committing himself or his government, succeeded in effecting what was the chief object of this mission, an extension of the armistice, although unable to procure its continuance beyond the approaching session of the Vermont legislature, which was to convene in June following.

While Allen presented to the council a full and public report of his successful arrangement in securing the exchange of prisoners, all reference in that document to the more important negotiations was studiously avoided. The knowledge of these measures and a participation in them, were limited to eight of the prominent citizens of the state and veiled from the public eye with an art and success only equaled by its duplicity. A surreptitious correspondence was maintained through this and the succeeding year, by the Allens as the organs of the Vermont leaders, and the British officials at Ticonderoga. By the agency of British soldiers, secret missives were constantly interexchanged at Sunderland, a distance of sixty miles within the American territory from Ticonderoga, between the Allens and the agents of England. In the darkness and secrecy of one night, letters were deposited at an appointed receptacle, and by the same channel answers were returned the evening succeeding. A trifling incident reveals with strong significance the actual relation which existed between the initiated in these measures, and the British government. A band of patriotic citizens proceeding from Manchester, with the design of demolishing the house of a suspected royalist in Arlington, were intercepted at Sunderland, an intermediate town, by Ira Allen and two of his coadjutors, by whose influence and persuasion they were with reluctance induced to relinquish their purpose. That very night and on the same ground, where this occurrence happened, Allen received a packet from Ticonderoga by the English guard that had been the active medium of this intercourse, and returned an answer.

In the autumn of 1781, St. Leger ascended the lake with a strong force, and again occupied Ticonderoga. These extraordinary and repeated oscillations of large bodies of troops between St. Johns and the Champlain fortresses, now known to have been connected with this negotiation, and intended to facilitate and strenghten it, at that time tended to excite the greatest alarm and agitation not only in Vermont but throughout the whole northern frontier. When they advanced, the militia were suddenly summoned from their homes, forts were armed and replenished, and great inconvenience and expense incurred by both individuals and the government. When they retired mysteriously, the apprehensions arose that the movement was designed to disguise other and more important operations. While these events were transpiring on Lake Champlain, an intercepted letter from Lord George Germaine to Sir Henry Clinton, partially disclosed to congress the character and designs of the secret intercourse between Vermont and the English commanders. About the same time, a circumstance occurred in the vicinity of Ticonderoga, which was calculated to confirm the growing jealousy of the people of Vermont in reference to the practices of their leaders and to augment the apprehensions which had long existed.

The agreement for the suspension of hostilities had never been openly proclaimed, and from this cause originated all the public and private embarrassments to which we have adverted. It was necessary, in order to avert suspicion from the bold game these parties were pursuing, to maintain an apparently hostile attitude. Among these subterfuges a pretended system of patrols between the armies was sustained by each. Between the pickets occurred an accidental collision. In the skirmish that followed, the sergeant that commanded the Vermont party was killed. The body was respectfully interred by the English, and his clothing restored by St. Leger with an open letter to General Enos, the American commander, expressing regret for the occurrence of the untoward circumstance. The facts connected with the secret arrangements had necessarily been imparted to Enos, and his subordinates, Fletcher and Walbridge. The letter of St. Leger, with private dispatches from these officers, was immediately transmitted to the council of war of Vermont by an agent ignorant of these designing machinations, who promulgated widely the contents of St. Leger's mysterious communication. The popular distrust, which already existed, was aroused by this incident into a vehement suspicion. The council, who were all initiated in the secret proceedings, on opening the dispatches, discovered that they contained intelligence in reference to the negotiations, which it was not safe to reveal to the public. While they were engaged in examining the papers, a Major Runnals entered the apartment, and demanded in the name of the people, and with warm excitement, an explanation of these events, and why St. Leger should regret the death of an enemy. Ira Allen sought to escape the inquiries by artful evasion; but pressed by the stern determination of the agitated people, he adopted, with his peculiar versatility, the expedient of effecting a personal altercation with Runnals. Attention was thus for the moment diverted from the council, and an important delay secured, which enabled them to suppress the original documents and to substitute others, simulated and relieved of all their dangerous contents. In that form they were submitted to the people by Governor Chittenden, and thus the impending danger of disclosure of these negotiations was temporarily averted. It is asserted that these modified dispatches were prepared by Nathaniel Chipman, who afterwards attained great professional and political eminence. The position of these men had become eminently perplexing and critical. It was evident that their devious practices could not longer be sustained. These ambiguous relations must be terminated, and the country exposed to the invasion of a powerful enemy, or by the unveiling of the transactions, those involved in them would be denounced by congress and probably condemned and repudiated by those who had been deceived by their intrigues. The salutary results they professed to have contemplated, would in either dilemma be defeated. At this moment of oppressive doubt and apprehension they unexpectedly derived relief from a most auspicious event.

The commissioners of Vermont in the interview of September, 1781, could present no plausible evasion to the final proposition of the British agents, which they insisted upon as an ultimatum, if the armistice was to be maintained. They proposed, that during the approaching session of the Vermont legislature, in October, the British commander should issue a proclamation from Ticonderoga, declaring Vermont a colony under the crown, and confirming the form of government which had been agreed upon by the negotiators, and that the legislature should accept the overture and adopt the appropriate measures to enforce it.[1] The British agents now insisted that the time had arrived for issuing the projected proclamation, and manifested a determination to act. While the affair was in this attitude, a rumor reached Vermont of the surrender of Cornwallis, and imparted such animation to the popular feeling, that Fay, one of the Vermont commissioners, seized upon the circumstance and addressed a letter to the British emissaries with St. Leger at Ticonderoga, urging them to suspend immediate action until the truth of these rumors, which must exert so important an influence on the negotiation, might be ascertained. The gates of Ticonderoga had scarcely closed upon the messenger bearing this appeal, when authentic intelligence confirming the report, reached the British commander. St. Leger hastened to lower, for the last time, the banner of England on the ramparts of Ticonderoga, and before the setting of the sun, embarked the garrison, and evacuated the fortresses on Lake Champlain. Since that period their mouldering walls have reposed in silence and solitude, only disturbed at intervals by the mimicry of war on festal occasions.

---

[1] *Thompson's Vermont.*

During the early months of 1782, Haldimand, in repeated efforts, attempted to establish a renewal of these negotiations, but his advances were received by Vermont in great reserve and coolness. Ira Allen, in July, proceeded to Canada, still under the pretense of effecting a cartel for the exchange of prisoners. He was received by the British agents with a renewal of the same conciliatory propositions, and while he was able to procrastinate a decisive answer, he adroitly succeeded in securing a continuance of the armistice, that conferred advantages so important on Vermont. The intervention of peace terminated all danger from British invasion; but these secret negotiations were pursued for several years, and were not terminated until Vermont ceased to cherish apprehension from the pretensions of New York.

The historians of Vermont, who are the apologists of these transactions, allege that the men who conducted them, never seriously contemplated a return to the allegiance of England, except as the only means of avoiding a greater and more detestable tyranny than British domination, the more odious, that it was nearer, more direct, and tangible; that the insidious attempts of British emissaries to tamper with the patriotism of Vermont, was turned against themselves, by artifices, that paralyzed the movements of an army of ten thousand men. The diplomacy was most consummate and successful, which could thus delude the English officials, and, at the same time, allow just light enough and no more, to fall upon these negotiations, than was calculated to alarm the fears of New York, and to restrain the adverse actions of congress. What would have been the judgment upon these practices by the rigid code of military law, it is now perhaps inopportune to inquire. Political casuistry will find it difficult to maintain the propriety of the representatives of a patriotic and intelligent people, deceiving the masses on a most vital question, by a deliberate system of artifices and evasion; or to vindicate either the moral or political integrity of holding clandestine intercourse with a foreign enemy; maintaining negotiations and forming treaties with a public foe, while in professed and solemn allegiance to a country struggling for liberty and existence. The length to which these secret relations extended, or how definitive the arrangements of the leaders became, will never probably with clearness be revealed.[1]

The views of Ira Allen himself, justly solicitous for his own fame and security, in regard to these proceedings, are evinced by the fact that he extorted from Governor Chittenden and other of his coadjutors, two explicit written declarations, in June and July, 1781, recognizing and ratifying his negotiations with the British emissaries.[2] No just mind will distrust the early patriotism of these men, and it must always be conceded, that if so unhappy a design as the conditional return to British fealty existed in their minds, it was inspired by a hatred of wrong and oppression, and the law, as they believed, "of self-preservation," the preservation not merely of political rights, but of their homes, and humble fortunes. They detested and opposed foreign tyranny, and the same spirit which stimulated that feeling, rendered them the more sensitive to the persecutions of a kindred people, and more determined in their resistance to domestic aggression. Whatever may have been the purposes or action of individual leaders, and these should be generously judged, with regard to their services and sacrifices in the common cause, and subsequent expo-

---

[1] Governor Clinton submitted to the legislature of New York, in 1782, a mass of facts and documentary evidence, in reference to these transactions, which present the action of the Vermont leaders in a most unfavorable light. These papers embraced affidavits from two individuals, detailing circumstances alleged to have occurred at different times and distinct places, tending to establish the existence of a matured arrangement by which Vermont was to be formed into an independent colony under the protection of England, and that Vermont was pledged to support, under certain contingencies, the British government, with an armed force, under Ethan Allen, consisting of fifteen hundred or two thousand men; and that she should remain neutral, unless the war should be carried into her own territory. I am not aware that their affidavits, perhaps of doubtful character, were fortified by any further corroboration.

[2] *The Stephens Papers.*

sitions, the people of Vermont, through all the trying scenes of the revolution, by their patriotic zeal and inextinguishable ardor, vindicated the undesigned eulogium of Burgoyne, when in bitterness and disappointment, he wrote: "the New Hampshire grants abound in the most active race on the continent, and hangs like a gathering storm on my left."[1]

CHAPTER XII.

THE SETTLEMENT, 1782–1849.

The fields which had been cleared and cultivated on the Boquet with so much labor, were abandoned from 1776 to 1784, and after peace restored repose and security, and the settlers returned to their former homes, they found that nature had almost reestablished her empire over the territory. Brambles and weeds infested the land, the roads had become impassable, the fences and bridges were prostrated and decayed. Much of the former toils of the colony were to be renewed.

The personal history of Mr. Gilliland, so intimately interwoven with the settlement and progress of the county, demands attention. In common with an innumerable class of patriots, who had freely lavished their fortunes upon the country in the hour of trial and effort, the peace

---

[1] The student of history will obtain all the elucidation this subject will ever probably receive, by consulting *Slade's Vermont State Papers, Almon's Remembrancer*, vol. IX, *Thompson's Vermont, Allen's Political History, Stone's Life of Brandt, The Haldimand Papers*, copies of which have been procured from England and are preserved at Montpelier in two manuscript volumes, the *New York Historical Documents*, and preeminently, the able and learned *Early History of Vermont* by Hon. Hiland Hall. This most valuable contribution to American annals has been published since the preceding pages were prepared for the press. Governor Hall has given great research to this obscure question. He seems to have extracted all the important elements of the *Haldimand Documents*, and presents a very forcible and earnest vindication of both the proceedings and designs of the Vermont statesman, who, with such vast ability, guided the early destiny of that state.

of 1783 found Mr. Gilliland deeply embarrassed in his pecuniary affairs. The acquisition of an estate of thirty thousand acres upon the borders of Champlain, with the disbursements incident to its improvement, had involved the expenditure of a large amount of his means. He had lived in great comparative affluence and splendor, dispensing munificent charities and a generous hospitality. Driven from his home by a protracted war, his estates were wasted, and for several years abandoned and unproductive.

In the progress of the contest he had been reduced almost to indigence and destitution. Arnold, in his progress through the lake, with characteristic rapacity and violence, had ravaged the property of Mr. Gilliland. He appealed to congress for remuneration of his advances, and indemnity for his various losses, but the exhausted treasury ot the country could afford no relief. Returning to his wide possessions, he saw them wasted and desolate. Abandoning his long cherished purpose of erecting his property into a manorial estate, he decided to sell his lands in fee. The first purchasers were Joseph Sheldon and Abraham Aiken, of Dutchess county, who went into the occupation of their lots in March, 1784, and were the pioneer settlers under the new arrangement, in the limits of the present town of Willsboro'. During that spring, fourteen other families purchased and occupied farms, and several other individuals bought lots, and commenced improvements.

The lumber required for their buildings was procured at Vergennes. The saw-mills at the Boquet, destroyed in the course of the war, had not, at that time, been rebuilt. Meanwhile, other embarrassments gathered around to darken and accelerate the decaying fortunes of Mr. Gilliland. In several of the claims purchased by him in good faith, and for valuable considerations, and regularly located, he had filed the requisite applications in the appropriate colonial offices. The confusion incident to the convulsed period which ensued, impeded, and finally prevented the consummation of these grants by patents. Others appropriating, as he alleged, a transcript of the boundaries of the premises, contained in his documents, had applied to the new government, and obtained patents of the territory embraced in his previous locations. Litigation ensued. The antagonist titles were sustained. Costs and expenses followed, which absorbed the remnant of his property, and led to his imprisonment upon the jail limits of New York.

He returned at length to his former residence, despondent, and cherishing a disgust at the cold ingratitude of many, who in brighter days he has fostered and protected, and partially alienated in mind, he wandered into the solitudes of the forest, and there perished, stricken by some sudden attack, or overcome by exposure. His lacerated hands and knees, worn deeply into the flesh, attested how long and fearfully he had struggled with hunger, cold and exhaustion. Thus died the pioneer of Essex county; the former possessor of a baronial domain, and the dispenser of munificent hospitalities.

A strong current of emigration from New England rapidly diffused a hardy and valuable population along the western shore of Lake Champlain, and gradually penetrated the interior. Ticonderoga and Crown point were settled by American emigrants at the close of the revolution. George and Alexander Trimble were among the earliest and most prominent of these settlers. Two lots upon Whallon's bay were occupied the same year by Amos and David Stafford. The name of Charlotte county was in 1784 changed to Washington, and the eventual arrangement of the Vermont controversy limited its territory in the Champlain valley to the western side of the lake.

On the division of Washington county, in 1788, a new county was organized, embracing the territory which now constitutes the counties of Essex, Clinton, and the eastern section of Franklin. The new county was called Clinton, and was divided into the four towns, Champlain, Plattsburgh, Crown point and Willsboro', which were incorporated at the same time with the organization of the county. The town of Crown Point, in its original limits, comprised the present town of that name, Ticonderoga, also Moriah, Westport, Elizabethtown, Schroon, Minerva, Newcomb, North Hudson and a part of Keene. Willsboro' embraced the residue of the present county of Essex, and three towns now included in Clinton. Each of the towns of Crown point and Willsboro', at the period of its organization, spread over a territory of about nine hundred square miles.

At the first town meeting of Willsboro', Melchior Hoffnagle was elected supervisor, and Daniel Sheldon town clerk. The first town meeting of Crown Point was held in December, 1788. At this epoch, the ordinary civil functions of incorporated towns were little regarded or enforced. A plan was adopted, and although not ratified by any legislation, was conceded by common consent, by which the town officers were apportioned to the various prominent settlements. Each locality, designated in a primary meeting the individuals who should receive the several appointments appropriated to them. A delegate bore the respective nominations to the general town meeting, in which they were almost uniformly confirmed. At the general elections, the polls were held on the two first days, one-half a day in a place, and on the third at some central or populous point. These expedients facilitated and secured as far as practicable, the exercise of their civil rights to the settlers.

A claim instituted by the Caughnawaga and St. Regis Indians in 1792, to a vast tract of land, embracing nearly the entire territory between the St. Lawrence and Mohawk rivers, was urged for many years with great pertinacity and earnestness. It was resisted on various grounds, without violating any principle of public justice and private rights; investigation amply established the facts, that these tribes had no original title to the district, but that it was held exclusively by the Iroquois, who had alienated it to the whites by sales to individuals and by cessions through public treaties.

Charles Platt was appointed the first judge of the newly organized county, and William McAuley, of Willsboro', one of the side judges. Plattsburgh was made the shire-town of the county. At this period no road had been constructed from Willsboro', north of the Boquet river. The traveler was guided solely by blazed trees over the Willsboro' mountain. The route thus indicated, extended through the forest to the Au Sable river, which was crossed at the High bridge, about three miles below the site of Keeseville. A wood road had been opened from that point to Plattsburgh. A similar track, it is probable, was the only avenue of intercourse between Crown Point and Split rock. The settlement at Ticonderoga was about seventy miles distant from Plattsburgh, at which place the inhabitants were compelled to appear, to assert their rights as litigants, or to discharge their duties as jurors and witnesses. Jay was incorporated as a town in January, and Elizabethtown in February, 1801. Chesterfield was organized in 1802, and Essex and Lewis, April 4, 1805.

In 1790, Platt Rogers established a ferry from Basin Harbor, and constructed a road from the landing to a point near Split rock, where it connected with the road made in an early period of the settlement. He erected, in the same season, a bridge over the Boquet, at Willsboro' falls, and constructed a road from that place to Peru, in Clinton county. These services were remunerated by the state, through an appropriation to Rogers and his associates, of a large tract from the public lands. The venerable Judge Hatch, who until recently, survived, was one of the earliest settlers in the interior of the country. He moved, in 1792, into that part of the town of Essex now known as Brookfield, which was surveyed and sold in 1788. "This district," he says, "was at that time chiefly in a state of nature." In 1804, he "removed to the village of Westport, then called North West Bay. The distance was eight miles, and the removal of his family occupied two days, and the labor of four men, to open a passage for a wagon. At Westport, a small improvement had previously been commenced, and one frame house, three log houses, a saw-mill, and one barn had been erected. No road extended south beyond the limits of that town. A track had been opened to Pleasant Valley, where an infant settlement had just been formed. A road which was almost impassable, extended to the new colonies, in Lewis, and Jay, and Keene.[1] The alarm and excitement which agitated the whole country at the defeat of St. Clair, in this year, and the apprehension of a general combination of the Indian tribes of the west with the Six Nations, extended to these humble hamlets.

A block-house was erected for the protection of the inhabitants, near the village of Essex. The enterprise of the pioneer of New England had penetrated the gorges of the mountains, and his keen eye had fastened upon rich and alluring districts far in the forest paths I have mentioned. The table lands of Jay, the fertile valleys of Schroon, and the ravines and slopes in Lewis, Elizabethtown and Keene, were all occupied previous to 1798. An exploring party from the east had reached an eminence in Elizabethtown, that looks down upon the beautiful vale now occupied by the county seat of Essex county, embosomed among a lofty group of mountains, and adorned by the branches of the Boquet, which glide through its verdant plains, and gazing in delight upon the scene, they pronounced it Pleasant Valley. It still preserves, by common sentiment, the name and the same preeminence. Schroon was settled about the year 1797, by Samuel Scribner, Thomas Leland, Moses Patee, Benjamin Banker and Simeon Rawson, who were all men of New England. Thomas Hinckley made the first purchase in the town of Lewis, in 1796. The most important measure designed to open and develop the interior sections of the country, was the enactment of laws which authorized the construction, by Platt Rogers, and others, of public roads. I have already referred to one. Another was authorized to be constructed

---

[1] *Letter Hon. Charles Hatch.*

from Sandy Hill to the Canada line, and passing along the Schroon valley, through Elizabethtown and Lewis, and crossed the Au Sable river at a fording place near Keeseville. This highway is still designated as the Old State road. Numerous appropriations, at more recent periods, have been made by the state, for the construction of public roads, which traverse the county in various directions. One of these, opened many years since, extending from Westport to Hopkinton, traversing Elizabethtown, the gorges of the Keene mountains, and the plains of North Elba, penetrated what was then denominated, the fifty miles woods. A road, constructed under acts of 1841 and 1844, from Lake Champlain to Cartharge, in Jefferson county, was gradually built by an application of specific road taxes. It passes through the towns of Crown Point, Schroon and Newcomb, penetrating the heart of the Adirondacs. These avenues are of the deepest importance in promoting the progress and improvement of the county. Rogers and his associates received an enormous grant of unappropriated lands, covering an area of about seventy-three thousand acres. It costs, in the construction of these roads, according to the estimates preserved by tradition, "one penny and two farthings per acre."

Essex county was organized in 1799, in the division of Clinton county, and is now bounded on the north by Clinton and Franklin counties, on the west by Franklin and Hamilton, on the south by Washington and Warren, and on the east by Lake Champlain. The area of this county embraces one thousand seven hundred and seventy-nine square miles, or one million one hundred and thirty-eight thousand five hundred acres. It is the second county in territorial extent in the state, being only exceeded by St. Lawrence. New towns, by repeated divisions, have been occasionally formed, as circumstances and the convenience of the population required. The county now comprises eighteen incorporated townships, several of which comprehend more territory than some of the counties in the state. Nearly all of them are too extended for the convenient exercise of their civil and political functions. The village of Essex was originally constituted the county shire, and the old block-house, mentioned before, was appropriated for the public use, and was occupied for these purposes, until the removal of the county seat to Pleasant Valley. By the census of 1800, the combined population of Clinton and Essex counties, was eight thousand five hundred and seventy-two, including fifty-eight slaves. The next decade exhibits a very decisive increase. Essex alone contained, by the census of 1810, nine thousand five hundred and twenty-five population, and Clinton eight thousand and two. The tabular exhibit, Appendix D, will present the progress of the county in population.

Essex county voted with Clinton, until after the census of 1800. Thomas Stower was the first representative of Essex, when voting independent of Clinton.[1]

The war of 1812, although it closed many of the ordinary channels of business in this county, accelerated its progress by the new demands created for all the products of industry and agriculture, and by the general and abundant diffusion of money it produced. The enemy appeared on several occasions in the waters of Essex county, and in the summer of 1813, entered the Boquet with two galleys and two barges for the purpose of seizing a quantity of government flour which had been deposited at Willsboro' falls. Landing at different points, and committing many wanton ravages on private property, they retired after a slight skirmish with a body of militia under General Wadhams near the former entrenchments of Burgoyne. The fire of the militia killed or wounded nearly all that were in the rear galley. She floated down the river a disabled wreck and was towed into the lake, by boats sent to her assistance.[1] After this repulse the British flotilla returned to the Isle aux Noix.

The citizens of the county exhibited promptitude and zeal in responding to the calls of patriotism, during the war, and particularly on the approach of the British forces,

---

[1] For the complete civil list of Essex county, see Appendix C.

in 1814, upon Plattsburgh. Many of the volunteers and militia of Essex, creditably participated in the events of that brief, although glorious campaign.

The masses of the settlers of Essex county were of New England origin, and in a congenial soil and climate, familiar to their habits and experiences, they implanted the usages and characteristics of their puritan fatherland. No county of the state embraces a population of higher intelligence, of purer morality, or more industrious and frugal habits. Its early history presents only a counterpart of the aspect of every new colony, where among the virtuous and worthy, there always drifts from more mature communities, the loose and reckless.

The disorganizing and demoralizing effects of the war of the revolution exerted a malignant influence upon the character of the frontier population. Essex county was not exempt from these consequences. The testimony before me, of aged citizens, presents a striking portraiture of the state of society, in some sections of the county, where the restraints of government were scarcely recognized and where laws seem to have administered only to evil passions. I quote the language of a judicious observer, in speaking of a town, now second to none in its high moral and social position : " When an individual wished to secure a piece of land, he erected upon it a cabin, and repelled others by physical force; if unsuccessful or absent, his cabin was prostrated, and the last aggressor took possession of the coveted premises, and claimed the title. The parties, with their partisans and a supply of whiskey, met on the soil, and 'tried their wager of battle.' The victor maintained the possession. To correct these evils an association was formed, and a system adopted, which required a person desiring to occupy a lot, to perfect a survey of the premises, and to file a transcript with the secretary of the society. The title thus established was held sacred, for the purpose of that community."[1] The vene-

[1] *C. Fenton, Esq.*

rable author, since deceased, of a communication, describing the primitive habits of the county states: "that justices' courts, at that period, were usually held in taverns the innkeeper himself being the justice. The most frivolous difficulties were nursed into lawsuits; these, attended amid intemperance and revelings, led to assaults, and trifling controversies which engendered further and debasing litigation.[1] Essex county presented in this rude and demoralized class of its citizens, a stage of society exhibited along every frontier of civilization. Wherever I have succeeded in tracing the history of the early settlement of this county, I almost universally have found one prominent feature developed, and which strongly marks the character and descent of the people. The first impulse, and almost instinct of the settlers, even when their cabins were scattered over a wide area of several miles, seems to have been to secure the erection of a school-house. For many years in the early stages of the settlements, these schools had no legal organization, and were sustained alone by the voluntary contributions of the people, unaided by the public bounty.[2] The school-house supplied the place of public worship. The missionary at an early day appeared in the midst of these settlements, superseding in the religious duties, the humbler offices of the private Christian. Churches were soon organized in various sections of the county. Many colonies were accompanied in their emigration by their own spiritual guides.

The cold season of 1816, which produced such universal distress and suffering, inflicted a scarcity upon this new country, that visited it almost with the horrors of famine. So close and pressing was the destitution, that the indigent, gathering from many miles about a mill, would crave the privilege of collecting its sweepings, to preserve the lives of their families. A few sufficiently provident to cut the corn in the sap, saved it sound enough for planting. In the succeeding spring, many traveled fifty miles to procure

---

[1] *Levi Higby, Esq.* [2] *John Hoffnagle.*

this seed. Partial failure of crops had before occurred, but the season of 1816 will long be memorable, as the only instance in the history of the county of extreme destitution and suffering.

Ticonderoga and Crown Point present, upon the margin of Lake Champlain, a low and beautiful tract gently undulating and gradually ascending as it recedes, and swelling towards their western limits into bold and abrupt eminences. Clay predominates in these towns in the vicinity of the lake, intercepted by occasional seams of sand, and in the interior the soil is generally a gravel or sandy loam. Several sections of these towns are distinguished for the great excellence of their meadow lands. A view of Westport, Essex, and Willsboro', from the lake, presents ranges of highly cultivated and fertile farms, mingled with a combination of hills and plains which beautifully adorn and diversify the scenery. The two former spread into the interior bosoms of choice land, more elevated, and which are environed by lofty hills and mountains. Willsboro' point is a low, flat peninsula, projecting several miles into Champlain, having the long estuary, formerly known as Pereu bay, on its western side. This portion of Willsboro' affords some of the best farms in the county. A ridge of high, warm and rich land traverses the town of Essex diagonally from near the lake to Whallonsburgh, embracing a territory of great natural fertility and inferior to few sections of the state in the advanced character and excellence of its tillage. The soil of these towns is very diversified, although a sandy loam is its prevailing character. Moriah and Chesterfield, both bordering upon the lake, are more broken and stony than the other lake towns and contain less arable and cultivated land. The former ascends abruptly, and in a series of terraces or high valleys, until it attains an elevation of several hundred feet a short distance from the lake. The soil of this tract is deep and strong. Chesterfield contains many ranges of sand and rocky districts, but embraces much territory of very superior land. Elizabethtown and Lewis, lying among the gorges of the mountains and intersected by various branches of the Boquet, expose chiefly a light soil, with some alluvial flats and valleys enriched by the debris of the upland, which form tracts of the choicest land. Parts of these towns are managed, in their agricultural affairs, with great skill and sagacity. North Hudson and Keene, while they include several fine farms, are, in the aggregate, broken and mountainous. The Keene flats are unsurpassed in beauty and fertility. The territorial limits of Schroon equals the area of some counties, and is exceedingly diversified in the face of the country and the nature of the soil.[1] The centre of the town forms a beautiful rich valley of warm alluvial soil, through which flows, along high and even banks, the waters of the upper Hudson. Successful cultivation has been extended into the ravines and recesses of the mountains traversed by tributaries of this stream. Fertile and cultivated tracts occur in various other sections of the town.

The town of Minerva was organized from a part of Schroon, and incorporated in 1817, when it comprised a few log cabins scattered over its wide surface. It is situated in the extreme south-western corner of the county. A very large proportion of this town is still occupied by the original forest. Separated by a high range of mountains from other sections of the county, connected with them by imperfect communication, and with little associations in their business affairs, this most valuable and interesting town has been little known or appreciated. In the general improvement of the town, in the appearance of the farms, the erection of new buildings, and its indus-

---

[1] This town derives its name from the lovely lake which it embraces. The legend is, that the lake was visited by the French in their military expeditions and in fishing and hunting excursions from Crown Point and Ticonderoga, and was named by them Scarron, in honor of the widow Scarron, the celebrated Madam Maintenon, of the reign of Louis XIV. Rogers mentions Schoon creek which was crossed in marching between Fort Edward and Lake George. The islands of this lake afford sites for elegant and retired villas and country seats, unsurpassed by the waters of Cumberland and Westmoreland, in picturesque beauty and romantic seclusion.

trial pursuits, no part of the county exhibited, to my observation, more decisive and gratifying evidences of prosperity and advancement. The physical formation of Minerva is peculiar and striking. The whole territory of the town is elevated, rising in a gradual ascent of a succession of lofty valleys, formed by deep, broad, and sweeping undulations. This formation, viewed from an eminence, communicates a rich rural aspect, and great beauty to the landscape. In the language of one of its inhabitants,[1] "Minerva is a rugged and mountainous town, containing about one-third mountain, one-third feasible land, and the residue rough and stony."

The town of Newcomb is high, spreading over an elevation — apart from the altitude of the mountains — ranging from one thousand five hundred to one thousand eight hundred feet, which presents a broken and rocky surface. Yet its slopes and elevated valleys comprise tracts of much natural vigor, with great depth of soil. These qualities of the earth are exhibited by the dense and stately growth of its primitive and magnificent hard-wood forests. Isolated farms have been occupied in different parts of this town, since an early period of the present century.

Jay was settled as early as 1798. Remote, and at that time nearly inaccessible from Lake Champlain, its great natural fertility and beauty attracted the emigrant, who, passing by lands contiguous to that great artery of the country, penetrated to this wilderness by a mere bridle path, and transported thither, on horseback, his family and effects. A large portion of this town is formed of high and precipitous hills and mountains, and its whole territory is elevated. In the valleys, the soil is light, but usually vigorous. Upon several parallel ridges, which traverse nearly its entire length, ranges of land occur, distinguished by a warm, quick, and highly productive soil. These tracts allured the early emigration to this

---

[1] *A. P. Morse.*

region seventy years ago, and they still preserve their high character for great and enduring fertility.

Wilmington and St. Armands, recently separated from it, occupy the north-western angle of Essex county. They are generally, in their topographical aspect, elevated, rough, and mountainous. The soil is sandy and gravelly, with occasional alternations of loam. These towns comprise numerous bosoms and flats of excellent land. The long slopes gradually descending from the mountains to the valleys of the streams, present a highly picturesque and beautiful scenery. Settlements commenced in Wilmington, in 1800, and in the district now forming St. Armands, not until 1829, by any permanent occupancy.[1]

The town of North Elba is environed, upon all except its western borders, by a lofty sierra, which separates it from the other sections of the county, by an almost insuperable barrier. It is now approached by a circuitous route through Clinton and Franklin counties by the road which penetrates the mountains at the Wilmington notch, or by the state road, which passes through the deep gorges, and along the high and broken slopes of the Keene mountains. North Elba has little assimilation to the other towns of the county, either in its topographical arrangement or in the character of its soil. The gigantic amphitheatre of mountains, which almost encircle the town, form in its outline an arc of nearly sixty miles in extent, and embraces within this area a territory of about one hundred square miles. Upon the west, the plains of North Elba mingle with that vast plateau, teeming with rivers and lakes and forests, which spread to the shores of the St. Lawrence. The grandeur and imposing beauty of these mountain bulwarks, which singularly blending with a landscape of lakes and rivulets, vales and hills, combine to form a scenery of surpassing loveliness and magnificence. From one position, the eye gazes on the lofty group of the Adirondac mountains. Mt. Marcy stands out in his perfect contour and

[1] *Elias Goodspeed.*

vast dimensions. Mt. McIntyre, Colden, McMartin, trace their outlines upon the horizon, and far towards the south-west, the group of Mt. Seward limit the view; on the north, the Whiteface envelops the plain, and on the east, tower the dark and rugged cliffs of the Keene mountains.

The western branch of the Au Sable river flows through the town, and nearly the whole distance along a wide alluvial valley, almost as broad, and apparently of fertility equal to the flats of the Mohawk river. The soil of this intervale is generally a deep alluvial. Ascending from the valley to the table land, the earth becomes a dark and rich loam free from stones and rock. The growth of hard wood upon this territory is in no part of the state surpassed in its size, quality, and density. Its maple, birch, cherry and beech, are as stately, and form as highly timbered woodland as in the most favored sections of the country. Slightly elevated above the table-land, and receding from the river, commence the plains, which expand far into the interior. This tract embraces, in its general character, a warm, rich sandy loam. This land is scarcely inferior to the other soils of the town in vigor, while it exerts an early and more impulsive influence on vegetation, and is more easily and cheaply tilled.

With a view of instituting a comparison between this rich and beautiful region, and some of the most highly cultivated and productive districts of Vermont, and thus to test the adaptation of the former from altitude and climate to agricultural purposes, I applied to the late venerable and distinguished professor of natural history, in the Vermont University, Rev. Zadock Thompson, for information on the subject. His reply is contained in a very interesting note in which he states that many of the most valuable and productive farms in Vermont are situated at an altitude of five hundred to one thousand two hundred feet. It will be understood that the elevations mentioned by Professor Thompson, are from the basis of Lake Champlain, which is itself ninety-three feet above tide water. The plateau, which embraces the arable parts of North

Elba, is estimated in the report of Professor Benedict, as ranging from one thousand four hundred, to one thousand eight hundred feet above tide. This town contains nearly eighty thousand acres of land, seven-tenths of which, it is computed, are susceptible of cultivation.

The great beauty of this town, its agricultural capabilities, and its peculiar history as well as the general absence of information relative to its character and importance, seem to require a somewhat extended view of its progress and condition.[1]

A few pioneers, near the commencement of the century, with their families, entered into this remote and deeply secluded region. They seem to have encountered severer hardships and trials than the ordinary privations incident to a frontier life. Divided from civilized society by a chain of almost impenetrable mountains, they probably reached the place then known as the Plains of Abraham, by the circuitous route, now traversed by a road, along the course of the Saranac. While they waited in expectation of the scanty harvest yielded by their improvident agriculture, they subsisted by fishing and hunting, and from supplies transported by their own labor from the nearest settlements. The numerous beaver meadows furnished an abundant supply of fodder and grazing for the cattle. Until 1810 little progress was made either in the agricultural or social condition of this remote colony. The construction about that period of the Elba Iron Works, by Archibald McIntyre and his associates, gave

[1] The vestiges of Indian occupation in North Elba, and the territory around the interior lakes which remain, leave no doubt that at some former period they congregated there in great numbers. I found in the county a obscure tradition that the partisan Rogers attacked and destroyed a village in the absence of the warriors, situated on the Plains of Abraham; that he was pursued and overtaken, and a battle fought on the banks of the Boquet, just below the village of Pleasant Valley. Relics of both European and savage weapons of war found on the scene of the supposed conflict, seem to corroborate the legend, or at least indicate the probability of an engagement between Europeans and Indians having occurred at that place.

a new aspect to the affairs ot this region. The history of that enterprise I shall narrate in another place. The requirements of these works created occupation for all the population in the vicinity, formed a domestic market, and attracted numerous settlers. Schools were established, religious ordinances observed, and an efficient and benign influence exerted by the benevolent proprietors. Unhappily for the progress and permanent prosperity of the district, nearly all the land in the township at this period was held by the state. The emigrant, when he arrived, selected his lot without perfecting a title, or even securing a preemption, relying upon his right and ability to do so at his convenience. This delay eventually defeated their occupation of the farms, and blasted all the anticipated rewards of the toil and privations of the pioneers. In the language of a citizen of the town, "a great landholder heard of this territory of state lands, came and inspected it, returned to Albany and made a purchase at the land office of the entire tract." The settlers, soon apprised of this event, so fraught with evil and calamity to themselves, sought to purchase of him their possessions. He announced to them that the lands were not, at that time, in market. They too well understood the purport of this intimation. They were not, however, disturbed in their occupation, but unwilling to continue a course of improvement, which might enure only to the benefit of a stranger, little further progress was made in the cultivation of their farms, and the land was gradually abandoned with the exception of a few lots.

In 1840, only seven families remained on the eighty thousand acres which now forms the town of North Elba. At this time the lands were offered for sale, emigration was again directed to the region, and the evidences of returning prosperity were restored. The public highways were again opened and improved. At this period a new episode occurred in the checkered history of North Elba. Mr. Gerrit Smith, who had become an extensive proprietor of the town, made gratuitous conveyances of a large number of quarter lots, embracing forty acres each, to colored persons, with the professed design, it was understood, of forming a colony, which should constitute an asylum for a peculiar class of African population. I found no difference of opinion in that region, in reference to the character and results of this movement. Whatever may have been the motive of the benefaction, the issue of the experiment has entailed only disappointment and suffering upon the recipients of the gratuity, while the act has exercised a depressing and sinister influence upon the prosperity and reputation of the country. The negro, ill adapted in his physical constitution to the rigorous climate, with neither experience nor competency to the independent management of business affairs, and adverse to them from habits and propensities, soon felt the inappropriateness of his position. He has abandoned his acquisition in disgust and disappointment, or became, in many instances, an impoverished and destitute object of public or private charity. A very considerable proportion of these freeholds have been sold for taxes; others have passed into the hands of speculators, and when I visited the district only a few if any of the large number of original grantees retained the occupation of the farms they received. A knowledge of these facts has been widely diffused, and although the whole scheme bore in its inception the inherent elements of failure, the result has been imputed not to these causes, but public opinion has ascribed it to an inhospitable climate and the sterility of the soil.

During the brief operations of the Adirondac works, the affairs of North Elba received a fresh impulse. A road cut through the forest, in the gorges of the mountains, gave to the inhabitants a winter communication with that place, where they enjoyed the advantages of a ready market, at liberal prices, for all their agricultural commodities.

North Elba was separated from Keene, and incorporated in 1849. The population of the town is steadily advancing, and now amounts to nearly four hundred souls. Lands may be purchased, which are adapted to farming purposes, for from one dollar to six dollars per acre, the price being governed by position, and the condition of the premises, in reference to improvements and cultivation.

CHAPTER XIII.

THE REBELLION, 1849–1861.

Essex county was agitated by the same admonitions which in every part of the republic disturbed and moved the popular heart and presaged the approaching conflict, when the collision of opinion and sentiment should be succeeded by the din of arms. Distant from the immediate scenes of the terrible events, that shook the foundations of the Union, her territory was exempt from much of the woe and suffering that desolated other sections of the country. But none met the responsibilities of the hour with greater vigor and promptitude, or more freely offered the libation of its wealth and blood, in the common cause.

It is a strange coincidence that in one of the most remote and politically unimportant counties of New York, and in one of its smallest and most secluded towns, separated from the world by vast mountain barriers, an individual should have resided, who impressed a momentous and startling episode upon the history of the nation, and impelled a vast stride in the procession of events, which culminated in the rebellion.

I have elsewhere described the romantic town of North Elba and its beautiful plateau, embosomed among the Adirondacks and encircled by its stupendous amphitheatre of rocks and mountains. Nature, in such a scene, would cherish the reveries of religious fanaticism and stimulate visions of a social or political enthusiast. We have referred to the abortive scheme of Mr. Gerrit Smith for establishing in Essex county a colony of emancipated negroes. Benign and worthy in its designs it bore the inherent elements of failure. It was evident that the experiment was languishing and must eventually fail. In the year 1849, a man called upon Mr Smith and representing to him, in reference to the project which had been announced in the public papers, that the negro, without experience in his contemplated occupation and unaccustomed to the climate, was not adapted to the intended colonization. He proposed to take up a farm in North Elba, and by affording the negroes instruction and partial employment to aid in the enterprise. Mr. Smith acquiesced in his views and promptly conveyed to him a lot. This person was John Brown. At that time he was a resident of Massachuetts, but the same or the next year, removed to North Elba with his family and flocks and herds. He ereceted a humble dwelling house on a slope of the Adirondacks, and almost beneath the shadow of their pinnacles. This was his nominal home during the eventful scenes of the succeeding ten years; his family continued to reside there until after his death and there in a picturesque spot which he himself selected, repose his remains.

A brief notice of this remarkable person seems to be imposed on me by his relations to Essex county. No one can resist the conviction, that John Brown, by the texture of his spirit, and the qualities of his mind, was no ordinary character. He was a lineal descendant from a pilgrim of the May-Flower, and appears to have been preeminently imbued with the stern religious enthusiasm, the ardent zeal, the self-reliance and the inflexible devotion to truth and the peculiar convictions of right and justice he cherished, that marked the early Puritan principles. His religious fervor was inflamed by fanaticism. He believed that he maintained direct communion with heavenly wisdom, and that he was guided by specific visions and spiritual teachings. His biographers represent him to have been a man of constant prayer, and that the Bible was uniformly consulted as the guide and counsellor of his course. Religious ordinances he not only observed in his own practices, but they were maintained and inculcated in his relations with others. In the wildest period of his

Kansas career, twice each day he observed public prayer, and at every meal offered a grace of thanksgiving and praise. He united in youth with the Congregational church, and at an early age commenced studying with a view to the ministry, but this purpose was arrested by a severe affection of the eyes.

Before his settlement in North Elba, he had engaged in varied business pursuits without any considerable success, and usually with decided reverses. In 1848, he visited Europe in the execution of a wool speculation, which resulted in a disastrous failure. During his sojourn in Europe, his native taste and love for fine stock prompted him to the inspection of the choice herds of the various countries he had visited. By this means he acquired a knowledge of their respective qualities and value, which rendered him subsequently a useful citizen and intelligent breeder in Essex county. Brown embraced at an early period the most vehement anti-slavery sentiments, and in 1839 imagined that by a divine consecration he had been constituted the liberator of the African race. This idea became the all absorbing passion of his life, and to its realization he subordinated every other feeling.

We may not assert that John Brown was insane, and on his final trial in Virginia he peremptorily refused to allow that defense to be interposed, although he admitted that in his maternal line a strong taint of insanity prevailed which had been frequently developed. It is certain that several members of that branch of his family were inmates of lunatic asylums, and that the mind of a son who perished in Kansas was disordered. On the subject of negro emancipation, it can scarcely admit of doubt, he was a monomaniac. This fervid enthusiasm had disturbed the balance of his powerful and ardent mind. An inherent predilection for military affairs, cultivated by historical reading, had apparently suggested the idea that he was predestinated to become the military leader of a slave insurrection. We can only conjecture of his proceedings before visiting Europe; but while in England, he sought intercourse with the prominent abolitionists of that country and exposed to them his plans. It is evident that these men did not approve or sanction his violent designs. In reference perhaps to his visions of military duties, he constantly attended reviews in England and upon the continent, and was a close and intelligent observer of the organization and tactics of the armies of the several countries. Stimulated by the same feeling and avowedly to prepare himself for an impending crisis, Brown visited many of the battle-fields of Napoleon, and with the self-complacent reliance on his own powers, or perhaps presumption, which was a striking trait of his character, freely criticized the campaigns of the great commander and often objected to his strategy. It is a singular fact that Brown, in his Kansas warfare, brought into practice on a diminutive scale the manœuvres he had theoretically preferred to those of the French emperor.

The first prominent appearance of Brown before the people of Essex county was in connection with the agricultural fair of 1850. The report of the society for that year, thus refers to the subject: "The appearance upon the ground of a number of very choice and beautiful Devons from the herd of Mr. John Brown residing in one of our most remote and secluded towns, attracted great attention, and added much to the interest of the fair. The interest and admiration they excited have attracted public attention to the subject, and have already resulted in the introduction of several choice animals into the region. We have no doubt that this influence upon the character of the stock of our county will be permanent and decisive.[1]

While a resident of North Elba his earnest and energetic character attracted jealous friends, and often aroused strong hostility. A peculiarity of temperament, which moulded his whole career, was a proneness to assert what he believed to be right and just, with no regard to any personal interest. An iron will and the determination of a self-reliant and decisive spirit sustained by great native intellectual

---

[1] *Transactions of New York State Agricultural Society*, 1850.

properties conferred those qualities by which he exercised a magnetic power over the masses.

When the disturbances arose in Kansas, four sons of Brown were already there, and he instantly hastened to the participation in events; and he went as to a congenial field, in which he recognized the first scenes of the opening drama of conflict and blood. In the council of the Free State party, he at once attained an ascendancy, and was prominent among its active and controlling spirits. He was everywhere present, in all the acts of lawlessness and violence which debauched both parties and demoralized society. He manifested no insignificant skill and science in organizing the forces and constructing fortifications appropriate to that warfare, and fought the battles of his party with great conduct and intrepidity. A partial subsidence of the turmoils in Kansas allowed Brown and his sons to return to the east, with the ostensible object of rejoining his family at North Elba. His traces were exposed in various sections of the northern states, as the active and efficient emissary of the free state agitation. At Boston he appeared by request, before a committee of the legislature, to whom had been submitted a proposition to extend material aid to Kansas, and delivered an elaborate and inflammatory address on the public affairs of that territory.

In the ensuing summer we again discern him in Kansas, and his advent was signalized by renewed agitation and conflicts. Soon after his return, Brown entered the state of Missouri with an armed band, and by violence liberated twelve slaves. He led them into Kansas and by a slow and scarcely disguised progress conducted them through Nebraska, Iowa, Illinois and Michigan, and placed them in security upon the shores of Canada. This extraordinary and lawless act astounded the country through its whole borders, and was severely reprobated by many of his own sympathizers. The governor of Missouri offered a reward of three thousand dollars for his arrest. The president of the United States proclaimed an additional reward of two hundred and fifty dollars, with the same object. Brown subsequently avowed, that a prominent motive which suggested this action, was the desire of demonstrating the practicability of a forcible liberation of the American slaves.

By the sole authority of his own name and influence, he assembled a secret convention at Chatham, Canada, composed of all classes of his associates. Its proceedings were private, and have never been clearly disclosed. A colored minister presided, and we are authorized to assume that an early invasion of the south was on that occasion discussed and arranged. From this convention emanated the constitution that proposed to establish within the United States a provisional government; Although this instrument professed in one article to denounce all interference with the existing state or federal political organizations, it was calculated to subvert both. The negro preacher, who presided over this assembly, was constituted president of the contemplated government. This fantastic and extravagant chimera, was accepted by Brown as an actuality. In his brief subsequent career, he professed to act under the obligations of the oath it imposed, and holding the appointment by its provision of a commander-in-chief, he signed with that designation the commissions of his subordinates. Large numbers of printed copies of this document, designed to be disseminated, were found in his possession at Harper's ferry. The movements of Brown from this period, until the final catastrophe closed his turbulent career, were more disguised than they had been, but were not less active or zealous. Occasional glimpses are detected, where he appears inflaming the abolition sentiment, haranguing public meetings, and never slumbering in his assaults upon the existence of slavery.

In the month of April, 1859, he was in Essex county, enlisting associates. Like Mahomet, he found his first and firmest proselytes in his own household and among his own kindred. Five certainly of the youth of North Elba, three sons, a son-in-law and a brother of the latter, embraced his views, and all but one son died amid the terrible scenes at Harper's Ferry. Brown devoted, it is believed, most of the eight months preceding the invasion of Virginia to the military organization of the escaped slaves, that had gathered in Canada. He caused several hundred spear heads, a weapon peculiarly adapted to the hand of an undisciplined negro, in the service he meditated, to be fabricated in New England and transported to Harper's ferry. That position had long before been designated in the plans of Brown as the point at which to initiate his proposed occupation of slave territory, and it was selected with unusual skill and forecast. He had been for many years perfectly familiar with the topography of that whole region. This sierra he designed as the base of the guerrilla war he proposed to maintain. Harper's Ferry was easily accessible from Canada and in intimate communication with the entire north. The seizure of the guns and munitions deposited at the arsenal would furnish, he conceived, all the means necessary for arming the slave population.

A large unoccupied farm, embracing three dwelling houses, and situated within a few miles of Harper's Ferry, was hired by Brown, under the name of Smith, and afforded a convenient rendezvous to the initiated, and a safe receptacle for the arms and ammunition which were actively but cautiously collected. The unusual deportment of these men excited no small attention and comment, but suspicion was eluded by the pretext, that they were preparing to form an extensive wool-growing establishment. The presence, among other females, of a daughter, and the wife of a son, attached plausibility to these professions. With the prudence and care which so singularly contrasted with his reckless and violent schemes, the safety of these women was secured by their secret return to North Elba, directly preceding the outbreak. Brown had designated the 24th of October, as the day on which to strike a blow, that he hoped would secure the fruition of all his dreams and toils. Either alarmed by a suspicion of treachery among his followers, or from a natural fear of detection, he was induced to anticipate the movement a week. This change in his plans, his friends allege, was fatal to their primary success. It deranged a concerted movement of the slaves, and defeated a co-operation from Canada, Kansas, and New England. Brown, himself, did not sanction by his language at Charlestown, this assertion.

The details of his designs are shrouded in profound and impenetrable mystery. He was too shrewd and cautious to leave anything to the revelations of paper, and maintained after his capture an inflexible silence, which he earnestly enjoined on his associates in their final interview. This course was the promptings of a determination not to prejudice by any disclosures the cause he had so earnestly cherished, and to shield his secret coadjutors from the consequences of a complicity in his acts. The dreams and purposes that excited his feverish mind are buried in his grave, and we now can only speculate upon the nature of designs, which, to the calm judgment of history, seem to have been suggested by a wild and insane fanaticism, that inspired the attempt, with seventeen white and five negro followers, to uproot a system the growth of centuries, and to oppose and defy the forces not merely of the southern states but all the powers of the federal government. The facts which have been disclosed warrant the inference, that the plans of Brown embraced the design of the surprise of Harper's Ferry; the capture of the arsenal; the seizure of prominent citizens to be held as hostages and ransomed by a supply of provisions or the liberation of slaves, and an escape to the mountains with the arms and ammunition he might secure. He hoped to maintain himself among the fastnesses of the mountains until he should be supported from the north and relieved by the general servile insurrection, he believed his presence would enkindle. He would possess ample means, with his rifles and spears, to arm the slaves. His schemes were admirably conceived, and the execution attempted with equal courage and skill.[1] All his designs were accomplished, as far as he advanced, except the last and most essential step. He failed to retreat into the mountains. For hours he held the ability to execute unopposed this measure; but his wonted vigor and promptness abandoned him, and while he hesitated, lingering in doubt, his foes enclosed him and the opportunity was lost. Brown asserts that this hesitation was prompted by motives of humanity; others conjecture that he cherished the expectation of an uprising of the slaves.

Enveloped by an overwhelming force of the militia of Maryland and Virginia and federal marines, Brown sustained his position with a mere handful of men in the arsenal building, until the second night, and when the door was at length burst open, he and three others alone survived. One of these was instantly killed and Brown himself cut down by frightful sabre wounds. A son and daughter's husband were dead, and another son expiring under a mortal wound lay before him. A small party, including a third son of Brown, which had been left in charge of the farm buildings, effected an escape. The remainder of the band were either slain in the streets or captured. Several citizens were also killed or wounded in the conflict. When the arrest of Brown, and the few followers who escaped immediate death had been effected, the popular exasperation was controlled by the authorities; no outrage was committed against them. Brown was removed to the jail at Charlestown, his wounds were nursed, his wants relieved and to his friends a free access allowed to his prison. Brown complained of the precipitancy of his trial; but under the circumstance it appears not to have been urged with any ungenerous haste, and although the weight of incontestible facts rendered it a mere form, it was conducted with justice and fairness. He was legally convicted

---

[1] "It is in vain to underrate either the man or the conspiracy * * * Certainly it was one of the best planned and best executed conspiracies that ever failed."—*Mr. Vallandigham.*

and justly executed, but no indignity offended the solemnities of justice. His body was respectfully delivered to the tender care of his wife and friends.

The ruling passion of the enthusiast was illustrated in his progress from the prison cell to the scaffold, when he paused to kiss and bless a negro infant. The transcendant and eccentric tone of his sentiment was exhibited in the desire expressed to his wife, that she should collect the bodies of their two sons and his own, place them on a funeral pyre, consume their flesh, transport the bones to Essex county, and inter them on the farm at North Elba. With just sensibility she removed the purpose from his mind. Mr. Washington, one of the hostages held by Brown, attested to his humane solicitude for their safety during the assault. The high intelligence and elevated sentiment disclosed in his conversations while in prison; his heroic resolution; and the steady firmness and unfaltering spirit with which he encountered his fate, extorted the admiration even of the enemies, upon whom his designs were calculated to inflict the direst woes.[1]

Romance rarely delineated a more impressive scene than is described by Mr. Washington: "Brown was the coolest and firmest man he ever saw in defying danger and death. With one son dead by his side, and another shot through, he felt the pulse of his dying son with one hand, held his rifle with the other, and commanded his men with the utmost composure."[2]

It is not my province to discuss the character or aspect of these events. Glancing at them as they constituted by the action of its citizens, a fragment of the history of Essex county, I have discharged my duty and yield to others their defense or denunciation. Deluded and stimulated by a

---

[1] "He is a man of clear head, of courage, fortitude, and simple ingenuousness. He is cool, collected, and indomitable, and he inspired me with trust in his integrity as a man of truth." "He is a fanatic, vain and garrulous, but firm, truthful, and intelligent."—*Governor Wise's speech at Richmond.*

[2] *Idem.*

frenzied zeal and blindly reckless as he was to the consequences of his enthusiasm, Brown apparently fostered, in the prosecution of his designs, no aspirations of personal ambition, nor was he impelled by any lust of wealth or by individual hostility to those he assailed. He believed himself to be a chosen instrument in the hands of God; and to the imaginary behests of duty he devoted his own life, and sacrificed the blood of his sons and the happiness of his family.[1] With feelings not insensible to the domestic affections he witnessed without regret, the deaths of his disciples: he felt no remorse for the blood of unoffending citizens by his acts, shed before their own peaceful homes, nor did he recoil from the certain horrors of a war of races, that he hoped to arouse. His mind, under the dominion of the wild visions and extravagant hallucinations that inflamed it, rejected all fealty to the federal constitution. He did not accept its paramount obligation; he did not recognize its sanctions and guaranties. A regard to social order and the restraints that secure protection to life and property were powerless to control or modify his course. All these emotions, sacred to most minds, were extinguished or subverted in the pursuit of his one great dominant passion.

The invasion of Brown will hereafter be recognized as an active cause in accelerating, if it did not produce, events which subjected the institutions of the Union to that ordeal they were predestinated at some period to encounter. The inherent jealousies of the people of the south were inflamed; they naturally regarded this attempt as a manifestation of a determined purpose in the north of armed aggression, while the very hopelessness of its audacity was calculated to intensify this alarm and excitement. They saw in this movement the barriers of the constitution crumbling in the progress of the abolition spirit. The death of Brown sup-

---

[1] In one small school district, hidden among the mountains, where we might hope that the strifes of the great world would never enter, and composed of scarcely twice that number of families, five were made widows by the tragedy at Harper's Ferry.

plied fuel to the enkindling fires of the anti-slavery sentiment in the free states. He was regarded by the disciples of his faith, not as a felon, but as a martyr, whose blood had consecrated a sacred principle. The hour of his execution was solemnized by a large class of the northern people with religious exercises and the tolling bell, and as his body was borne through many a village the solemn knell proclaimed the deep sorrow of his sympathizers. An immense concourse formed from every grade of society, dignified his obsequies. Such exhibitions of adverse feeling tended to deepen the alienation between the sections; to excite stronger antagonisms, and to hasten the appeal to the terrible arbitrament of arms. The presages of Brown were singularly accomplished when, before even the moss had gathered upon his solitary mountain grave, the armed tread of thousands was moved by an anthem inspired by his blood, and which so often sounded above the clangor of the conflict and the shoutings of the battle-field.

The tide of patriotic enthusiasm which rolled over the northern states, when the national banner had been fired upon at Fort Sumter, rose high among the mountains of Essex. No section of the state responded with superior zeal and alacrity to the requisition by the government for aid. When counties subsequently found it expedient to claim credit on their military quotas, it was ascertained that Essex county had been prejudiced by this promptitude, and had in the early stages of the war supplied troops much in excess of her just proportion. Neither was the county surpassed in the fervor and decision by which the popular sentiment sustained the military measures of the government. Public meetings were immediately assembled in most of the towns to promote enlistment by both influence and contributions. Women of every class combined their labors to furnish clothing and every requisite for the comfort and efficiency of the volunteers. Few families declined to impart from their household goods, when called upon by committees who visited every district, to relieve the wants of the soldiers, which the government at that period could not adequately supply. The national flag or patriotic symbols floated from nearly every dwelling.

The proclamation of the president announcing the call for the first seventy-five thousand volunteers had scarcely reached the county when in various sections the enlistment of five different companies was simultaneously commenced. These companies were in a large proportion, but not exclusively, recruited from Essex county, while numbers of her sons enlisted in different organizations both in New York and other states.

A company was recruited in Keeseville, and composed in about equal proportions of residents of Essex and Clinton counties. Gorton T. Thomas was elected captain of this company, and Oliver D. Peabody 1st lieutenant, and Carlisle D. Beaumont 2d lieutenant. Another company was raised in Schroon from the southern towns of Essex and parts of Warren county. The officers elected were Lyman Ormsby, captain, J. R. Seaman, 1st lieutenant, and Daniel Burgey, 2d lieutenant. A third company was recruited in Moriah, and other eastern towns, and elected Miles P. S. Cadwell captain, Edward F. Edgerly and Clark W. Huntley, first and second lieutenants. These companies were distinguished as Companies C, I, and K, of the Twenty-second regiment New York Volunteers, in which they were incorporated on its organization upon June 6th, 1861. On the promotion of Captain Thomas, Lieutenants Peabody and Beaumont were respectively advanced a grade, and Charles B. Pierson appointed 2d lieutenant of Company C. A company raised in Crown Point and the adjacent towns, embracing one hundred and eight men, of which Leland L. Doolittle was elected captain, Hiram Buck, Jr., 1st, and John B. Wright 2d lieutenant, was mustered into service as Company H, of the Thirty-fourth regiment of New York Volunteers. Before the departure of this company for Albany, it was supplied with every equipment except arms, at an expense of $2,000, by the characteristic patriotism and munificence of the people of Crown Point.

The fifth company, recruited in Elizabethtown and the central towns of the county, was incorporated as Company K, into the Thirty-eighth regiment, and was the last company accepted from New York by the government under the first proclamation. Samuel C. Dwyer was elected captain of this company, William H. Smith 1st, and Augustus C. H. Livingstone 2d lieutenant. To describe adequately the services of these troops, and the other organizations which the county yielded to the exigencies of the country, would demand a narrative of the campaigns in which they participated. I can only attempt to present very summarily a general view of the endurance, the toils and achievements of the volunteers of Essex.

CHAPTER XIV.

The Volunteers.

The Twenty-Second New York Volunteers.

On the 16th May, 1861, this regiment was accepted by the government, and Walter Phelps, Jr., of Glen's Falls, commissioned colonel, Gorton T. Thomas of Keeseville lieutenant-colonel, and John Mc Kee, Jr., of Cambridge, major. It left Albany for Washington on the 28th of June, and while passing through Baltimore on the night of the 30th, was assailed at the depot by an armed mob. A private[1] was killed, but the regiment was promptly formed, and returned the fire, wounding several of the assailants. Order was soon restored by the city police, and the troops proceeded on their march without further molestation. The 22d was employed until the April following, in garrison duty and occasional reconnaissances in the vicinity of Washington. Through the several months following,

---

[1] Edward Burge, Company I, of Pottersville, Warren county.

it was occupied in services, that most severely try the spirit, the constancy and endurancy of the soldier. It was constantly engaged in marches and changes of position amid rain and darkness, or rushed from station to station, upon open and comfortless cars, and upon tedious and fruitless expeditions.

At length, the ardent aspirations of the regiment for active service seemed about to be gratified, when as a part of McDowell's corps it was ordered to advance in support of the army of the Potomac, but arrested on the threshold of this movement, McDowell was directed towards the Shenandoah. After the battle of Cedar mountain, the regiment participated in the continuous engagement, which extended through several successive days in the vicinity of that field. On the 27th of August, it marched with its divisions from Warrenton in the direction of Gainesville with the design of intercepting the retreat of Jackson, who had attempted to penetrate to the rear of the Union lines, and of breaking up his command. Ignorant of the position of the enemy, the divisions advanced slowly and with extreme caution. On the second day of its march Jackson was discovered near Gainesville in great force. The federal troops consisted of King's division, and were commanded by McDowell in person.

The line of battle was promptly formed and an action immediately and about an hour before sunset, commenced. McDowell's position was upon the Gainesville pike, while the rebels occupied a wood about a half a mile in front, with open fields between the two armies. The engagement was opened by a furious cannonade on both sides. The rebels had secured an accurate range of the road, and swept it by a continual storm of shells, and with fearful accuracy. A battery, supported by the Twenty-second regiment, was silenced and almost instantly annihilated. A ditch running parallel to the pike afforded a protection to the regiment, while the shells and shot, passing just above them, completely furrowed and tore up the road. For an hour this firing was maintained with unabated vigor, when the enemy emerging from the woods in a magnificent line a mile in length, charged, uttering the wildest yells as they rushed upon the Union position. All the Federal batteries directed by McDowell personally, which could be brought to bear, opened upon them, with grape and cannister. At every discharge, broad gaps were visible in their ranks. The Wisconsin brigade attached to this division poured upon them a terrible volley, and along both lines the fire of musketry was incessant and severe. The rebels paused in their advance, but stubbornly sustained their position until dark, and then slowly and defiantly withdrew, leaving the Union troops in possession of the field. They remained on the ground until midnight, and then, in order to receive rations, fell back to Manasses Junction. The Wisconsin brigade lost nearly half its strength in killed and wounded; but the Twenty-second regiment owing to its protected position, escaped with only slight casualties.

While the Twenty-second with its brigade, was reposing in this brief bivouac, Fitz John Porter's corps, early on the 29th, marched past them to the front, and was soon after followed by the brigade. The fighting raged through the day, Jackson gradually falling back, towards Thoroughfare Gap. The Twenty-second was not engaged, until towards evening; King's division was then ordered to charge the retreating enemy, and to complete their fancied defeat. With loud and exultant cheers, they were pursued the distance of half a mile, in apparent great disorder, when the Union troops were suddenly arrested by a withering discharge of small arms. The division, instead of being deployed to meet this attack, was massed in solid order and attempted to advance at double quick. In this form and unable to fire except in the front, it received destructive discharges, in front and from a wood upon the left flank. The troops by their formation were rendered almost powerless for offensive action. Darkness was approaching; the men began to give way, and the promise of victory was soon converted into an utter rout. This engagement was known as the battle of Groveton or Kittle run.

After this disaster, the division was attached to Porter's corps. Cannonading and skirmishing continued along the whole front, through the 30th, until about two P. M., when the entire line was ordered to advance in a simultaneous charge. The brigade, to which the Twenty-second belonged, was in the van of this division. The charging column of the division was two regiments deep; the Fourteenth New York, on the right, and the Thirtieth New York on the left, and followed by the Twenty-second and Twenty-fourth New York, at a distance of about twenty yards, Burden's sharp-shooters being deployed as skirmishers. This force constituted the brigade. The Union troops charged through a wood into an open field. The rebels were entrenched about two hundred yards in advance, behind a rail road embankment, and immediately opened a heavy fire with grape, cannister, solid shot and shell, supported by a terrible discharge of musketry. The roar of cannon was deafening, and the air was filled with missiles, but the gallant brigade rushed forward. The Twenty-second became intermingled with the Thirtieth, when within fifty yards of the enemy's line, and was compelled to halt. At that moment the rebels were abandoning their works, and scattering in every direction; many throwing down their arms, came into the federal ranks. But the pause was fatal to the promised success. The troops of the brigade hesitated to advance, and commenced a rapid and disordered firing. The confidence of the rebels was restored by this hesitancy, and they immediately reoccupied their strong position. The fire of the enemy, which had been partially suspended, was now resumed with increased intensity. The Union troops were rapidly falling, and it was next to impossible to remove the wounded from the field, as both flanks were swept by the enemy's guns. At this juncture, a brigade was ordered to the support of the troops, in their perilous and terrible position; but it had scarcely emerged from the wood, before it broke and fell back. The firing on both sides continued rapid and unremitting.[1]

The remnant of the brigade able to fight continued to fire until their ammunition was all expended, and then slowly withdrew, closely pursued by the enemy. The whole army soon after fell back upon Centreville. On the retreat there was neither panic nor rout, but the troops sternly retired, fighting as they retreated.

The casualties of the Twenty-second in the battles of these bloody days were severe almost beyond a parallel. On the 29th, its effective strength was six hundred and twenty-six men. Its loss in killed, wounded and missing, according to the record of the military bureau, was five hundred and four. The regiment entered the field with twenty-five officers, and on the night on which it fell back to Centreville, it retained only one captain and four lieutenants. Colonel Frisbie commanding the brigade on the 30th was killed, while urging the troops to advance.

Lieutenant Colonel Gorton T. Thomas was mortally wounded, and soon after died in the hospital.[2] Among the other losses of the regiment, were, in company C. Lieutenants C. D. Beaumont killed and Charles B. Pierson,

---

[1] It was a bright and clear day, and the smoke disappeared rapidly. On looking back upon the field, it appeared like the surface of a pond in a rain storm; the dust being kept in continual agitation by the pattering of the bullets. * * * The roar of cannon was so great that a man could not hear the report of his own gun. Indeed, instances occurred of soldiers continuing to load after their pieces had missed fire, until they were charged to the muzzles and rendered useless. There was no difficulty in procuring others, as the ground was strewn with them. Many changed their muskets, as the barrels had become so heated by the rapid firing, that they could not be held.—*Captain Edgerly's letter.*

[2] Lieutenant Colonel Thomas was shot in the body, but maintained his seat, until, incapable of controlling his horse, he was borne into the ranks of the sharpshooters, and there by a singular concidence, when falling from the saddle, was received into the arms of two neighboring boys attached to that regiment. He was carried by them to a house in the vicinity, and from thence was removed to the hospital at Washington, where he died of internal hemorrhage. No braver spirit or truer patriot moved on the battle-fields of the rebellion. The name of Colonel Thomas was the first attached to the enlisting roll in the valley of the Au Sable.

mortally wounded, and Captain O. D. Peabody, wounded; in Company I, Captain Lyman Ormsby and Lieutenant Daniel Burgey, wounded; in Company K, Captain M. P. S. Cadwell, killed, Lieutenants E. F. Edgerly and C. W. Huntley, wounded, the former twice. These companies averaged in these actions, a loss of nearly thirty men each.[1]

On the 6th of November, the Twenty-second moved from its encampment at Upton's hill to act in the Antietam campaign. Its feeble relics of one hundred and twenty-six combatants fought at South Mountain, were closely engaged and suffered heavily. The entire brigade in this action and at Antietam was under the command of Colonel Phelps. At Antietam the regiment was constantly exposed to a raking artillery fire, and out of sixty-seven, its whole remaining strength, it lost twenty-seven men. It was engaged, with its ranks restored to two hundred and ten effective strength, at Fredericksburg and afterwards at Chancellorville, and although conspicuous in its conduct in those actions its casualties were inconsiderable. After the disaster at Chancellorville, the brigade acted as rear guard to the army and gallantly covered its retreat. On the succeeding 19th of June, on the expiration of its term of enlistment, the Twenty-second was mustered out of service at Albany.

Subsequent to the desolation it sustained in the battles of the 29th and 30th of August the regimental organization was restored by the appointment of Major McKie, lieutenant-colonel, and Thomas M. Strong, major. The changes which occurred in the companies connected with Essex county, from their excessive losses, were numerous. In Company C, Beaumont and Pierson were succeeded by Gorton T. Thomas, Jr., and James Valleau; in Company C, Lieutenant Burgey was promoted on the resignation of Seaman and B. F. Wickham appointed second

[1] I have indulged in more minute details in reference to these events than my space usually allows, but it was the first great sacrifice that the district offered to the war, and its people will always cherish a deep and peculiar, though sad interest in the gloomy narrative.

lieutenant; in Company K, Lieutenant B. F. Edgerly was promoted to the captaincy. Sergeant John I. Baker was appointed first lieutenant in place of Huntley, discharged from disability on account of wounds, and Charles Bellamy, sergeant, promoted to second lieutenant.[1]

Officers attached to the Twenty-second Regiment when mustered out of service, June 19*th*, 1863.

Walter Phelps, Jr., Col. brevet Brig. Gen. U. S. V.	Benj. F. Wickham, Captain.
Thomas J. Strong, Lt. Col.	Edward F. Edgerly, "
Lyman Ormsby, Major.	Amos T. Calkins, 1st Lieutenant.
Malachi Weidman, Adjutant.	A. Hallock Holbrook, "
James W. Schenck, Q. M.	Wm. H. Hoystradt, "
Elias L. Bissell, Surgeon.	Gorton T. Thomas, "
Austin W. Holden, Assist. Surg., brevet Major N. Y. V.	Henry Cook, "
Henry J. Bates, Chaplain.	Warren Allen, "
Addison L. Easterbrooks, Capt.	James H. Merrill, "
Matthew L. Teller, "	John J. Baker, "
James W. McCoy, "	Asa W. Berry, "
Oliver D. Peabody, Capt., brevet Major and Lieut. Colonel.	Patrick McCall, 2d Lieutenant.
Lucius E. Wilson, Captain.	James Valleau, "
Daniel Burgey, "	Charles H. Aiken, "
Fred. E. Ranger, "	George C. Kingsley, "
Duncan Cameron, "	Salmon D. Sherman, "
	George Wetmore, "
	Lester A. Bartlett, "
	Charles F. Bellamy, "

Resignations and discharges of officers attached to Essex County Companies.

Joseph R. Seaman, 1st lieutenant, resigned Feb. 26th, 1862. Clark W. Huntley, 1st lieutenant, discharged Feb. 6th, 1863, on account of disability.

The first regimental flag of the Twenty-second was lost at second Bull Run. Another which was borne through its subsequent battles is deposited in the military bureau.

---

[1] Besides official documents to which I had access, I am indebted to information from the officers of the Twenty-second, and especially to Captain E. F. Edgerly for the facts I have referred to in the text and incidents.

Perforated by forty-six bullet holes, and its staff wounded by a ball, it is an eloquent witness to the perils and endurance of the regiment.

The Thirty-fourth Regiment New York Volunteers.

This regiment, to which the company raised in Crown Point, commanded by Captain Doolittle, was attached as company H, was organized on the 24th of May, 1861, by the elections of William La Due, colonel, James A. Suitor lieut. colonel, and Byron Laffin, major. The original officers of Company H left the service at an early period. Capt. Doolittle resigned October, 1861. Lt. Buck was not mustered in, and Lt. Wright, having been promoted to fill these vacancies, 1st lieutenant May 11th, and captain November 11th, resigned on the 28th November, 1861. James McCormick of Crown Point was appointed 2d lieutenant, September 29th, 1862, and promoted 1st lieutenant May 8th, 1863. Simeon P. McIntyre was appointed 2d lieutenant January, 1863, and George B. Coates December, 1862. Each of these officers was mustered out with the regiment June 30th, 1863. The Thirty-fourth arrived at Washington the 5th July, 1861. It was soon after assigned to duty on the upper Potomac. It was attached to the brigade then commanded by General Stone. The regiment was ordered to Ball's Bluff, but only arrived in time to aid in the removal of the wounded. Until the following spring it was occupied in continual harassing marches, and participated in all the hard services, which were at that period encountered by most of the army. The regiment at this time became attached to the first brigade commanded by General Gorman and the second division of the second corps, and remained in this organization during its subsequent services.

The Thirty-fourth landed at Hampton at the initiation of the peninsula campaign on the first of April, 1862. It was actively engaged in the siege of Yorktown, and was the first regiment in the enemy's works at Winne's mills. At Fair Oaks it was eminently distinguished, and was warmly engaged for nearly three hours, with a loss of ninety-four killed and wounded. The Thirty-fourth participated in most of the operations of this campaign, and at Glendale and Malvern Hill lost more than one hundred men, and was compelled in the first action to abandon its killed and wounded to the enemy. It was now subjected to a series of the most vigorous picket and field duties, and on the withdrawal of the army of the Potomac from the peninsula, the regiment endured the terrible forced march from Harrison's Landing to Newport News. The Thirty-fourth was transferred from that point by water to Alexandria, and was at once advanced to the front, encamping without tents or shelter, amid a furious storm of wind and rain. On the eventful 30th of August it was efficiently engaged in covering the retreat of Pope's army. At Antietam the Thirty-fourth entered the field on a double quick, and was moved directly to the front, where it was exposed to a wasting fire from infantry, in front and on both flanks, and by artillery on its left; but maintained its position, although abandoned by a supporting regiment, until ordered to fall back by General Sedgwick personally, who received two wounds while giving the command. In another period of the action, the regiment was again exposed to a destructive cannonade. During this bloody day, the Thirty-fourth sustained a loss of one hundred and fifty men, amounting to one-half of the effective strength with which it went into action. Through the remainder of the campaign, the regiment was employed in constant and arduous services, in severe marches, reconnaissances and picketing. On the 11th December, it led the van of the brigade, at that time commanded by General Sully in the passage of the Rappahannock at Fredericksburg, when the enemy were driven from the town. The regiment lost on this occasion more than thirty men from the fire of the enemy's batteries. After this action, the Thirty-fourth remained in camp during the winter, its repose being frequently interrupted by picket duty. At Chancellorville and Fredericksburg the ensuing spring it was present, but only slightly engaged. On the expiration of its enlistment the regiment was mustered out at Albany on the 30th June, 1863. The Thirty-fourth had participated in seventeen battles and numerous skirmishes. In all these scenes, Company H had sustained a conspicuous and honorable attitude, and worthily received, in common with the regiment, the official encomium "that it never failed in duty to its country, or devotion to its flag."

The Thirty-eighth New York Volunteers.

This regiment, under Col. J. W. Hobart Ward, was mustered into service at New York, in June, 1861. The company enrolled in Essex county, of which Samuel B. Dwyer was elected captain, William H. Smith first lieutenant, and A. C. Hand Livingston second lieutenant, was incorporated with the regiment as Company K. The Thirty-eighth regiment left the state on the 19th, and reached Washington on the 21st of June, and was soon after attached to Wilcox's brigade, and Heintzelman's division. It advanced with the Union army to Bull Run, on the 21st of July. and was engaged in that battle, suffering a loss in killed, wounded, and missing of one hundred and twenty-eight men. It was distinguished by its heroic bearing. During four hours it was in close action and exposed for a long time to a deadly fire of artillery both in front and on its flanks. Such an exposure affords the severest test to the constancy and courage of fresh troops. The regiment bore the heat and dust with all the suffering of the early part of the engagement, with the highest soldierly resolution, and when confronted with the enemy, it firmly met and successfully repulsed the attacks of his infantry. When compelled by the disasters of the day to abandon the field, the Thirty-eighth retreated in comparative order, and returned to the encamping ground from which it had marched in the morning. Company K, in this action, was in charge of Lieutenant Smith and Lieutenant Livingston, owing to the absence from sickness of Captain Dwyer. In this initial battle of the war, Company K was the only organization from Essex county engaged, and although none were killed on the field, it seems proper to record the names of the wounded and captured. Orlando R. Whiting, captured and died in prison; James A. Coburn, Henry Van Ornan, killed at Chancellorville; Patrick Waters, Pitt A. Wadhams, killed at Fredericksburg; Loyal E. Wolcott, John M. Gladden, George Boutwell, James McCormick, died in prison; and Wesley Sumner, killed at Fredericksburg. Lieutenant Smith resigned August 2d, 1861, Lieutenant Livingston, four days afterwards. The officers who subsequently served in this company, were Fergus Walker, second lieutenant August, 1861, promoted first lieutenant May 1862, promoted captain August, 1862; and William Warren second lieutenant May, 1862, promoted first lieutenant December, 1862.

Until the opening of the peninsula campaign the Thirty-eighth was employed in picket duty and the construction of field works for the defense of Washington. In August, the regiment was assigned to Gen. Howard's brigade. This brigade, known as the third brigade, was successively commanded by Generals Sedgwick and Birney. Upon the organization of the army of the Potomac, the division to which this brigade was attached constituted the first division of the third corps, and these various designations were retained during the subsequent service of the regiment.

The Thirty-eighth was at the siege of Yorktown and sustained in the operations before the works some slight casualties. Its bearing at the battle of Williamsburgh was highly conspicuous, and it encountered there a loss of eighty-six men. In this engagement, the gallant Captain Dwyer, of Company K, fell mortally wounded, and died a few days afterwards at St. Johns Hospital in Philadelphia. His body, claimed by the popular enthusiasm, was borne to the village of Elizabethtown, in his native county, of which he was a prominent citizen, and there buried with the imposing and touching obsequies due to his patriotic devotion.

The regiment was engaged in all the battles that immediately followed on the peninsula. It also fought at second Bull Run, Chantilly, Fredericksburg and Chancellorville. On the 21st December, 1862, the remnants of the ten companies of the Thirty-eighth regiment was consolidated into six companies, and marked from A to F inclusive, while the Fifty-fifth New York Volunteers was also consolidated into four companies, enumerated from G to K, and annexed to the Thirty-eighth regiment. A large proportion of the regiment reenlisted, embracing a considerable part of Company K, and when it was mustered out on the expiration of the term of service June 22d, 1863, these men were transferred to the Fortieth New York Volunteers. This regiment, both before and after the consolidation, was ranked among the most distinguished regiments of the state volunteers. In noticing the departure from the field of the Thirty-eighth regiment, the commander of the third corps in a special order paid the highest tribute to its service and reputation.

The Forty-fourth Regiment New York Volunteers.

A happy inspiration suggested the idea of forming a regiment to be composed of chosen men to be selected from the various towns and wards of the state, and organized and known as The Ellsworth Avengers. The design proposed at once to appropriately commemorate the name of the young hero, who was the earliest martyr to the Union cause, and to animate a just and patriotic military spirit throughout the state. Essex county promptly responded to the invitation, and most of the towns sent their representatives to the regiment. It was mustered into the service on the 24th September, 1861, as the Forty-fourth New York Volunteers. The services of the Forty-fourth were active and conspicuous in the varied operations of the army of the Potomac, and it is believed that its name and associations rendered it to the rebels an object of peculiar hostility and vindictive assault. The gallantry of the Forty-fourth was eminently conspicuous at Hanover C. H., where four times its flag was cut down by balls, and as often triumphantly raised. When the color-bearer fell, the standard was promptly raised by another hand. In the midst of the fierce and terrible conflict, which the Forty-fourth in connection with the Second Maine: "How many men," was demanded of a captain of the former, "will follow me to the charge." "Every man," was the Spartan reply, "save the dead." Such was the character and spirit of this regiment. The staff of the torn and faded flag, deposited in the military bureau, had about eighteen inches with the eagle and top shot away at Spottsylvania. When the Forty-fourth was mustered out of service, October 11th, 1864, the veterans and recruits were transferred to the One Hundred and Fortieth and One Hundred and Forty-sixth regiments, New York Volunteers.

The Seventy-seventh Regiment New York Volunteers.

This regiment was mustered into service November 23d, 1861, for three years at Bemis's Heights, Saratoga, and by the suggestions of the spot appropriately numbered seventy-seventh. At this organization, James B. McLean was elected colonel, Joseph A. Henderson, lieut. colonel, and Selden Hetzel, major. Two companies attached to the seventy-seventh, designated A and I, were principally enrolled in Essex county. Company A was recruited in the towns of Westport, Jay, and Keene. It was inspected on the 15th of September, and two days later proceeded to Saratoga. The company was organized by the election of Renel W. Arnold captain, William Douglass first and James H. Farnsworth second lieutenant. It originally mustered ninety-five men and received fifty recruits, chiefly nonresidents of Essex county, during its service. Lt. Farnsworth resigned January 5th, 1862, and Charles E. Stevens was promoted to second lieutenant. Captain Arnold resigned April 3d, 1862, and was succeeded by 1st Lt. George S. Orr of Company G. In December following, Lt. Stephens was appointed first lieutenant and Orderly Sergeant William Lyon was promoted to his post. Captain Orr of Company G was wounded at Cedar creek and mustered out with the regiment at the expiration of its term. Lt. Stevens was promoted to the captaincy of consolidated Company E, October 15th, 1864. Lt. Lyon was killed at Spottsylvania May 10th, 1864. Charles H. Davis was promoted second lieutenant October 16th, 1864, and appointed first lieutenant Company E, November 15th, 1864, and captain, April 25th, 1865. Company I was recruited in the northern towns of Essex and the adjacent towns in Clinton county. Mr. Wendell Lansing was largely instrumental in the enrollment of this company, but on its organization was transferred to the commissary department, in which he served about one year. The company officers on its organization were Franklin Norton captain, Jacob F. Hayward and Martin Lennon first and second lieutenants. Capt. Norton was promoted August 18th, 1862, to lieut. colonel of the One Hundred and Twenty-third New York Volunteers, and died on the 12th of May, 1863, of wounds received in the battle of Chancellorville, on the 10th December, 1862. Lt. Lennon was appointed captain of Company I, and January 3d, 1863, Lt. Hayward was promoted to quarter master and remained in that capacity until the term of enlistment expired. John W. Belding was made first lieutenant, March 17, 1863, was promoted to the captaincy of Company K, but never mustered in as such, and died October 27th, 1864, from wounds received in action. On May 19th, 1863, Orderly Sergeant Carlos W. Rowe was appointed second lieutenant. Lt. Rowe entered the service as corporal in Company I. At the organization of Co. I, William E. Merrill was corporal. He was made a sergeant July following, and orderly sergeant February, 1863. He reenlisted in February, 1864, was severely wounded at Spottsylvania, was made second lieutenant September 19th, 1864, and promoted to first lieutenant April 22d, 1865, and was mustered out with the regiment, at the close of the war.

Immediately after being organized, the Seventy-seventh started for the field of active service, and reaching Washington in December, 1861, went into camp on Meridian hill. The regiment was incorporated with the army of the Potomac on its first organization, and continued connected with it until its disbandment; it participated in all the fortunes of that army, from the commencement of McClellan's campaign to the close of the war. Its earliest experience of battle was in the charge upon the enemy's works, at Mechanicsville, in which a youth from Keeseville, Clifford Weston, a private in Company I, was killed, the first offering of the regiment to the country to be succeeded by a long and heroic line of sacrifices. The Seventy-seventh was conspicuous throughout these services, and no part of it was more distinguished than the two companies from Essex county. The regiment belonged to the immortal sixth corps, and its torn and fragmentary flags and guidons, and their shattered staffs deposited among the archives of the state, prove its worthiness of the association.

I do not possess the materials from which to form a narrative of the specific services of the Seventy-seventh, nor indeed could its movements be properly separated from the general operations of the army. That its services were severe is attested by the records of thirty distinct battles, and that they were gallantly performed is evident from the bloody decimation of its ranks. One or two instances will illustrate the character and endurance of the regiment. In the battle of White Oak swamp, the division to which the Seventy-seventh was attached, was suddenly assailed by a superior force of the rebels. The regiment was stationed some distance from its brigade, and could not be approached owing to the severity of the enemy's fire. Although not directly exposed to this fire, it was in imminent danger, from its position, of being cut off. "Not proposing to move without orders," as one of its gallant members writes, the regiment maintained its post. A slight suspension of the action enabled an aid to reach it, with orders to change its ground. This order was promptly executed, but only in time to save the regiment from capture.

At the battle of Spottsylvania, May 10th, 1864, the Seventy-seventh was selected with several other regiments to form an assaulting column, to charge the enemy's lines. The attack continued scarcely more than fifteen minutes, but was of the fiercest and bloodiest character. The position assailed was extremely formidable, and the attacking column was not sufficiently strong to maintain it. They were compelled to fall back and abandon the position with their dead and severely wounded to the mercy of the enemy. Twenty members of the Seventy-seventh were left upon this field. In the terrible conflict at Spottsylvania, the regiment lost seventy-four men, about one-fourth of its strength engaged. Lt. Lyon of Company A was killed in the charge, and Lt. Rowe of Company I was taken prisoner.

The regiment participated in the eventful scenes on the peninsula. At Mechanicsville it captured a guidon belonging to a Georgia regiment; it was at Gaines's Mills, Savage's Station, and in all the operations before Richmond, which terminated at Malvern Hill. Transferred from that field it was engaged at second Bull Run, Crompton Pass and Antietam, closing the services of that year at

---

[1] Lt. Rowe made his escape. The story in its detail is full of interest from its romantic incidents and the adroitness and courage by which success was secured. The fifth day after his capture, he began a march with about twelve hundred prisoners, in the direction of southern prison houses. On the second day of the march, they were compelled to ford a stream, which was waist deep. In effecting the passage the line became scattered. The guard was comparatively small, and in the confusion, Rowe was able soon after crossing to plunge into a thicket and secrete himself behind a heavy cluster of bushes. He was concealed in this covert until the whole detachment had past. He had procured a map from a fellow prisoner, and aided by this and a pocket compass, he deliberately marked out the route he should pursue to regain the Union lines. Pursuing for a while nearly the course of the party from which he had escaped, he at length diverged and crossing the Richmond and Gordonsville rail road and then the Gordonville and Lynchburg, proceeded by a long circuitous route. He traveled in seven days and principally in the night, a distance of one hundred and fifty miles, and succeeded on the thirteenth day after his capture in joining the Union forces at Fredericksburg. In his perilous journey he encountered innumerable hair-breadth escapes, endured extreme suffering, and had no other subsistence than he secured from his own efforts and the kindness and charity of the negro people.

Fredericksburg on December 13th. In January, 1863, it encountered the horrors of the "mud campaign." At Marye's Height, on the 3d of May, it captured the flag of the Eighteenth Mississippi; it fought at Fredericksburg, Gettysburg, Rappahannock station and Robinson's tavern. In the campaign of 1864, it was at the Wilderness, Spottsylvania, Coal Harbor and Fort Stevens. Transferred to the Shenandoah valley, it was engaged in the battle of the 19th September in which Captain Lennon, of Company I, and Lieutenant Belding were mortally wounded, and died, the former on the succeeding 1st November, and the latter the 29th October. It was at Fisher Hill September 22d, and at Cedar Creek on the 19th of October, gallantly aiding in the achievement of that crowning victory. In this engagement Captain Orr of Company A was severely wounded.

In November, 1864, at the expiration of its term of enlistment, the regiment was mustered out of service; but it left in the field a battalion composed of veterans who reenlisted, formed from the original organization and new recruits. This was designated the 77th Battalion New York State Volunteers. The relics of Companies A and I were consolidated into a new company designated C, and attached to the battalion. This company embraced eighty-five men and was formed of nearly equal proportions of the original companies. The officers of Company C consisted of Charles E. Stevens captain, appointed major but not mustered in as such; 1st lieutenant Charles A. Davis, and 2d lieutenant William E. Merrill. The battalion was engaged in the final siege of Petersburg and in the assault of the 2d April its flags and guidons were the first colors on the enemy's works.[1] It was mustered out, in June 27th, 1865. The regiment had fourteen hundred and sixty-three on its rolls, of whom seventy-three were killed in battle, forty died of their wounds and one hundred and forty-eight of disease.

The different banners of this regiment in their torn and shattered condition, which are deposited in the Bureau of

---

[1] *Flag Presentations.*

Military Records at Albany, are invested with deep and peculiar interest. In the charge up Marye's Height, one of the color guards of the regimental flag was killed, and the banner torn into shreds by a shell. A national flag borne in many fields, is half gone, its ends ragged, its field in ribbons. The top of its staff was shot off at the battle of the Wilderness. In the battle of Chancellorville its field was torn by an enemy's shell. Among its bearers in battle, Corporal Joseph Murray was killed at Antietam, Michael McWilliams in the Wilderness.. Corporal Horicon of the color guard was killed at Cedar Creek, and Corporal Myers shot through the hand in the Wilderness. Its inscription was placed upon the flag by the order of General Sheridan.

Officers of Seventy-seventh mustered out on expiration of original term of enlistment, Dec. 13th, 1864.

Lt. Col. Winsor B. French.
Major Nathan S. Babcock.
Q. M. Jacob F. Hayward.
Surgeon George T. Stevens.
Asst. Surg. Justin T. Thompson.
" " Wm. A. Delong.
Chaplain Norman Fox, Jr.
Captain George S. Orr.
Joseph H. Loveland.
1st Lt. Alonzo Howland.
" Henry C. Rowland.
" Lewis T. Vanderwarker.
" William W. Worden.
2d Lt. David Lyon.
" Carlos W. Rowe.
" George W. Gillis.

Officers mustered out on discharge of Battalion, Seventy-seventh New York Volunteers.

David J. Caw, brevet Col. U. S. V.
Q. M. Charles D. Thurber, brevet Capt. U. S. V.
Surgeon John G. Thompson.
Capt. Isaac D. Clapp, brevet Major U. S. V.
Capt. David A. Thompson.
" Charles E. Stevens, appointed major but not mustered in as such.[1]
Capt. George M. Ross.
1st Lt. William E. Merrill.
" Thomas S. Harris.
" Adam Flansburgh.
" Robert E. Nelson.
" James A. Monroe.
2d Lt. Sorrell Fountain.
" William Carr.
" William H. Quackenbush.
" Thomas M. White.

---

[1] I am under peculiar obligations for the facts I have embodied in the account of the Seventy-seventh to Major Stevens, Lt. Rowe, and Mr. W. Lansing. My researches, not only in respect to this, but every other

Brevet Commission issued by Governor to Enlisted Men.

Hospital Steward Alexander P. Waldron, 2d Lieutenant.

The Ninety-sixth New York Volunteers.

This regiment was wholly enrolled in the northern section of New York. Only a single company, as appears from the documents which I have been able to collect, originally organized, belonging to the Ninety-sixth, was enrolled in Essex county, although large portions of other companies were recruited in the county, and towards the close of the war, numerous drafts from the county joined this regiment. Essex was therefore largely represented in the organization. Captain Alfred Weed enlisted principally in Ticonderoga, a company which he commanded, and of which Thomas W. Newman was second lieutenant. This company was attached to the Ninety-sixth as Company G, George W. Hinds, of Au Sable, was captain, February 18, 1862, and promoted to major, March, 1865. Earl Pierce of Jay, originally attached to Company K, of the One Hundred and Eighteenth, was appointed first lieutenant of the Ninety-sixth, January 27, 1864, and promoted to captaincy, January 20, 1865. The regiment was organized at Plattsburg, and departed for the field, March, 1862, under the command of James Fairman, Colonel Charles O. Grey, lieutenant-colonel, and John E. Kelley, a veteran of the regular army, major. Nathan Wardner of Jay was appointed chaplain of the organization, John H. Sanborn, quarter-master, and Francis Joseph D'Avignon, of Au Sable Forks, surgeon. The Ninety-sixth, in the early stages of its services, was severely depressed, through the unfavorable auspices by which it was surrounded, but after the brave and accomplished Grey was placed in command, the regiment rapidly attained a very high reputation. It had been precipitated by ill-advised councils into active ser-

---

military organization of the state, have been enlightened by the invaluable report of Adjutant General Marvin, 1868. For a copy of the work, I am indebted to the courtesy of Hon. Smith M. Weed.

H. B. Hall.

Col. Charles O. Gray

96th N. Y. Vol.

vice, without the advantages of any adequate drilling, and was hurried into the peninsula campaign before the habits of the troops were adapted to field duty, and while they were yet unacclimated. Company G marched from Fortress Monroe, comprising more than seventy combatants, and when it entered the conflict at Fair Oaks, it retained only eighteen men fit for duty. The remainder had been stricken down by diseases incident to hard service and a malarious climate. This fact illustrates the general condition of the regiment, the efficiency of which was also deeply impaired for a season, by dissensions among its officers. A number of the subordinates had resigned from this and other causes. Captain Weed, immediately previous to Fair Oaks, was compelled by severe sickness, to relinquish his command, and Lieutenant Newman, who was discharged in May, 1862, had already left the regiment.[1]

The company for a time was in charge of Orderly Sergeant Patrick English, and was ultimately consolidated with Company C of Clinton county.

Major Kelly was killed in a picket skirmish, immediately before the battle of Fair Oaks. In that action the losses of the Ninety-sixth regiment were extremely severe. The services of the regiment, throughout the peninsula campaign, were marked by great perils and hardships, and elicited from General Peck, the commander of the division, warm and unusual encomiums. It was afterwards ordered to Suffolk, enduring all the trials and sufferings of that field, and was subsequently engaged in the North Carolina expedition, and gallantly participated in all the hard services of that vigorous campaign. In the battle of Kingston, December 14th, 1862, Colonel Grey, who had already, although a youth of twenty-four, achieved a brilliant fame, was killed while charging at the head of the regiment over

---

[1]Lieutenant Newman afterwards joined a Maryland regiment, and remained in the service during the war. Captain Weed, after his health was restored, enlisted as a private in the Ninety-third New York Volunteers, and did not return to civil life until the spring of 1865.

the bridge on the Neuse, and in the act of planting its standard upon the enemy's works. Three weeks before, in presenting a new flag to the Ninety-sixth, he had uttered a glowing and eloquent tribute to its old flag, and now this enveloped his coffin, as his remains were borne from his last battle-field to its resting place among his familiar mountains. That venerated flag is deposited in the military bureau. After this event the Ninety-sixth regiment was for a short term under the command of Colonel McKenzie.

Early in 1864, the regiment was transferred to the army of the James before Petersburg, and attached to the same brigade with which the One Hundred and Eighteenth was connected. It was incorporated with the eighteenth and afterwards with the twenty-fourth corps. The Ninety-sixth was engaged in all the subsequent operations of the eighteenth corps. At Coal Harbor, and the assault on Fort Harrison its casualties were appalling. In the attack upon Fort Harrison, the Ninety-sixth and the Eighth Connecticut formed the assaulting columns, with the One Hundred and Eighteenth New York, and Tenth New Hampshire on their flanks as skirmishers. The division approached the works in close order, and in a distance of fourteen hundred yards was exposed to a plunging and galling fire of artillery and musketry.[1]

It steadily advanced to the base of the hill, which was crowned by the enemy's work. Here the column, exhausted by its rapid progress, paused. The enemy perceiving the point of attack were meanwhile pouring reenforcements into the menaced works. The crisis was imminent, and General Stannard commanding the division sent an earnest order for an instant assault.[2] The head of the column charged up the hill, and scaling the parapet,

---

[1] *Gen. Stannard's Report.*

[2] General Stannard claims that this order was carried by Captain Kent his aid. Other authorities state that it was communicated from General Burnham by Lieutenant Campbell, of the One Hundred and Eighteenth, who was on his staff. Perhaps the orders were coincident.— *Butler's Address to the Army of the James.*

drove the enemy from their guns. Sergeant Lester Archer of the Ninety-sixth and the color bearer of the Eighth Connecticut, simultaneously planted their respective regimental flags upon the ramparts. The Rev. Nathan Wardner, chaplain of the Ninety-sixth, charged with his regiment in the advancing columns, prepared to administer spiritual consolation on the very field of carnage.[1] The captured guns of the fort were turned upon the retreating enemy with terrible effect. The Ninety-sixth was conspicuous in opposing the repeated, resolute and desperate attempts of the rebels to recover this important position.[2] The death or wounds of four superiors, placed Colonel Cullen of the Ninety-sixth, at the close of this sanguinary battle, in command of the division.

The Ninety-sixth continued near Fort Harrison in camp with its brigade, after the capture of that work, until the 24th of October, when the entire division, marched against Fort Richmond, at Fair Oaks. It bivouacked that night, about three miles from the fort. While the skirmishing party of the One Hundred and Eighteenth was engaged in the perilous and hopeless assault of the enemy's line, the next morning the Ninety-sixth, in common with the remainder of the division, stood idle spectators of the slaughter of those troops, although little doubt now exists, that a combined and energetic attack of the fort, when the One Hundred and Eighteenth advanced and while it was occupied by a force wholly inadequate to its defense, would have secured a glorious success. A designed feint had been converted into a real and sanguinary assault, and the character of this bloody field, conspicuous for its profitless and murderous losses, was only redeemed by the valor of the troops.

For two long and trying hours, after the repulse of the One Hundred and Eighteenth, the residue of the division

---

[1] *Butler's Address.*

[2] I more particularly describe these events in noticing the services of the One Hundred and Eighteenth on the occasion.

stood under arms, in front of the enemy's lines, with no orders, either to advance or retreat, while the rebels were observed, eagerly rushing troops into the fort, on foot and upon horseback. Horses were constantly perceived hurrying up at their highest speed, bearing three riders, and as they approached the works, two leaping from the horse would enter the fort, while the third returned at the same speed, to bear back another freight of defenders. At length, when the lines by this delay had been rendered impregnable to an attack, the division was madly hurled upon the works. It was bloodily repulsed. The casualties of the Ninety-sixth were in the highest degree severe. Its last colonel, Stephen Moffit, of Clinton county, who continued in the command until the regiment was disbanded, lost a leg in this action, while gallantly leading in the fruitless and disastrous assault. He was borne from the field by Captain Earle Pierce of the Ninety-sixth, and Capt. M. V. B. Stetson, of the One Hundred and Eighteenth, the latter of whom was wounded in the generous act.

The ground upon which these unfortunate operations occurred, had been signalized by the sanguinary battle of Fair Oaks, during the peninsula campaign. The works erected by McClellan were still discernible, and as the federal troops moved to the assault, they disturbed and trampled upon skulls and bones and other ghastly memorials of the former conflict. The Ninety-sixth participated in the brilliant closing scenes of the war around Richmond and its final consummation.

I should not close this notice, which I regret is so inadequate, of this gallant regiment [1] without referring to the memory of one of its members, who was alike distinguished for the ability and zeal with which he performed his official duties, and his warm hearted and generous sensibilities. Francis Joseph D'Avignon was placed at the head of the medical corps of the Ninety-sixth at its

---

[1] I have made every effort to obtain information, but generally with very unsatisfactory results.

organization. His skill and courage early attracted attention, and led to his promotion. He was made surgeon-in-chief to a division, was captured at Drury's Bluff and remained a prisoner for several months. He was confined for a short term in Libby Prison and encountered its rigors, but was soon released from confinement and allowed with slight restraints to mingle freely with the Union prisoners, and minister to them his professional services. He was mustered out on the expiration of his term of service, March 14th, 1865. Surgeon D'Avignon had been a Canadian patriot, and was involved in the perils of 1837. He fled into the states from the scaffold, and yielding to his republican instincts became an American citizen. He married and permanently resided at Au Sable Forks.[1]

Officers of the Ninety-sixth mustered out with the Regiment, February 6th, 1866.

Col. Stephen Moffitt, brevet Brig. Gen. U. S. V.
Lt. Col. George W. Hinds, brevet Col. N. Y. V.
Major Courtland C. Babcock, brevet Lt. Col. N. Y. V.
Q. M. Allen Babcock.
Surgeon Robert W. Brady.
Chaplain Nathan Wardner.
Capt. Earl Peirce.
Moses Gill.
Moses E. Orr.
Henry C. Buckham, brevet Maj. N. Y. V.
William B. Brokaw, brevet Major N. Y. V.
Merlin C. Harris, brevet Major N. Y. V.
Thomas E. Allen.
Oscar B. Colvin.
1st Lt. William B. Stafford.
" Thomas Burke.
" Charles H. Hogan.
" Orlando P Benson.
" Lyman Bridges.
" George J. Cady.
" Lucien Wood.
" Alexander M. Stevens.
" Alonzo E. Howard.
2d Lt. Washington Harris.
" Stanford H. Bugbee.
" Alexander McMartin.
" Charles Sharron.
" Amos S. Richardson.
" Silas Finch.
" Judson C. Ware.

[1] A brother officer in the regiment, himself as well as Surgeon D'Avignon, since deceased, remarks of the latter: "He stood very high in the army, and was beloved by both officers and privates."

Enlisted Men of the Regiment to whom Medals of Honor have been Awarded by the Secretary of War.

Sergeant Lester Archer.

The archives of the state present the following brilliant record of the services of the Ninety-sixth: Gainesville, second Bull Run, South Mountain, Antietam, Mine Run, Fredericksburg, Chancellorville, Gettysburg, Wilderness, North Anna, Mattapony, Spottsylvania, Bethesda Church, Petersburg, Weldon Rail Road, Chapel House, Hatcher's Run, Yorktown, Williamsburg, Fair Oaks, Seven Days' Battle, Blackwater, Kingston, Whitehall, Goldsboro', Siege of Newbern, Drury's Farm, Port Walthall, Coal Harbor, Battery Harrison, Charles City Road.

Fifth New York Cavalry.

At the opening of the war of the rebellion, the government suffered severely from the absence of an efficient cavalry arm. In this force, the rebels were far superior, both in numbers and efficiency. A wide defection among the cavalry officers of the army, in one instance, embracing almost an entire regiment, and the peculiar equestrian habits of the southern people, which rendered most men expert riders from early youth, combined to furnish materials for an immediate and powerful organization of mounted troops. Directly after Bull Run, the government addressed itself to the task of remedying this deficiency. Agents appeared throughout the north, arousing the chivalric spirit of the country, and urging everywhere the formation of cavalry companies and regiments. This appeal reached the town of Crown Point, which, as I have mentioned, had but recently, by private munificence, equipped an infantry company, and was responded to with an ardor and promptness that has few parallels in all the incidents of enthusiasm that characterized the times. The fervid zeal that was inspired could not be restrained to await the formal preparation of enlisting papers, or for a regular mustering in, by the usual machinery of the department. But a written compact was at once prepared, by which each man was pledged to serve the government for three years in the mounted service, and in an incredibly short period it received the signatures of one hundred and twenty-seven of the youth of that town and its immediate vicinity.[1] They constituted the bone and muscle of the community. To each name is attached the age and occupation of the signer. Nearly all were between the ages of twenty and thirty years, and most of them were either farmers or mechanics. Almost every signature was an autograph; thus affording evidence of an intelligence and education rarely found in a body of soldiers hastily recruited. Of such materials, Cromwell formed his memorable Ironsides, and these young men of Essex carried with them into the service, the resolute qualities and the exalted spirit that made the troopers of the English enthusiast invincible on every field.

Under this compact, to which all implicitly adhered, the company, without officers and without any other restraint, proceeded to New York, and were there regularly mustered into the service. The entire body of men were accepted as privates, nor were their officers elected until the company joined the regiment on Staten island. John Hammond was commissioned captain, September 14, 1861; major, September, 1863; lieutenant-colonel, March, 1864; colonel, July, 1864, and brevet brigadier-general, May 22, 1866. Jonas A. Benedict was commissioned first lieutenant, and James A. Penfield second lieutenant of the company, the 22d of October, 1861. Lieutenant Benedict died in the next December, and was succeeded by Penfield, who was appointed captain in July, 1863, and resigned in May, 1865. John G. Viall

[1] This instrument, so novel and remarkable in its character and so illustrative of the patriotic ardor that pervaded the country, is worthy of the choicest preservation. This is its exact language: "We, the undersigned, hereby agree to serve the government of the United States in the mounted service for three years, unless sooner discharged, subjecting ourselves to all the rules and regulations governing troops in that branch of the regular service."

was appointed second lieutenant, December, 1861; first lieutenant, September, 1862, and captain, April, 1864. Elmer J. Barker was appointed second lieutenant, September, 1862; first lieutenant, November, 1863; captain, March, 1864; and major, November, 1864. Eugene B. Hayward was appointed second lieutenant, November, 1863; first lieutenant, March, 1864; and captain, November, 1864. Lucius F. Renne, appointed first lieutenant, November, 1864; and Clark M. Pease, second lieutenant, November, 1864. This catalogue embraces all the changes in the officers of the company during its service. The company was collected mainly by the zeal and earnest exertions of John Hammond, of Crown Point. The father of Mr. Hammond, Charles F. Hammond, Esq., advanced the funds for the purchase of all the original horses, amounting to one hundred and eight, supplied the company. These horses were selected with extreme care, in reference to their adaptedness to the service, and were probably superior to those of any troop in the army.[1]

This body of men was organized as Company H of the Fifth New York Cavalry, commanded by Colonel Othniel De Forest of New York. The regiment employed the winter of 1861 – 62, at camp Harris near Annapolis in constant and thorough drilling, and acquired the discipline and proficiency, that rendered its subsequent service so efficient and so valuable to the country. This narrative proposes to trace the movements of Company H distinctively and the operations of the regiment, where that company or the soldiers of Essex were prominently connected with them. In April, this company was detached to Luray Valley on special service. Here, in frequent skirmishes, it gradually prepared for the toils and the scenes of peril and hardships which were approaching. It rejoined the regiment in May, and did not participate in some of its

[1] These animals were delivered in New York by contract, at one hundred and thirteen dollars each; but such was the spirit of the men, that they frequently paid from their own means, from five to twenty-five dollars in addition, to secure to themselves a horse they particularly desired.

John Hammond
Col Comdg
5 N.Y.V.C.

earlier achievements, but was with it in the disastrous campaign of General Banks, and the terrible retreat through the mountains, incident to it. A part of the regiment, including Company H, acted as flankers to the army in this retreat, and was exposed perpetually to severe fighting.[1] Throughout the month of July, the regiment was engaged in frequent skirmishes, and was in constant motion, often sufering severely from the want of rations and forage.

On the second of August a brigade composed of most of the Fifth and the First Vermont approached Orange C. H., from the east under the command of General Crawford. The streets were silent and apparently deserted, as the troops entered; but a sudden and heavy fire poured upon them announced a concealed enemy, and while confused by its effect they were repulsed and driven back from the town. Captain Hammond had been detached in charge of Companies G and H across the country to the Gordonsville road which penetrates the village from the southwest. He reached the road, and was approaching with no knowledge of the assault and repulse of the brigade. The Confederates were equally ignorant of his presence. Ordering his command to draw sabres, he said to them: "This is the first favorable opportunity you have had to try your sword; use your hardware well and we will take the place

[1] A single incident will illustrate the character of this service. Captain Hammond, while in the advance with ten men, marching upon the flank, noticed a superior body of rebels in front, and immediately pursued. Leading his men he soon personally came up to their rearmost man, a strong and completely armed soldier. They exchanged several shots, which were without effect, owing to the great speed with which they were riding. Captain Hammond's pistol had become foul and useless, while his antagonist had two chambers undischarged. Hammond lost his in attempting to strike him with the butt, but determined to secure the rebel he seized him by the collar with both hands and tore him from his horse. In the struggle, Hammond's horse also went from under him, and they both fell to the ground. Hammond above, one hand grappling the throat of the rebel and the other hold of his pistol hand, while the rebel was attempting to shoot Hammond. At this moment a private of Company F came up and by Hammond's order fired at the rebel. The ball grazing his head, brought him to surrender.

or die in the attempt." They rushed at full speed upon the enemy in an impetuous charge and with a wild shout. Although surprised, the Confederates met them by a withering discharge of musketry; but the enthusiasm of the cavalry was irresistible. The enemy were driven back to an open space, where they rallied for a moment and then broke and fled in utter disorder. More prisoners were taken than the feeble force were able to secure.

The charge was most gallantly executed and terrible in its effect. The area, in which the rebels made their last stand, was strewn with the killed and wounded, and with unhorsed men bearing fearful evidence of the force of the sabre's blow. When the cavalry, after these events, advanced along the street, they were first apprized by the dead and dying, men and horses, of the preceding combat. Lieutenant Penfield of Company H was peculiarly conspicuous in this brief conflict, by his chivalric bearing. The enemy's force was composed of the celebrated Virginia horse, which had been organized by Ashley.[1]

Soon after this action, a part of the regiment was engaged in the battle of Cedar Mountain. During the month of August it was occupied with brief relaxations, in toilsome marches, reconnaissances and various harassing and exhaustive duties. It participated with great gallantry in the warm engagements at Kelley's Ford and Waterloo, and on the 27th of August was broken up into detachments to perform escort services to different generals. Duties of this character, patroling, observing roads and guarding trains constitute an important part of the operations of

[1] The ludicrous and comic sometimes relieves the grim visage of war. As the command was advancing to the charge, Captain Hammond advised the company's cook, Henry Spaulding, who was leading a pack horse, loaded with frying pans, kettles, and all the paraphernalia of his office, to remain in the rear; but this, he was unwilling to do. Guiding his own and leading the pack horse, with sabre in hand, he kept well up and boldly rushed into the thickest of the affray. The gallant officer who furnished me with the anecdote, remarked that he often doubts, whether the strange din of the kettles combined with the shouting of the men, was not as effective as their sabres.

O'Neill N.Y.

Louis N. Boudrye,
Chaplain 5th N.Y. Cavalry.

cavalry, acting in a campaign under the circumstances which surrounded both armies in the war of the rebellion; but like the trench duties of the other arms of the service, these operations were far the most irksome and onerous imposed upon the mounted regiments, attended often with greater hardships, toils, and perils than actual combats; they were not sustained by the excitement and glory of battle. The movements of the Fifth, with a few brief interludes of repose, were incessant and generally severe. Its history from May, 1862, when it entered into active duty, to April, 1865, presents a remarkable and scarcely parallel series of severe services and hard fought battles. Besides the toils and endurance of this special service, it was engaged in a mass or by detachments in one hundred and eighteen skirmishes and fifty-three battles, necessarily varied in their importance and severity.[1]

The scope of my work will permit me only to glance at some of the most prominent of these events. The Fifth was on the bloody fields of second Bull Run, Chantilly and Antietam. Major Hammond conducting an expedition in October, came in collision with the Confederates at Leesburg, Upperville and Thoroughfare Gap, and engaged in a running fight while pursuing their cavalry from Haymarket to Warrenton. The opening weeks of 1863, were devoted by the regiment to unremitting picket duty charged to oppose and repel the incursions of the guerrillas, that thronged the front of the Union lines. On the 26th January, a detachment was ordered in pursuit of a party which had captured a picket of the Eighteenth Pennsylvania, and at Middleburg, Major Hammond, who was in command, executed a brilliant charge through the town, captured twenty-five of Mosby's cavalry, and dispersed the party. A fortnight later, Captain Penfield in command of

[1] The interesting *Historic Record of the Fifth New York*, by the Rev. Louis N. Boudrye, its chaplain, exhibits a tabular statement of the skirmishes and battles in which the regiment was engaged, with the date and locality of each.

Companies F and H, was engaged in warm skirmishing with large detachments of the enemy at New Baltimore and Warrenton. On the 9th of March, Mosby by a bold movement surprised, at Fairfax C. H., nearly six miles within the Federal lines, an Union detachment and captured thirty prisoners, including General Stoughton and Captain Augustus Barker, of Company L, and fifty choice horses, belonging to the Fifth. These men had been detached from the regiment, and were acting under the command of the provost marshal. The brigade pursued the enemy by different routes, but with no success. On the 23d, the regiment experienced another severe and mortifying reverse. The rebels making a feint attack on a picket retreated rapidly, pursued by a part of the Fifth, in charge of Majors Bacon and White. The pursuers were arrested by a barricade across the road, and suddenly assailed by a sharp fire in front and flank. At this moment Mosby dashed upon them in an unexpected impetuous charge. The cavalry broke and precipitately retreated, with a loss of five killed and wounded, and thirty-six prisoners, including one commissioned officer. It was at length rallied by the efforts of the officers, and reenforced; it in turn repulsed and pursued the enemy a distance of several miles. Yet the chagrin and mortification of the defeat remained. Whatever lustre was lost to the fame of the Fifth by this reverse was gloriously restored on the 3d of May. Early in the morning, the First Virginia cavalry while dismounted, were surprised by Mosby with a detachment of the Black Horse Cavalry and a guerrilla force. Separated from their horses, the First retreated to a house, and courageously defended themselves, refusing to surrender. Mosby then ordered the building to be fired. At that critical juncture, the Fifth, which, without the knowledge of the rebels, was bivouacking in a neighboring grove, burst upon them, under the command of Major Hammond. A furious fight ensued; but the Confederates fled, broken and scattered, sustaining a heavy loss in killed, wounded and prisoners. This gallant exploit was noticed in warm commendation by a special order of the division commander.

On the 30th of May, the rebels, by an adroit expedient, arrested a train advancing by the Orange and Alexandria rail road to the Rapidan, heavily ladened with army supplies, and opened upon it a fire from a twelve-pounder mountain howitzer. The infantry guard upon the train, unable to oppose the storm of cannister, dispersed, and the whole train with its contents was consumed. The Fifth, with the First Vermont and Seventh Michigan cavalry was stationed on the road, and through their encampment the train had just before passed. They were startled by the report of the gun, and those not engaged on picket duty directly mounted, and taking different routes marched across the country with the hope of intercepting the rebel retreat. The Fifth first came upon them and immediately charged; but was repulsed by a discharge of small arms and the howitzer, at close quarters in a narrow road which the guns completely commanded. The officer in command of the Fifth, Capt. Hasbroock, judiciously hesitated on renewing the assault, but Lieutenant Barker of Company H, unwilling to allow the enemy to escape in their triumph, and calling on the men to follow in the charge upon the gun, he dashed up a steep hill at the head of less than a score of volunteers, and when they had nearly reached the howitzer it poured forth a withering shower of cannister, by which the young leader was stricken down with two shot through his thigh, another severing the sole from his boot; his horse received three grape and two pistol balls in his body. Three of the little band were killed and most of the others severely wounded; but before the piece could be reloaded the survivors were sabreing the gunners at their post. After a brief but fierce conflict the howitzer was recaptured, for it had been taken at Ball's bluff, and to the captors it was a proud and grateful trophy. The rebels lost two officers and several men, wounded and captured. In this movement Mosby first introduced his use of artillery.[1]

Soon after this occurrence, the cavalry division to which the Fifth was attached, joined the army of the Potomac in the Gettysburg campaign. On the last day of June, the cavalry division of Kilpatrick, with two batteries of artillery, were defiling through Hanover, Penn. Each regiment, in its passage, was regaled by the patriotic citizens. While the Fifth was in the act of participating in this hospitality, a cannon sounded from an adjacent height. For the moment it was supposed to be connected with the demonstration, but it proved to be a signal gun, and its echo had scarcely ceased, when Stuart, at the head of a large party of cavalry, rushed in a furious assault upon the Eighteenth Pennsylvania, which held the rear of the brigade. Stuart was unexpectedly present with three thousand horse, supported by artillery, and was in occupation of the surrounding hills. With consummate coolness and judgment, Major Hammond, then in command of the Fifth, which in the street received the first shock of the attack, instantly formed the regiment, faced to the rear in column, and charged the enemy's front. A fearful hand to hand conflict in the narrow street succeeded, when the rebels, broken and repulsed, with a heavy loss, sought the protection of their artillery. The casualities of the Fifth were forty killed and wounded, and a few missing. Adjutant Gall was killed while charging in the street, and Major White slightly wounded. The trophies of the Fifth included the commander of a bri-

---

[1] The age of nineteen was attached in the compact I have mentioned to the signature of Elmer J. Barker. On the 9th of February, preceding this action, he suffered a severe contusion by the fall of his horse while charging in the fight at New Baltimore. After receiving the wounds mentioned in the text, he was first carried to the hospital at Fairfax C. H., and subsequently in haste to Alexandria. From thence he was removed to New York, nursed and tenderly cared for by two ladies whose husbands were in the regiment. From New York he was brought by the wife of a distinguished officer to his native mountains, where he recovered from his wounds and returned to the army.

gade, and a battle flag, and a few prisoners. The division was engaged in the afternoon of the 2d of July, with the enemy's cavalry on the left of their line at Gettysburg. Custer, with the second brigade, retained that position through the 3d. The First brigade including the Fifth, under Kilpatrick and Farnsworth, marched all the night of the 2d, and reached the right flank of the rebels about ten o'clock on he 3d, and maintained a vigorous contest through the day. Repeated charges were made upon the enemy's infantry line, in one of which General Farnsworth, the commander of the brigade, gallantly fell. The Fifth, during a part of these events, was left in support of Elder's battery, and exposed to a tremendous cannonade.

On the night of the 4th, the cavalry division intercepted upon the summit of South mountain the enemy with an immense train transporting the spoils of Pennsylvania. After a sharp contest the entire train was captured with fifteen hundred prisoners and two hundred wagons burnt. On the 6th, the division was engaged in the defense of Hagerstown against the attacks of Stuart's cavalry, and in the afternoon of that day retreated before Hood's infantry towards Williamsport amid continuous and severe fighting. In one of the charges in these conflicts the horse of Captain Penfield of Company H was killed under him, and while attempting to extricate himself from the fallen animal he received a fearful sabre cut upon the head, and was taken prisoner. He suffered in the southern prisons until March, 1865, and resigned soon after his exchange. The third division, united with Burford's, maintained on the 8th upon the plains near Antietam creek a severe engagement with Stuart supported by Hood. The conflict was desperate and sanguinary, but in a final charge by the Union cavalry towards the close of the day, the rebels were swept from the field with a heavy loss. On the 14th the division attacked the rear of the retreating enemy near Falling Water, and captured a brigade of infantry under General Pettigrew, who was mortally wounded, two flags and two pieces of cannon. During the remainder of the summer and far into autumn the regiment was incessantly engaged in the severest field duties, attended with frequent bloody collisions with the enemy's horse. On the 10th and 11th of October, the division was involved in a most critical position from a formidable attack by infantry and cavalry in the neighborhood of Culpepper, and near Brandy Station. Surrounded by the enemy, it was only extricated by one of the most daring charges led by Kilpatrick, Davies and Custer that signalized the war. The enemy was checked, and the division united with Burford's, and at night fell back across the Rappahannock. During these operations, Major Hammond, with half of the Fifth, was in support of a section of Elder's battery, while Major White was supporting the other section with the remainder of the regiment, and by a bold and opportune charge they saved the battery from capture. On the 10th of December, Major Hammond and Captain Krom were ordered home on recruiting service, and returned to the regiment before the middle of March, having enlisted five hundred men by great efforts and personal disbursements. A large part of the regiment at this time reentered the service on a new enlistment.

At the approach of the new year of 1864, the Fifth were permitted to construct near Germania Ford its winter quarters; but this promise of repose resulted in only slight actual relaxation of their active patrol service. On the 28th February, the entire third division marched upon a raid of more than usual importance towards Richmond. A detachment of the Fifth was detailed to serve in the subordinate and unfortunate expedition of Colonel Dahlgren, but it embraced no member of Company H. The division encountered in its movement extreme suffering and toil, at length reached the Union lines near Yorktown, were transported to Alexandria, and from thence reached its former camp at Stevensburg. Towards the close of April, the regiment broke up its nominal winter quarters and prepared for the impending campaign. On the 4th of May, the Fifth leading the division forded the Rapidan; the first regiment in this campaign that crossed that stream. Early the next morning a heavy column of infantry appeared on its flank, and a furious conflict immediately commenced. This action was the initiative of the memorable battle of the Wilderness. Colonel Hammond after holding his ground three hours, advised General Meade of the evidently large force in his front, with the assurance that he would "hold them in check as long as possible." By voice and example he maintained the regiment resolutely in hand. A portion of it was dismounted, and assailed the enemy with the Spencer rifle with terrible effect. Until relieved by a part of the sixth corps, the Fifth, with unsurpassed firmness and devotion, confronted for five hours the assailing column, and slowly and defiantly falling back. It performed most valuable service to the army but at a fearful sacrifice to itself. After this brilliant achievement, the Fifth was ordered to bivouac near the Wilderness Tavern, to be under the immediate orders of General Meade.

On the 7th, the Fifth, in conjunction with two other regiments, all under the command of Colonel Hammond, was again in the advance, intrusted with the responsible duty of guarding the fords and picketting the roads. In the afternoon, the command was attacked by cavalry and artillery, and a part giving way, Hammond was compelled to make a rapid retreat down the river. When Grant effected his first flank movement, the Fifth was the last regiment that left the Wilderness. It was in the rear of Burnside's corps, and the command of Hammond, subsequently formed the rear of Hancock's corps. Colonel Hammond was reenforced on the 17th, by the First Massachusetts, twelve hundred strong, with direct orders from General Meade, to destroy the Guineas station, and make a reconnaissance on Lee's flank. He found the enemy strongly fortified on the banks of the Potomac, and a warmly contested action occurred, without dislodging their force. Four days later, the regiment had another severe fight on the Mattapony. On the 23d, it encountered the enemy in large force, near Mt. Carmel church. A furious fight ensued, that brought on a general engagement between the armies, which resulted in the rebels being driven from their strong position on the North Anna. The brigade, on the 1st of June, met the rebels in a conflict of unusual severity, at Ashland station. Although inflicting a heavy loss upon the enemy, it suffered itself severely. Major White of the Fifth, was dangerously wounded, and Colonel Hammond received a ball just above the ankle, that had flattened upon his scabbard. On a previous occasion he had been wounded in the hand. At Salem church the brigade was again engaged, and on the 15th, near White Oaks Swamp, the division suddenly encountered a heavy Confederate column, and after a severely contested action, the division was overwhelmed by superior numbers, suffered heavily, and was compelled to fall back.

General Wilson, who had succeeded Kilpatrick in the command of the Third division, aided by Kautz's brigade of cavalry, and fourteen pieces of flying artillery on the 22d of June, commenced his remarkable raid which was designed to sever the enemy's communications below Richmond. Rushing with the utmost celerity along devious roads and through unfrequented bypaths, it accomplished a vast work of devastation. It first struck the Weldon rail road; it next reached the South Side road; here and everywhere on its march destruction marked its track. Near the close of the second day, it was met by a strong force of the enemy; a sharp engagement followed, protracted long into the night. The Fifth was in the skirmish line, and fought with its usual ardor and efficiency. On the 24th the expedition reached and effectually broke up the Danville road. The next day Kautz was repulsed in an attempt to burn the bridge over the Staunton river. Up to this point, ten important and several smaller stations and depots had been destroyed, and fifty miles of rail road track with their bridges and culverts. The course of the expedition was now describing a wide circle gradually tending towards the Union line. The 28th, it reached the Weldon road, and through the night with brief pauses was engaged in a fight with an infantry force. On the eighth day of its march it again approached Ream's station. The Fifth was leading, and a mile and a half in advance of the column. Here the harassed troops had the assurance of meeting a support, but instead of succor and friends, they were confronted by an impassable barrier, supported by a force of overwhelming strength. The decision was promptly made to attempt a retreat to Rowanty creek and there fortify while scouts should penetrate the rebel lines and apprise General Grant of the critical position of the command. The execution of the plan was attempted, but while the main body was in bivouac it was irresistibly assailed by the rebels on its flanks and rear and utterly routed. I am unable to trace the incidents by which the command, broken up and scattered, reached the Federal lines by detachments, in small parties and individually, many after several days of severe suffering. The artillery, wagons and trains were lost. Many of the troops were slain and numerous prisoners and horses left in the enemy's hands. Hundreds of slaves, who had gathered in joyous exultation around the column, were abandoned to their fate.

The shattered Fifth, after its fearful endurance in this expedition, was allowed a brief period of repose, but on the 6th of August, the whole division was embarked on transports at City Point and transferred to a new field of action with the army of the Shenandoah. A number of the regiment, who were disabled or had lost their horses in the raid, had been previously sent to camp Stoneman near Washington, participated in the series of battles fought the month of July in upper Maryland. The Fifth was soon after actively engaged in picket duty, in aiding to cover Sheridan's retreat from Cedar creek, slowly falling back amid incessant conflicts. On the 25th of August, the first and third divisions of cavalry met a heavy force of the enemy under Breckenridge, and after a protracted engagement were forced to retreat. The regiment lost a number in killed and wounded, including Lieutenant Greenleaf commanding Company A; mortally wounded. At night it moved to the Potomac, and crossing at Maryland heights on a pontoon bridge, it did not pause until it reached Antietam creek. Two days afterwards the division recrossed the Potomac and with the army again assumed an offensive attitude.

The term of Colonel Hammond's service having expired and private duties constraining his return to civil life, on the 30th of August, he bade a formal farewell to the noble regiment he had so long commanded and led through a series of such brilliant services. An infinitude of toils and privation, of perils and triumphs and a common fame, had united the officers and men of the Fifth by no ordinary ties of cordial affection, and fraternal sympathy. As no man had entered the service of the country from loftier impulses than Colonel Hammond, so no officer of his grade left the army with a higher reputation. He was succeeded in the command of the regiment by Lieutenant Colonel Bacon.[1]

In the early part of September, the brigade was constantly engaged with the enemy's forces, and on the 13th captured at Opequan the South Carolina Eighth with its colonel and standard. On the 19th, it was engaged in the terrible battle near Winchester, and during that day executed five distinct charges, four of which were against the close serried ranks of infantry. Its losses were heavy, but its bearing was eminently conspicuous. Advancing in the pursuit of the enemy, the regiment was exposed near Ashbury church to a furious shelling, such as it had never before experienced; but it maintained its position

[1] The application of Colonel Hammond to be mustered out, was approved by General Wilson, in an endorsement from which I make the following extracts: "Colonel Hammond is a most valuable and worthy officer, and has served with great credit to himself, and benefit to the service." General Torbet in his approval writes: "I am pleased to mention from personal observation, that he is one of the most accomplished officers I have known in the service, and the country can ill afford to lose the services of such an officer at this time."—*Boudrye.*

with unfaltering firmness and tenacity. Through the month of September it had trifling relief from incessant and harassing duty in patroling, forming escort, and in actual conflict. During this period, one of the most sad and revolting services was imposed on the Fifth, that the harsh severity of warfare exacts from the soldier. A Lieutenant Meigs of the Union army had been barbarously assassinated by unknown persons residing near Dayton. The government deemed a stern retaliatory example demanded, and ordered every edifice to be burnt in an area of three miles. The regiment was detailed to execute this fearful retribution. Numerous splendid mansions and happy homes were consigned to the torch, without any discrimination between the innocent and guilty; but the impulses of compassion at length prevailed and the order was arrested before the devastation reached the pleasant village of Dayton. During several successive days, the regiment was employed in the burning of forage and grain and the destruction of mills; a ruthless necessity of war, that marked the course of Sheridan's army with ashes and ruin.

Determined to arrest the harassing assaults of the enemy upon the Union pickets and rear, Custer, with the Third division on the 9th of October turned back upon and attacked them in one of the most spirited cavalry actions of the war. Amid the animating clangor of the bugles along the whole front, sounding the charge, the entire line rushed forward; Custer himself at the head of the Fifth dashed upon the rebel's strong central position. The issue formed a brilliant success to the federal troops. On the 19th, the division was lying at Cedar creek with the Union army, and indulging in its fatal security. It endured the common disasters incident to the surprise and rout, and fully participated in the crowning victory wrought by the marvellous inspirations of Sheridan. Near the close of the day, the Confederates made a final and desperate effort to redeem its fortunes, by a cavalry attack upon the flank of the Union army. This movement, Custer was ordered to repel. Torn by the Union artillery, and at sundown assailed by the whole line, the rebels broke and fled in a disordered rout. At that moment, the Third division burst upon them in a merciless pursuit. There was no cheering; no sounding of trumpets, and the flying enemy were admonished of impending slaughter only by the trampling of pursuing horses. At length they halt and pour a volley upon the Union cavalry. Then the bugles sounded and Custer and his men were in their midst, and a scene of carnage ensued that had scarcely a parrallel in the war. A bloody track, weapons broken or abandoned, the bodies of the dead and wounded, attested the horrors of the flight. For five miles the pursuit continued, until darkness spread its compassionate mantle over the frightful spectacle. Captain Barker of Company H, by the personal command of Custer, had led the charge. The Fifth, commanded in the field by Major A. H. Krom, gleaned immense spoils from the common harvest of the great victory.[1]

The Second and Third divisions of cavalry while engaged in a reconnaissance on the 22d of November, near Mt. Jackson, were involved in a hard fought battle, and again the Fifth was peculiarly distinguished, in repelling by a bold and vigorous movement a flank attack on the column by the Confederate cavalry. On the 25th, the regiment was ordered into camp near the headquarters of the commanding general, and a few days after was allowed to construct its winter quarters near Winchester. On the 27th of February, 1865, Sheridan moved with the cavalry

---

[1] This is attested by the official receipt: "Received of the Fifth New York Cavalry commanded by Major A. H. Krom, twenty-two pieces of artillery, fourteen caissons, one battery wagon, seventeen army wagons, six spring wagons and ambulances, eighty-three sets of artillery harness, seventy-five sets of wagon harness, ninety-eight horses, sixty-seven mules, captured in action in the battle of the 19th October, 1864, at Cedar Creek, Va. A. C. M. Pennington, Jr., colonel commanding brigade." General Custer, in an enthusiastic address to the Third division, among other high panegyrics on its achievement, exclaims: "Again, during the memorable engagement of the 19th, your conduct throughout was sublimely heroic and without a parallel in the annals of warfare."

of the Shenandoah towards Staunton, and on the 1st of March at Waynesboro', nearly annihilated the relics of Early's army. Fourteen hundred prisoners were among the fruits of this victory. Sheridan decided to transfer most of these to the Union rear, and the Fifth, under Colonel Boice, with broken parties of other regiments, amounting in all to about one thousand men, was detached as their escort. The distance was more than one hundred miles, through a country infested by guerrilla bands, and occupied by General Rosser, an alert and energetic rebel leader. The service was difficult and perilous, but was successfully executed. Rosser made a vehement effort to rescue the prisoners, but was repulsed with a severe loss, leaving a number of his troops to augment the aggregate of prisoners. General Sheridan had detained about his own person a small detachment of the Fifth, selected for special duty. These accompanied him on his trying march to the James; participated with their wonted efficiency in the closing battles of the war, and were present at the surrender of Lee.

The main body of the regiment performed on the 19th of May its final service in an expedition to Lexington, Va., to effect the arrest of Governor Letcher, and on the 19th of July it received its last general orders, directing its return to New York, to be there mustered out of service and discharged. By an auspicious fortune the Fifth had fought at Hanover, Pa., the first battle on free soil; it was the first Union regiment that crossed the Rapidan in Grant's campaign; it received the first shock at the battle of the Wilderness, and was the last to leave the field.[1]

The One Hundred and Eighteenth New York Volunteers.

This gallant regiment was recruited entirely in the sixteenth congressional district, and throughout its whole

[1] Besides official documents, I am largely indebted to the Rev. Mr. Boudrye's *Historic Record of the Fifth* for the facts I have embodied in the preceding pages. I have also received valuable information from officers connected with the regiment.

career, was an object of peculiar pride and solicitude to the people of that district. Its organization embraced three companies from Warren county, A, D, G; three from Clinton county, B, H, I; three from Essex county, C, E, F; and one, K, from Essex and Clinton. The latter company was enrolled chiefly in the Au Sable valley; a part in Peru, and a small portion, including the captain, were residents of Jay. The regiment, with great appropriateness designated the Adirondac, was mustered into service the 29th August, 1862, with Samuel F. Richards of Warrensburg, colonel, Oliver Keese, Jr., of Keeseville, lieutenant-colonel, and George F. Nichols, of Plattsburgh, major. By the successive resignations in both cases from severe sickness, of Colonel Richards in the summer of 1863, and Keese, in May, 1864, Major Nichols was promoted to the command of the regiment, and led it with distinguished skill and courage in many of the severe conflicts it encountered. Colonel Keese, during his command of the regiment, was usually in the performance of active duty in the field. At the mustering in, the officers of Company C were James H. Pierce of St. Armands, Captain Nathan L. Washburn of Wilmington, first, and George M. Butrick of Jay, second lieutenant; the two latter resigned in 1863, and were succeeded by George F. Campbell and Luther S. Bryant. Of Company E, Jacob Parmerter of North Hudson was captain, Joseph R. Seaman of Schroon, first lieutenant, who was promoted to the captaincy of Company A, and came home in that command; and John Brydon of Crown Point second lieutenant, who succeeded Seaman, was promoted to the command of Company K, was afterwards in the ordnance department and general staff, and brevetted major. Sergeant Edgar A. Wing succeeded Brydon and Sergeant J. Wesley Treadway, promoted to second lieutenant; in November, 1864, first lieutenant Company A. Corporal M. V. B. Knox was promoted second lieutenant Colored Volunteers, and left the service with rank of captain. In Company F, Robert W. Livingstone of Elizabethtown, was captain, and received the brevet of major; John L. Cunningham, of Essex, first lieutenant, was promoted in 1863, to captain of Company D, and to major in 1864, and brevetted lieutenant-colonel; and William H. Stevenson of Moriah, second lieutenant, who succeeded Cunningham. Henry J. Northrop was appointed second lieutenant in 1864; Daniel A. O'Connor was promoted to first lieutenant in 1864, and came home in acting command of company. Charles A. Grace was promoted to second lieutenant. Henry J. Adams and Nelson J. Gibbs were promoted from this company to lieutenancies in Companies G, and I. Adams was afterwards advanced to captain and commissioner of subsistence and brevet major, N. Y. V. Rowland C. Kellogg, promoted to second, soon after first lieutenant Company D, and in 1864 appointed captain in commissary department. The officers of Company K were John S. Stone of Jay, captain, John H. Boynton of Peru, first lieutenant, resigned in spring of 1864 and succeeded by Sam Sherman of Company D. Henry M. Mould, of Keeseville, second lieutenant resigned in 1863 and succeeded by Charles W. Wells, who was promoted to captaincy of Company C, and came home in command. Philip V. N. McLean was promoted from this company to second lieutenant Company D. Charles E. Pruyn was adjutant of the regiment on the organization. Patrick H. Delany, quarter master; John K. Mooers, surgeon, James G. Porteous, assistant, promoted to surgeon in Forty sixth, and Charles L. Hagar, chaplain.

The One Hundred and Eighteenth regiment entered the service with an aggregate of nine hundred and eighty-three men; it was reenforced at intervals, by three hundred and fifty recruits, but returned from the field at the expiration of its term with only three hundred and twenty-three in its ranks, embracing both officers and privates. Immediately upon joining the army the regiment commenced a series of active and incessant duties. It formed a part of Peck's force, in the memorable defense of Suffolk, and was employed in the arduous raids along the

Black river. It was warmly engaged through two days and often under heavy fire, in a continued skirmish with the rebel sharp-shooters near Suffolk, and participated in the feint upon Richmond in June, 1863. The brigade to which the One Hundred and Eighteenth regiment was attached was in the advance, and the regiment was ordered to destroy parts of the Richmond and Fredericksburg rail road. While the regiment was engaged in executing this service, two companies, A, Captain Norris, and F in the absence from severe sickness of Captain Livingstone commanded by Lieutenant Cunningham, were advanced as skirmishers along the rail road, towards the South Anna river, and after cautiously proceeding about one mile came in contact with the rebel pickets. The command continued to advance in line under a sharp and constant fire, the enemy slowly retiring, and speedily in addition to small arms they opened a fire on the Union troops from batteries in front commanding the line of the rail road and on a flank. The companies under this concentrated fire were compelled to retreat and fell back in order, assuming a strong position in a wood, behind a ditch with an open field in front. During this movement, Lieutenant Cunningham received a painful wound from a spent ball, but did not leave the field. Major Nichols soon after appeared on the ground with two fresh companies, D, Captain Riggs, and a company of the Ninety-ninth New York. These companies deployed on either side, and the line thus formed made a rapid advance. A warm action ensued in which the command was subjected to a heavy fire of mingled bullets, shot and shells. The enemy were at length driven back along their whole front, except at one point in their position, which was obstinately maintained and appeared to be fortified. This point, which proved to be a breastwork of plank, Lieutenant W. H. Stevenson of Company F proposed to capture; and calling for volunteers for the service, selected five of the first who offered. He rapidly advanced in the dark behind a screen of bushes, which flanked the rebel's position on the right, and with fixed bayonets and loaded guns rushed upon the breastwork with a wild shout. Although surprised, the enemy attempted a resistance, but the gallant Stevenson killed one with his revolver, wounded a second and captured the remainder of the party consisting of thirteen men, who were brought into the Federal lines. This dashing exploit initiated the brief though brilliant career of the stripling hero. The constancy and resolution of the regiment was first tested on this occasion, and the conduct of the officers engaged and the steadiness and discipline of the troops received the highest encomiums.

The One Hundred and Eighteenth continued attached to the column of the James until the spring of 1864, and was engaged in operations near Norfolk and Bermuda Hundred. It composed a portion of Wistar's command, when it advanced to Bottom's Bridge from Williamsburg, in an attempt upon Richmond.

It at this time constituted a part of the second brigade, first division of the eighteenth corps. General W. F. Smith commanded the corps, Brooks the division, and Burnham the brigade. All these officers were eminently distinguished by their fighting qualities and high reputation. Early in May, the army marched upon the ill-omened expedition against Fort Darling on the James, which was terminated by the fatal results at Drury's Bluff. The march from the commencement to its disastrous issue, was a constant scene of fighting and skirmishes. On the tenth, Companies D, F, and K, were advanced in a skirmishing line, the last held in reserve, while the remainder of the regiment was deployed. The coolness and bearing of Lieutenant Stevenson of F, and Kellogg of Company D, were conspicuous, and the steadiness of the whole line was eminently distinguished.[1]

The One Hundred and Eighteenth, four days after, captured with small loss a series of rifle pits, redoubts and batteries, which formed a strong advance line of the enemy.

---

[1] The firmness and constancy of the skirmishing line drew out from Burnham's adjutant general, the emphatic tribute: "There is a line the rebels can't break."

This work from the form of its construction afforded no protection to the Federal troops. The enemy occupied a short distance in front, far more formidable works mounted with heavy guns, and during the whole day the second brigade was exposed to a severe fire of shells from this work. One of the missiles crushed the head of Sergeant Place of Company K, a brave and intelligent soldier. Throughout Sunday, the 15th, the brigade maintained this exposed position, which was soon to acquire a dread and bloody prominence in one of the darkest pages of the war. Heckman's brigade, lying to the right of the Second, formed the extreme right of the army line. Between Heckman's brigade and the James, there was an interval of a mile in length, which was left unoccupied, except by a few feeble and scattering posts of colored cavalry. No entrenchments had been constructed either in front of the Union lines or on the flank; excepting such as were hastily thrown up, under the direction of commanders of particular brigades or regiments. The ground had been previously occupied by the Confederates, by whom scattered and irregular redoubts, trenches and rifle pits were constructed; but these were so arranged that they afforded no protection to the Union troops in their present position. The line held by the second brigade, stretched along a deep excavation which had been made by the rebels, and at this time was filled with water. A standing place was formed for the brigade, by levelling a narrow space, between this ditch and the embankment created by the earth thrown up in its construction.[1] Slight bridges were at short intervals thrown across the Trench. These precautions proved a few hours later of infinite importance. The embankment was thus converted into an imperfect defense, which in the subsequent action afforded great protection to the troops. General Brooks conceived the novel and happy idea of

[1] Contrary to the prevailing opinion I am assured by an officer who participated in the campaign that the One Hundred and Eighteenth, at least was supplied with entrenching tools.

extending a telegraph wire in front of the brigade; but unfortunately, Heckman's brigade was without even this feeble protection, and lay totally exposed to the assault of a vigilant foe.[1]

At three o'clock on the morning of the 16th, the One Hundred and Eighteenth was aroused and at its post, in conformity to special orders, or its established practice. The air was loaded with a thick, dank fog, which the opening dawn but slightly dissipated. As sun-rise approached, the advance or movement of troops was noticed in front, but in the obscure light, the color of their uniform could not be distinguished, nor their evolutions determined. A few shots from Belger's artillery, in front of the brigade, were thrown into the ravine along which these troops were advancing, and they were seen to halt and lie down. A staff officer, who at that moment appeared on the field, pronouncing them to be federal pickets retiring, and ordered the firing to cease. Small white flags or signals were distinctly discerned, waving in the mist, and voices shouted from the obscurity, " Don't fire on your friends." The musketry had already become sharp on the right, but the second brigade had received no orders of any kind. There was a period of fearful suspense and hesitation. Captain Ramson of Company I, unable to restrain his impatience, leaped upon the embankment, and firing his revolver, exclaimed: " This is my reception of such friends." The last chamber was scarcely exploded, when he fell, pierced by a ball that passed through his body, and shattered an arm. Doubt no longer existed of the character or purpose of these troops, and the One Hundred and Eighteenth instantly poured a volley into the advancing line. The front rank of the enemy now rushing impetuously forward, and in the dimness of the light, stumbled over the wires, and those in the rear pressing after them, all were hurled together

---

[1]The inspiration I have imputed to General Brooks has been also ascribed to other sources.

in a promiscuous mass; their ranks broken and thrown into inextricable disorder. Many of the enemy involved in this confusion, threw down their arms and surrendered, and were sent to the rear. Up to this point, the One Hundred and Eighteenth had achieved a success. It was vigilant, and the contemplated surprise had been defeated; but Heckman's brigade was surprised and nearly flanked, from the undefended space on its right. It had fallen back, and at one time the whole brigade were prisoners; but in the tumult, and amid the dense mist and smoke, escaped. The Eighth Connecticut, next on the right of the One Hundred and Eighteenth, was attacked in flank, doubled up and disappeared from the field. The One Hundred and Eighteenth was now exposed to a crushing fire in front and upon the right flank. The extemporaneous traverses which it had constructed at this crisis, were most effective, affording a partial protection, and for awhile the resistance of the regiment appeared to be successful; but it was enveloped by an overwhelming force, and a terrific and sanguinary conflict ensued. In this desperate aspect of the battle, each man was directed to gain the rear without regard to discipline. A few embraced the opportunity to retreat; others still sustained the fight, while the wounded implored their comrades not to abandon them, and more than one noble life was sacrificed to preserve these sufferers from the horrid calamities of a hostile prison house. The regiment was soon after rallied, and made a gallant stand; but was compelled to fall back: again advanced a short space, and ultimately retreated in order. Captain Dominy, the senior officer, succeeded to the temporary command of the regiment, on the disability of Colonel Nichols.

The dire aceldama was ennobled by deeds of daring heroism, and instances of exalted devotion. An intrepid young lieutenant, Henry J. Adams, of Elizabethtown, at the moment the regiment was breaking, seized a standard, and shouting the words so familiar to scenes of home and festive joyousness: "Rally round the flag, boys," attempted to arrest the retreat, and essentially aided in rallying the troops. Captain Robert W. Livingstone of Company F, early in the action, moved from the cover of the embankment in order to communicate with Colonel Nichols, and while standing a moment exposed, was struck down by a frightful wound in the shoulder. His gallant young lieutenent, W. H. Stevenson, who was behind an embankment and in a situation comparatively secure, saw him fall, and calling on the men to bring in their captain, rushed out to Livingstone's assistance, accompanied by four of the company. Livingstone admonished them of the great exposure they incurred, and urged that he might be left; but Stevenson persisted in his generous purpose, and in a moment after fell dead at his commander's side, a sacrifice to duty and friendship. Two of the brave men[1] were prostrated by wounds, were captured and died in southern prisons. Livingstone, as he was borne from the field, was struck by another shot, that terribly lacerated his foot and leg. He languished in great suffering fourteen months in a hospital, before his severe wounds permitted a return to his home, a mutilated and disabled soldier.[2]

The regiment was not pursued by the severely punished enemy and was immediately rallied by its own officers. It maintained a bold and defiant attitude until most of its wounded were borne from the field. In that conflict, scarcely extending over the space of half an hour, the One Hundred and Eighteenth out of the three hundred and fifty men engaged lost one hundred and ninety-eight privates and thirteen officers in killed, wounded and prisoners. Amid all these disasters and sacrifices, the regiment had captured and secured two hundred prisoners,

---

[1] George Miller and William Huff. Their names are worthy of commemmoration.

[2] Captain Livingstone gives utterance to this just and feeling tribute to the memory of Stevenson: "No more gallant and generous spirit was offered among the victims of the war." No praise of Lieutenant Stevenson—his gallant ardor—his dash—his generous friendship, can be misplaced.—*Major Livingstone's Letter.*

a greater number than it retained men fit for duty. Among the killed on this fatal day was Captain John S. Stone of Company K.[1] Lieutenant Stevenson was killed and Lieutenant Edgar A. Wing, Company E, a youth of high promise who had joined the company only a few days before, was mortally wounded, taken prisoner and died the next day. Lieutenant Colonel Nichols was slightly wounded in the side and hand, from which his sword was stricken by a shot; and his clothing, as was that of several other officers, was riddled by bullets. Adjutant John M. Carter lost an arm and was captured; Captain Livingstone and Ransom were severely wounded; Lieutenants Treadway and Sherman were wounded, and Captain Dennis Stone, Company A, and James H. Pierce, Company C, taken prisoners. The army on the same day fell back to Bermuda Hundred and fortified; but the stricken and fragmentary One Hundred and Eighteenth were exempted from the toil of entrenching.

On the 29th of May the eighteenth corps, embracing the One Hundred and Eighteenth, embarked in transports, and passing down the James, ascended the Pamunky and landed at the White House. Directly upon disembarking it was rushed to the front, and on the 1st of June joined the army of the Potomac. On that day near Coal Harbor commenced a battle which continued until the 3d, and was one of the most severely contested and sanguinary engagements of the war; but its incidents and results have been singularly veiled from the public eye. The Eighteenth corps occupied a position in front of the Union army. The One Hundred and Eighteenth was engaged in the bloody scenes of these conflicts, but not unconnected with its corps. Its casualties were extremely severe. At times exposed to a heavy fire in front and enfiladed by a battery and rifle

---

[1] Captain Stone, before entering the army, was pastor of the Presbyterian church at Au Sable Forks. Although singularly modest and retiring in his habits, he was disposed from the impulses of duty to engage in the conflict, and when a large number of the intelligent and energetic youth of the vicinity offered to enlist under his command, he freely and promptly offered his services to the country.

pits, to escape annihilation the troops were compelled to lie prone upon the earth, while a tempest of minie balls, shot and shells, hurtled just above them. The dead could neither be removed nor buried, and their corpses were thrown upon the breastwork, with a slight covering of earth strewn upon them, and thus their decaying bodies aided to form a bulwark for the protection of their living comrades. The taint from the decomposing mass became almost insufferable, before the corps was withdrawn from the trenches.[1] The sufferings of the regiment through the trying ordeal of those eight days were extreme. It lost at Coal Harbor seventy men and officers. Among the casualties were Lieutenant Michael Reynolds of Company A, killed, and Captain Jacob Parmerter of Company E severely wounded with the loss of a leg.

An impregnable line in front arrested all advance by the Union army, but the enemy was held in an equally tenacious and unyielding grasp. The eighteenth corps sustained its exposed position, and in the end formed a curtain behind which, on the 12th, General Grant accomplished his perilous and memorable flank movement which effected the change of his base. When this bold and remarkable operation had been accomplished, the Eighteenth, also, hastily abandoned its entrenchments and fell back unopposed to White House, and returned to its previous field of duty. On the 15th of June, the One Hundred and Eighteenth was engaged in the attack on Petersburg. Here it suffered a heavy loss in the death of Major Charles E. Pruyn, who was in temporary command of the regiment. While standing in an exposed position, and in the act of surveying the works he was preparing to assault, he was struck and horribly mutilated by a shell. He had acted as adjutant in the organization of the regiment, and its singular proficiency and high disci-

---

[1] An intelligent and gallant officer who was present in some of the most severe battles of the war, said to me that the terrible fighting at Coal Harbor "far exceeded anything he had witnessed; that the field was literally swept by the storm of bullets, and that a hat raised a short space from the ground would instantly be riddled by balls."

pline were chiefly imputed to the skill and assiduity of his services, sustained by the field officers preeminently by the military attainments and persistent zeal of Colonel Keese.[1] Lieutenant Rowland C. Kellogg was also wounded by the explosion of a shell. Captain Levi S. Dominy of Company B succeeded to the immediate command of the regiment.

The fierce and protracted siege of Petersburg exacted from the One Hundred and Eighteenth the most arduous and exhaustive duties. Night succeeded the day, days rolled into weeks, and the weeks formed months, but their toils had no mitigation, while their endurance and dangers were perpetual. Now exposed to the burning sun and breathing the arid sand, and now struggling in mud and water; often suffering for drink, seldom able to wash, and never changing their clothing for rest. Constantly shelled and frequently enfiladed by new batteries; burrowing in the earth to escape projectiles, against which ordinary entrenchments afforded no protection, the troops were yet joyous, patient, enduring and full of hope. Amid all these exposures and suffering, after it had recovered from an almost universal prostration by chills and fever at Gloucester point, and although moving in a malarious region, the One Hundred and Eighteenth was always vigorous and healthy. The rigorous ordeal to which it was now subjected, continued with brief relief until the 29th of July, when the regiment was withdrawn to aid in the support of the storming column, which was designed to assail the enemy's works, on the explosion of the long projected mine. They witnessed in sadness and humiliation the disastrous failure of that magnificent experiment. On the 27th of August, after a term of two months, the second brigade was relieved from its arduous trench duties. During the long period of one hundred and thir-

[1] Major Pruyn had been first lieutenant in the Ninety-seventh, but resigned and became attached to the One Hundred and Eighteenth. In the summer of 1863 he was appointed major, on the recommendation of a large part of the line officers of the regiment, a majority of whom held senior rank.—*Major Livingstone's letter.*

Chas. E. Pruyn

teen days, the One Hundred and Eighteenth had marched and toiled, and endured, with no enjoyment of quiet repose, and almost incessantly subjected to the fire of the enemy.

A single month, the One Hundred and Eighteenth was permitted to repose, after its prolonged and severe service, in a pleasant encampment near the southern banks of the James. In that interval, the Ninety-sixth had been attached to the second brigade. This brigade, by the proficiency of its drill, its exact discipline, and general efficiency, had become conspicuous and universally esteemed second to no other in its distinguished corps. On the 27th September, every indication presaged the renewal of active duty. Rations for two days were ordered to be prepared. An unusual earnestness and activity were manifested by the generals and their staffs. The next night, the tattoo, suggestive of repose, had scarcely sounded, when the brigade was ordered to move promptly and in profound silence, leaving their tents standing. Previous to breaking camp, the One Hundred and Eighteenth and the Tenth New Hampshire had by a special order exchanged their Enfield guns for the Spencer repeating rifle, a tremendous weapon in the hands of resolute and expert marksmen. This selection by the corps commander was a distinguished recognition of the efficiency of the preferred regiments. At three o'clock on the morning of the 29th, the division led by the second brigade, was passing over the James upon a pontoon bridge, which had been completed the same hour. The sound of the movement was suppressed by earth or other substances strewn upon the bridge. On reaching the north bank of the river, the One Hundred and Eighteenth and Tenth New Hampshire were thrown out as skirmishers and flankers, while the remainder of the command was advanced along the road in column. Soon after daybreak a brisk fire was opened by the enemy's pickets which fell back on their reserves, and the whole were forced rapidly back through a dense wood, for the distance of more than two miles, when the Union column entered upon open ground. A strong earth work was now revealed in front, and mounted with heavy guns. This formidable work, was Fort or rather Battery Harrison, and General Stannard instantly ordered Burnham to take it by assault. The Ninety-sixth and Eighth Connecticut forming the storming column were supported by the First and Third brigade of the division with the One Hundred and Eighteenth New York, and Twelfth New Hampshire as skirmishers on their flank. The column rushed impetuously forward, along the open space, met by a furious plunging fire from the enemy's lines. When it reached, after this rapid advance along a distance of nearly three-fourths of a mile, the base of the eminence upon which the works were erected, the column breathless and exhausted, paused in a position comparatively protected. As we have already seen, the enemy was hastening reenforcements to the point of attack, and the commander both of the division and brigade, alarmed at the posture of affairs, sent a member of his staff to order an instant assault. Lieutenant George F. Campbell, Company C, One Hundred and Eighteenth, aid to General Burnham, dashed across the plains exposed to the whole range of the enemy's fire and unhurt communicated the order. In the strong tribute of the official address, this was pronounced a most gallant act. The two regiments impetuously scaled the hill, mounted the parapet, and their gallant color-bearers planted simultaneously their flags upon the works. The enemy precipitately abandoned the lines, falling back to other works, while their own guns were turned upon them, with deadly effect. In the act of training one of these guns upon the fugitives, General Burnham was mortally wounded and died in a few minutes after.

While these events were in progress in the centre, the skirmishing support had approached the fort, and used their terrible rifles in picking off the gunners in the works, and demoralizing the defense. Lieutenant-colonel Nichols, with the One Hundred and Eighteenth, after being distinguished "for his cool conduct of the skirmish lines in the general assault, captured two redoubts on the right of the fort, during the main assault. Lieutenants N. J. Gibbs and H. J. Adams, were the first men in the redoubts, and promptly turned the captured guns upon the retreating enemy. Surgeon F. G. Porteous, of the One Hundred and Eighteenth, was officially noticed with strong recommendations for bravery and attention to duties, being the only surgeon in the brigade, advancing with his regiment in the charging column."[1] The second brigade now moved upon two entrenchments in front, and captured them successfully, driving the enemy back upon their third and last defense on this line of works. Fort Harrison had thus been snatched from the jaws of the Confederate army, which lay in great force immediately contiguous, and was too important a position to be relinquished without a desperate struggle. The last line captured by the Union troops was exposed to the fire of the enemy's gun-boats and to assault, and it was deemed expedient to fall back upon Fort Harrison. The enemy vigorously pursued, and in this movement both Colonel Donohoe and Lieutenant-colonel Nichols were severely wounded. The night and the succeeding morning were assiduously employed in extending and strengthening the works, which now acquired the form and strength of an enclosed fortification. A second and third time the onset was repeated, and met in the same courageous spirit, and with similar results. On the last assault, those of the assailants who survived the withering fire of the federal troops, threw down their arms and surrendered. About noon the next day, rebel troops had been massed in three heavy columns, and covered by two batteries, rushed upon the new federal lines with heroic impetuosity. The One Hundred and Eighteenth and Tenth New Hampshire were stationed at salient points in the works, and the fatal power of their new weapons was frightfully demon-

[1] These notices of the One Hundred and Eighteenth, I extract from the address of General Butler to the army of the James. He also refers with warm approbation to the conduct of Corporal Michael Finnigan, and Private Frank Jandrew, of the regiment.

strated upon the Confederate ranks. Gun-boats were constantly, but with trifling effect, shelling the Union position. This formidable assault was repulsed by musketry alone, and the rebels falling back to cover, abandoned their numerous dead and wounded upon the field.

In the critical period between the two first assaults, a gallant act occurred that reflected the highest credit upon the bravery and zeal of Captain Brydon of the One Hundred and Eighteenth.[1] Twenty-two pieces of cannon, several battle flags and numerous prisoners were among the results of this enterprise which secured to the Union army an important position that was never relinquished. The confederate loss was known to be very large. Clingman's North Carolina brigade was almost annihilated. The federal loss amounted to nearly one-fifth of their combatants engaged. Besides Lieutenant Colonel Nichols, Captain Dobie and Lieutenant Treadway of the One Hundred and Eighteenth were wounded.

The One Hundred and Eighteenth moved with its division from the quarters near Fort Burnham where it had remained since the capture of that work, on the 26th of October, to a position within about three miles of Fort Richmond, erected on the former battle-ground of Fair Oaks. The regiment at that time was composed of two hundred and five men for duty including supernumeraries. At dawn the succeeding morning it advanced. That part of the regiment embracing more than half which was

---

[1] "Finding that my ammunition was getting low — I had a few minutes before sent a staff officer with orders to bring up a wagon from my ordnance train: the wagon came just at the right time, during the second assault, and was driven up to the sally-port of the fort by Captain John Brydon, One Hundred and Eighteenth New York Volunteers, A. O. O., of the division, and kept there until the action was concluded. It was in full view and but short musket range from the enemy, yet Captain Brydon gallantly held his mules, three of which were killed and three wounded while he was thus occupied, while Lieutenants Burbank and Cook of my staff distributed the ammunition to the command."— *General Stannard's Report.* For this gallant feat Captain Brydon received from the governor, with words of warm encomium, the brevet of major.

armed with Spencer rifles, was thrown in front as skirmishers, and the remainder held in reserve. Passing a covert of woods, the skirmishers entered upon a cleared field, which extended to the fort a distance of about one-fourth of a mile. Over this space, they made a rush upon the work, in the face of a terrible fire, and succeeded in approaching it within about one hundred yards. The enemy's lines at this moment were only slightly manned, but the entrenchment was heavy and formidable, and wholly unassailable by the feeble skirmishing force. Major Dominy, an officer conspicuous for his fighting qualities, commanded the regiment, and at this time passed an order for the troops to lie down, seeking any cover that presented itself, for protection against the irresistible tempest of shot and balls that was hurled upon them. Soon after, they were directed to fall back singly to an excavation on a road in the rear. The regiment made no further advance, but after the repulse of the assaulting column mentioned in the notice of the Ninety-sixth regiment, retreated to its former encampment.

The losses of the regiment were greater in proportion to its strength than on any previous occasion. The skirmishing party entered into action with nine officers: three of these, Major Dominy, Lieutenants McLean and Gibbs returned in safety, but Captain J. R. Seaman, Company A, was seriously wounded. Lieutenant M. J. Dickinson was wounded and taken prisoner, with Lieutenants Saunders, Potter, O'Connor, and Bryant. Captain M. V. B. Stetson in the reserve was also wounded while aiding to remove Colonel Moffitt of the Ninety-fifth from the field. When the regiment reached its former quarters, scarcely forty men had gathered to its standard, but others returned until the aggregate was increased to nearly one-half the number who had marched out the day preceding. The One Hundred and Eighteenth remained in camp through the winter, and on the march upon Richmond the ensuing spring, its relics were engaged on picket duty and advanced as skirmishers, covering the third division of the twenty-fourth corps. It was the first organized Federal regiment that entered Richmond. The One Hundred and Eighteenth bore the noble inscription upon its national flag: "Suffolk—South Anna—Coal Harbor—Fort Harrison—Bermuda—Swift Creek—Petersburg — Fair Oaks — Drury's Bluff— Crater — Richmond." This attests its military glory, but its high moral qualities are still more illustrated by the remarkable fact, that not a single member of the regiment was known to have deserted to the enemy. In more authoritative language than I can use, General Devens, in recapitulating its services, pronounces this eulogium upon the One Hundred and Eighteenth at Drury's Bluff: "This regiment distinguished itself for great valor and pertinacity, and won the reputation it has since enjoyed, of being one of the most resolute regiments in the service." He adds: "With this weapon (the Spencer rifle) they will return to your state armed, and it is a most appropriate testimonial of their efficiency."[1] I have been guided essentially in the brief survey of the operations of the One Hundred and Eighteenth by official documents. I owe my acknowledgments, also, to a series of articles first published in the *Glen's Falls Republican* as to other authentic newspaper correspondences, but particularly to officers of the regiment from whom I have derived the most valuable information; among these I may enumerate Colonel Nichols, Majors Livingstone and Brydon, and Lieutenant McLean.

Officers of the One Hundred and Eighteenth Regiment, when mustered out of the service, June 13*th*, 1865.

Col. George F. Nichols, brevet General U. S. V.
Lt. Col. Levi S. Dominy, brevet Col. N. Y. V.
Major John L. Cunningham, brevet Lt. Col. U. S. V.
Surgeon William O. Mansfield.
Asst. Surg. J. C. Preston.
Chaplain Charles L. Hagar.
Adjutant Clifford Hubbard.
Q. M. Henry J. Northrup, brevet Captain N. Y. V.

Company A.

Capt. Joseph R. Seaman, brevet Major U. S. V.
1st Lt. J. W. Treadway, brevet Captain N. Y. V., from Co. E.

Company B.

Capt. George F. Campbell, brevet Major N. Y. V., from Co. C.

---

[1] General Devens to Governor Fenton.

1st Lt. Jas. A. Garrett, brevet Captain N. Y. V., from Co. A.

2d Lt. Merril Perry, brevet Captain N. Y. V., from Co. A.

Company C.

Capt. C. W. Wells, brevet Major N. Y. V., from Co. K.

1st Lt. L. S. Bryant.

2d Lt. N. H. Arnold, from Co. E.

Company D.

Capt. John W. Angell, from Co. E.

2d Lt. Philip V. N. McLean, from Co. K.

Company E.

Capt. Henry S. Graves, from Co. I.

1st Lt. George H. Potter, from Co. A.

2d Lt. William T. Bidwell, late Hospital Steward.

Company F.

Capt. Robert W. Livingstone, brevet Major N. Y. V.

1st Lt. Daniel O. Connor, Asst. Hospital Steward.

2d Lt. Charles A. Grace, from Co. A.

Company G.

1st Lt. James H. Pitt, from Co. H.

Company H.

Capt. David F. Dobie, brevet Major N. Y. V.

1st Lt. F. Saunders.

Company I.

Capt. Martin V. B. Stetson, Major N. Y. V.

1st Lt. Nelson J. Gibbs, brevet Captain N. Y. V., from Co. F.

Company K.

Capt. John Brydon, brevet Major N. Y. V.

1st Lt. John W. Calkins, from Co. K.

2d Lt. George Vaughan, from Co. I.

Officers connected with Essex County Troops who resigned or were discharged.

Samuel T. Richards, Col., July 8th, 1863.

Colonel, Oliver Keese, Jr., resigned Sept. 14, 1864.

Captain James H. Peirce, discharged Feb. 9, 1865.

1st Lieutenant Nathan S. Washburn, discharged February 14, 1863.

2d Lieutenant George M. Butrick, discharged February 14, 1863.

Jacob Parmerter, discharged Nov. 15, 1864.

1st Lieutenant John S. Boynton, resigned March 12, 1864.

1st Lieutenant Sam Sherman, discharged Oct. 19, 1864.

2d Lieutenant Henry M. Mould, resigned Aug. 1, 1863.

Brevet Commissions issued by the Governor to Enlisted Men of this Regiment.

Sergeant Cass C. La Point, 2d lieutenant.

Sergeant Major Ashley S. Prime, 2d lieutenant.

Sergeant Joseph A. Hastings, 2d lieutenant. Sergeant Freeman D. Lindsay, 2d lieutenant.

Enlisted Men of this Regiment to whom Medals of Honor have been awarded by the Secretary of War.

Private Franklin Jandro.

The One Hundred and Fifty-third Regiment N. Y. Volunteers.

This regiment was recruited from various sections of the state, and mustered into service October, 1862. Thomas Armstrong of Clinton county received the appointment of lieutenant-colonel at its organization, and resigned February, 1863. A large part of a company which was attached to the One Hundred and Fifty-third as Company I, was enrolled by John F. McGuire of Keeseville, from Clinton and Essex counties, and in it he was appointed second lieutenant. By the successive resignations of the superior officers he was promoted in December, 1863, to the command of the company. The regiment immediately after its organization was ordered to Alexandria, and subsequently at Washington was employed in provost duty. Company I was specially detached in that service. Early in 1864 the One Hundred and Fifty-third was transferred to Louisiana and incorporated with the nineteenth army corps. It was engaged in the Red river expedition and participated in all the hardships and disasters of that campaign. When the Union forces, after the battle of Sabine Cross Roads, fell back, Company I was the rear company in the retreat of the army. The nineteenth corps sailed from New Orleans on the 3d of July, with sealed orders; but its destination proved to be the Chesapeake. The One Hundred and Fifty-third and four companies belonging to other regiments, the advance of the corps, on their arrival at Fortress Monroe, were instantly ordered, without disembarking, to the defense of Washington, then menaced by Early's incursion. These troops were hastened through the city amid the deep excitement and alarm of the people, to a position at Fort Stevens, where they went into immediate action. After the repulse of the rebels, the One Hundred and Fifty-third joined in their pursuit across the Potomac into the Shenandoah valley, but was suddenly recalled to the vicinity of the capital to oppose another apprehended advance of the enemy. The regiment was soon after engaged in the battle of Winchester, and Company I here sustained some slight casualties. It participated in the engagement at Fisher Hill and in the pursuit of the Confederates from that field.

The Nineteenth corps was at Cedar Creek and suffered heavy losses incident to the surprise and early catastrophies of that eventful day. The One Hundred and Fifty-third formed part of the picket line that enveloped Washington after the assassination of Mr. Lincoln, and discharged guard duty at the arsenal on the military trials that succeeded. In June, 1865, the regiment was ordered to Savannah, where it performed provost duty until its discharge. Captain McGuire of Company I, brevet major N. Y. V., during that service acted as adjutant provost marshal of the city. In the succeeding October, the One Hundred and Fifty-third was disbanded at Albany.

Brevet commissions issued to enlisted men of this regiment.

Sergeant James C. Bullock, 2d lieutenant.
Private Melchior H. Hoffnagle, 2d lieutenant.

The Second New York Cavalry.

The last organized company in Essex county was enrolled in Ticonderoga in the summer of 1864, of which William H. Sanger was appointed captain, James McCormick first, and George B. Coates, second lieutenant, each on the 8th of September, 1864. They had both belonged to the Thirty-fourth New York Volunteers. It was attached to the Second New York Cavalry as Company E,[1] with the army of Sheridan, and performed excellent services in the Shenandoah valley, attended him in the perilous march to

[1] When the original members were mustered out, and the veterans and recruits were organized into four new companies.

the James, and was engaged with his command in the battles that preceded the surrender of Lee. This regiment was ultimately associated with the Fifth in the achievements of the Shenandoah campaign. Lieutenants McCormick and Coates were both wounded, the former very seriously at the battle of Cedar Creek. Lieutenant McCormick was discharged May 1st, 1865. Coates was promoted to first lieutenant but not mustered in as such, and remained with the regiment until it was disbanded June 5th, 1865. Captain Sanger was made brevet-major New York State Volunteers and discharged May 15th, 1865.

Medals of Honor were awarded to the following enlisted men:

Frank Miller. J. S. Calkins.

List of brevet commissions, second lieutenant issued to enlisted men.

Private John J. Morse. Private Burnet Galloway.
Sergeant Fred. A. M. Ball.

An approximation only can be reached of the number of troops contributed by Essex county to the Union army. The official military records and the census returns which are known to be imperfect, are far below the reality, exhibits a total of one thousand and three hundred and six. These records do not embrace the large numbers who were mingled in the various other organizations of the state, and the census returns must most inadequately exhibit the true amount. Many other residents of Essex county, estimated at the time to amount to several hundred in the aggregate, were enlisted by the active zeal of agents from several of the New England states. The excess of seven dollars per month pay, offered by Vermont, allured large numbers of the youth of the county, who enlisted into the line of that state. The archives of New York show that from the recruits credited on the quota of Essex county, three hundred and sixty-six deaths occurred on the field of battle from wounds, accidents, and diseases incident to the exposures of the service. The actual casualties among the citzens of Essex were far heavier, and can never with any degree of accuracy be computed.

An attempt to ascertain the expenses and disbursements in their infinitely varied forms, is still more difficult and unsatisfactory. The amounts actually authorized by the board of supervisors to be raised by the county and the several towns, at different sessions and without the accumulation of interest reached a total of $553,871.47. This great sum does not include the vast amounts realized by the liberal contributions derived from personal and local efforts, nor the money expended in recruiting and equipping the early volunteers. Nor the supplies of provisions, clothing, medicines and other subscriptions essential to the health and comfort of the troops. Heavy sums were aggregated by the individual payment of the $300, by an early act authorized to avoid the draft, and by the purchase of substitutes. Private liberality and patriotic zeal expended in silence and secrecy vast amounts which were unknown and incomputable. The magnitude of all these contributions and expenditures can never be known, nor will human pen ever record the extent and value of these efforts.

The following tabular statements exhibit interesting statistics illustrative of the devotedness and responsibilities incurred by the towns of Essex county: [1]

Table No. 1. *Number enlisted by several towns.*

Chesterfield,	92	North Elba,	27
Crown Point,	192	North Hudson,	24
Elizabethtown,	105	St. Armands',	19
Essex,	60	Schroon,	94
Jay,	93	Ticonderoga,	128
Keene,	47	Westport,	58
Lewis,	115	Willsboro',	43
Minerva,	50	Wilmington,	64
Moriah,	157		
Newcomb,	8	Total,	1306

[1] I have obtained these materials through the research and courtesy of Major R. W. Livingstone.

Table No. 2. Died, etc.

Town		Town	
Chesterfield,	28	North Elba,	6
Crown Point,	44	North Hudson,	...
Elizabethtown,	19	St. Armands,	7
Essex,	16	Schroon,	28
Jay,	25	Ticonderoga,	45
Keene,	9	Westport,	24
Lewis,	35	Willsboro',	17
Minerva,	12	Wilmington,	16
Moriah,	34		
Newcomb,	1	Total,	366

Table No. 3. Town Indebtedness.

Town		Town	
Chesterfield,	$16,192 33	North Elba,	
Crown Point,		North Hudson,	$1,100 00
Elizabethtown,	3,777 91	St. Armands,	2,000 00
Essex,	1,275 00	Schroon,	200 00
Jay,	12,300 00	Ticonderoga,	
Keene,		Westport,	2,600 00
Lewis,	6,600 00	Wilmington,	900 00
Minerva,	3,500 00	Willsboro',	3,858 00
Moriah,	9,860 00		
Newcomb,	600 00	Total,	$64,763 74

The towns which appear blank in the above statement, made separate provision for their local liabilities.

CHAPTER XV.

Grants and Patents.

I have reviewed in preceding pages, the circumstances connected with the grants of territory contiguous to Lake Champlain, in accordance with the ordinance of the king of France, in the year 1676. The action of the colonial government, under the British proclamation of October 7, 1763, authorizing grants of land to be made in such colonies as they might prefer, to the reduced officers and soldiers who had served in the regular army, in the Canadian campaigns; and transactions connected with such grants, I have fully discussed. The purchasers of these rights usually located their lands in the names of the grantees, but not apparently in all cases. William Gilliland embraced in one body, the entire tract from the Boquet to Splitrock, under several distinct rights, and other purchasers pursued the same course. All these locations, many of which were established as early as 1765 and 1766, and authenticated by appropriate legal formalities, have been perpetuated and still exist, under the names of the original grantees. In many instances, the officers and soldiers located and perfected the titles themselves to these lands.

The history of the grants and the change of policy connected with them possess no inconsiderable value and demands a brief attention. The quantity of these grants contemplated by these proclamations was the concession of five thousand acres to a field officer; to a captain three thousand acres; to a subaltern staff officer two thousand acres; to a non-commissioned officer two hundred acres, and to a private fifty acres. These grants were conferred by parchment patents, under the great seal of the colony and impressed with the royal arms. They reserved to the king "all mines of gold and silver, and all pine trees fit for masts of the growth of twenty-four inches diameter and upwards of twelve inches from the earth." These grants were held for ten years "in free and common socage exempt from all quit rents, and after the expiration of that term, rendering and paying in the custom house in New York, at Lady Day, the yearly rent of two shillings and sixpence sterling, for each and every hundred acres of the granted land." The farther conditions imposed the settlement "of as many families on the tract as shall amount to one family on every thousand acres thereof," and "to cultivate at least three acres for every fifty acres susceptible of cultivation." Both of these conditions were to be performed within three years from the date of the grant. "No waste was to be committed on the reserved timber; the grant to be registered at the secretary's office and docketted at the auditor's office in New York." A neglect to perform either of these conditions worked a forfeiture of the grant. We may trace in the land papers serious consequences resulting from these delinquencies. The council seems to have possessed certain powers to control the nature and form of these proceedings. In February, 1765, it adopted a rule, that no soldier was entitled to a grant "unless disbanded on the reduction of the regiment." By minutes in 1770, 1771, it required grants to be taken out in three months after the petition had been presented, and in the last date ordered names of delinquents to be stricken from the list of grants. Most of these grants were located in the vicinity of Lake Champlain, and a large proportion upon the eastern side, upon what is now the territory of Vermont. In the confusion of the agitated period that preceded the revolution, numerous cases of these petitions remained in an inchoate condition; and in others, although the proceedings had been regular and ample, were not consummated by patents from the colonial government. In most of these instances the succeeding state government refused to ratify the proceedings of the claimants, and large estates, as we have seen illustrated in the notice of Gilliland, were lost. The state constitution of 1777, by a provision which has been incorporated in the constitutions of 1821 and 1847, abrogated all royal grants after October 14th, 1775.

Deep interest attaches to those ancient grants, the rewards of military services, while strong romance has gathered about a portion of them. We recognize the peculiar justice and appropriateness, that conferred on the gallant men who participated in the terrible scenes, which impressed on the region its gorgeous historic associations, these acknowledgments of their services from the territory won to their country by their blood and sufferings.

A small part only of the great area of Essex county was occupied in the location of these grants. Since the revolution, large tracts of unappropriated lands, belonging to the state, have been patented to individuals. The remainder, at an early period of the present government, was run out into tracts and townships by the state, and subdivided into lots, which have been sold in any amount desired by the purchaser. These lands were devoted to the accumulation of an educational fund, and the proceeds of the sales have been appropriated to that beneficent purpose. The state yet retains a large extent of this domain. Much of it possesses considerable value from the wood and timber forests it embraces, but other portions, constituting as they do, the rocky upheavals and mountains of the Adirondacs, are worthless, except for the mineral wealth that may be hidden in their recesses.

I am indebted for most of the materials upon which I have founded the following account of the grants and patents of the county, to the zealous and careful investigations of a learned legal friend, whose professional studies have constrained a thorough research into the land titles of the district. With such aid I have made the notices I now present, of the origin and history of these patents and grants as accurate and complete as I believe so intricate a subject admits, but I am aware that the execution is necessarily imperfect. The long list of the patents I have endeavored to make full and correct, but it may be found defective.[1] The magnitude of many of these grants will attract attention. Land was at that period the most abundant of all commodities, and the government felt that it controlled a "whole boundless continent." In the voluminous *Land Papers*, documents frequently occur, referring to surveys of "that small piece of land," sometimes embracing five hundred and often two thousand acres.[2] The *Southier Map*, to which I shall make frequent reference, was prepared under the direction of Governor Tryon, and published in London, 1779.

Abeel. James Abeel, for himself and twelve others February 3d, 1773, petitioned for a grant of thirteen thousand acres of land lying on the west side of Schroon lake in

[1] I have received peculiar aid from the examinations of Mr. F. C. Hale, in the archives of the office of secretary of state.

[2] The *Calendar of Land Papers*, and the *Catalogue of Maps and Surveys*, shed a flood of light on the history of these grants and patents.

Totten and Crossfield's purchase.[1] Southier's map has a tract with this name and corresponding with the above description, which would embrace the present Schroon Lake village. From the frequent appearance of his name in the *Land Papers* it may be inferred that Abeel was engaged in large and numerous land operations.

Benzel. Adolphus Benzel has been already mentioned as a prominent official in the county and a weathy resident of Crown Point. He seems to have acted largely as surveyor in locating the ancient patents. He was conspicuous in the New Hampshire grant controversies, and necessarily highly obnoxious to the settlers there. The reply of the Bennington committee to Governor Tryon, in reference to Colonel Reid's action, speaks of " the vicious and haughty aid of Mr Benzel, the famed engineer."[2] He was among the reduced officers embraced in the royal proclamation. Southier lays down two patents in his name, one in Moriah between Small's and Legg's; the other in Crown Point adjoining south of the garrison grounds. The former is known as Springer patent of three thousand acres, and the latter as Benzel's of one thousand acres. We conjecture that the former may have been applied for by Benzel, but subsequently issued to Springer and others.

Benson. Richard Benson, and a number of other privates reduced from the Eightieth, Sixtieth, and Forty-fourth regiments, received a patent for five hundred and fifty acres Oct. 29th, 1765, which was located in the present town of Willsboro' north of Wreisburg and west of the Montressor patent. It appears that the Benson and also the Montressor patent were occupied only by squatters until 1819. In that year both were purchased by Seth Hunt of Keene, New Hampshire. The validity of the original patent and his title were soon after established and his rights judicially enforced. Many individuals, who had been innocent purchasers under the spurious titles to these patents, were severe sufferers by this adjudication.

---

[1] *Land Papers*, XXXIII, page 25. [2] *Hall's Vermont.*

Bruyn. Two patents granted to Lewis Bruyn, are laid down west of Schroon lake on Southier's map.

Campbell, Allen. A reduced field officer, is thus described: "having served in N. A., during the late war in Second battalion of our Royal Highland regiment of Foot." Campbell united in a petition with Lt. John Kennedy, praying for a grant of seven thousand acres. The boundaries indicated "extending from the first mountain west of the carrying place at the foot of Lake George" along said mountain to where it touches Lake Champlain near Crown Point, and thence to the mouth of the outlet from Lake George. Kennedy's grant embraces a portion of this highly desirable territory, but Campbell's was located elsewhere. His patent for five thousand acres, dated July 11, 1764, was laid out in Crown Point, on the lake shore: Benzel and Legg on the north, and Grant on the south.

Campbell, Donald. The petition of Donald Campbell, December 17th, 1763, describes him as late lieutenant in the Royal American regiment, and claims two thousand acres. The land his petition indicated was nearly identical with the last. Another petition, Feb. 18, 1773, of Quarter Master Donald Campbell, asks for two thousand acres on the south-west side of Lake George, near the garrison grounds. On November 1st, 1784, Donald Campbell filed a petition for a confirmatory grant of a tract of land surveyed for him in 1764, pursuant to the Royal proclamation. No action appears upon record on this petition, but on the 25th of May, 1786, the return was filed of a survey of two thousand acres north of N. Sutherland's tract to Donald Campbell, for which he paid on the following 28th of June, one hundred pounds. A tract is laid down on the map, under this designation between Grant's on the north, and Southerland's on the south.

Connelly. John Connelly presented a petition for a grant as surgeon's mate and belonging to a military hospital. A patent was issued April 13th, 1765, for two thousand acres.

---

[1] *Land Papers,* LII, 45.

It lies in Willsboro, and Essex, and is one of the grants located by William Gilliland.

Deal. Samuel Deal, a merchant of wealth in the city of New York, embarked in heavy land operations in the present county of Essex in 1767, and purchased about that time a tract of five thousand acres between Lakes George and Champlain. His connection with the Kennedy patents, I shall notice in its proper place. He received July 12th, 1769, a grant for one thousand acres, which was located by him in Ticonderoga and west of the village of Lower Falls. Another tract, adjoining the above, is called and designated on the county map as Deal's patent.

Field. John Field was a surgeons mate and applied by petition April 14th, 1764, for a grant of two thousand acres in pursuance of proclamation. The patent was issued April 15th, 1765, and the land surveyed on the south side of the Boquet by Gilliland as assignee of Field immediately after.

Franklin. Joseph Franklin, late sergeant in Twenty-seventh regiment, united with Sergeant Benjamin Porter, in a petition, July 9, 1764, praying a grant to each of two hundred acres, described as "bearing west north-west thirty-nine chains from the salient angle of the King's bastion, fronting the lake half a mile, and then west north-westerly, until it completes the said number of acres." Mr. Benzel, the engineer, made a note of the survey. The patent to Franklin issued July, 1765, and was laid out in conformity with the petition between the Porter and McKensie's tracts, and embraced Cedar point at Port Henry. On the 5th of March, 1792, Franklin conveyed his title to James Graham, and April 15, 1792, Graham devised it to his daughter, Ann Eliza. Graham was a fur trader, and the mother of this child was a half breed. The daughter, in 1802, executed a will in New York, devising the property to St. Peter's (Catholic) church of that city, in trust for the school of the church. The church conveyed it to Mr. J. B. Spencer, under this will, whose title was judicially sustained.

Friswell. John Friswell applied as late lieutenant in the navy, and having acted as midshipman on board the Princess Amelia, at the siege of Louisburg and Quebec, February 15, 1765, for a grant of three thousand acres of land on the west side of Lake Champlain. On the May following a return of a survey was filed of two tracts, containing two thousand acres; one in Plattsburg, and the other of one thousand acres nearly west of "Splitten Rock," and lying upon the lake. This is one of Gilliland's locations.

Frelegh. A certificate of location of six hundred acres of land to George Frelegh, on the west side of Lake Champlain, appears in *Long Island Papers*, XLVI, 41, February 3, 1789, and a patent in Willsboro' and Essex, bears this name.[1] It is not on Southier's map, and must have been granted subsequent to the revolution.

Gilliland. A Gilliland patent is laid down on Southier, west of Benson's grant in Willsboro'. James, a brother of William Gilliland, about 1767, settled upon a lot on the north bank of the Boquet.[2]

"*William Gilliland & Matthew Watson.*" Their tract which appears on the large county map, contained two hundred acres, and began according to the certificate of location, seven chains north of the south-west corner of James Judd's patent, June 22, 1789, and was surveyed under a title from the state.[3]

Grant. Robert Grant is described in a patent for three thousand acres issued August 7th, 1764, as late captain in the Seventy-seventh regiment. He was promoted to major and killed at the battle of Hubbardton July 7th, 1777. A return of survey with map of the location in the town of Crown Point was filed in the colonial office, August 3d, 1764, *Land Papers*, XVIII, 8. About twenty years after the death of Grant, a spurious agent appeared in the city of

[1] *Calendar*, 777.

[2] *Champlain Valley*, 41, etc. It is probable that this may have been his location.

[3] *Land Papers*, XLVII, 33, 34.

New York, and pretending to hold authority from him, deeded the patent, as such, with an agreement that the grantee and agent should participate in the avails. The sisters of Major Grant, more than half a century after his decease, instituted proceedings as heirs at law for the recovery of the patent. Under a commission issued in the suit and sent to Scotland in the year 1830 among other witnesses examined, was Lieut. General Thomas Scott then eighty-four years old, who swore, that he saw the dead body of Grant on the battle-field at Hubbardton and witnessed its interment at that place with military honors, and that he brought back to Scotland relics of Grant which he delivered to the brother of Grant. The claimants necessarily recovered the premises. This patent embraces a large portion of the most valuable part of the town of Crown Point.

Guise. William Guise and three others non-commissioned officers in the Fifty-fifth regiment of foot, received a grant of eight hundred acres, Jan. 5th, 1773. On the county map, this grant is placed on the east side of Schroon lake near the county line. It is not on Southier. By the survey and map for Guise and associates, the location of the patent was on the north-east branch of the Hudson on the boundary between Schroon and Warren county.[1]

Hasenclever. Peter Hasenclever and others petitioned June 30th, 1766, for a grant of fifteen thousand acres, on the east side (?) of Lake Champlain, and praying a resurvey of Franklin, Porter and McKensie's patent (inMoriah) so as to admit a passage to the lake and land for store house. On Southier's map the patent is laid down north of Small, but it does not appear on the county map, and the present Iron Ore bed tract is bounded by Small's patent on the south. This grant was probably confiscated if ever actually consummated.

Hicks. John Hicks is described as " gentleman, a reduced staff officer," and " surgeon in one of our independent com-

---

[1] *Land Papers,* XXXII, 91. [2] *Idem,* XXI, 51.

panies of Foot," Patent April 15th, 1765, for three thousand acres. Lies in Essex and located by Gilliland.

Judd. James Judd, described as "gentleman, reduced officer and surgeon's mate in our military hospital." Patent issued April 15th, 1765, for two thousand acres, with boundaries "beginning at Cloven or Splitten Rock, etc." Lies in the town of Essex.

Kellett. Roger Kellett "gentleman, a reduced subaltern officer," late lieutenant in Forty-fourth regiment. The grant was surveyed August 2d, and patent granted August 7th, 1764, for two thousand acres.[1] This patent situated in Ticonderoga with those of Stoughton and Kennedy, were selected with great judgment by officers familiar with the beauty and value of the territory.

Kelly. John Kelly appears to have been a large operator soon after the revolution, but I find no traces of him anterior to it. A tract of land in Essex and Westport known by this name, is probably the same described as lying west of Split rock or Northwest bay, for which he proposed to pay on April 15th, 1793, two shillings per acre, and contained about three thousand acres.

Kennedy. John Kennedy, "gentleman, reduced subaltern officer," lieutenant in the Sixtieth regiment. Patent granted August 7th, 1764, for two thousand acres. It lies in Ticonderoga, and extends from the lower falls along the north side of the stream to the fort ground, thence across to Lake Champlain and down its shore, and sweeping into the interior included a large part of the valuable plateau in the north section of the town.[2] At the death of the grantee, the property passed to "his oldest brother, Henry Kennedy, surgeon," who sold it September 26th, 1765, for one hundred and fifty pounds sterling, to Abraham P. Lott and Peter Theobaldus Curtenius, "merchants of the city of New York," and they sold it December 16th, 1767, for one hundred and eighty pounds, lawful currency to Samuel Deall "merchant, etc."[3]

---

[1] *Catalogue,* 155. [2] See Allen Campbell patent. [3] *Cook's Ticonderoga.*

Legge. The singular incidents connected with the history of this patent have attached peculiar interest to it, and no portion of Essex county has been the subject of more bitter and protracted litigation. Francis Legge, who I infer belonged to the family of the Earl of Dartmouth, was a captain in the Forty-sixth regiment. Under the royal proclamation, he received a concession on June 26th, 1769, of five thousand acres which had been located in the present towns of Moriah and Crown Point by a survey returned the 6th of April preceding. The early action of Legge in reference to his grant, is enveloped in considerable obscurity. A mandamus was issued by the king in council September 5th, 1765, for five thousand acres to be surveyed to Francis Legge, captain of the Twenty-sixth, in one continuous tract in the province of New York.[1] On the 3d of November, 1766, Captain Francis Legge presented "a petition for five thousand acres of land on the west side of Connecticut river, with specific boundaries."[2] He made a similar application for a grant of five thousand acres in the township of Norwich in a wholly different section from the preceding. The identity of the name and the quantity of land solicited, seem to warrant the conclusion, that the several applications if made by one individual, rested upon the same claim; but it is difficult to determine, why all should have been advanced. In 1809, a William Legge, assuming to be the heir of Francis, conveyed or pretended to convey this patent to one Winter, who afterwards deeded it to Shaw. One of them caused the tract to be subdivided into lots, and sold a portion of these to settlers. Subsequently, Shaw brought ejectments against occupants who refused to admit his title. Another claim, known as the James Brown title, was founded upon a deed dated in the year 1818, and purporting to have been executed by John Legge in Ireland, who also claimed to be heir of Francis, to two persons, mother and son, by the name of Sinclair. They conveyed to James Brown, who

[1] *Calendar*, 377. [2] *Idem*, 204.

also brought ejectments, and some suits under this title are said to be still pending.

In 1831, suits were brought against some of the occupants upona claim some times called the "Cape Ann title." It was asserted, that, in the year 1770, Francis Legge, while at Ipswich, Mass., residing with a Dr. Manning, executed a deed of the whole patent, to one Rowe, then a child of four or five years. One of these suits was against Brown and an occupant, was tried, with a verdict and judgment for the plaintiff, but this was reversed in the court of errors. On the trial of this suit, proof was introduced by defendants, tending to show, that Legge died and was buried in Troy, N. Y., in 1780. In 1860, a commission issuing out of the United States circuit court, was executed in London, by which the following series of facts were established, from records in the war office and those of the state paper office and the colonial office, the registry of the court of probate, in doctor's commons, and by exhibits and the examination of proper officials, that Francis Legge, was appointed lieutenant, in Thirty-fifth Foot in 1754, captain in Forty-sixth in 1756; that at this time he was serving in America; that he was major in 1767; lieutenant in Fifty-fifth Foot in 1773, and appointed governor of Nova Scotia in August, 1783; that he was recalled, and his conduct as governor investigated in 1786; that he was buried in the parish of Primer, Middlesex, England, in 22d May, 1783; that his will dated April 18th, 1769, was proved the May following by his executors, the Earl of Dartmouth and William Baillie, Esq., and that the Earl of Dartmouth, whom he styles in his will "his much esteemed friend," was his principal legatee and devisee. Personal property was left by the will to various relations. The record of his burial described him as "Lieutenant Colonel Francis Legge, late governor of Nova Scotia." It is not my province to discuss the singular features of this case.

Miller. Paul Miller, a corporal in Sixtieth regiment of foot, located a patent dated April 16th, 1765 of two hundred acres on the south side of the Boquet. It lies in Willsboro'.

Mallory's Grant. Nathaniel Mallory, on March 25th, 1799, entered the return of a survey or tract of land on west side of Lake Champlain containing nine thousand nine hundred and seventy-three acres, situated in Jay, Keene and Wilmington.[1]

Mathews. This patent was granted October 30th, 1765, to James Mathews and seven others, privates, for four hundred acres. It lies in Ticonderoga.

Maule's. This tract, comprising forty-two thousand nine hundred and fifty-seven acres, was patented to Thomas Maule, August 21st, 1800. Embracing large sections of Chesterfield, Jay, and Willsboro', it also occupies a portion of Au Sable and Black Brook, in Clinton. In March, 1803, Maule and wife conveyed to five persons in trust about twenty thousand acres of this patent in Chesterfield and Jay. This trust was for the benefit of the Farmers' Society, a benevolent organization, intended, as is now understood, to supply mechanics and others in moderate circumstances with freehold farms; but as the scheme proved a failure, there is no object for tracing its history. The trustees executed a mortgage for fifty thousand dollars on the purchase. This mortgage came into the hands of Edward Livingstone, who assigned it to his sister, the widow of General Montgomery; and the surviving trustees, conveyed, or released the property to her. She devised it to Edward Livingstone, and on his death he devised it to his wife. By these various owners, parcels were conveyed to numerous settlers.

McIntosh. Alexander McIntosh, late captain of Seventy-seventh regiment August 3d, 1764, filed the return of a survey of three thousand acres between Crown Point and Ticonderoga. Patent issued August 7th.

McBride. Patent issued April 23, 1765, to James McBride, late sergeant in Forty-seventh foot, for two hundred acres.

---

[1] *Calendar*, 1010.

Lies in Willsboro', and is bounded south and west by the Boquet, and east by the lake.

McDonald. Three tracts bearing this designation appear on Southier's map, lying west of Schroon lake and river. On December 1, 1773, Captain Lieutenant (he is thus described more than once in the land papers) Alexander McDonald and associates, presented a petition for three tracts of land, containing in the aggregate thirty thousand three hundred and sixty acres, and lying "within the bounds of Totten and Crossfield's purchase."

McKensie. Alexander McKensie, sergeant in the Fortieth regiment, received two patents, October 29, 1765, one of a hundred acres adjoining the Franklin patent, and fifty acres called the Grove. Both are situated in Moriah, in which town a grandson and numerous descendants reside; a descendant lives upon the original patent. I am aware of no other instance, except that of William Gilliland, in which the family of an original patentee of these ancient grants have remained in the county.

Montressor. Patent issued June 6th, 1765, to John Montressor, Francis Mee and Robert Wallace for three thousand acres, "called Ligonier point, as also four small islands called Les Isles des Quatre Vents, in the lake eastward of Ligonier point."[1] This is the beautiful tract now known as Willsboro' point.[2] The original petition also asked for Schuyler's island. Some doubt exists in reference to the origin of the name Ligonier. I venture to refer it to Sir John Ligonier, who, about the date in which it must have been applied, was commander-in-chief of the army in Great Britain.[3]

Old Military Tract. An act was passed May 5th, 1786, as a memorial of public gratitude, to remunerate military service in the revolution, devoting to the purpose, a large territory known as the Old Military Tract, lying north of Jessup's purchase and beginning thirty miles from the north-east corner of lands granted to Philip Skene, 6th

---

[1] *Land Papers*, XIX, 31. [2] *See Benson.* [3] *Doc. Hist.*, X, 705 *note.*

July, 1771, and extending twenty miles in width and to the north bound of the state, a computed distance of sixty miles. It was run out into large townships. Nos. 11 and 12 constitute St. Armands and North Elba. Nos. 1 and 2, were also embraced within the present bounds of Essex county. These townships were subdivided into lots, known as the Thorne and Richard's surveys.

Ord. Lieutenant Colonel Thomas Ord, Royal regiment of Artillery, was granted, December 23, 1774, a patent of five thousand, acres part of lot 27, in Totten and Crossfield's purchase. This patent lies in Newcomb.

Porter. Benjamin Porter, late sergeant in Twenty-seventh regiment, obtained a patent July 5th, 1765, for two hundred acres.[1] Port Henry is situated on this tract.

Potts. This patent, issued in the name of William Potts, April 26th, 1755, for two thousand acres, located by William Gilliland. Essex village stands on the line of Potts and Hicks patents.

Ross. Patent issued to James Ross, "late apothecary's mate in our military hospital," for two thousand acres April 16th, 1765. The patent is bounded on the Boquet. It was occupied in 1766 by two persons, Wilson and Goodrich, who established an agency at Flat Rock bay, which they called Burton. The scheme was abandoned the February ensuing, and no further occupation in Willsboro' north of the Boquet occurred until 1790, except one slight improvement near the river.

Ryerse Grant. In 1791, the state granted to one Vredenburgh a tract of three hundred acres, the title of which became vested in Gozen Ryerse. On the compromise with Massachusetts, this territory was embraced in the new preemption line of that state. In compensation to Ryerse for this loss, New York in 1800 patented to him a tract of eighteen hundred acres lying in the centre of Wilmington, and now known as Ryerse grant.

---

[1] See Franklin.

Stoughton. A patent was issued to John Stoughton, late lieutenant in New York independent company, July 25, 1774, for two thousand acres lying on both sides of the outlet of Lake George. Stoughton was drowned in Lake George, leaving a widow and only child. This child became the wife of Governor Wolcott of Connecticut, and the valuable estate of Edward Elice in this patent was derived from her by purchase.[1] A question was agitated for a period in reference to the legitimacy of this child, but this has long since subsided, and the estate which had not been previously sold is now held by an indisputable title by Mr. Charles Wheeler of Ticonderoga.

Skene. I have adverted sufficiently to the history of Skene. The patents were granted to Major Philip Skene July 5th, 1771, one for two thousand four hundred acres, situated in the present town of Westport, and embracing a part of the village of Westport, and the other for six hundred acres, lying in Moriah and formerly referred to as the Iron Ore tract. The property of Philip Skene was confiscated under the attainder of Philip and Andrew Skene, and the patent in Moriah was sold by the commissioners of forfeitures under the act of 1786.

Small. John Small, late captain in the Twenty-first regiment, on April 5th, 1774, received a patent for five thousand acres. It lies in Moriah, and is occupied by Moriah Centre and part of the village of Moriah. Grants were also issued to Small by the New York colonial governor, which were located in Vermont. His name appears as plaintiff in a test suit brought in the New York court, to establish the validity of these grants.[2]

Sutherland. Patent issued to Nicholas Sutherland, late captain of Seventy-seventh Foot, August 7th, 1764, for three thousand acres. Lies in Ticonderoga.

Springer or Sharp. On the 10th November, 1766, John Springer, Elizabeth Springer and Ann Chadarin Partin, afterwards Sharp, filed a petition for three thousand acres,

---

[1] *Cook's Ticonderoga.* [2] *Hall's Vermont.*

in the county of Albany, or on Otter creek. The basis of this claim appears to have rested upon rights vested in Adolphus Benzel and his associates. Elizabeth Springer was a sister-in-law of Adolphus Benzel. A return of the survey of three thousand acres on the west side of Lake Champlain, is on record April 6th, 1772. A warrant authorizing this survey had been issued 1st May, 1771. In April, 1785, the parties presented a petition to the new government, "for land already ordered to be surveyed for them between the Legge and Small patents." On the 10th November following, Zephaniah Platt filed a certificate of location of the same tract, praying for a grant of the same. His claim seems to have been founded on the delinquency of the original claimants, but after considerable controversy it was withdrawn March 13th, 1786, and 1st May following the patent was granted to Elizabeth Springer and Ann Catharine Sharp, for the consideration of £150 paid the state. It is situated in Moriah.

Soldiers' Rights. On Southier's map, a tract is laid down, commencing about a mile and a half from the flag-staff at Ticonderoga, and extending along Lake Champlain, from a mile and a half to two miles wide, upon which is inscribed, "Soldiers." A map has been exhibited to me by the distinguished professional gentleman already referred to, which seems to have been executed more than sixty years ago, in which the seven tracts are laid down, in conformity to Southier, beginning with William Douglass on the north, succeeded by four others, of one thousand acres each; one of seven hundred acres, and one of four hundred acres, making an aggregate of six thousand one hundred acres. It appears by the *Land Papers*, that a return was filed February 8, 1772, of a survey for "William Douglass and others, noncommissioned officers and private soldiers of sundry tracts of land containing together six thousand one hundred acres on the west side of waters running from Wood creek to Lake Champlain." On the county map, six of these rights are laid down in Essex county.

Stevenson. James Stevenson, December 7, 1765, applied for a patent in right of his father, James Stevenson, commissary of ordnance, etc., for three thousand acres; but it was not granted until the 11th of July, 1776. This patent lies in Ticonderoga, and is usually called, the Kirby patent.

Stewart. A tract of fifty acres, granted May 2d, 1772, to James Stewart, is situated on Lake George, in Ticonderoga, and south of Tomlin's patent.

Summervale. This tract of fifteen thousand one hundred and twenty acres, was surveyed in 1771, but a patent to Goldsboro' Banyar, and others, was not granted until August 14, 1786. The tract lies in Crown Point and Ticonderoga.

Totten & Crossfield. Experience had proved, that transactions for the acquisition by private individuals of Indian lands were fraught with infinite mischief and injustice. At an early period, the instructions to the colonial governors, and at length, soon after the cession of Canada, a peremptory proclamation of the king, prohibited every purchase of the kind, and declared that all purchases of lands from the Indians should be made by the crown.[1] The same wise and beneficent policy was engrafted in the state constitution of 1777, and those which have succeeded.

On the 10th of April, 1771, Joseph Totten and Stephen Crossfield, shipwrights, residing in the city of New York, presented a petition to the council, asking for a license to purchase from the Indians a tract of land lying on the west side of the Hudson, and on the 7th June following the license was granted. In accordance with this privilege a treaty was held in July, 1772, at Johnson Hall, with all the peculiar solemnities of such occasions and under the auspices of Sir William Johnson, for the purpose of perfecting the contemplated purchase, with the Mohawk and Caughnawauga Indians. The purchase was made for the consideration of about one thousand one

---

[1] *Doc. Hist.*, VII, 571.

hundred and thirty-five pounds New York currency, and a deed formally executed for the tract, embracing about eight hundred thousand acres and with boundaries carefully designated by courses and land marks, but singularly vague and obscure. This interesting document is still preserved in the office of secretary of state, among the *Land Papers*, vol. XXXII, 45. A written agreement of association was entered into March 27th, 1772, between "the intended proprietors of lands about to be purchased by Ebenezer Jessup in behalf of Totten and Crossfield and their associates," and on January 14th, following, a further agreement was executed and a ballot made of twenty-four of the townships in the purchase. A catalogue of the lots drawn, with the proprietors' names annexed, is on file in the secretary's office.[1]

Ebenezer Jessup, a large operator in lands at that period, was the active agent in these arrangements, and purchased the tract for Totten and Crossfield and their associates. This Indian deed conveyed no legal title, the absolute fee in the land existing in the crown. It undoubtedly protected them against intrusion and conferred rights probably analogous to the preemptive rights existing at the present day. The government recognized these rights and issued patents in subordination to them. Jessup advises Governor Colden, December 27th, 1774, that he had agreed with certain individuals for Totten and Crossfield to convey ten thousand acres to them in the purchase, and requested that letters patent should be granted, in conformity with the agreement, which was soon after done.[2]

The territory comprised in the Totten and Crossfield purchase lies in the counties of Essex, Warren, Hamilton and Herkimer. The west and part of the north lines were surveyed in 1772, with an outline of a portion of the township, each of which included about twenty thousand acres.

---

[1] *Land Papers*, LIX, 9, 10, 88. This volume is occupied exclusively with papers referring to this tract.

[2] *Land Papers*, XXXIX, 157.

Slight vestiges of these surveys may still be traced. The colonial government issued patents for a few townships previous to the revolution, some of which I have mentioned, but none of these extended to lands in Essex county. Among these patents, the return of a survey of twenty thousand acres for Sir Jeffrey Amherst appears among the *Land Papers* under date of March 27th, 1774. Sufficient evidence exists upon which to form an estimate of the market value of these lands at that period. Jessup executed December 3d, 1772, a receipt to Philip Livingstone for two hundred and six pounds and eight shillings, the purchase money of two townships; in July he gave another receipt to Thomas Lewis for fifty-one pounds, in payment of three thousand acres, and on 8th April the same year another to Chris. Duyckinck for one hundred and three pounds "in full of twenty-four thousand acres." These are preserved among the *Land Papers*. The action of the proprietors at a meeting, January 14th, 1773, in reference to the construction of a road, indicates that their measures for the improvement of the territory were active and judicious.

On the 21st of April, 1775, and only a few months preceding the day established by the constitution of 1777, from which all royal grants were abrogated, Dartmouth wrote to Tryon, that the king would confirm by letters patent to Totten and Crossfield and their associates, "their lands, on humble application" and "a disavowal of all association" with the nonintercourse measures of the colonists.[1] The two former, at least probably yielded their adhesion to the government. Tradition asserts that these estates were confiscated. It is certain that a large portion of the purchase reverted to the state government. The imaginary lines of all the townships were laid down on Southier's map, although a part only had, at that time been practically surveyed. In the years 1785 and 1786, numerous petitions were presented to the state for grants of large

[1] *His. Doc.*, VIII, 570.

tracts in this territory, and many by the original proprietors, who thus asked the confirmation of their former claims. These applications were generally conceded, the claimants usually paying the state a valuable consideration for their grants.

Tomlin. Thomas Tomlin obtained a grant of two hundred acres May 2d, 1772, located east side of Lake George and adjoining Stoughton. On the old map referred to,[1] this patent is thus located.

Wharton. A patent was granted to John Wharton, Esq., late captain in Sixtieth regiment, April 16th, 1765, for three thousand acres, which was located by Gilliland in Essex.

Wriesburg. On the same day a patent was granted to Daniel Wriesburg, late captain Sixtieth Foot, and was located by Gilliland, in Willsboro'.

---

[1] See Soldier's Rights.

PART II.

PHYSICAL GEOGRAPHY.

The physical formation of Essex county combines peculiar and striking characteristics. The beautiful and picturesque are singularly blended with the magnificent and imposing. Exhibitions of impressive grandeur, scarcely transcended by the magnificence of Niagara, are combined with scenes of incomparable sylvan beauty and romantic seclusion. A very large proportion of the county is formed by a general upheaval, which produced a common elevation of the whole region, except along the shores of Lake Champlain, and some of its tributaries. It may be pronounced in the aggregate, a broken and mountainous territory. Many districts, however, embracing large portions of entire townships, exhibit a very high degree of native fertility and adaptation to tillage. The surface of these tracts is usually level, or presents gentle and agreeable undulations. Extensive valleys, lying elevated among the mountains, possess the richest soil, formed by the accumulation of ages, from the debris of the higher steeps. Alluvial flats of great extent and natural fertility, spread along the margin of numerous streams, and surround the hidden lakes and ponds in the interior.

The hills and mountains, far up their slopes, often afford a rich and generous soil, yielding the choicest pasture and meadow lands. Although these advantages may mitigate its general character, the country presents a vast surface, rock bound and inaccessible in its cliffs and heights, and impracticable to cultivation. A large portion of this territory, stamped by nature with ruggedness and desolation, and closed against the approaches of agriculture, teems with immeasurable wealth in its forests and mines.

Several detached and broken ranges of mountains enter the county from the south. These mountains appear to lose their distinctive peculiarities as a system or general range, and are thrown together in promiscuous, massive groups. Two of these disturbed ranges reach the limits of the county at Ticonderoga. They are not high, but exceedingly abrupt and jagged. One suddenly terminates at Mount Defiance, and the other subsides into slight eminences, in the vicinity of Lake George. Two other ranges, loftier and more important, exhibiting the same dislocated character, traverse the county in nearly parallel tracts. They both terminate in bold and majestic promontories upon Lake Champlain, and spread their lateral projections over the county. These lofty promontories, at some points upon the lake, present a high and nearly perpendicular wall, and at others, their huge and beetling cliffs impend over the water. These impressive spectacles of mountain scenery are exhibited at Moriah, Willsboro', Westport and Chesterfield.

Peaks occur along the line of these sierras, which in other regions would be regarded as conspicuous landmarks, but here, associated with loftier and more imposing summits, they have neither names nor notoriety. Among the class of secondary mountains within the county, are Pharaoh, in Schroon, Mount Dix, in North Hudson, and the Bald mountain, in Moriah, which attract attention, and are admired for their position and formation. The Bald mountain rises to an altitude of more than two thousand feet. By its proximity to the lake, and its isolated position, one standing upon its bald peak may trace the sinuosities of the lake, studded with its islands and promontories, distinctly revealed in a course of more than forty miles. The villages and mountain scenery, with the intervening plains on both sides of the lake, form a brilliant picture, while directly beneath, the eye rests upon the elevated plateau in Moriah, "all dressed in living green," and the busy scenes that surround the numerous ore beds. This peak will soon be reached by a convenient ascent, when the explorer may enjoy, without any great effort or fatigue, one of the most impressive and beautiful panoramic views afforded by this region of forests, mountains and lakes. In the Adirondac group, situated chiefly in the towns of Keene and Newcomb, a cluster occurs of the loftiest and most remarkable mountains east of the Mississippi. Less elevated than individual summits of the White hills of New Hampshire, or the Black mountain of North Carolina, they far exceed any entire range in the gigantic magnitude of their proportions, and in the grandeur and beauty of their structure. It is extraordinary, that the public should, until so recent a period, have been in comparative ignorance of this remarkable group of mountains, and of the deeply interesting and romantic country they envelop in their mighty folds. They are within forty miles of Lake Champlain, the great avenue of northern commerce, and so familiar to the fashionable tourist. Their highest peaks are visible from Burlington, and the altitude of Mount Marcy has actually been determined from that point. The idea, however, is inaccurate, that this tract had not been explored until a recent date, or that these mountains were unknown until a late discovery. Most of these scenes have been, for many years, familiar to innumerable hunters, pioneers and surveyors. Most of these prominent summits are visible through a wide territory (which has been occupied for more than half a century), not in the obscurity of distance, but in the full exhibition of their majesty and glory.

Mount Marcy, the monarch of these wilds, towers above the surrounding pinnacles, in a beautiful cone, and in one view nearly an acute apex. Ascending above every contiguous object, and piercing with this striking formation far upward no one can contemplate it without recognizing the force and appropriateness of its name, in the energetic and beautiful nomenclature of the Indians. They called the towering mountain projecting its acute top toward the heavens, Tahawus, *The Cloud-splitter*. The height of this mountain, above tide water, is 5,467 feet. Another eminence, Mount McIntyre, supposed to fall a little below Mount Marcy in altitude, perhaps surpasses it in ponderous magnificence, and presents a more uniform, massive and compact structure. The Dial mountain, Mount Seward, McMartin, Colden, and other peaks unmeasured, of apparently equal if not greater dimensions, mingle in this cluster, and impress a stamp of Alpine grandeur upon the scenery.

A lofty range known as the Keene mountains, presents a peculiar aspect; dark, broken, and frowning. The White-face mountain, in the majestic Indian dialect Waho-partenie, an eminence of 4,855 feet,[1] stands remote from the other groups, and occupies the northern extremity of the huge mountain belt that encircles the town of North Elba. This peak from its rare and admirable proportions, its bald summit, solitary isolation, and the vast preeminence of its height above surrounding objects, is a beautiful and conspicuous landmark, over a wide horizon. A few years since it presented a spectacle of unequaled sublimity. In the heat and drought of midsummer, the combustible materials upon its summit were fired by accident or design, and during one whole night the conflagration raged, exhibiting to the gaze of hundreds, almost the splendor and awfulness of a volcanic eruption in its wild vehemence. A convenient pathway has been constructed to the summit of the mountain from which a magnificent view is commanded over a wide expanse of territory.

Public sentiment will not ratify the acts of private men, who would obliterate the aboriginal names of the great physical features of this continent, and substitute those of individuals, however eminent their political position, or excellent and esteemed their private characters. The Indian nomenclature is singularly rich in its force and

---

[1] A recent observation gives to White-face about the same altitude as Mount Marcy.

euphony, and in the beauty and illustrative appropriateness of its designations. The names they have attached to physical objects will soon be the only vestige of their existence. They will leave no other monuments of their former presence upon the land they once possessed, and fondly deemed their own peculiar heritage.

Lakes.

Lake Champlain. In an early part of this volume, I glanced at the military aspect and commercial importance of Lake Champlain. The rare and exceeding beauty of its scenery arrests and delights the observer. On the east it is bounded by an undulating plain, rich in a high and luxuriant culture, whilst beyond this, the horizon is limited by the bold and broken outline of the Green mountains. On the western border, the dark and towering Adirondacs, spread far into the interior, here and there projecting their rugged spurs into the bosom of the lake, and often forming lofty and inaccessible headlands, covered with forests, or exposing bleak and frowning masses of naked rock. The lake ranges in width, from one mile to fifteen miles. It is studded by innumerable islands; some of which are mere rocky projections; others clothed in their native green woods, rest like gems upon the waters, and others formed by alluvial deposits, are unsurpassed in their native loveliness, or in their exuberant fertility.

The severity of a northern climate closes the navigation of this lake no inconsiderable portion of the year. The ice usually forms upon the broadest part about the 1st of February, and remains, in an average of years, until near the middle of April. The navigation is suspended for a longer period by the ice forming earlier and remaining later at each extremity.[1] The lake occasionally remains open the entire winter. The transition from navigation to the transit of the lake upon the ice, is often amazingly sudden; teams having crossed its broadest part, upon the ice

[1] *Iddo Osgood, Esq.*

the fifth day after it had been passed by a steamer. The ice often attains great thickness. The spectacle, frequently afforded by this vast expanse of icy surface, is singularly beautiful and exhilarating. It furnishes for several weeks the great highway of business and pleasure. Roads diverging from every point, are animate with activity and excitement. Long trains of teams, freighted with the commodities of the country, glide easily over it, whilst the pleasure sleigh bounds along its smooth and crystal field, breaking the stillness by the music of its merry bells. Little danger occurs in the transit of the ice, except in the passage of the cracks or fissures, which starting from the various points and headlands, rend the ice asunder with a sound and concussion like the reverberation of thunder, or the prolonged discharge of ordnance. These fissures entirely separate the ice, and are designed by the wise purposes of providence to strengthen it, by affording an escape to the pent up air beneath.

The balmy atmosphere and warmer sun of approaching spring, affect and gradually weaken the ice. Traveling on it, then becomes hazardous, and is often attended with great jeopardy and frequent loss of life and property. The inhabitants, residing upon the shore of the lake, are habituated to these perils and familiar to the modes of assistance. On the alarm of accidents, they rush to the point of danger, with prompt and efficient zeal bearing ropes and boards and other requisite articles, and rarely fail to extricate the sufferer, when the scene can be reached.

The final breaking up of the ice in the spring often affords a spectacle of intense interest. The evidences are readily recognized, which portend the event. Its surface exhibits several marked and peculiar phases, which indicate the progress of decay. Its usual transparent and brilliant clearness yields to a dark and clouded aspect. This is succeeded by a soft and snowy color, as the moisture leaves the surface and penetrates the mass. The next stage in its dissolution is exhibited as the body of ice becomes porous and losing its buoyancy, sinks to the level of the water.

Its appearance then is black and portentous, and can scarcely be contemplated without a feeling of awe and dread. The fissures now open and expand. The ice separates into larger bodies, and driven by the winds in immense fields, is broken up, and often piled in huge masses upon the shores where it remains late in the spring, a memorial of the passed empire of winter. At other times, the ice continues nearly entire, until saturated with water, it at once, in a moment as it were, disappears, dissolving into its original element. In the progress of dissolution of the ice, a singular phenomenon is revealed. The mass at this time, exhibits a combination of an infinitude of parallel crystals or icicles, arranged in a perpendicular formation, and each distinct and perfect, extending from the lower side to the surface, or in other words, from the water to the atmosphere. These particles separate from each other in the process of disintegration.

A day of jubilee and rejoicing succeeds, when these icy fetters are finally broken up, and intercourse is restored. The advent of the first steamer of the season, always rejuvenated during the winter, and fresh from the hands of the painter, is hailed at each landing by joyous shoutings and often by the booming of artillery.

Interior Lakes and Rivers.

The numerous lakes and gem-like ponds, that stud the surface of the country in such profusion, not only diversify and adorn the scenery, but are the source of the vast water power so essential to the industrial interest and prosperity of the country. This water, chiefly arising from springs, is usually cold, clear, and pure. Schroon lake, lying partly in Warren country, is ten miles long and one and a half broad, and is remarkable for its quiet and romantic beauty. A high, precipitous shore encloses it on the east, and on the west a cultivated and delightful tract spreads its fertile fields down to the brink. This lake forms the reservoir to the waters of the upper Hudson. It is already the channel of a valuable traffic, and will become highly important to the rapidly increasing manufacturing business of the district.

Paradox lake is situated in the same valley, and is separated from Schroon lake by a drift or alluvial, of apparently modern formation. Paradox lake occupies the basin of hills that environ it in a gentle ascent, except the narrow passage at its outlet, which is a confluent of the Schroon river and nearly on a level with it. The river, swollen by the mountain torrents, often rises higher than this lake, and pours its waters into the basin, presenting the paradoxical appearance of a stream rushing back upon its fountain head. The lake derives, from this singular fact, its unique but not inappropriate name. Directly east of Schroon lake, and elevated above it several hundred feet, lies Lake Pharaoh, an important body of water, surrounded by a group of dark and gloomy mountains. In this vicinity cluster numerous ponds, the fountain heads of valuable streams.

The miniature lakes and ponds, which repose in almost every valley among the Adirondacs, and form the head springs of the Hudson, possess indescribable romance and beauty. Now they are embraced and hidden by dense and unbroken forests, and now encompassed by lofty mountains, whose inaccessible precipices descend into their waters by a nearly vertical wall, and now slumbering in the bosom of some lovely and picturesque nook, their mirrored surface, reflecting this varied scenery, is alone broken by the leaping of a trout, the gambols of a deer, or, at far intervals, by the oar of the solitary hunter. These gentle and subduing beauties of nature, combined with the awe-imposing and thrilling grandeur of their mountain spectacles, with the pure, invigorating and health-inspiring air which envelops them, must render these solitudes among the most desirable and attractive resorts, to the philosopher, the invalid and the tourist of pleasure.

Lake Placid, situated principally in North Elba, just touches that beautiful valley, in the incomparable landscape of which it forms a conspicuous and very essential feature. Its great expanse, its deep and transparent waters, its beautiful proportions, stretching its sinuosities along bold headlands far into the recesses of the mountains, until in the distant view, its waters seem to lave the base of Whiteface, although in fact separated from it by a rich valley of two miles in width, unite to render Lake Placid one of the most delightful and attractive objects in this land of loveliness and silence. A small pond connects with the lake by a narrow channel; this pond has no other inlet or outlet, and is distinguished by a singular circumstance. The water flows for a period of two or three minutes from the lake into the pond; an interval of a few seconds succeeds, with no apparent motion of the water; after this, for the same time, it flows back again into the lake. This ebbing and flowing is, I believe, perpetual.[1] Lake Placid is one of the most important heads of the Au Sable river. The manufacturing interest on the line of that stream, has erected at the outlet of the lake, an expensive and ponderous dam. This work forms the lake into a capacious reservoir, and secures a permanent supply of water, at all seasons, to the immense works moved by the Au Sable.

The Au Sable ponds form the loftiest as well as most important reservoir of the South branch of the Au Sable river. Lying amid the acclivities of the Adirondacs, and buried deeply in the solitudes of forests, which have yet scarcely been disturbed by the movements of enterprise, these waters are calculated, when more fully known, to attract the attention of the tourist and sportsman, by their solitariness, their beauty and sporting wealth. They are four or five miles from civilized habitations. Small boats have been placed upon them, to facilitate access to Mt. Marcy, towards which they afford one of the most direct routes. The Upper pond is classed among the most beautiful lakes of the region. The state some years ago

---

[1] *T. L. Nash.*

erected a dam on the outlet of these ponds, to aid the manufacturing interests of the district, but it yielded to the pressure of a sudden and extraordinary accumulation of water, which contributed to produce a flood, that poured upon the Au Sable valley, in wide and terrible desolation.[1]

I may here appropriately refer to a fact of some philosophical interest and great practical importance. In the progress of my survey, I have observed, in repeated instances, the ruins of mills and dams, which, in the early occupation of the county, had ample water power, not a vestige of which now remains but a deep and worn ravine that once formed its channel. As the progress of agricultural and manufacturing improvements — before which forests are leveled, the country opened, and the earth exposed to the influence of the sun and atmosphere — advances, springs and streams will be dried up, and it will become imperatively necessary to adopt artificial means to control and preserve the water power of this county.

Rivers.

The elevated and extended highlands of Essex county, naturally form the great water shed of an extended territory. In their recesses, the sources of the Hudson almost mingle with the waters that flow into Champlain and the tributaries of the St. Lawrence. A rivulet gurgling towards the Hudson, discharges from one extremity of the Indian pass, and a branch of the Au Sable from the opposite. A pond lying amid the rocks, hundreds of feet above the pass, pours its waters into a confluent of the St. Lawrence. The streams of a district, like Essex county, broken and mountainous, will be numerous, but turbulent and precipitous. These characteristics are eminently useful in the aspect of a manufacturing interest. Wherever the demands of business require water power in the county, it exists or can be at once created.

---

[1] *Mr. George S. Potter.*

The tributaries of the Hudson traverse every section of the southwestern portion of the country, and afford illimitable facilities to various mechanical and other industrial occupations. Putnam's creek, formed by the lakes and ponds in the mountains of the interior, courses a distance of twenty miles, supplying the power to numerous works and enters the lake at Crown point. The Boquet interlaces, by its numerous branches, the central portion of the county, and affording, in a course of forty-five miles, unnumbered water privileges, discharges into the lake at Willsboro'. Several of the most extensive and valuable manufacturing works in the county are established upon this stream. The Boquet was formerly navigable to the falls, a distance of three miles, by the largest vessels upon the lake. Its channel, now changed and obstructed, only admits, at favorable periods of the year, the lightest crafts.

Lake George penetrates Essex county several miles, and discharges through an outlet of about three miles and a half in length, into Lake Champlain, by a strong, deep, and equable stream, which is navigable to the lower falls. This stream, in its course from Lake George to the falls, forms a most extraordinary water power, in some peculiarities, without a parallel. It discharges per second a volume of water, exceeding four hundred feet, along a natural canal of one mile and a half in length, making chiefly by a gradual descent, a fall of two hundred and twenty feet. Through almost its whole course water wheels, connected with machinery, may be dropped from its elevated rocky banks, into the stream, and propelled almost without any artificial arrangement. The sloping banks of Lake George form an immense receptacle where the excess of water is accumulated, and gradually discharges. Hence, no freshets can endanger the works upon its outlet, but a uniform and permanent supply of water is secured at all seasons, and under all circumstances. This stream rarely varies three feet from its ordinary level.

The warmth of the water, and the rapidity of the current prevent every obstruction from ice to the wheel. The water may be diffused laterally, and its power multiplied to any extent. The great and rare purity of the water renders it particularly adapted to those manufactories which require dyeing, bleaching and printing facilities. In combination with all these singular advantages, this position commands the commercial thoroughfare formed by the lakes; it may reach the immense forests extending far into the interior, spreading on each side of Lake George; it has, within its own environs, a rich and abundant mineral region, and has near and easy access to the vast iron deposits of the Moriah district.

Such harmony in its arrangements, so great and remarkable advantages in the bounties of providence, are rarely combined. The utilitarian spirit of the age, the interests of business and enterprise, would long since have converted these neglected privileges into elements of prosperity and wealth; but the blight of foreign ownership has paralyzed those high bounties. The cupidity or grossly mistaken and pernicious policy of these proprietors has imposed terms so exacting, as to repel through a long term of years almost every purpose of an adequate occupation of these advantages.

The two main branches of the Au Sable river, nearly equal in size and importance, rise principally in the western part of Essex county, and by their numerous and wide spread confluents drain a territory of about eight hundred square miles. These branches unite at Au Sable Forks and roll along the Au Sable valley a motive power that impels varied and extensive industrial pursuits equal to any other stream within the state of no greater extent and capacity. The river Saranac penetrates Essex county from Franklin near the line that divides the towns of North Elba and St. Armands, and crossing the latter diagonally, enters Clinton county. Gliding along high level banks, with scarcely a perceptible current, it exhibits almost the form and aspect of an artificial canal. It is navigable in Essex county about fifteen miles by small boats, and probably by slight improvement might be adapted to the passage of the smaller class of screw steamers.

Natural Curiosities.

Indian pass. The mighty convulsions which have upheaved the lofty mountains of this region, or rent asunder the barriers that enclosed the seas, which washed their cliffs, have left impressive vestiges of their power, in the striking natural phenomena spread over the country. None of them afford more wonderful exhibitions of those terrific agencies, or more imposing beauty and magnificence, than a remarkable gorge, known as the Indian pass, in the impressive aboriginal Otneyarh, the Stony Giants. It occupies a narrow ravine, formed by a rapid acclivity of Mount McMartin on one side, rising at an angle of forty-five degrees, and on the opposite by the dark naked wall of a vertical precipice, towering to an altitude of eight hundred to one thousand two hundred feet from its base, and extending more than a mile in length. The base itself is elevated about two thousand five hundred feet above tide water. The deep and appalling gorge is strewn and probably occupied for several hundred feet, with gigantic fragments hurled into it from the impending cliffs, by some potent agency. The elements still advance the process. So exact and wonderful is the stupendous masonry of this bulwark, that it seems, could human nerve allow the effort, a stone dropped from the summit, might reach the base without striking an impediment. The pencil cannot portray, nor language describe, the full grandeur and sublimity of this spectacle. The deep seclusion, the wild solitude of the place, awe and impress. Many miles from human habitation, nature here reigns in her primitive silence and repose. The eagles form their eyries amid these inaccessible cliffs, and seem like some humble bird as they hover over the deep abyss. The heavy forests that clothe the steeps of McMartin, and shroud the broken and confused masses of rock in the gorge, add to the gloom and solemnity of these dark recesses. A tiny rivulet just starting from its birthplace amid these solitudes, chafes and frets along its rocky passage, in its course to the Hudson. A ravine lying among the Adirondacs, near Keeseville and known as Poke-O-Moonshine (the origin or meaning of this euphonious name I have not been able to trace), presents a feeble copy of the Indian pass in reduced proportions.

The Wilmington Notch. The western branch of the Au Sable breaks through its mountain bulwarks, in a scene almost as thrilling and impressive as the Indian Pass. The river compressed within a narrow passage of a few feet, in width, becomes here an impetuous torrent, foams and dashes along the base of a precipitous wall, formed by Whiteface mountain, which towers above it, in nearly a perpendicular ascent of thousands of feet, whilst on the other side it almost laves the abrupt, naked and rugged crags, of another lofty precipice. Bursting through this obstacle, it leaps into an abyss of more than one hundred feet in depth, so dark and impervious from mantling trees, and impending rocks, that the eye cannot penetrate its hidden cavern. A road which has been recently constructed through the pass, renders this remarkable spot easily accessible to the tourist; and I can imagine few scenes more attractive by its wild and romantic beauty, or its stern and appalling grandeur. Nearly the whole course of the Au Sable and its branches presents a series of falls, cascades and rapids, which, whilst they adorn and animate the scenery, afforded innumerable sites of water power, rarely exceeded in capacity and position.

Walled Banks of the Au Sable. The passage of the Au Sable river, along its lofty and perpendicular banks and through the chasm at the High bridge is more familiar to the public mind, than most of the striking and picturesque features in the interesting scenery of that romantic stream. The continued and gradual force of the current, aided perhaps by some vast effort of nature, has formed a passage of the river through the deep layers of sandstone rock, which are boldly developed above the village of Keeseville, and form the embankment of the river, until it reaches the quiet basin below the high bridge. In the vicinity of Keeseville, the passage of the stream is between a wall upon either side of fifty feet in height; leaving these it glides gently along a low valley, until suddenly precipitated over a precipice, that creates a fall of singular beauty. Foaming and surging from this point, over a rocky bed until it reaches the village of Birmingham, it then abruptly bursts into a dark, deep chasm of sixty feet. A bridge with one abutment setting upon a rock that divides the stream, crosses the river at the head of this fall. This bridge is perpetually enveloped in a thick cloud of spray and mist. In winter, the frost work encrusts the rock and trees, with the most gorgeous fabrics, myriads of columns and arches, and icy diamonds and stalactites glitter in the sunbeams. In the sunshine a brilliant rainbow spreads its radiant arc over this deep abyss. All these elements, rare in their combination, shed upon this scene an effect inexpressibly wild, picturesque and beautiful. The river plunges from the latter precipice, amid the embrasures of the vast gulf, in which for nearly a mile it is nearly hidden to observation from above. It pours a wild torrent, now along a natural canal, formed in the rocks in almost perfect and exact courses, and now darts madly down a precipice. The wall rises on a vertical face upon each side from seventy-five to one hundred and fifty feet, whilst the width of the chasm rarely exceeds thirty feet, and at several points the stupendous masonry of the opposite walls approaches within eight or ten feet. Lateral fissures, deep and narrow, project from the main ravine at nearly right angles. The abyss is reached through one of these crevices by a stairway descending to the water by two hundred and twelve steps. The entire mass of these walls is formed of laminæ of sandstone rock, laid in regular and precise structure almost rivaling the most accurate artificial work. The pines and cedars starting from the apertures of the wall, spread a dark canopy over the gulf. The instrumentality, which has produced this wonderful work, is a problem that presents a wide scope for interesting, but unsatisfactory speculation.

A report of the state geologist asserts, "that near the bottom of the fissure at the High bridge, and through an extent of seventy feet, numerous specimens of a small bivalvular molusca, or lingulæ," are discovered, and "that ripple marks appear at the depth of seventy or eighty feet."

Split rock. Travelers in passing through Lake Champlain, observe in the town of Essex, a remarkable point, known to the French as *Rocher fendu*, and to the English, as Split rock. It contains about half an acre of land, and rising thirty feet above the water, in a bold, precipitous front, is separated from the promontory by a fissure of ten feet in width. Its slope and position have created the belief, that it has been detached from the adjacent headland by its own weight, and in some shock of nature, although it has probably been separated in the gradual attrition of the earth and disintegrating rocks, by the action of the elements. It is a striking and interesting formation. Guide books, and some works of high pretensions, describe an abyss of five hundred feet in depth, dividing the rock from the promontory. I visited it last autumn, and walked through the fissure, two feet above the level of the lake.

Near Port Kendall, in Chesterfield, another of these remarkable phenomena occurs, to which frequent allusion has been made. The outlets of several ponds upon these highlands, unite in a stream which forms at this place, a very superior water power, directly upon the margin of Lake Champlain. The water rushes a distance of forty or fifty rods above the falls, through a chasm, which appears to have been opened by some mighty physical convulsion. It presents a gulf sixty or seventy feet wide, with a depth of thirty or forty feet.[1] At the extre-

---

[1]*Levi Higby, Esq.*

mity of this passage, the stream plunges into the lake over a precipice of about forty feet. A similar spectacle known as Split rock, is exhibited near Pleasant valley, where the whole volume of the Boquet rushes through a ravine of this character.

The Rainbow Falls. This remarkable cascade is situated in Keene within a mile of the romantic Au Sable ponds and forms a striking feature of that wild picturesque region. It is upon Rainbow brook, a small tributary of the South branch of the Au Sable river. The fall is computed from careful observation to be one hundred and twenty-five feet in sheer vertical descent. The site is separated from the Keene flats, the nearest human residence, by a dense forest three or four miles in extent, and is hidden in the recesses of the vast wilderness of the Adirondacs. It is embraced in the extensive tract of timber land recently purchased by Messrs. Thomas & Armstrong, and is now first revealed to general knowledge. The falls are at present only accessible by a path through the forest; but they have already excited the attention of the artist and explorer, and it is in contemplation to immediately open by convenient roads, a district that will be regarded not among the least attractive or interesting in the Adirondac region, to the sportsman and the worshiper of nature, in her secluded temples.[1]

The Hunter's pass. This gorge lies in the town of North Hudson, and is formed by the deep, parallel precipices of Dix's peak and Nipple top, which are among the highest and most sequestered mountains of the Adirondacs. It is similar to the Indian Pass, and second only to that amazing exhibition in its sublime and imposing features. This pass is rarely penetrated even by the hunter, and at a very late period only has been visited for the specific purpose of exploration. It is buried several miles deeper in the mazes of these forests and mountains than the Au Sable ponds or Rainbow falls, but is sufficiently near these points to enhance the attraction of the district, when it shall have

---

[1] *Almon Thomas, George S. Potter.*

become a new object of interest and resort. The scene can now only be reached by the severest toil of several miles (but the feat has been achieved by brave and delicate woman) and when this is accomplished, the dense forest, the masses of rocks and their mosses, and their debris gathered for ages, renders the gorge almost impenetrable.[1] These successive revelations in the physical aspect of the county, illustrate the profound seclusion and great extent of the wilderness, and warrant the opinion, that other objects of deep interest remain in its recesses yet to be unveiled. It is believed that several of the most secluded peaks of the Adirondacs have never been ascended. This circumstance becomes still more impressive, if upon a map of the state, one point of the dividers graduated at one hundred miles, is placed at the Capitol, and we find on describing a circle, that it traces a line through the central part of the Adirondac group. Mount Marcy and other prominent objects we have noticed, lie scarcely beyond this circle.

Two very remarkable subterranean passages in the town of Schroon near Paradox lake are worthy of examination. The first of these forms the channel of a small rivulet, by a natural perforation of some hundred feet through the massive rock, ten or fifteen feet below the surface, over which passes the public road, as if by an artificial bridge. The other, which I find referred to in early works on the topography of this region, is a highly curious and interesting exhibition. The explorer enters a lofty arch, several feet below the surface, carved out of the solid rock. It presents, at some points, the appearance of nearly an exact gothic structure, and at others, broken and ragged sides and canopy. This dark and gloomy cavern extends a number of rods, and is from four to twelve feet in width, and ten to fifteen in height. It constitutes the sluice way of a large stream, which propels a

---

[1] *The Elizabethtown Post.*

mill just above the entrance, and foams and dashes through the rocky and precipitous descent.

Trout are often found in pools within this passage, which are formed by the obstructions to the stream in its course.

Inflammable Gas. A striking phenomenon is noticed in Schroon lake. In parts of that picturesque and beautiful sheet of water, inflammable gases are emitted from the bottom, where the water is eighteen or twenty feet deep. When the surface is frozen over, the gas collects in various insulated bodies beneath the ice, where it can be readily discovered. If a small aperture is cut in the ice above one of these collections, the gas rushes forth with violence, and when a match is applied to it, the gas ignites and flames up in a brilliant fiery column eight feet high, and continues to burn, usually, from five to fifteen minutes or until the receptable is exhausted. In the summer, the gas rises to the surface at intervals, producing a strong ebullition of the water, which continues about five minutes, when it ceases and the lake becomes as calm as usual. Sometimes burning shavings have been thrust into the gas before it is dissipated, when it instantly takes fire and bursts into a flame that ascends several feet high and spreads along the surface of the lake frequently two rods.[1]

THE WILDERNESS OF NORTHERN NEW YORK.

This remarkable territory has not, until a comparative recent period, attracted any considerable public attention. The mind can scarcely comprehend the fact, that a district equal in size to the superficial area of several of the separate states of the Union, lies in the bosom of New

---

[1] I am indebted to Hon. Joel F. Potter for the above statements. In his note he mentions the following additional facts: "A neighbor of mine cut a large opening in the ice, but was somewhat slow in lighting his match. When he did apply it, the gas had accumulated and he was thrown back by its sudden ignition about eight feet, with the lost of whiskers and eye-brows." He relates another experiment in which the gas was collected

York, touching on one extremity the long occupied and densely populated valley of the Mohawk, and encircled by a highly cultivated and matured country, is still shrouded by its primeval forest, and remains almost as it came from the hands of its Creator. This territory embraces nearly all Hamilton county, and parts of Herkimer, Oneida, Lewis, St. Lawrence, Franklin, Essex, and Warren, and extends over one hundred miles in length, and about eighty miles in breadth.

Nature reigns in this wilderness, in her primeval seclusion and solitude. The daring hunter alone formerly penetrated its mazes in pursuit of its only denizens, the moose, the bear, the panther, and deer. The fisherman, whose ardor leads him to the deep recesses of the forest, breaks the quiet repose of these lakes and rivers, but within the boundaries of this sequestered region, man has scarcely an abode, in his civilization and improvements. A portion of this territory is mountainous and impracticable to culture. Here, as I have already remarked, the highest group of mountains east of the Mississippi, lift their pinnacles to the skies. The sheer and lofty precipice, the dashing torrent, the sylvan lake and the boundless ocean of forest, combine to form a scenery, which is unrivaled in its magnificence and beauty. The votaries and admirers of nature will learn to visit these scenes, and will gaze on them with wonder and delight.

The existence of this range of mountains, imposing and magnificent as it is, enveloping in its gigantic folds, the rich and beautiful region beyond, and to the approach of which it seemed to impose an impenetrable bar, has given rise to the opinions and estimates of that entire territory, which prevail. Eminent men, in supreme ignorance of the character of this district, have sneered at it, as the

---

and retained in a rude receptacle. "We have cut a hole in the ice, and placed a barrel over it, with the lower head on. Around this, snow was piled, and a gas burner attached to the upper head of the barrel, protected by a glass lantern. With this apparatus the gas from one of the collections referred to has burnt nearly a whole night."

Siberia of New York, little aware of the illimitable wealth which must be revealed, not only in its immense forests, of the most valuable wood and timber, and its boundless mineral riches, but in the adaptation of large sections of it to agricultural purposes. Other men, impelled by their example, have habitually indulged in sarcasm and ridicule, upon the character and resources of northern New York. These and similar views, have created impressions relative to the soil, the capabilities and climate of this territory, which have arrested emigration, and induced the board of land commissioners of the state, in an unwise and mistaken policy, to sacrifice by inadequate sales a large proportion of the public domain, which had been consecrated by our fathers, to a noble and glorious purpose — the education of our children.

I am anxious to correct those opinions, where I regard them to be false, and briefly to describe the physical features, the topographical arrangement, the agricultural and industrial capacity of this wilderness district. It is known that a part of this tract is situated within the limits of Essex county, and that it embraces the loftiest mountains of the Adirondacs. This range, stretching into Hamilton and the southern section of Franklin counties, partially bounds the table land on the south.

The fertile and beautiful plains of North Elba, on the eastern side of this district, are encircled by a lofty amphitheatre of these mountains. This territory, I have sufficiently described in another place, and have attempted to show by an analogy with some sections of Vermont, of nearly the same altitude, and which constitute a part of the most valuable and productive districts of that state, the great importance and adaptedness of these plains to cultivation. These mountains abound with ores, and are mantled to their summits by forests of the heaviest timber and choicest varieties of wood. Such is the present condition and aspect of this region, in the county of Essex, and these are some of its natural resources. Beyond the confines of this county, it reveals another appearance. The broken and rocky range of mountains subsides into a high plateau, with a fertile soil, adapted by its ingredients and formation to tillage and more particularly to grazing. The plains of North Elba extend to, and unite with this territory, forming an expansion of the plateau, in the bosom of the mountains over an area of about one hundred square miles.

The systems of lakes, which extend over this territory and yield to it so much beauty and animation, and almost mingle their waters, form the sources of the Hudson, of many affluents of the Mohawk and the Black river. Here also, are the fountain heads of the Oswegatchie, the Grass, the Raquette and St. Regis rivers, large and important streams, which discharge into the St. Lawrence, and the Saranac, Au Sable and Boquet, which flow into Lake Champlain.

The project of forming, in the connection of these streams and lakes by slight artificial constructions, an inland water communication, designed to open to enterprise and emigration the solitudes of this wilderness, I shall notice elsewhere.

The Black River canal skirts this territory on the west. The existing and proposed rail roads from Utica and Rome, in a northern direction, traverse its western borders. The Saratoga and Sackets Harbor rail road, now in progress, and which has been fostered by a magnificent bounty of five hundred thousand acres from the state lands, will, it is estimated, penetrate for a distance of one hundred and twenty miles through the heart of an unbroken wilderness. It will thread the mazes of this sequestered tract, along the base of lofty mountains (towering above it thousands of feet), through dense forests and amid the loveliest lakes and rivers. The original contemplated route of this road traverses the south-western section of Essex county, through the rich and important town of Minerva, and approaches within a few miles of the Adirondac works, and will thus render accessible the boundless wealth of that amazing district.

The most effective and decisive work, however, for the development of the entire region, would be created by the extraordinary reconnaissance referred to on another page. This subject I propose to notice elsewhere.

On every side, the slow but constant progress of improvement and cultivation is invading the wilderness. The pioneer of agriculture is each year occupying the haunts of the hunter, and gradually supplanting him. The valuable town of Greig, in Lewis county, now embracing a population of about nineteen hundred inhabitants, has within comparatively a few years, been carved from the silent forest.

This wilderness is distinguished for the healthiness of its climate. There prevails in the atmosphere, which envelops these mountains, a pureness, an elasticity and vitality that imparts health, and affords an indescribable physical enjoyment in the mechanical process of inspiration; the lungs are filled, and perform their functions without effort or labor. In my explorations of the country, I have met with repeated instances of individuals, who had reached their forest homes, in advanced stages of pulmonary affection, in whom the disease had been arrested, and the sufferer restored to comparative health. They uniformly imputed the change to the influence of the atmosphere, and to the soothing and invigorating effect of the peculiar property referred to. No invalid enters these solitudes without experiencing upon his system this strengthening and renovating influence. The atmosphere can be impregnated by no noxious miasmas, but is poured down from the summits of these stately mountains, fresh and pure, and life giving as it comes from the laboratory of nature.

Parts of the southern section of this territory in Warren and Hamilton counties, particularly where the lofty group of Mt. Seward upheave and dislocate the surface, are high, broken and mountainous. With this exception, and the portions of Essex county already described, the altitude of the country is lower than the plains of North Elba, but it still has an elevation which sensibly affects the climate; far less, however, than has been imputed by an erroneous public opinion. That this severity is not extreme, or such as to repel occupation, may be judged from the fact, that for many years, while the visitors to this region were limited, the hunters and guides were accustomed to procure their supply of potatoes from the spontaneous growth of the vegetable, gathered in the earth, and which had sprung from the peelings left upon the surface the preceding year.

Like every new country, in northern latitudes, which is shrouded by a thick and heavy vegetation, this tract is now far more liable to the effects of cold and frost, than it will be, when the advance of improvement has removed the massive forests, and exposed the earth to the influence of heat and light. The face of this country is represented by those who have thoroughly explored it, to be formed of a series of plains, or high valleys, distinct in their arrangement, and slightly elevated one above the other.

The streams, particularly those which are affluents of the St. Lawrence, flow in a strong, but neither rapid nor violent current, generally between high banks, and through a level and beautiful country. The land bordering upon these streams is chiefly occupied by dense and stately forests, comprehending the most magnificent and valuable evergreen timber, and the choicest varieties of hard wood. These forests are not unfrequently interspersed with wide and beautiful wet prairies, or natural meadows, spreading along the margin of the rivers, and presenting in their luxuriant herbage or native grasses, the appearance of highly cultivated fields. Myriads of deer graze and fatten upon these meadows.

The soil, whether sustaining its towering growth of primitive wood, or revealing the natural meadows, is represented as possessing native fertility and adaptation to agriculture, seldom surpassed by any districts of equal altitude, and in as high parallel of latitude. Such I know, from personal inspection, to be the character of the lands in North Elba. Specimens of soils, from the alluvial flats, upon the Au Sable river, and the loam from the uplands in that town, which were analyzed by Professor Salisbury, indicate the highest degree of native fertility. In some sections of this territory, a white silicious earth predominates, which is evidence of a light and rather sterile soil; other parts of it are, doubtless, rocky and broken; but a large portion of the land is susceptible of useful cultivation, and much more will be found congenial to grass and grazing.

The general face of this region may be inferred from the circumstance, that tourists speak in their description of it, of seeing, while floating upon the remote lakes and rivers, the summits of the Adirondacs, towering above the surrounding plateau, at a distance of thirty, and even fifty miles.

The nearness and facility of access to various markets, which must soon exist, is a most important and obvious advantage, which this country will at an early day possess. When the different public improvements, existing or contemplated, are accomplished, and that result is morally certain, every section of this region will enjoy an easy access to the Hudson, to the marts of the St. Lawrence and to Champlain. But the emigrant to this territory need not place any reliance upon remoter markets, while an infinitude of forge fires illuminate the recesses of the Adirondacs, the banks of the Saranac, and the valley of the Au Sable, and the varied other manufactories exist, which are springing into importance along the whole confines of this wilderness. These immense and increasing consumers will always secure a certain and prompt demand, at the highest prices, for all the charcoal that can be made, for every animal that can be raised upon these hills, and every production of agriculture that the earth can yield. Already, as the pioneer reaches the outline of the wilderness, we see the manufacturer and the lumberer press on his track, requiring the coal he produces in clearing his land, the timber he falls and every article of consumption he produces, at prices often exceeding those of the Atlantic cities. This domestic market will never be exhausted, but must constantly augment.

Large appropriations have been applied by the state, to the improvement of the navigation of several of the streams, which flow from this region, to facilitate the transportation of logs. Many of them are now navigable for this purpose, from the lakes where they rise, to their mouths. The incalculable amount of saw logs, embraced in the wilderness, may by these channels be transported at an insignificant expense, in their direct course to market, to points where they are fabricated into lumber, for exportation. The same spirit has cherished and will continue to foster the constructing of rail roads calculated to develop the affluence of this region. This wise policy of public munificence is calling into practical existence and utility an immense aggregate of property, which has been hitherto inaccessible and valueless. While it will administer to the efforts of private enterprise, and supply new fountains of individual wealth, it will return to the treasury of the state, tenfold, the expenditures, by opening the vast public domain to market and by the immense accession to the business of the public works it must create. Hence, it is manifest, that the labor of the settler, which removes the forest and reveals the earth to cultivation, also prepares the coal for the manufacturer and the timber for transportation; and thus, while he is remunerated for his toil, he is enabled to pay for his farm and adapt it to tillage. In addition to the pine, spruce and hemlock timber, which occupies this territory and which may be computed by millions of saw logs, it comprehends a vast amount of excellent cedar, and several varieties of oak, birch and cherry, that attain an immense size, and are in great request by the manufacturer, for choice fabrics, and coal wood, that can be estimated by tens of millions of cords.

Iron ore is known to exist here in large deposits, sufficient, probably, for all its requirements; but if this opinion should prove to be incorrect, aside from many other sources of supply, its most remote sections will soon, by means of the contemplated works, join hands with the exhaustless masses of the Adirondac deposits.

The unrivaled fish, which throng these waters in the utmost profusion, and now afford an article of such exquisite luxury, may be made an important and valuable commodity of exportation, when the means of a rapid and certain transportation are established. An immense quantity of venison is every season sent from the wilderness to the southern and eastern cities.

The price of land, in this territory, ranges from one dollar to six dollars the acre.

The wisdom of the development by the state of the resources of this region, and the promoting of its settlement by every liberal and fostering policy, is so apparent and imperative, that its expediency can scarcely be enforced by any argument. Let avenues be opened into it; let the navigation be perfected, and the rivers made more available for the floating of saw logs, and it will soon be colonized by sturdy and energetic emigrants, and the silent and gloomy wilderness will resound with the din of labor and industry. False and deceptive public sentiment has shed a blighting influence over this territory, and created obstacles to its occupation, more impracticable than its mountain barriers, or all the impediments with which nature has surrounded it.

Mineral Springs.

Numerous springs of mineral water occur in Essex county, but a few only are known to possess any high or peculiar medicinal properties. The Adirondac springs, consisting of a cluster of four fountains, lying within a small circle, are situated upon premises formerly owned by Mr. Stevenson of Westport. About two years since, the property was purchased by Mr. George W. Spencer, who gave the springs their present appropriate name. They are beautifully situated upon a slope of the Adirondacs, about half a mile from the lake, and command an extended view of its course, with a magnificent mountain scenery on both shores, and a landscape formed by a highly cultivated and picturesque country. The site of these springs is about four miles and a half from Port Henry, and the same distance from the village of Westport, and is approached in both directions by excellent roads, through an interesting and beautiful district. Mr. Spencer has erected, at large expense, convenient structures about the fountains. These waters have been known and celebrated in the region during the last forty years, for their singular efficacy in relieving various diseases and affections.

In the year 1852, while acting under my appointment by the State society, I procured a gallon of the water from each of the springs mentioned below, and submitted them to Professor Salisbury, at that time the chemist and geologist of the society. After a careful examination, he returned to me the subjoined result. I may properly remark, that the appearance of the springs and the vicinity, disclose the presence of minerals in an extraordinary degree. The deposit of a substance that appears to be chiefly magnesia, through which the Cold spring ascends, is about ten feet thick; and the concretion formed by the water of the Sulphur spring has been opened eighteen feet in depth without reaching the base. These encrustations are very similar to the High Rock spring in Saratoga. This residuum of the waters may be traced along their course several feet, after the discharge from the fountain. In its first stage, before induration, it is about the consistence of putty, soft and unctuous, and without grit to the touch. This substance, while soft, has been used constantly, and with remarkable success, as an external application in cutaneous affections. The Sulphur spring is characterized by the constant, and often quite active ebullition of a gaseous substance. The following are the analyses of Professor Salisbury:

	1 gal. water from Sulphur spring.		1 gal. water from Cold spring.	
Sulphuretted hydrogen,..............	16 cubic inches.		......	
Organic matter, ...	8.64 grains.		8.16 grains.	
Sulphur, ...	2.88	"	......	
Lime, ...	10.32	"	12.88	"
Magnesia, ...	2.24	"	3.12	"
Potassa, ...	1.36	"	1.20	"
Soda, ...	1.12	"	0.88	"
Iron....	1.04	"	1.44	"
Chlorine, ...	trace		0.48	"
Sulphuric acid, ...	0.88	"	1.52	"
Phosphoric acid,......................	0.32	"	2.48	"
Carbonic acid, ...	1.36	"	1.44	"
Silicic acid, ...	0.40	"	0.48	"
Total solid matter in one gallon,...	30.64	"	34.08	"

" One distinguishing character of the Sulphur spring is the large quantity of sulphuretted hydrogen its waters contain. A portion of the alkaline basis is also combined with sulphur, forming sulphides.

The water designated in the analysis, as No. 3, was taken from a spring upon the premises of L. Pope in Chesterfield, and No. 6 from a spring in Jay, situated almost within the water line of the Au Sable river. In relation to these waters, Prof. Salisbury remarks: " On removing the cork, I found in No. 3 a mere trace of sulphuretted hydrogen; in No. 6 no trace of this gas, or carbonic acid gas could be detected. They both contained a very small quantity of a ferruginous sediment. No. 6 has a slightly bituminous odor. No. 3 a slight fetid odor."

A gallon of water from No. 3 contains 12.16 grains of solid matter, and from No. 6, 6 grains of solid matter. Of this solid matter 100 parts gave of

	No. 3.	No. 6.	No. 5.
Organic matter,..........................	31.98	41.32	19.73
Magnesia,..........................	23.39	14.64	16.14
Sulphuric acid,..........................	10.13	5.28	23.32
Lime,..........................	11.03	17.34	4.75
Potassa,..........................	6.01	7.98	20.33
Soda,..........................	3.32	0.27	2.34
Carbonic acid,..........................	6.40	4.01	3.59
Phosphoric acid,..........................	5.11	5.32	4.18
Chlorine,..........................	1.82	2.31	3.79
Iron,..........................	0.51	1.19	4.18
Silica,..........................	9.23	0.14	0.11
Sulphuretted hydrogen,..........................	trace	......	......
	99.93	99.80	99.86

The spring from which the water marked No. 5 was taken, is situated almost within the shadow of the giant wall of the Indian pass. A fountain of health, sufficient to constitute a "watering place," within the pure and invigorating atmosphere of the Adirondacs, and amid scenes where nature reigns in profound seclusion, and in such imposing and terrific grandeur, would possess infinite attractions and interest. One gallon of this water gave of solid matter 12.64 grains, and 100 parts of this solid matter gave the preceding analysis. "The analysis shows No. 5 to be a magnesia potassa water. The magnesia and potassa are probably mostly in the form of sulphates. No. 5 has a slight earthy odor."

The discovery of a spring near Schroon lake has recently been announced. The locality is almost as imposing and picturesque and even more beautiful than that in Indian pass, and if the properties of the water prove as valuable as is claimed, and the purpose of erecting a hotel is accomplished, I can imagine no resort more delightful or attractive.

PART III.

NATURAL HISTORY.

ANIMALS.

Champlain, and the early explorers of the environs of Lake Champlain, allude to the abundance and variety of the game and wild animals found in that region. The reminiscences of the living recall the prevalence in vast numbers of these animals, at their first settlement of the county. Fearful legends are still rife of exposures of the original settlers, and their terrific encounters with the panther, the bear, and wolf.

The moose within a late period has been discovered in the recesses of the interior wilderness. The panther and wolf still prowl in these wilds, but rarely, and by solitary individuals. The small black bear exists in small numbers among the fastnesses of the Adirondacs, but are seldom seen in the more inhabited sections of the county. The bear, wolf and fox, in the early occupation of the county, committed the most destructive depredations upon the flocks of the pioneers. They literally occupied and infested the forest, and by their great prevalence seriously retarded and embarrassed the introduction of sheep. The howling of wolves around the solitary cabins of the settlers, is described as having been most appalling. In the language of an aged pioneer,[1] "the deer, sixty years ago, were more abundant in our fields than sheep." Venison was then the cheapest food of the settler, and at different periods, their almost exclusive dependence. A bear cub was esteemed as delicate and luscious as the fattest lamb.

---

[1] *Mr. Leavitt, Chesterfield.*

Deer still abound in the interior solitudes, and are annually destroyed in vast numbers, in the mere wanton and brutal instincts of slaughter. Under the influence of public sentiment and a determined purpose of enforcing the stringent statutes for the preservation of game, the cruel extinction of both deer and fish, has been in some measure suppressed in this wilderness. Sometimes expelled from their retreats by the attacks of wolves, their ferocious foe, they appear in the older settlements, and in their extreme terror, occasionally dash into a village; but only to find man as merciless as the savage beast. Thus, torn and devoured by wolves; chased by dogs, and overtaken when their sharp and tiny hoofs penetrate the crust of snows, and they helplessly flounder in their depths; hunted by torchlight, and pursued in the lakes and ponds of their native wilds, this beautiful, timid and gentle creature, now affording so much beauty and animation to these forests, and such luxury to the table of even our metropolitan epicures, must soon be extirpated, or greatly diminished in their numbers.

The beaver was found in great abundance throughout the region, by the first occupants. They no longer exist, it is believed, in the territory of Essex county. The skeleton of probably the last patriarch of the race is still preserved. Numerous vestiges exist of their former habitations. The evidences remain throughout the county of their wonderful architectural works, and of the amazing sagacity that approached human intelligence. The skill with which the beaver selected the position of his dam, the untiring industry and great vigor exhibited in prosecuting his work, the exactness of its capacity to the required object, and the great beauty of its structure, excite the deepest admiration and wonder. The water obstructed by these dams flowed over extensive flats, destroying the trees and vegetation which had flourished upon them. These were carefully removed by the beaver, as they decayed, leaving the surface as clear and unobstructed as if the work had been accomplished by the nicest labor of human industry. These clearings were ultimately occupied by a spontaneous growth of natural grasses. The beaver meadows of the county, formed by this process, were of incalculable benefit to the early settlers, preparing for many of them in advance, an abundant supply of excellent fodder.

The hunter who penetrated deeply into the solitudes, beyond the western limits of this county, until recently found the moose in considerable abundance.[1] Individuals occasionally appeared among the nearer Adirondacs. A solitary bull or a cow and calf, usually selects in autumn a hill or spur of a mountain, where abounds the mountain ash and striped maple, his choicest food. Here he hibernates in what the hunter terms his yard. As the snows deepen, he industriously keeps open the paths leading to the various sections of his domain. He uniformly traverses the same route, and thus preserves a beaten track in the deepest snows of winter. In this seclusion he passes the season, feeding upon the tender branches of his favorite shrubs, until spring returns, and the voice of nature invokes him to seek new companions. During the summer they frequent the vicinity of ponds and marshes, feeding upon aquatic plants. The roots of the pond lily they greedily devour.

The pursuit of the moose is among the most animating and attractive sports of the huntsman. The senses of this animal are supposed to be peculiarly acute. He discovers afar off the approach of danger, and breaks from his covert and flies with incredible celerity. His stately horns thrown back upon his shoulders, his nose projecting, and with the gait and action of a fast trotting horse, he dashes amid the forest, over mountains and through morasses, with a speed that defies pursuit, unless the crust of snow yields to his enormous bulk, when he is readily overtaken. Although naturally a timid animal, he then turns at bay, and with immense power and indomitable courage faces his foes, and

---

[1] *A. Ralph.*

woe betide the hunter or dog who falls within the reach of his horns, or the trampling of his hoofs. He is then the very symbol of savage ferocity. His aspect is terrific; his eyes glare, his mane erect, every hair, long and protruding, seems to expand and become animate. His defiant roar resounds among the mountains; he defends himself to the last throe with unyielding energy. The meat of the moose is considered a choice and rare delicacy.

The fox and the muskrat are abundant, and, with the minx and martin, are yet pursued for their pelages. The lynx is occasionally found. The squirrel, in most of its varieties, exist in great numbers. Small colonies of the flying squirrel are found in some localities. Its singular construction and great beauty render it an object of much interest. A peculiar incapacity alike for defense and escape, makes it the victim of innumerable enemies. A remarkable fact in natural history is observed in relation to these animals, and particularly of the common red squirrel. A district of country, which has been nearly exempt from their presence, is suddenly thronged by innumerable multitudes. Every tree and bush and fence seems alive with them, until they at once and as mysteriously disappear. This circumstance affords undoubted evidence of the migration of the squirrel, but to what extent the habit prevails is unknown. Popular opinion assumes, that they traverse Lake Champlain in these progresses. The autumn of 1851 afforded one of these periodical invasions of Essex county. It is well authenticated, that the red squirrel was constantly seen in the widest parts of the lake, far out from land, swimming towards the shore, as if familiar with the service; their heads above water, and their bushy tails erect and expanded, and apparently spread to the breeze. Reaching land, they stopped for a moment, and relieving their active and vigorous little bodies from the water, by an energetic shake or two, they bounded into the woods, as light and free as if they had made no extraordinary effort.

Fish.

Lake Champlain embraces most of the species of fish, usually found in fresh water lakes. Several varieties, formerly abundant in these waters, are now rarely found or have totally disappeared. My work does not pretend to the dignity of science, and I propose to glance only at the subject of the fishes of the region in a few general observations and in familiar language. Champlain, whose veracity, researches always vindicate, speaks of a remarkable fish, which many have supposed to be fabulous. Alluding to other fish, he continues "among the rest, there is one called by the Indians chaousarou, of divers length. The largest, I was informed by the people, are of eight and ten feet, I saw one of five feet, as thick as a thigh, with a head as big as two fists, with jaws two feet and a half long, and a double set of very long and dangerous teeth. The form of the body resembles that of the pike and is armed with scales, that the thrust of a poniard cannot pierce, and is of a silver grey color. The point of the snout is like that of a hog." Professor Thompson believes the original of this description to have been the Bill-fish (*Lepirostrus oxyurus*), a fish still existing in the lake, but rarely taken. Prof. Agassiz appears to have found traces of the same fish in the upper lakes. The muskalonge, to which the fish of Champlain bears a slight analogy, and supposed by some naturalists to be an enormous growth of the pickerel, frequents some sections of the lake and often attains the weight of thirty or forty pounds.

The early settlers of the valley of Lake Champlain, found the streams upon both sides filled with salmon. They were very large, and among the most delicate and luscious of all fish. At that period they were abundant, and so fearless as to be taken with great ease and in immense quantities. A record exists of five hundred having been killed in the Boquet in one afternoon,[1] and as late as

---

[1] *Levi Higby, Esq.*

1823 about fifteen hundred pounds of salmon were taken by a single haul of a seine, near Port Kendall. They have been occasionally found within the last twenty years, in some of the most rapid streams, buthave now totally disappeared. The secluded haunts they loved, have been invaded; dams have impeded their wonted routes; the filth of occupied streams has disturbed their cleanly habits, or the clangor of steam boats and machinery has alarmed their fears. Each of these causes is assigned as a circumstance that has deprived the country of an important article of food and a choice luxury. The subject is not unworthy the inquiry and investigation of the philosopher of nature.[1]

The LAKE SHAD (*Coregonus Albus*). In the absence of the salmon the shad will be classed as the choicest and most valuable fish belonging to the waters of Lake Champlain. Owing to its shyness and the peculiarity of its habits, its natural history is little understood. It appears not to resort promiscuously to every section of the lake, but only frequents or abides in chosen haunts. It delights in clean, sandy or gravelly bottoms. In the early spring, it is taken in considerable quantities, lying at night along the shores. Practical fishermen state that as the water grows warmer and recedes, the shad retires into the deeper channels of the lake. This fish abounds chiefly in the lower parts of the lake, and in particular localities is taken by the seine in great abundance throughout the season, and in some years and at favorable sites sufficient for barrelling. When its haunts and habits are better understood its pursuit may become an important branch of industry. It rarely takes the spoon or bait in trolling. The clam, used as a bait, an amateur sportsman informs me, sometimes attracts it. It is occasionally caught by dropping the hook in deep water, so that it lies on the bottom. It is supposed that the fish is usually hooked while playing with the bait in that position, rather than in attempting to swallow it. The spawning season of the shad is be-

---

[1] *Documentary History.*

lieved to be in autumn or winter. The ground it selects is uncertain, but observers of its habits incline to the opinion, that it seeks for the purpose, the deepest and coolest pools. After the most careful inquiry, I can obtain no information or facts in reference to the fry of this fish. No person with whom I have conversed has ever seen them. The appearance of young shad eight or ten inches long is not uncommon. They are most difficult to be obtained, and from the singular delicacy of their organization would hardly bear transportation.

The PICKEREL (*Esox reticularis*). This fish is a favorite object of pursuit in both trolling and spearing. In the spring, directly after the dissolution of the ice, when the rising water of the lake sets back upon the marshes and low lands, it is taken in those places, at night, by the jack light, in great numbers. During the day in pleasant weather it is prone to lie near the surface, basking in the warm vernal sun, and is then shot with great facility. The pickerel does not rank among the best fish in the lake for the table. To many it seems infected by an unpleasant odor, and its taste is sometimes strong with a muddy taint, and yet its great size and beauty, its extreme eagerness at the bait, and its powerful and determined resistance in the taking, renders it very desirable sport and attractive trophy. The pickerel is often and with uniform success transferred to other waters. When introduced into the lakes and ponds of the interior all its qualities are transformed. The cold and clear waters of the mountain springs, and the novel and abundant food it rejoices in, seem to remove its objectionable properties; it becomes hard-fleshed, pleasant and high flavored, and almost approaches the exquisite delicacy of the trout. In these favorable situations it attains a great size, and by its wonderful fecundity and rapid growth, in an incredibly short period throngs the waters into which it has been translated and every contiguous stream which connects with them. By the myriads it soon produces, and its remarkable voracity and pugnacious habits, the pickerel very rapidly extirpates almost every other variety of fish. For this reason its introduction into lakes and streams, which have been the abode of the trout, is always deprecated by sportsmen. This fish is distinguished by a peculiarity, which possibly, although I am not aware of the fact, may be common to some other species. It seeks in the spring the shallow waters upon marshes and swamps which at that season are overflowed, and deposits its spawn not upon the bottom, but on the small bushes and rushes then submerged, and to these plants the spawn is made to adhere by the glutinous substance that enfolds it. If the water, as frequently happens, subsides before the eggs are hatched, they of course must perish. Fishermen recount marvelous tales of the discovery of the spawn of the pickerel in this condition, and estimate the quantity by measure, instead of any infinity of numbers. The incalculable prolificness of the fish is evinced by the myriads of the fry, which will be observed in the summer thronging the small brooks, that are usually discharged from the places frequented by it in the spawning season. Instinct, doubtless, retains them in shallow water, which affords a protection from indiscriminate destruction by their voracious parents. The pickerel is an example of the changes which are constantly observed among the fishes of the lake; a frequent increase of one species, and a diminution of another. A few years since, the pickerel was the prevailing large fish, and the pike was rare in the waters of Champlain. At this time the former has perceptibly decreased, while the latter has become abundant.

The STURGEON. Two species are found in Lake Champlain. One, the *acipenser rubicandus*, Mr. Thompson states, is of a large size frequently reaching six feet in length and a hundred pounds in weight. The other species is smaller. The flesh, although not highly esteemed, is palatable. It is not, however, pursued for its edible qualities and is only captured incidentally in drawing the seine. In some parts of the lake it is said to be very abundant. It runs in schools and often in vast numbers. We hear sometimes remarkable tales of the foremost files of those schools being projected on a beach or shoal and stranded by the momentum of the enormous masses pressing in their rear.

The YELLOW PERCH is the most abundant of the smaller class of fish. It often reaches an unusual size, and is highly valued as a pan fish. The exuberance of the perch is nearly incredible. In a serene sunny afternoon, they often seem to collect in vast shoals near the surface, animating and rippling the water in an area of acres, either by their gambols, or in the pursuit of insects. At such times the skill and industry of the angler have no success.

The BULL POUT is also very common and abundant. It is often taken a foot in length, and although repulsive in its form and general appearance, is an excellent article of food when manipulated by scientific hands.

Several varieties of EELS abound in the lake and its tributaries, and are taken in large quantities, both by the hook and in seines.

The BLUE LAMPREY is a small, odious parasite, often captured in seines, and usually adhering, by its peculiar construction, to the bodies of other fishes. It possesses more of the qualities of the blood-sucker than of the fish. It fastens, by the suction powers of its mouth, upon a larger fish, and thus preys on its living flesh. No effort of the suffering creature can displace its tormentor, which usually adheres to its victim until it dies from pain and exhaustion.

The LING or METHY (*Lota maculosa*), occupies one of the lowest positions in the scale of animated nature. Its form is loathsome, and its habits so sluggish and inert, that it seems to crawl along the bottom, as it slowly moves up the little brook it has selected for its migration. Notwithstanding this appearance, Mr. Thompson, in his *Natural History*, states it to be remarkable for voracity, and that he found its stomach gorged with small fish, to the utmost capacity of its huge abdomen. These it must have seized by art rather than dexterity. Its annual migration is performed in the winter, when the ling, in greatest profusion ascends its favorite stream in long procession. Although tough, tasteless, and disagreeable, it is taken in immense numbers, and salted by the poorer classes, for winter food. Holes are cut in the ice, and as the fish passes beneath it is pierced by a fork or any pointed implement, and is even seized by the hand. Bushels of lings are often thus thrown out in an incredible short time. At night, which is the most favorable time, a brilliant fire is enkindled on the ice at the opening, and the fish is thus taken in great abundance, and with ease.

The SMELT, a small but very fine fish, of marine origin and migratory habits, have recently appeared in the lake and are taken through the ice in large quantities. Varieties of the bass and pike are among the most valuable and delicious of the lake fish and are taken in great numbers. Many of the lake fish are highly esteemed, and secured in ice, are exported by rail roads to the southern cities and watering places, where they command exorbitant prices.

In early spring, when the rising water has formed an open space between the shore and the ice, the shad and indeed most of the larger fish of the lake are pursued with keen avidity, by the spear and with torch-light. This very exciting and pleasant sport also occurs at the season in which the fish seek the estuaries and the lower grounds covered by the shallow water which have overflowed from the lake. In a calm night (and if dark more certain the success), the boat impelled by a single paddle glides silently through the water, bearing an iron jack at the bow, loaded with light wood, which emits a bright flame, shedding an illumination far in advance. The spearsman, with poised weapon, stands behind the light, with full opportunity of seeing the fish, that sleeping quietly or attracted by the gleaming of the fire, lies unconscious of danger, and is easily approached and killed. Every part of the lake adapted to this sport, presents at the season a brilliant and animated aspect and glowing with hundreds of these fires.

Trolling is a favorite and highly exciting sport of the amateur fisherman upon these waters. This mode is adapted to deep water, and is conducted by towing the line some distance behind the boat, in a sea somewhat agitated. Fish, of extraordinary dimensions, are thus frequently taken in large numbers. Fishing by seines and nets is much and successfully used in the lakes and more important streams. Several varieties of the most choice trout occur in great profusion, in most of the innumerable streams, ponds and lakes which are scattered among the forests and mountains of the interior. The salmon trout is peculiarly distinguished for the great size it attains, and the superior delicacy and excellence of its qualities.

Two distinct species of the trout, in popular language designated the lake and the brook trout, prevail in the lakes and streams of the interior. These are supposed to ramify into a number of varieties. They differ very perceptibly in color and appearance, and the distinctions which science detects, are very clear and marked. The color of the flesh, which is either red or white in both species, is not characteristic of either, but seems to be an individual peculiarity. The lake trout, fierce and voracious in its habits, is the tyrant of the waters. It attains a very great size, and specimens have occasionally been taken, which weighed fifty pounds. These are rare, and fish of ten to twenty pounds are deemed choice sport. The brook trout seldom exceeds three pounds. The former spawn from the 15th to the 25th of October, and the brook trout about ten days earlier. The two species run in separate schools, and although found associated, they appear not to amalgamate. The brook trout frequents the streams, and near the entrances and outlets of the lakes. The fry of both remain on the spawning ground until the ensuing spring. Notwithstanding the avidity with which these fish are pursued, their marvelous fecundity preserves them from apparent diminution in these lakes. The acquaintance with men, however, renders them shy, and thus is enhanced the pleasure and excitement of the sport, by exacting additional skill and perseverance for their capture. The procreative habits of these fish are peculiar and interesting. The female prepares the bed, and entering upon it for a brief period each day, gradually deposits the spawn, ejecting a part on every visit, through the entire spawning season. In her absence, the male daily occupies the bed, and for a short time remains upon it in the performance of his functions. It is believed that a large proportion of the spawn is not fertilized.

My attention has been called by gentlemen peculiarly familiar with the fish of these lakes, to another trout, which, although I have no specimen to examine, I am inclined to regard as a distinct species, or certainly a different variety. This fish appears late in the fall, in great abundance, but long after the other species have left the fishing grounds. It is rounder in its form, longer and more slim than either the lake or brook trout, in proportion to its weight. It is distinguished by a brighter and more silvery coloring; has brilliant spots on its sides, indiscriminately red or yellow; seldom reaches a pound and a half in weight; is taken by any kind of bait or fly, and either by trolling or still line. Unlike the other species it spawns in the spring. In its edible qualities, it is equal to either of the others.

These waters are singularly deficient in other classes of fish. Few are found in them except the perch and the coarser kinds, as the bull pout or sun-fish, except one of remarkable habits and appearance, and known to the sportsman as the white or frost fish. This fish usually appears about the 1st of November, near the outlets of the lakes, or in shallows, in immense shoals, at times, and in places, literally thronging the waters in myriads. They are small, weighing about four to the pound, and are light colored, with large scales that cleave from the body at the slightest pressure. They persistently refuse the hook, and every contrivance of bait, but are taken in great quantities by the grapple and nets, and afford, in the absence of the trout, excellent sport to the angler. They supply a good article of food. These fish appear in numbers at no other season, and are supposed to resort to the deep waters of the lakes, from whence they are expelled by the periodical return of the trout.

No country offers to the sportsman more delightful and diversified attractions, than this region of lakes and ponds. It is deeply to be deplored, that the same barbarous and ruthless improvidence that formerly depopulated with such rapidity the forests of deer, has hastened in some districts the extinction of the trout. They have been not only pursued in utter wantonness, and in the passion of destruction at the legitimate seasons, but they were mercilessly followed by the net, the fly and the spear, to their spawning bed, where, in the extinction of one life, the embryo of thousands is annihilated. Laws are plenary in their stringency and severity, but have not been adequately enforced. Even now in many lakes the most exposed to such ravages, these fish are nearly extirpated. Happily these remarks are more applicable to the recent past than the present. As I have before stated these practices are now becoming generally restrained.

A striking and very curious difference occurs in the character of the fish occupying lakes which lie in close proximity. One body of water in its normal condition is filled to exuberance with the choicest trout; whilst another situated in the same lofty valley, fed by the same mountain springs, and mingling its waters in the same stream with the former, is destitute of every variety of fish, except the hardier and coarser kinds. At periods when these latter lakes are extremely low, numbers of the dead bodies of the fish which occupy them, are found floating upon the surface of the water. These facts, well established, attracted my attention as interesting in the physiology of these creatures, and an important feature in natural history. The result of my examinations of the subject was conclusive to my mind, that this effect is produced by foreign and noxious substances impregnating the waters. On inspection I discovered in every instance, where the phenomenon occurred, the presence of native copperas, other sulphates, and incidentally arsenic largely developed in deposits within the surging of the water, or in its immediate vicinity.

Reptiles.

The rattle-snake formerly infested several localities in this county in horrid profusion. In the early settlement of the region, they were seen in vast numbers basking in the sun, near their dens. A mountain, in the vicinity of Lake George, is pointed out, where the legend says eight hundred were killed in a single season. These reptiles are now almost exterminated. No other snake of a venomous character is found in the county. The other reptiles, birds, insects, and bugs, which prevail, are familiar to the popular mind, to science, and the practical farmer and gardener.

Wild Bees.

The hunting of wild bees has been, in parts of Essex county, a pursuit of considerable importance, and as exciting and amusing, as it often is profitable. It is still continued to a limited extent. The wild bee, although similar in appearance and habits to the domestic bee, is undoubtedly a native of the forest, and indigenous to the country. It appears to be adverse to the vicinage of man, and recedes into the deeper wilderness as cultivation approaches its secluded and hidden haunts. The hives of the wild bee are found far in the solitudes of unoccupied tracts, removed from the habitations of men, and occupying the most sequestered retreats. It selects, for the location of its hive, an elevated position, far up some retired and shady ravine, in the midst of hills or mountains, and in the vicinity of a body of water. If the country is flat, the bees establish their domicile upon the margin of a lake or stream, in as much seclusion as possible. They appropriate usually, for this purpose, the hollow of a tree, generally selecting one of great magnitude; but occasionally they construct their hives in the crevices of rocks. They enter the opening in the tree by a small orifice, which very essentially protects them from observation and discovery. Here they remain for years, in possession of the same abode, models of laborious and untiring industry, accumulating hoards of their luscious treasures, and annually casting off new colonies. These retreats are found with difficulty, and by the exercise of much skill by the hunter; and when found, are often very difficult of access. They are exposed, not only to the merciless ravages of man, but insects and animals, particularly the bears, commit great depredations upon them.

The professional bee hunter, when engaged in this pursuit, provides himself with a quantity of honey comb, strained honey, and a small light box, about six or eight inches long, and four inches deep and four wide. This box has two slides, one at the top, and the other in the centre. The slides move in grooves. In the upper lid he arranges a piece of glass; the lower compartment contains comb filled with honey. Thus equipped, the hunter proceeds, late in autumn, to a district, which by previous observation, he has ascertained is frequented by the bees, in pursuing their labors. Two modes are adopted by the hunter for procuring the bees, which he uses to discover the position of the hive. By the first, and this is the most common, when he detects a bee upon a flower, which is generally a wild plant, known to the hunter as the frost blow, that blooms late in October, he places the box beneath the insect with the upper lid drawn, and by a quick and dexterous movement thrusts it into the first compartment, and the lid being closed, the bee is seen through the glass. The lower lid is then drawn and the glass darkened, when the bee immediately settles upon the honey and commences its feast. It is now left undisturbed, with both lids open. After having supplied itself, the bee leaves the box, and, rising above it, seems to take a particular note of its locality, flying around in circles, which grow wider at every gyration; the bee constantly ascending, until at length it takes an air line for its hive. This crisis tests the skill and vigilance of the hunter.

The course of the bee is carefully watched and the distance of the hive is computed by the length of its absence. The hunter estimates this by allowing three miles to the minute, for its flight and return. The bee is allowed to make the journey several times, when it is again secured and the hunter proceeds in the direction of the hive, as indicated by the course of the bee's flight. It seems to communicate its discovery to the hive; as frequently on its return it is accompanied by others. The hunter often finds it necessary to catch and mark an individual bee, so as to identify it in his operations.

After advancing as far as he deems it expedient, the hunter opens the box, a second time, and allows the bee to escape. It repeats the same reconnaissance as before, and then takes its line for the hive. If this, as often occurs, has been passed, the fact is indicated by the bee returning on the hunter's track. It frequently becomes necessary, when the position of the hive has been disguised, with more than usual adroitness and success, for the hunter to make several lines in this manner, when he determines the locality of the hive, by ascertaining the point where the different lines intercept. A number of bees from the hive are often in the box together, and occasionally those from different hives, as appears from their making distinct lines, on rising from the box.

The other mode pursued by the hunter is this: Upon a cleared spot in an elevated situation, he builds a fire and heats some flat stones; on these, some of the comb is burned; the odor of the burning comb will attract the bee; fresh comb, containing honey, is then placed on the stone, upon which the bee is allowed to feed. When it leaves, the comb is removed from the stone and the box substituted in the same place; the bee, on its return, alights upon the honey in the box and is thus secured; afterwards the hunter proceeds by the same process as before. The tree, which contains the hive, is then felled and the whole family of bees are exterminated, usually by burning straw. This ruthless work, the hunter considers necessary, as well to protect himself from their assaults, while securing the honey, as to prevent his being thrown on a false line, by wandering bees from the same hive, who would bring him back to the already ravaged tree. This often happens.

Bee hunting, my informant[1] remarks, in closing, "is a most exciting sport, and when pursued by a skillful hunter, is also very profitable. I have known of over a ton of honey having been procured in a single month by three persons, myself being one of the number, besides more than four hundred pounds of wax. This honey was sold in Boston for fifteen dollars the hundred weight, and the wax for twenty cents the pound." "We discovered in this excursion fifty-seven hives, which yielded from thirty-five to one hundred and fifty pounds of honey each, depending on their age and size." [1]

In the south-western section of the town of Chesterfield, and amidst a rude and mountainous tract of country, I am informed, an immense colony of bees existed, consisting of numerous hives. Their abodes were in the crevices and fissures of the rocks and inaccessible. The whole atmosphere in the vicinity, it is represented, was filled with the bees. Various attempts by excavation and blasting have been made, to reach the deposits of honey, but without success. Owing to these annoyances and many disturbances, the bees became so exasperated and ferocious, and they were so formidable from the infinitude of their number, that it was hazardous to approach their retreat. It is supposed, that this remarkable and most interesting colony, has been destroyed by the conflagrations, which in recent years have swept over that district.

A singular fact in the nature and habit of the bee is remarked by hunters. While they permit some persons to approach their habitations with perfect impunity, they evince towards others the most determined and inveterate instinctive hostility.

---

[1] Mr. James M. Weston, Chesterfield.

Forests.

The woodlands of this region afforded to the early settlers a ready and available resource, and still afford a most important element in the business and prosperity of the country. When the wilderness was penetrated and the forest fell before the woodman's axe, in most parts of the country, he collected the bodies of the trees into log heaps, reduced them to ashes, and with the simple chemistry of the woods, and in the rude laboratory that necessity had invented, manufactured them into potashes. This commodity commanded a prompt and high price in the Canadian markets, and was received by the local merchant in exchange for merchandise and provisions required by the settler.

The several species of the pine, the spruce and hemlock constituted the great glory and magnificence of the original forests. We still see vestiges in their remaining stumps and roots that indicate their immense size. These giants of the forests were at an early day only incumbrances upon the soil, and were destroyed by a careless hand. The native of the county, to whom I have referred, informs me that he has seen white pine trees girdled and left to fall and rot upon the earth in the process of preparing ground for a potatoe field, which would now be worth one hundred and fifty dollars upon the stump. Similar enormous trees are still found in the interior wilderness. A gentleman lately stated to me, that he had seen a pine log, which in floating down the Raquette river, had become stranded in a cove, which measured nearly six feet in diameter.

The beauty and magnificence of the forests upon the islands and shores of Lake Champlain, excited the admiration of its discoverer. His description of the scenery in this particular evinces the singular accuracy which characterises his entire work. He speaks of "the quantity of vines, handsomer than any I ever saw." The wild grape is still found upon these islands, and upon the mainland, in the greatest profusion, and in numerous varieties of color and flavor. They spread their tendrils far and wide. often overtopping the loftiest trees in their luxuriance and beauty, and forming barriers in their tangled branches, impervious to man or beast. In the month of July, when Champlain first visited the lake, he could only see and admire the splendor of the vegetable growth, without being able to judge of the quality of the fruit.

The shag bark hickory, the hazel, the butternut, and the chestnut, now rarely found, but formerly very common in the southern sections of the county, are indigenous to the county. The various species of the maple, birch, beech, elms and oaks, are all natives of these woodlands, and often attain in the primitive forest a magnificent growth. The white cedar of great beauty and size abounds in the swamps, and often appear in large numbers on the uplands. I noticed them, far upon the acclivities of the Adirondacs, of immense proportions, but observed, and was assured that the fact was uniform, that, although beautiful in their exterior appearance, they were defective and hollow at the core. The red cedar was discovered at the first occupation of the country, but is nearly extirpated. Several varieties of the maple and birches, the black walnut, the black cherry and butternut, often stately and splendid trees, are highly valued in the arts and manufactures, and are exported in considerable quantities for the purpose. The oaks (particularly the white oak), were formerly of great importance, and still continue to a considerable extent, as articles of exportation, at one period, to Canada, but now to the southern markets. The larch or hackmatack, is abundant and highly valuable. This timber with the cedar and oak, affords most excellent material in ship building. The juniper flourishes in great abundance in many sections of the county, indicating, however, by its presence a thin and sterile soil. It spreads, a few inches elevated above the earth, a thick and perfect umbel, often several feet in diameter, mantled by a deep and rich green foliage. Standing in solitary plants or in clusters, it imparts an unique and highly ornamental feature to the scenery.

The product of wood, in the primitive and vigorous forests, is vast; upon exuberant soils, sometimes exceeding one hundred cords to the acre, and among the rocks and broken acclivities, seldom yielding less than twenty cords. Within an area of several miles around manufacturing works, the value of the wood, standing, ranges from twenty-five cents to one dollar and a half the cord, controlled in its price by its quality and position. This estimate refers to localities where the advantages of transportation authorize the erection of manufactories, and not to regions more remote and inaccessible. Such districts are happily rare in the county, and are rapidly diminishing before the progress of improving facilities of intercourse. At one period, a large demand existed for wood to be used as fuel in steam boats.

The quantity of wood in Essex county, consumed for manufacturing purposes, has been immense, and can only be computed by a rough approximation. It probably should be estimated by hundreds of thousands of cords. A great change has in late years occurred in the substitution, in many manufactories and generally with steam boats, of mineral coal for the charcoal and wood. This is due to the increasing scarcity and enhanced price of wood, and to other economic views. In extensive districts of the county where the wood has been cut exclusively for coaling, and the land is not required for agricultural pursuits, a second spontaneous growth rapidly shoots up, soon mantling the earth with a luxuriant product, which in the term of fifteen or twenty years, yields a heavy burthen of wood and timber. This growth rarely contains plants of the original forest, but is usually composed of trees of a totally dissimilar character. Pine is usually succeeded by hard wood, and the site of a forest of the latter is occupied by evergreens. Different sections of the county produce in this aspect, irregular and various results. The aspen, yellow poplar, white birch, and oaks, generally succeed the pines; but in the vicinity of the Adirondac works, the small red cherry is almost the exclusive second growth succeeding the stately hard wood forest. The dry and loamy plains contiguous to the Elba works, of a past generation, which were cut over to supply them with fuel, are now clothed with forests of spruce. The latter fact is remarkable and worthy of reflection, as the habits and peculiarities of the spruce in its natural position adapt it to a totally different soil. This recuperation of the woodland, which nature thus bountifully provides, may in connection with the waste and broken territory, afford, by judicious economy and management, a certain and permanent supply of fuel, to all the arts for many ages.

I observed in my investigations relative to this second growth, circumstances that excited my attention, and which I deem entitled to consideration. In the fastnesses of the Adirondacs I perceived entire groves of the young cherry trees, loaded with a black excrescence, similar in appearance to the disease which has been so destructive in our plum orchards. In other sections of the county, I noticed large tracts of the black cherry and birch, dead and dying, and presenting in their blackened and blasted bark, the aspect of the pear and apple trees which have been visited by the destroying fire blight. If, as I conjecture, these diseases are identical with those known to our gardens (their results are certainly very analogous), does not the fact open an interesting field for the researches of science, as to their origin, causes, and operations?

The chestnut groves, which so beautifully adorn some of the northern towns of Warren county, only enter the confines of Essex. The sweet walnut is, however, widely scattered over various sections of the county, and flourishes in great profusion and beauty, in the lovely tract that spreads from the cliffs of Lake George to Champlain. When the early frosts of autumn have opened the husks, and their luscious treasures are poured upon the earth, the bright, shouting, joyous groups of nutting children, which gather beneath their boughs, communicate to the landscape a most primitive and pastoral scene.

Spreading from the warm soil that borders Champlain, to the Alpine summits of the Adirondacs, where almost the rigors of the frigid zone are stamped upon the climate, the soil of Essex county, naturally imparts a great diversity to its botanical productions. There is nothing, however, so distinct or novel, as necessarily to require notice in a work of this character. The cryptogamic plants are exceeding rich and exuberant.

Climate and Winds.

Grave senators who have pronounced northern New York the Siberian district of America, exhibit more fancy on the subject, than intelligence. No climate is more salubrious, or better calculated to secure enjoyment and comfort to man. The atmosphere, clear, elastic and invigorating, bears no miasmatic exhalations. The winters of this climate are often severe but equable. The summers are warm, and yield a rapid impulse to vegetation, that promotes an early maturity. The heat of summer is modified by the cool and exhilarating breezes of the lakes and mountains. A signal difference occurs in the climate and seasons of the territory bordering upon the shores of Lake Champlain and that of a few miles in the interior. The influence of that large expanse of fresh water mitigates equally the rigors of the winters and the heats of summer. The territory bordering upon the lake has usually an exemption of at least two weeks from the late frosts of the spring and the early frosts of autumn, to which the interior is exposed. The fact is well authenticated, although its philosophy may not be so readily explained, that premature frosts often occur in the meridian of Pennsylvania when the valleys of Essex county are totally free from its effects. The snows accumulate among the mountains and in the higher valleys to the depth of several feet, although in most parts of the county they are less abundant than in the western or central sections of the state; they remain, however, longer upon the earth. An excess of snow is a rare event, although the want of it often embarrasses the operations of business.

The absence of snow as well as rain is peculiar to the valley of the Au Sable, and in many seasons, essentially affects its agricultural and manufacturing prosperity. No part of the country is visited more frequently by protracted and blighting draughts than this district. The circumstance is universally remarked, and may satisfactorily be imputed to the influence of the mountains and lake upon the atmospheric currents. These aerial currents, governed by much the same laws which control the course of all fluids, are involved in eddies created by the gorges and ravines of the mountains, are arrested by their airy summits, and often receive a direction from these causes. Clouds, not unfrequently, are perceived approaching the valleys, bearing rain and portentous of thunder and lightning, when in a moment their course is changed, and skimming along the acclivities of the mountains, they pour upon them their contents. Hence, in a dry season when nature elsewhere is parched and seared, the slopes of these mountains smile in verdant and luxuriant beauty. The movements of these atmospheric streams, witnessed from the valleys embosomed by lofty mountains, are often beautiful and sublime exhibitions.

A valued correspondent[1] furnished me with several highly interesting facts illustrative of this subject. The amphitheatre of mountains that nearly surround North Elba, is imperfect on the western side from whence the plateau spreads far into the interior. Volumes of clouds often advance from that direction, until entering within the influence of these currents, they suddenly divide, the dissevered masses passing to the north and south, along the brows of the respective mountains. He describes a scene of singular grandeur and sublimity, that occurred at North Elba in 1847, and strikingly elucidates this remark-

[1] *T. L. Nash.*

able influence. On a still and sultry evening of summer, when not a breeze moved the leaf, a dark and heavy bank of clouds suddenly appeared in the western horizon, and gradually approaching, menaced an immediate and violent storm. Whilst gazing upon the advance of the impending tempest, he beheld in a moment the masses rent asunder. One column rushed along the crest of Whiteface, and the other amid pealings of thunder and torrents of rain, careered over the lofty summits of the Adirondacs, whilst in the valley, an instant before threatened by the tornado, all was serene and calm, and the moon and stars beamed softly upon it, through the riven canopy of black and flashing clouds. I introduce these impressive incidents to illustrate the powerful agency which is exerted on the elements, by these lofty pinnacles.

The winds in the vicinity of Lake Champlain are materially modified in their direction by its influence.

The aurora borealis, displayed in the latitude of Essex county in transcendent splendor and effulgence, exerts, it is believed, at times a decisive effect upon the course and character of the atmospheric current. The exhibition of that phenomenon is generally, if not uniformly succeeded by a prevalence of southerly winds. The duration and severity of the one seems proportionate to the intensity and expansion of the other.

The climate of northern New York, has, since its discovery, gradually, but very decidedly ameliorated. The improvements which have removed the forests, and exposed the earth to the action of the sun and atmosphere have eminently tended to promote amelioration. The winters are pronounced by aged settlers to be at this time, far less rigorous and protracted, than in their early recollections of the country. The rains are now more equally diffused through the mild seasons, and not falling as formerly in periodical and severe tempests.[1] The autumnal season is the glory of this climate, often lingering late into

---

[1] *John Hoffnagle, Esq.*

November, and clothing the forests with its gorgeous and brilliant robes. It is, to all animated nature, the most delightful and joyous period of the year, fraught with blessings and pleasure, and bearing the inspiration of health and vigor.

Hardy stock is often turned off by the 1st of April, although the 20th of that month may be regarded as the average period when grazing may be relied upon. The commencement of foddering usually ranges with the varieties of stock, from the 15th of November to Christmas. Plowing commences in a series of years, about the middle of April, and usually terminates in November, although in some seasons it is extended into the last days of the year.

The table which the following is a copy, has been formed by the careful observation of Mr. Alvin Colvin at Port Kent for a series of years, and exhibits very interesting facts in illustration of the climate and seasons on Lake Champlain.

Trips between Burlington and Port Kent, each year.

Last Trips.			*First Trips.*		
Steamer Saranac,	Jan.	1, 1845	Steamer Winooski,	April	1, 1845
Schooner LaFayette,	Feb.	3, 1845			
Steamer Saranac,	Jan.	3, 1846	" Winooski,	April	7, 1846
Sloop Cashier,	Feb.	1, 1846			
Steamer Saranac,	Jan.	5, 1847	" Saranac,	May	7, 1847
" John Gilpin,	Feb.	8, 1848	" Ethan Allen,	March	30, 1848
" Ethan Allen,	Jan.	6, 1849	" Saranac,	April	16, 1849
" LaFayette,	Jan.	11, 1849			
" Saranac,	Jan.	15, 1850	" Saranac,	March	26, 1850
Sail boats ran all winter.		1850			
Steamer Saranac,	Jan.	25, 1851	" Saranac,	April	1, 1851
" Boston,	Jan.	25, 1852	" Boston,	April	25, 1852
" Boston,	Feb.	10, 1853	" Boston,	April	15, 1853
" Francis Saltus,	Jan.	23, 1854	" Saranac,	April	19, 1854
Sloop Danl. Webster,	Jan.	24, 1855	" Boston,	April	20, 1855
Steamer Francis Saltus,	Jan.	19, 1856	" Boston,	April	21, 1856
" Montreal,	Jan.	9, 1857	" Montreal,	April	10, 1857
" Montreal,	Feb.	1, 1858	" Montreal,	April	7, 1858
" J. Clark,	Feb.	7, 1858			
" Montreal,	Jan.	9, 1859	" Montreal,	April	2, 1859
Sail boat ran to,	Jan.	25, 1860	Schooner Excelsior,	March	28, 1860
			Steamer Montreal,	April	4, 1860
Steamer Boston,	Jan.	10, 1861	" Boston,	April	15, 1861
" Boston,	Jan.	1, 1862	" Boston,	April	28, 1862
Sail boat ran to,	Feb.	1, 1862			
Steamer Boston,	Jan.	21, 1863	" Montreal,	April	27, 1863

Last Trips.			*First Trips.*		
Sail boat ran to,	Jan.	28, 1863	Boat J. G. Weatherbee,	March	30, 1864
Steamer Boston,	Feb.	13, 1864	Steamer Montreal,	April	8, 1864
Steamer Montreal,	Jan.	14, 1865	" Montreal,	April	7, 1865
Lake closed,	Jan.	18, 1865			
Schooner Excelsior,	Jan.	21, 1866	Boat Oregon,	April	11, 1866
			Steamer Montreal,	April	12, 1866
Steamer Montreal,	Jan.	11, 1867	" Montreal,	April	15, 1867
Sail boats run all winter.					
Steamer Montreal,	Jan.	4, 1868	" Montreal,	April	17, 1868
Lake froze to Burlington,	Jan,	11, 1868			

MINERALOGY AND GEOLOGY.

The Adirondac District.

The field of researches presented by Essex county in these departments is so expanded and rich, that the labor of years would be required for its competent examination.

The mineral wealth of Essex county is not limited to iron ore, but comprehends numerous other minerals of great interest and value. Iron, however, in immense deposits, constitute its predominant resource. In many sections of the county, it forms the basis of the entire structure of the earth, and occurs not merely in veins, nor even masses, but in strata which rise into mountains. The surface is often strewn with boulders of iron ore, weighing from a few pounds to many tons, as ordinary rocks are scattered in other districts. The Adirondac district is probably surpassed in no region in the extent of its deposits of iron, and the higher qualities and varied properties of its ores. The ores seem to concentrate in the vicinity of the village of Adirondac, and here literally constitute the formation. The cellars of their dwellings, in many instances, are excavated in the massive beds.

The discovery of a mineral deposit, extensive and valuable, as the Adirondac Iron District, is an event so rare and important, that it seems appropriate in a work of this character, to perpetuate its minute history. An Indian approached the late David Henderson, Esq., of Jersey city, in the year 1826, whilst standing near the Elba iron works, and taking from beneath his blanket a piece of iron ore, he presented it to Mr. H. with the inquiry expressed in his imperfect English, "You want to see 'um ore, me fine plenty—all same." When asked where it came from, he pointed towards the south-west and explained "me hunt beaver all 'lone, and fine 'um, where water run over iron dam." The Indian proved to be a brave of St. Francis tribe, honest, quiet and intelligent, who spent the summers in hunting amid the wilds of the Adirondacs. An exploring party, consisting of Mr. Henderson, Messrs. Duncan and Malcolm McMartin, John McD. McIntyre, and Dyer Thompson, was promptly arranged, who submitting themselves to the guidance of the Indian, plunged into the pathless forest. The first night they made their bivouac beneath the giant walls of the Indian pass. The next day they reached the site of the present works, and there saw the strange spectacle described by the brave; the actual flow of a river over an iron dam, created by a ledge of ore, which formed a barrier across the stream. The reconnaissance revealed to their astonished view, various and immense deposits of ore, equal almost to the demands of the world for ages. A glance disclosed the combination in that secluded spot of all the ingredients, and every facility for the most extensive manufacture of iron, in all its departments. In close proximity existed an illimitable supply of ore, boundless forests of hard wood and an abundant water power. The remote position of the locality formed the chief impediment to the scheme, which was adopted at once by the explorers. Having accomplished a hasty but satisfactory examination of the deposit, the party with no delay that might attract attention, the same night and in intense darkness and a driving storm, retraced their path through the forest, after having carefully concealed the evidences of their work. Messrs. Henderson and McMartin, taking with them the Indian, of whom they did not deem it safe to lose sight, proceeded directly to Albany, and there effected the purchase from the state of an extended tract embracing the scene of this remarkable discovery.[1] A road was soon constructed to the site with slight aid from the state, at great expense, through a dense uninterrupted forest of thirty miles in length. The purpose was pursued with untiring energy and strong enthusiasm, by the proprietors, Archibald McIntyre, Archibald Robertson and David Henderson, Esqs. A settlement was soon commenced and an experimental furnace constructed. Iron was produced of rare and valuable qualities, rivaling almost in toughness and strength the best products of the Swedish furnaces. A small blast furnace was soon afterwards erected, together with several forge fires and a puddling furnace. Bar iron was subsequently fabricated to a considerable extent. Iron produced from this ore has proved admirably adapted to the manufacture of steel, and has been extensively used for that purpose by the steel works of the Adirondac Company at Jersey city.[2] I need only refer in addition to the report of Mr. Johnson which exhibits the triumphant display of that steel at the World's Fair. A magnificent blast furnace was completed about 1850 at the Adirdondac works, of the largest dimensions, perfect in its construction and powers, and most judiciously adjusted in all its arrangements. The first furnace had been erected in 1848.

Numerous ore beds exist within an area of three miles, and nearly all are comprised within half that distance from the works. They are singularly distinct in the appearance, nature, and quality of the ores.[3] The Millpond ore bed is situated in so immediate proximity with

---

[1] *Mr. Henderson's Journal.*

[2] See J. Dellafield's address, page 142, *State Agricultural Transactions*, 1851.

[3] I derive much of my information relative to the history and minerals of the Adirondacs, from the valuable manuscripts prepared at my request, by Alexander Ralph and Robert Clark, Esq. I have before me a copy of the original journal of Mr. Henderson, furnished me by Mr. Clark, now of Cincinnati. I regret that my space will not allow me to publish these highly interesting documents.

the furnace erected by the company, that its foundation rests upon a section of the vein. The length of this bed, ascertained by the actual mensuration of Professor Emmons, is three thousand one hundred and sixty-eight feet, and the width seven hundred feet. An opening of forty feet in depth has been excavated, and at that point, the ore is found more free from rock, and richer than at the surface. Its hardness is not of that character which constitutes the hard iron of the mines, nor does it communicate that quality to iron which it yields. Slight injections of serpentine in irregular veins, crystals of green feldspar, seams of carbonate of lime, and the common rock, are mingled with this ore, and incidentally, small particles of sulphuret of iron may be traced, although too minute to injure the quality of the ore. This bed has afforded nearly all the ore used in the furnace.

The *Sanford Bed* is situated about two miles from the former, and occupies the slope of a hill, which terminates upon Lake Sanford. The elevation of the bed is six hundred or eight hundred feet above the lake, but is approached by a gradual and easy ascent. This ore is less coarse than the preceding, and of a dark, black color. It has, when exposed in the bed, almost the appearance and form of a stratified rock. It possesses great and unusual purity, and is almost entirely exempt from stone. The ore may be projected from the bed to the lake, by an inclined plane, or it may be transported by teams loaded within the bed. The width of this vein is five hundred and fourteen feet, and its length along the centre, one thousand six hundred and sixty-seven. At each extremity it does not terminate, but passes beneath the rock. No correct or proximate calculation can be formed of the probable contents of this vast deposit. The minimum estimate exhibits the immense amount of 6,832,734 tons, which may principally be raised without blasting. This would yield 3,000,000 tons of the purest iron.[1] Personal

[1] *Emmons's report.*

examination, corroborated by the opinions of highly practical and intelligent men, warrants the conjecture that this estimate is below the real amount of ore. Ores, exhibiting similar qualities, crop out at different points, along an extension of the same course. One of these indications present a face of thirty-two rods in length, and fifteen rods in width. Such facts suggest the conclusion, that these veins are a prolongation of the Sanford deposit, and that its true magnitude may embrace a distance of two miles and a half in length, with a proportionate width. Another important deposit, known as Mount Magnet, apparently forms the mass of an eminence directly east and fronting the village. This is distinguished as the fine grained ore bed. This is very marked and peculiar in its characteristics. Although it is generally firm, with grains closely cemented together, it often becomes extremely friable when exposed to atmospheric influence. The oxidation makes it appear as if mingled with rock. On the surface it has an aspect of leanness, although singularly rich, free from impurities, and probably of more practical value for the furnace, than either of the preceding veins.[1]

This vein is remarkably uniform and regular, and extends in length five thousand seven hundred and forty-two feet, and in width about seventy feet.[2] It exhibits a strong appearance of stratification in the bed. The divisional seams are very distinct at the surface, but like those in the hyperstene rock, they are the result of a law of nature analogous, if not identical, to the principle of crystalization. A small vein, or probably a branch of this bed, occurs in the same hill, and is designated the crystalized ore bed. This vein is lined on the sides by a wall a few inches thick, formed of pure hornblende. A rare and peculiar formation. On the eastern slope of the same eminence, another vein of fine grained ore is developed, and probably of equal extent with that already noticed.

---

[1] *R. Clark.* [2] *Professor Emmons.*

The Cheney bed, situated about three miles west of Lake Sanford, yields the finest grained ore of the district. It occurs in gneiss, and differs from every other vein in that peculiarity. Numerous other veins are known to exist in proximity to these, but have only been superficially explored. A supply of ores, that the consumption of centuries cannot exhaust, immediately encompasses these works. Little doubt can exist that the entire district constitutes one vast formation of ore, concealed by a narrow and slight encrustation of earth and rock. I found, in the centre of the Indian pass, a specimen of ore, closely analogous to the ore of the Sanford bed. These ores are all varieties of the black oxide of iron, exhibiting a mechanical mixture of the protoxide and peroxide of iron.

I propose to deviate from the formal arrangement of my subject, in order to present in one group, the varied and interesting topics embraced in this important district. An exhibition in one view, of its striking features; of its geology and mineralogy, the peculiar harmony and adaptation of its resources to sustain its great predominant interest, will enable the reader more distinctly to apprehend the nature, the varied capacities, and singular advantages of this extraordinary region. When appropriate avenues, equal to its resources, shall connect it with the marts of commerce, the Adirondac iron district, it is adjudged, is capable of being made, and will probably attain a position among the most extended and wealthiest iron manufactories of the earth. This strong declaration is predicated upon the facts, that these ores, so singularly and distinctly varied in their properties, that they are adapted to the manufacture of every iron fabric; that they are inexhaustible and of the easiest access for working; that the stately forests which mantle the mountains, encircling these works, are nearly as boundless as the ores; and that every material, almost essential to the manufacture, are embraced within the district. Clay prevails contiguous to the works, of a quality, it is believed, adapted to the manufacture of the required brick. Lime is abundant, and, although partially affected by native impurities, may be converted to the desired purposes. The hydraulic power will ever remain, and be always adequate to every demand. The resources of this region will ultimately compel the construction of appropriate avenues to it.

The upper works, and the village of Adirondac, are situated upon the river, midway between Lakes Henderson and Sanford, in a narrow ravine, embosomed amid the lofty pinnacles that surround it. This neat little village realizes to the mind our ideality of a Swiss hamlet, its lake, its river, its mountains "crowned with their coronal of snow." Lake Henderson, in exceeding loveliness, slumbers in quiet and beauty at the foot of the giant Santonine, and is almost enveloped in a mountain screen. These works, by the existing circuitous road, are about fifty miles removed from Lake Champlain.

A ponderous and costly dam erected by the Adirondac Company, at the lower works, a distance of ten miles, throws back the volume of water to the very base of a dam erected at the upper works, in connection with the furnace completed in 1861. This fact affords striking evidence of the formation of the country. An excellent water communication is created by this improvement between the upper and lower works. At each extremity of the navigation, wharves, cranes, and every other appliance, are constructed to facilitate the transportation of heavy commodities. A survey has established the existence of a practicable and cheap route for either a rail road or a plank road, from the lower works to the Schroon valley, a distance of only eighteen miles. The wants of an industrious community, and the exigencies of general business, must secure the construction of a rail road through that valley to the Hudson. When this most desirable project is accomplished, the furnaces and ore beds of the Adirondac district will be separated by a land transportation of only eighteen miles from New York. The rail road at this moment approaching Essex county through Warren, promises still more practical result, by penetrating in its proposed route, within a few miles of the Adirondac mines.

The lofty group of mountains which occupy this region formed almost exclusively of the hyperstene rock, which has been rendered somewhat familiar to the scientific world by the reports of the state geologists. This rock, in different proportions, is diffused through almost every section of the county. The mineral hyperstene from which it derives its name, is incorporated in it, in very minute quantities, whilst the labradorite or opalescent feldspar constitutes its most conspicuous element. Although essentially granite, the hyperstene does not exhibit the ordinary appearance of that rock. Its color, as revealed in the quarry, is a smoky gray. In some quarries it is lighter, and in others it presents a strong green tinge, which forms a predominant shade. On the surface this rock is seamy to so great a degree, as to present almost an appearance of stratification; deeper in the quarry it is thrown out in large and firm blocks. Its beauty is greatly enhanced when lines of lighter color occur, by which it is traversed. Experiments have been successfully made in sawing and polishing slabs from this rock. If it yields blocks sufficiently firm and consolidated for this purpose, it will prove a most valuable and desirable material for the structure of the delicate and ornamental fabrics, to which the choicest marble is only appropriated. No Egyptian stone surpasses it in its beautiful and variegated colors, or in the brilliancy of its lustre. The hyperstene is equal to the granite as a building material. The labradorite is an exquisitely beautiful mineral, rivaling the plumage of the peacock in its brilliant iridescence when wet or polished, and exposed to the action of the light.[1] Highly opalescent specimens are not common, although that characteristic is partially exhibited in every crystal. Blue is the predominant shade, at times mingled

---

[1] *R. Clark.*

with green. The green seldom occurs alone, but is exceedingly brilliant and beautiful. Gold and bronze specimens are occasionally discovered, and rarely, crystals are found combining all these colors in a splendid iridescence. At times the crystals are striated, each alternate stria showing the opalescent reflection. Occasionally two colors alternate in the same crystal; both are seldom seen in the same direction of light. The bed of the Opalescent river, which derives its name from the circumstance, abounds in this mineral, and when the sun shines at the cascades through the clear water, the whole rock seems to beam and glow with the refulgence of the beautiful gems.[1] Bright opalescent specimens, polished and in settings, are highly valued in jewelry. This mineral was discovered by the Moravian missionaries in Labrador, and when originally introduced into England, commanded most exorbitant prices. There are but few foreign minerals enclosed in the hyperstene rock. Some of the feldspar taken from a vein near the works are peculiarly beautiful; they exhibit a remarkable glittering, spangled appearance. Crystals of iron have been found in this vein, similar to the crystalized ore. Serpentine is also sparsely mingled in it.[2]

Graphite exists in this locality, but has not been discovered either in sufficient extent or purity to give it value, although often found in very beautiful radiated nodules. It usually occurs in small quantities at the juncture of the gneiss and primitive limestone rocks. Slight veins of trap are numerous, and, I may add, to avoid recurrence to the subject, that this rock is prevalent in almost every section of the county, sometimes exhibiting extensive walls, and forming the dyke of most of the iron ore beds. At Jay, lower village, it spans the river in a massive dam. Remarkable developments of trap dykes occur both on Mt. McMartin and Mt. McIntyre, on the former its disintegration has formed a huge gorge, which, at its entrance, is

---

[1] *R. Clark.* [2] *Idem.*

one hundred feet wide and one hundred and fifty feet deep. This gorge beautifully discloses the entire stratification of the rock. The debris from the gorge, in large masses, was deposited in Avalanche lake. This lake is a fountain head of the Hudson, situated two thousand five hundred feet above its level, and is probably the most elevated body of water in the state. Its cold element is only inhabited by a small lizard.

The Adirondac Company was originally incorporated with a capital of $1,000,000. Large sums have been disbursed in the progress of these improvements, in opening the wilderness, and in a series of experiments upon the ores of this district. The tragic death of Mr. Henderson in the midst of these scenes, which his great energy and spirited enterprise had tended so much to animate and reveal, impeded these efforts. Not a sound, not a pulsation of business indicates the heart of a region boundless in the wealth of nature.

The lofty upheaval, that embraces the immense deposits of iron ore, which have been revealed in the Adirondac district, extends northerly through Essex and into Clinton county, and includes the town of Minerva at the south. The rocks and general geological formation throughout this extended territory are closely assimilated. In Clinton county, this range is the site of most of the valuable ore beds belonging to that district.

The town of Minerva, lying directly south of Newcomb, exhibits the evidence of great mineral wealth, although but one bed of iron ore has been actually opened and partially worked. In the language of a correspondent; "Minerva may already be regarded as a mineral town, with wood equal to the supply of charcoal, for fifty years." The bed which has been opened, lies on lot 21, township 25, Totten and Crossfield purchase. It is owned by a company, composed of Hon. E. H. Rosekrans, J. C. Durand, and other prominent and energetic men. On the surface, the ore is somewhat impregnated with sulphur, but as the excavation penetrates the deposit, the quality of the ore obtained is pure, rich, and highly magnetic. It is easily reduced, and is pronounced better adapted for making pig, than bloom iron, but has produced in the forge, the best quality of iron.[1] The abundant presence of ore on the adjoining lot No. 28, and upon most of the contiguous territory, is satisfactorily ascertained. In comparing the results of my examinations of the ore beds fifteen years ago, with their present condition, I observe many striking changes in the characteristics of the ore. In the ores from several of these mines, sulphates, phosphates and other foreign substances were then incorporated; but in almost every instance in which the mines have been worked to any considerable extent, the ore is now wholly or nearly so exempt from the impurities.

SCHROON.

The *Schofield Bed* is situated in the town of Schroon, near the head of Paradox lake, and was opened in the year 1828, by Horace Hall. Bar iron was at that time made in the Schroon forge from the ore of this mine, which was worked by various proprietors, until 1845. In this year, I infer, operations were suspended at the bed. An average of two hundred tons of iron was made during the above period, which established and maintained the highest character in market. The bed has been again worked during the last year by the present owner, Mr. John Roth, and the ore has been used in both of his forges in Schroon, with decided success. The ore yields fifty per cent of iron of the first class. The vein is only from three to four feet in thickness, and has been worked about two hundred and fifty feet in length and from twenty to sixty feet in depth. Horse power is used in hoisting the ore, but the pit is pumped by steam.

The *Skiff Bed* lies about two miles from Paradox lake. It was opened by A. P. Skiff in the year 1857, but is now owned by Mr. Roth. This ore, like that from the Scho-

[1] *E. F. Williams.*

field bed possesses the highest qualities, but the same embarrassments impede at present its successful and remunerative development. The vein is small, where it has been disclosed, and is compressed between walls of rock, that immensely enhance the difficulties and expense of working it. The energetic owner, under the conviction that a wider vein exists and can be reached, has already expended many thousands of dollars, in the construction of a tunnel at the base of a mountain, in the hope of revealing such a vein. If this enterprise, which is still to be pressed, results in the discovery of a large deposit of ore equal to that which has been worked, this bed will probably be made one of the most valuable in the region. The ore furnished by both of these mines is generally conceded to be equal to any in the country.

CROWN POINT.

Near the boundary line between Schroon and Crown Point two iron ore beds of great value are located, which were included formerly by the state geologists in the Moriah district. They are of the magnetic type, and appear to possess inexhaustible deposits of the mineral. They are known as the Hammond, and Penfield mines. These mines are situated about ten miles from Lake Champlain.

Hammond Bed. The existence of this mine was ascertained as early as 1827, but it was not worked extensively until 1845. It is situated on lot No. 278 in Paradox tract, and is now owned by G. & T. Hammond and E. S. Bogue. It has been constantly worked since 1845, and produces an average of about four thousand tons of ore annually, which is consumed in the blast furnace of the proprietors, for making pig iron. It requires no separating. It is a black magnetic ore, of a close, fine grain or texture, with very pure white quartz in small particles disseminated very evenly through it. The ore is hard to drill and sledge. Worked in a blast furnace, it yields a fluid glassy cinder, and makes a superior quality of pig iron. The ore has no infusion of sulphates or phosphorus. There are two pits opening out of this mine; one descends, at an angle of about forty-five degrees to the depth of four hundred feet, and the other, recently opened, has reached a descent of about fifty feet. The ore is raised by horse power. In 1852, I saw teams loaded alongside of the breast of ore. The Hammond ore possesses the highest qualities of peculiar strength and softness, and is eminently adapted to the purposes of the foundery and the fabrication of machinery. The harder parts of the pig metal are particularly calculated for the manufacture of car axles and malleable articles. The extreme fluidity of this iron, and the long time it remains fluid, renders it highly valuable in the manufacture of these fabrics.

Penfield Bed is about half a mile from the Hammond bed. The ore is very similar, and the mines are probably parts of the same deposit. The Penfield bed was first opened many years since, but not worked to any extent until 1824, when it was opened by Messrs. Penfield & Taft. Since that period, it has been in constant operation. It was subsequently carried on by Penfield & Son; afterwards by Penfield, Harwood & Co., and at present by Penfield & Harwood. Although worked for so long a term, this mine exhibits no appearance of exhaustion. The ore excavated is used in the forges of the proprietors in Crown Point. I regret that I have been unable to procure more in detail statistics of this highly important mine. The description, however, of the characteristics and qualities of the Hammond ore has a general application to the ore of this bed. I shall refer to the properties of the iron it produces, in my notice of the Irondale forge.

In the south part of Crown Point large deposits occur of magnetic iron ores, but these are strongly impregnated with sulphurets. In the central part of the town an ore bed, known as the Saxe bed was worked about forty years ago by Jacob Saxe, and used in a blast furnace, of which he was the proprietor, that stood at the mouth of the Salmon river in Plattsburgh. The furnace has long since been abandoned and fallen into ruins. The bed has not recently been worked, and is superseded by mines yielding richer and more desirable ores. The Saxe bed and ore are fully noticed in the *Natural History* of the state, part 4, *Geology*, page 232.

TICONDEROGA.

The development of iron ore in the eastern part of the town of Ticonderoga has not been favorable. Graphite appears at present to be the prominent mineral of the district. A bed known as the *Vineyard* possesses a large deposit of iron ore, but it is so impregnated by sulphur as to be unavailable for practical purposes. A vein of red oxide has been opened, from which about one thousand five hundred tons of ore have been taken, but it is too hard in drilling to be remunerative. A vein of magnetic ore about two feet wide upon Mount Defiance is being opened by Weed & Burleigh. A shaft is excavating, in the hope of discovering a large expansion of the vein. Upon the Tub-mill property five veins of iron ore have been partially opened, and afford evidence of large deposits of good ore. They are situated ten miles from the lake, and have been only partially developed.

MORIAH IRON DISTRICT.

This tract, scarcely, if at all subordinate, to the Adirondac district in the extent of its deposits, perhaps superior in the quality of its ores and far more eligibly situated, is calculated to excite the wonder and admiration of the observer. The immense aggregate of iron ore which has been dug from those rugged hills, instead of affording any evidence of appreciable diminution, seems to prove the boundless magnitude of this source of enterprise and wealth. As these excavations widen and deepen, and the quantity of the mineral appears to augment, its quality almost universally improves. An air of life, of prosperity and success animates the whole scene. Activity and effort are everywhere impressed upon the character of the people. Idleness in this stirring community has no tolerance. Brain and muscle are put upon their highest tension. I propose to present a brief outline of the progress, and present condition of each of the ore beds in this district separately, and although I have made every effort to obtain ample information on the subject, the interests are so diversified and my materials so incomplete, I fear the result of my labor will appear inadequate and unsatisfactory.

The Cheever Ore Bed. A knowledge of the existence of ore in this locality appears to have been almost cotemporaneous with the settlement. The first child born in the township after the revolution, who is still living,[1] states, that his earliest recollections are associated with this ore. It cropped out so prominently on the surface, as to attract the notice of any casual observer. Local legends refer the earliest working of the mines to squatters upon the land without title. Ore is known to have been procured from the bed in the year 1804, but the subject excited slight interest, and no appreciation existed of the vast magnitude and incalculable value of the deposit. In 1820, '21, it was leased to a Charles Fisher, at a rent of two gross tons of bloom iron, worth at that time, one hundred dollars per ton.[2] I have found it difficult to trace the varied ownership of the property, but ascertain that between thirty and forty years ago the title was in a person named John Coates, to whom Dr. Abijah Cheever as guardian of minor children, had loaned certain funds. Dr. Cheever was ultimately obliged with great reluctance to accept this property, either in payment or as security for the debt. It is a striking incident in the history of its progressive value, that this ore bed, now almost beyond price in the hands of the present owners, should in a comparatively recent period, have been urged upon the market by Cheever, and offered at scarcely above a nominal price without a purchaser, and ultimately sold, it is said, at five thousand dollars. This sale was made in the year 1838, to Horace

---

[1] *Alexander McKensie.* [2] *Hon. John A. Lee.*

Grey of Boston. The statement of the amount of the price paid for the property varies from two thousand five hundred dollars to six thousand five hundred dollars. I have adopted that which appears to be the most authentic. In 1840, Mr. Grey transferred his interest to the Port Henry Iron Company, and leased from them in 1846, the furnace property and the Cheever ore bed. In the fall of 1852, Mr. Benjamin T. Reed of Boston purchased all the property of the Port Henry Iron Company, and in the following year transferred the ore bed to the Cheever Ore Bed Company.[1] Mr. John O. Presbrey is the present resident agent and manager of the mines. The bed has been owned and worked since 1853, by that company, which is an incorporated organization composed of gentlemen of affluence residing in Massachusetts. It is situated on the J. Williams tract, formerly called the Rogers Ore Bed patent, about three miles from Port Henry, and less than three fourths of a mile from Lake Champlain. Since the occupation by the present proprietor, the mine has been worked without intermission, and yields annually from fifty thousand to sixty thousand tons of ore. A large per centage of this ore is used by the furnaces of the Bay State Iron Company at Port Henry. The remainder is exported to Massachusetts, Pennsylvania, and to various points in New York and other sections of the Union. The ore is found in a regular vein and perfectly developed, from five to fifteen feet in thickness. The vein is reached by five different shafts or pits, one of which descends vertically to the depth of three hundred and fifteen feet. The work of opening has been pursued from the several pits and shafts, until a breast work of nearly one thousand and five hundred feet of ore has been formed and is now worked. From the foot of the perpendicular shaft, four distinct rail tracks have been constructed, which enable cars to transport the ore a distance of about two hundred feet. At the shaft, the ore is tipped into iron buckets, capable of holding about a ton

---

[1] *Mr. W. T. Foote, and W. F. Gookin.*

and a half of ore. These are hoisted to the surface, where by the action of appropriate machinery, the buckets are discharged into cars which carry it by a rail road along an inclined plane to the company's wharf, at the lake, or by the same machinery, the ore may be deposited on a platform, ready to be conveyed away by teams. The ore is conveyed on the rail trains in the pits by cars from the breast, and discharge into boxes, which are hoisted up the slide or inclined plane, to the platform above from which it is transported. These slides require ropes seven hundred feet long to connect with the drum in the engine room. Steam is the motive power, created by three stationary engines, for all the movements and elevating of the cars, buckets and boxes with ore about the mine. The rail road, which conducts the cars to the lake, is about three-fourths of a mile in length. From the wharf it is shipped for exportation. This ore does not require separating. No stone appears in it, except an occasional slight cleavage from the wall rock. The following is the analysis of this ore in 1856, by Prof. A. A. Hayes:

Proto and peroxide of iron,	90.54
Phosphate of lime,	3.80
Amphibole,	2.80
Silicic acid,	1.60
Pilanferous iron,	1.26
	100.00

About two hundred men are constantly employed in this mine. I descended the perpendicular shaft in an iron bucket, accompanied by Mr. John O. Presbrey, the courteous agent at the mine. The stopping of the bucket at the foot was so gentle and noiseless that I was scarcely aware the descent of more than three hundred feet was ended. A strange, wierd and thrilling spectacle was revealed. There was no noise but the ceaseless clink of the hammer, and the jarring of the machinery. Along the different chambers a series of twinkling lamps, shining more and more dimly, as the long lines receded in the deep darkness, were sufficient to reveal the low, dark arched roofs supported by massive and glittering doric columns. These columns stand about one hundred feet apart, and average sixteen feet square. They are chiefly formed of solid ore, a most costly material, as each column contains about one thousand tons of ore. At the remotest extremity of one of the galleries I noticed a single light moving, and inquired the cause. It was a lantern carried by one in pursuit of powder, kept in that retired spot in small quantities for immediate supply, and to guard against accidents. With every precaution, frequent serious catastrophies occur in blasting, through the carelessness or inadvertence of the workmen. Several years ago, the pillars of ore left to support the enormous burthen of rock and earth above a chamber previously worked yielded to the weight, and the whole mass was crushed together. The concussion is represented to have been not unlike an earthquake, rending the earth and dislocating the massive rocks for acres. I was struck by the singular freeness of this mine, in its deepest recesses, from dampness, and by noticing the pure and dry atmosphere which pervades it. In summer the temperature is cool, but in winter the cold is severe in the pits. A remarkable and unusual effect was produced, when, in the progress of the work, the different passages were connected. A strong current of air, precipitated down one pit and rushing in a powerful draft through the mine, ascended at the opposite extremity of the bed by another opening. The volume of air was so great, that it became necessary to erect partitions in the mine, to protect the workmen from the cold, and to prevent the extinguishing of the lamps. The Cheever mine was one of the first opened in the town of Moriah. It has occupied and will probably maintain the highest rank in respect to reputation and value, both by the quality of the ore and the position and locality of the bed.

Goff Bed lies in the vicinity of the Cheever, and possesses a great similarity of ore. It is situated near the margin of the lake, and has connected with it a wharf and separator. This bed was opened in 1845, and was formerly owned by Hon. George W. Goff, but three or four years since was purchased by its present proprietors, known as the Champlain Ore and Furnace Company. Besides its advantageous location on the lake shore, this mine enjoys another great and rare facility in being penetrated by nearly horizontal openings. It has three of these openings, one of which follows the vein almost eight hundred feet. A mule car is employed in the transportation of the ore from the mine. This bed is not at present worked, but when in operation it yields about four thousand tons of ore annually. The ore is magnetic, and about one-half taken from the mine requires separating. It is exported to various markets. When both this bed and the furnace at Westport, owned by the same company, are in operation, they give employment to about one hundred men. This is esteemed a valuable ore.

Port Henry Ore Bed is situated in a ravine between two hills, about one mile west of Cheever bed. This mine is owned by George B. Pease, and has been but partially developed. About one thousand tons have been raised. Prof. Hayes has made the following analysis:

Metallic Iron,....................................	64.15
Oxygen with it,....................................	34.15
Silica, ...	4.10
Lime and Magnesia, ...	1.10
Phosphate of lime,...	6.20

He remarks, "the ore is very much like the covering ore of the Cheever bed, and will doubtless as it comes from a deeper point, exclude much of the earthy minerals now found with it. It is a soft ore, working easily."

Cleveland Mine, formerly known as the Sherman bed, is located near the above, and is owned by a company in Cleveland, Ohio. It has been worked the last three years with an annual production of ore from eight to ten thousand tons, which is principally conveyed to Cleveland for puddling purposes. A shaft has been sunk about two hundred feet. Steam is used as the motive power, in hoisting the ore and pumping the mine. From thirty to one hundred men are employed about the mine and in connection with the business. Most of the ore requires separating.

About six miles west from Port Henry and upon an elevation of nearly fifteen hundred feet above the lake is situated a cluster of pits and shafts which open into several different ore beds; but occupying the corners of several lots, they stand within a space embraced by an area of five acres. These shafts descend into a deposit of ore, that can be divided by no visible lines; but beneath the surface there exists a uniform and unbroken mass of ore. The operations in several of these pits have so nearly approached, that the sound of the implements in one may be distinctly heard in another. When this ore was first worked, it was conjectured that it formed an enormous pocket; a term used by miners, to designate an isolated and limited body of ore, without the formation of a vein and liable to sudden exhaustion; but as the pits descend and expand, it is asserted, that the evidence augments of the presence of an inexhaustible deposit. The opinion seems to be warranted, that all this extended eminence has been formed by a vast upheaval of iron ore, and that the whole formation of these hills is charged with the mineral. The terrific power of the agency which wrought this work, is indicated by the position of the disturbed and dislocated rocks of the vicinity. The whole district is barren, broken and distorted. The worthlessness of the territory, as estimated by an ordinary standard, appears from the fact, that most of this land was originally sold at fifty cents the acre.

Indications of the presence of iron ore in Moriah were revealed at an early period, in the occupation of the town. When the Kellogg survey was made in 1810 of the territory, appropriately designated the Iron Ore tract, strong attractions disturbed the magnet, and particularly along the common lines between lots Nos. 21, 23, 24 and 25. No openings were made on any of these lots until

1824, although large specimens of ore had been found ten years before on lot No. 25.

The Old Sanford Bed is situated on lot No. 25, of the above tract, and is about six miles from the wharves at the lake. The subject of ore upon this lot excited some degree of attention in the summer of 1824. Messrs. Harry Sherman and Elijah Bishop proposed at that time to Mr. D. E. Sanford, the owner of No. 25, to become associated with him in exploring the lot, and that each should pay him one hundred dollars for an undivided one-fourth interest in the property. The terms were accepted and operations were immediately commenced by the parties, near the north-east corner of the lot, and ore was discovered about one foot below the surface. Other places within a few rods were explored with the same result. A few rods south of the first opening, a large boulder of iron, as it was conjectured, was found embedded in the earth, with many smaller pieces strewn upon the surface. On attempting to remove this supposed boulder, it was ascertained to be the outcropping of a vein, or the index, as it proved, to an enormous body of ore. It was followed down, the excavation being enlarged about a rod square. The explorers still believed it to be a limited deposit of ore, but their work was in fact the opening of the old Sanford bed. Ore from this bed was tried in a blast furnace at Port Henry, in the year 1834, but the experiment from injudicious management was unsuccessful. Two years later, Mr. G. W. Goff used at the same furnace some of the lean ore, which had been thrown out, at the bed, and was purchased by him at fifty cents per ton. Mixed with the Cheever and other ore, it produced good iron. In the spring of 1846, the property came into the possession of John A. Lee, George Sherman and Eliphalet Hall. Mr. Hall sold his interest the same year to Mr. A. J. Rosseau of Troy, who transferred his title in 1849, to Messrs. S. H. & J. G. Weatherbee. When I first examined this bed in 1852, teams were driven into it, down a slight depression of the ground, and loaded directly alongside of the breast of ore. At that time, the length of one of the openings was two hundred and fourteen feet, with an average width of thirty feet. The breast of ore worked was about eighty-two feet. The ore was then stratified, easily drilled; a single blast not unfrequently threw off thirty tons of pure ore. A large infusion of phosphate of lime was at that time disclosed in this ore. Another breast was worked in the mine that exhibited a face of ninety-nine feet; sixty feet in length and an average depth of twenty-five feet. This bed is now entered by three distinct shafts. One of these requires a rope five hundred and fifty feet long; another a rope of two hundred feet, and the third opening is one hundred and fifty feet deep. The ore is raised by cars on an inclined plane of about forty-five degrees. The cars are hoisted by a wire cable, moved by the agency of a drum and steam power, to a platform at the mouth of the shaft, where they are made to discharge themselves by a simple apparatus. The ore falls upon a large sieve, which separates the coarse from the finer particles. The lumps are destined for puddling furnaces, and the fine for other purposes. The average yield of this bed during the last six years has been forty-three thousand and three hundred tons of ore. It is used in forges, furnaces, and rolling mills, and requires no separating. The Sanford ore is inclined to be cold, short, and is extensively used as a mixture with ores of an opposite quality to render them neutral.[1] We descended into this mine by a box along the inclined plane escorted by the agent, Mr. Tifft. The depth is about two hundred and thirty feet. The area worked in this bed, from the nature of the ore, has acquired a different and more compact form than the chamber of the Cheever bed. The distance from

[1] Red or hot short iron, is ductile when cold, but extremely brittle when heated, a defect caused by the presence of a small quantity of sulphur. Cold short iron is ductile when hot, but brittle when cold; caused by a small quantity of phosphorus. Neutral iron is exempt from both of these defects.

the point where the ore passes under the cap rock, to the bottom of the present working, about thirty degrees, is three hundred and fifty feet, and the length of the bottom from east to west is two hundred and fifty feet. The shaft is about one hundred and fifty-five feet deep to the ore. Drifts have been run north and south from the bottom of the shaft, making a breast of one hundred and seventy-five feet. The base rock has not yet been reached, and the thickness of the breast is therefore still to be determined. The Miller pit is a few rods north of the old bed, the vein dipping at forty-five degrees. The depth from the light hole is about one hundred and fifty feet, length of breast two hundred feet and height about forty feet. The roof which has been left in excavating the old bed is lofty, and supported by eleven corresponding pillars, averaging fifty feet high and thirty feet square, and computed to contain already one hundred thousand tons of ore. Among numerous other explanations of their processes, Mr. Tifft described the methods pursued in working the mine. Commencing at one extremity, a prescribed depth is excavated, which is preserved to the other extremity and laterally throughout the opening. By this system a nearly level surface is maintained, and the size and foundations of the pillars preserved. My attention was directed in this mine to the working of a diamond drill, and the implement with its operations was courteously exhibited and explained to me. It may be pronounced a vast improvement in economy, efficiency and safety to the usual drilling by manual labor. The instrument is operated either by hand or steam power. In the process I witnessed, two men turned the propelling wheel, and the instrument bored into the hard ore with great ease and incredible rapidity. From two hundred and fifty to three hundred men, including teamsters, are employed in connection with this bed. Two large steam pumps draw off the water from the two deepest pits. I noticed in this mine the same singularly low temperature

I observed in the Cheever bed. The following is the analysis of this ore:

Metallic iron,	72.09
Insoluble silicious matter,	.34
Phosphorus,	.01
Oxygen and moisture,	27.56
	100.00

Bed on No. 21. In the year 1829, parties by digging a shaft about twelve feet deep, discovered ore on this lot. It was then owned by Jonas Reed and Elias Smith of Moriah, and Allen Smith of Addison, Vt., who had purchased it of the original proprietors for a merely nominal sum. The latter sold his one-half interest about this time for the sum of one hundred and twenty-five dollars, and Messrs. Sanford, Bishop & Sherman, with a view of avoiding competition, acquired a title to a majority of the different interests, and paid as the consideration for their purchase, "five hundred tons of old bed ore in the ground." No further operations occurred at this bed, until the year 1846, when it came into possession of Messrs. Storrs & Rosseau. The actual and practical opening of the mine is referred to this epoch. The entire interest in the property had previously been divided into small fractional shares. Mr. Storrs secured a preponderance of these shares. In 1846, the parties resumed operations in the shaft, which had been opened and abandoned more than twenty years before, and after sinking it about thirty feet, reached the body of ore. In 1852, a judicious observer wrote me, in reference to the bed and the indications of ore in the vicinity: "It would be difficult to obtain an approximation to the quantity of ore, in this single deposit, without estimating the contents of the entire hill."[1] The result has vindicated the accuracy of this judgment. Messrs. Storrs & Rosseau succeeded in raising about one thousand tons of ore, and in 1853 conveyed their interest to the American Mineral Com-

[1] *J. P. Butler, Esq.*

pany. This company erected extensive separating works for the purpose of extracting the phosphates from the ore, while separating the latter for market. They did not succeed in procuring the phosphates in sufficient purity for agricultural uses, and after an expenditure of several thousand dollars in the experiment, the scheme was relinquished. The company was at the same time engaged in mining the ore for market. This association passed through various changes.

On the organization of the *Port Henry Iron Company*, that company, under various agents, furnished a large amount of ore for market, until 1864, when Weatherbees, Sherman & Co., having purchased personally one-fourth of the capital stock, became the managing and selling agents. This position they still occupy. The shaft which we descended, accompanied by Mr. Goff the superintendent, is two hundred and thirty feet in depth. The track upon which the ore boxes move, is supported by heavy timbers, which traverse the chasm. Looking down from the box, in which one is slowly gliding in the descent, into the hideous cavern, where the lamps are flickering far below, a spectacle is revealed, grand and imposing, but calculated to disturb ordinary nerves. The magnitude of this deposit will appear from the fact that the area of the opening is nearly two hundred and twenty-five feet from the base of the slide on the north end, to the first pillar on the south side, and about one hundred feet on the bottom from east to west. The solid ore on the south side, is vertically about one hundred feet high. Drifts have been driven on the north side, at right angles under the rock one hundred feet. Other drifts have been driven east and west from the pillar. The length of the opening in that direction is two hundred and twenty-five feet. Above a part of the opening, the superincumbent rock and earth have been removed. The roof is high and apparently formed of the cap rock, and supported chiefly by columns of the same material. An average of thirty-six thousand tons of ore is yielded annually by this bed. The annexed is an analysis of the ore:

Protoxide of iron,..... } (yielding metallic iron, 69.82)	25.29
Peroxide, " " }	71.65
Alumina, ...	40
Oxide of titaneum,..	Trace
Phosphate of lime,......................	.39
Magnesia, ...	.05
Silica and insoluble matter, ...	2.22
	100.00

The pay roll, embracing this mine and those on Nos. 23, and 24 comprises from two hundred and fifty to three hundred names.

In this, as in every mine I have explored in Moriah, I was impressed by the quiet, discipline and regularity, in which its vast operations were conducted. This harmony and subordination conveys a most favorable idea of the judgment and efficiency of the system of management that prevails. It is said that laborers prefer a situation in these mines to toiling on a farm or in lumbering occupations.

Beds on Lots 23 *and* 24. These lots are contiguous to Nos. 25 and 21 which embrace the ore beds above described. In the year 1824, while the development of the mine on No. 25 was in progress, Jeremiah Cook, the owner of No. 23, began an exploration on his side of the dividing line between the two lots. He associated with him, Solomon and Hiram Everest, to whom he sold one-half of his interest for two hundred dollars. This was the earliest opening of lot No. 23. After effecting this opening, the parties commenced disposing of interests in the mine, as minute as $\frac{1}{16}$ and possibly $\frac{1}{32}$ on a valuation of four thousand dollars for the entire bed. Mr. Rosseau, the partner of Mr. Storrs, secured a majority of these shares, as the latter had obtained those of No. 21. Old pit on 23 was opened in 1823 and Brinsmade shaft on the same lot in 1865. These are the only openings upon this lot. There is one shaft on No. 24 which was opened in 1845, but not extensively worked until 1864. The annual yield of No. 23 for the last six years has been an average of nine thousand four hundred tons of ore, and that of No. 24 since 1864 has been nine thousand seven hundred tons. The ores from these beds are used in forges, furnaces and rolling mills. I have seen no analysis of the ore, but understand that the quality of No. 23 is similar to that from the old bed on No. 25 as they lie in direct contact. Old pit on 23 is three hundred and fifty feet deep. Brinsmade shaft is one hundred and fifty feet deep with a breadth one hundred and seventy-five feet from north to south. The shaft on No. 24 is two hundred and thirty feet. A steam engine of twenty-four horse power is used at these beds for raising ore and running a pump for draining the pits. The vein on 23 grows thicker as it advances south, and it is conjectured that it extends to No. 21, a distance of six hundred feet.

New Bed. The deposit, which is now known by this name was discovered by E. E. Sanford in the south-west corner of lot No. 24, in the year 1844, and was opened by him the following season. The sale already mentioned of the Old Bed by Mr. Sandford to Sherman & Hall, embraced his title to the New Bed. Mr. Hall the same year (1846), sold his interest to Mr. A. J. Rosseau, who in 1849 conveyed the same interest to Messrs. S. H. & J. G. Weatherbee. The bed was first practically worked in 1845, and has produced, during the last six years, an average of six thousand seven hundred and twenty tons of ore annually. The ore is in large demand for forges and blast furnaces. The following is an analysis of this ore:

Pure metallic Iron,................................	71.19
Insoluble silicious matter,.........................	1.12
Phosphorus,..	a trace
Oxygen and moisture,.......	27.69

About one-third of this ore requires separating. It is inclined to be red short and when mixed with the ore of the Old Bed, produces a neutral iron of exceeding tenacity. It is stated that the demand for the New Bed ore is larger than can be supplied. The pure ore from this bed is pronounced by those interested, to be the richest ore known to exist in this country. "Perfectly formed crystals weighing more than an ounce, are often found, the plane surface of which resembles burnished steel, rather than iron ore." The bed contains the celebrated shot ore, and on my former examination I found it difficult to obtain a large specimen, from the fact that it disintegrated by the touch. The depth of this bed, measuring along the slide from the light hole to the base is seven hundred feet on a slope of forty-five degrees, with a thickness at right angles with the vein varying from fifteen to thirty-five feet. A seventy-five horse power engine is required for hoisting the ore and pumping the water from the bed. This mine is about six and a half miles from the lake and possesses the same facilities as the other bed, for the transportation of ore.

A separator and saw-mill are propelled by the steam power, which hoists the ores. At the saw-mill all the lumber and plank are produced, which are required for the mines and plank road. From fifty to seventy men are employed about the mine and separator.[1]

Barton Bed. This mine is situated on Lot No. 34, Iron Ore tract, and is about seven miles from Port Henry. It was opened previous to 1850, and was formerly owned by Caleb D. Barton. This ore has been highly esteemed by forge holders. In 1863 the mine was purchased by the Port Henry Furnace Company, and is now owned by the same individuals, under the corporate name of the Bay State Iron Company. A large proportion of the ore yielded by this bed, has been used in the manufacture of pig iron. About eight thousand tons of ore is produced per annum, and an average of thirty-five men, including

---

[1] I am chiefly indebted to the zeal and public spirit of Mr. W. F. Gookin for the statistics embraced in the above notices.

teamsters, are employed about the bed. The following is the analysis of the Barton ore:

Magnetic oxide of iron,	51.418
Oxide magnesia,	Trace
Titanic acid,	0.110
Aluminium,	0.329
Magnesia,	0.159
Lime,	0.498
Silicic acid (quartz, with a very little hornblende),	47.433
Phosphoric acid,	0.050
Sulphur,	0.003
	10.000

Quantity of metallic iron,	37.24
Phosphoric,	22

The Barton ore is used by the Bay State Iron Company furnace, at Port Henry, in combination with the Cheever ore, and in about equal proportions. The ore from the Barton bed is slightly mixed with silex.

Fisher Hill Bed. This mine was opened at an early period in the history of Moriah, by Fisher, and was sold by him to Eliphalet Hall. During a long term of years, the title was involved in a remarkable and exciting litigation, which was ultimately settled by a compromise. The mine is situated about seven miles from the lake. It was purchased by its present proprietors, an eastern company, in the year 1863, at seventy-five thousand dollars. The ore is lean and silicious, and requires separating, but is classed among the best ores of the district, and is in great requisition among the forges of the vicinity. It finds market also with the iron manufacturers along the Hudson, and in various other localities.

The mine has three shafts; two of which are now worked. Shaft designated number one, has a descent of five hundred and fifty feet, and number three has a descent of five hundred feet. The latter presents a breast of fifty feet and twenty-five feet in height. The ore is said to become of a purer quality as the mine is developed, and is reputed to be well adapted to the fabrication of wire and steel. Horse power is used in raising the ore. This bed was sold to the present proprietors in 1863, for seventy-five thousand dollars. It is now owned by eastern capitalists. Mr. O. Hall is the resident manager.

The Cook, or M. T. Smith Shaft. The revelation of this valuable mine was a striking triumph of practical science and determined perseverance, that has few parallels in mining operations. The bed is situated on lot 37, Iron Ore tract, and about six miles from Port Henry. The site of this ultimate great success was an open range, and the particular locality a sandy knoll in a pasture, where not the slightest appearance was disclosed on the surface of the presence of ore, although its existence at the place had been long suspected, from an unusual magnetic attraction. The needle, when passed along an area of about forty rods square, was drawn as much as possible to a vertical position. During the term of fifteen years, before the enterprise of Mr. M. T. Smith, several attempts to reach ore on the lot had been made and abandoned. Mr. Smith and an associate finally made an arrangement with Patrick Cook, the owner of the lot, to open the mine. In consideration of their services and disbursements, they were to receive a conveyance of two-thirds of the property. They commenced their labor, and, following the indications of the magnet, excavated a shaft ten feet square, through a hundred feet of earth, without finding any additional evidences of ore. Here they struck hard pan, but undeterred by these adverse results, they persisted with unabated zeal. At length they reached and passed through a very thin vein of ore, and this the croakers pronounced the cause of the attraction. But Mr. Smith, wisely judging the deposit too small to have produced effects so powerful, and with unyielding confidence in the assurances of the needle, continued the excavation, and after penetrating through rock and hard pan eighty feet further, he revealed a fourteen feet vein of ore, of the first quality. The mine was opened in June, 1866. In the first year it produced eight thousand tons, and in 1868 yielded fourteen thousand five hundred tons. The breast now wrought is two hundred feet in length, and averages fifteen feet in width. The ore is exported to Troy, Hudson, Pittsburg, and various other manufacturing localities. It is raised by horse power, but the water is pumped out by steam. No separating of the ore is necessary. The mine is worked both night and day, and requires the labor of thirty or forty persons. The future of this bed promises results which must secure an ample remuneration to the skill and energy of the enterprising explorers.

The impurities which affected most of the ores of Moriah were chiefly phosphates and white flint; but all these ores have become purer and softer as descents have been made in the mines. The first separator erected in the town was built in 1842, by Eliphalet Hall. In the year 1853 Lee & Sherman consolidated their interests with S. H. & J. G. Weatherbee. The firm of Lee, Sherman & Weatherbees continued until 1862, when Mr. Lee retired, selling his title to Weatherbees, Sherman & Co., who also purchased the remaining small interest, and are now the sole owners of the old and new beds. Mr. George R. Sherman is a member of this firm. The Port Henry Iron Ore Company, consisting of the above firm, and Messrs. John A. Griswold and H. Burden & Son of Troy and Bech, Tower & Brinsmade of Pokeepsie, now owns the mines, designated Nos. 21, 23 and 24, with ore rights on the west end of lot 25. The ores from these and the adjacent mines have been transported for several years by a plank road, extending to the wharves of these companies at the lake. Immense loads, averaging about five tons, and sometimes it is stated reaching nine tons, along nearly an uninterrupted descent, are conveyed by this medium. The Lake Champlain and Moriah Rail Road Company, formed of the above companies, is now constructing a railway along the same route, which will be completed in the summer of 1869. It will supersede the plank for teaming, and must effect a great economy in transportation of ore. This railway overcomes an ascent of fourteen hundred feet in about seven miles, on the extraordinary grade of two hundred feet to the mile.

A cloud seems to have rested upon the mines of Moriah for some period after their discovery. A distrust prevailed in regard to the character of the ore, and it required the struggle of several years before the confidence of the iron manufacturers could be secured. The sales of ore from these mines during the first three or four years amounted to scarcely two hundred tons annually, and then decreased to half that quantity. The aggregate of ore which had been sold, when Lee, Sherman & Hall came into possession of their interest, was about six thousand tons, at prices ranging from fifty cents to two dollars and a half, at the beds, payable in barter or on such terms as the purchaser proposed. The first specific trial of these ores was made at Ticonderoga, with a load sent there for the purpose. This issue was favorable, and about three hundred tons were raised the same year, only a part of which was sold, but the next year an increased interest in the ore was manifested by a more animated demand for it, by their iron works in Vermont. From that period, the sales of ore have been rapidly progressive. In 1847 Lee & Sherman effected a sale of twenty thousand tons to F. H. Jackson of the Sisco furnace at Westport. This was the first sale made of ore to be used in furnaces. About the same time their ores were introduced in furnaces at Troy and other points on the Hudson. The mines owned by this firm produced between the years 1846 and 1854, about fifty thousand tons of ore. A competent authority estimates the aggregate of ore raised from the mines of Moriah from their development up to January 1st, 1869, at one million and one hundred thousand tons, of which one-third has been raised during the last six years. These ores are used in all the manufacturing districts of New England and the middle states, and largely at the west and south. A heavy supply of the ore is constantly maintained at the depot in Cleveland, Ohio, to meet the demand in that state and Western Pennsylvania. The ores of Moriah are all magnetic and chiefly cold short, and are in request to combine with the red short ores of other districts to form a neutral iron. This trade is steadily increasing, while in Moriah new mines are constantly developing. The product of the several ore beds in the town in 1868 is as follows:

	Tons.
The Cheever bed,	68,000
Mines of Port Henry Iron Co.,	59,000
" Weatherbees, Sherman and Co.,	59,500
" Lake Champlain Mining Co.,	2,500
" M. T. Smith,	14,500
" Fisher bed,	6,500
	230,000

Most of these companies have supplied their different openings with improved hoisting power. The Port Henry Iron Ore Company and Weatherbees, Sherman & Co., are now prepared, if the demand justifies the effort, to raise one thousand tons daily from their various mines.[1] In the summer of 1869, a fresh activity seems to animate the business of Moriah. A fleet of vessels assembled about the wharves at Cedar Point, loading or awaiting their turns. Fifteen hundred tons, in part the accumulation of the winter, are daily shipped, while five hundred tons are delivered from the beds by teams. In the above aggregate of two hundred and thirty thousand tons of ore, it is computed that eighteen thousand tons are consumed by the works in Moriah, leaving two hundred and twelve thousand tons for exportation.

Spear and Butler Bed. In a former work, I used the following language in relation to this mine. This bed lies about a mile and a half from the lake. The ore is a mag-

[1] I owe these statistics to a very intelligent paper, supplied by W. F. Gookin, Esq.

netic oxide, impressed with a hermatite type. The vein has been traced by a magnet nearly one-half a mile. It has been opened about ten rods in length, and about twenty feet in depth, presenting a breast of nine feet, widening as it descends. This ore is very peculiar and of great value from its malleability and toughness. It is mixed with silex and carbonate of lime; requires separating, but works freely and reduces rapidly in a common force fire. The bed was discovered in 1848. The first analysis of the ore was made at my request by Professor Salisbury, and presents the following results:

	Butler's Magnetic ore.
Peroxide of iron,	56.53
Protoxide of iron,	28.49
Silica,	13.81
Alumina,	1.62
Carbonate of lime,	......
	99.85
Percentage of pure iron in the per and protoxides,	61.202
Percentage of oxygen in the per and protoxides,	23.318

I learn that this bed has never been worked, but remains in the same condition as when I examined it.

The Elizabethtown and Westport District.

The territory included in this designation, is a continuation of the same mountainous range, which embraces most of the important iron mines in Moriah. Similar in its general characteristics, it is identical in geological formation, and it seems to exhibit a prolongation of the same veins and deposits. A large number of mines have been already discovered, and the presence of iron ore in almost every section of the district is disclosed by evidence existing upon the surface, and the unerring indications of the magnet. Most of these mines have been but partially opened;

neither have such indications in all instances been efficiently pursued. Although the magnitude of the deposits has been confidently asserted, their full development has been impeded by unfavorable circumstances. These beds are generally remote from the facilities of commercial intercourse, and the character of most of the ores for practical purposes is yet to be determined. They necessarily have been depressed in competition with mines enjoying every convenience of access, and with ores, whose high qualities have been established by long experience and the severest tests. A cautious observer remarks in reference to the ore beds of this district: "All that is wanting to render at least nine out of ten of these beds profitable and valuable, is means of transportation and a market." I have been unable to collect the materials necessary to a just and competent account of the mines of this district, and am constrained to present scarcely more than a bare enumeration of them. For the limited statistics I have received, I am indebted to the zeal of a gentleman who possesses no pecuniary interest in the property.

Elizabethtown.

Castaline Bed was discovered and worked to some extent about the year 1800. Considerable quantities of ore were transported from this mine to Hinesburg, Vermont, and used in the iron works at that place at an early day. The bed is situated on land owned by M. J. Post, but the heirs of W. D. and H. H. Ross are proprietors of the ore. The following is an analysis of the Castaline ore:

Black oxide of iron,	95.04
Silex alumina,	3.12
Lime and magnesia,	1.84
	100.00

Ross Bed is located on lot No. 72, Roaring Branch tract, and about one mile north-east of the above. It was discovered about the same period, and is very similar in its qualities to the Castaline. The ore has been partially worked and makes good iron. The declination of the vein under or into a mountain, prevents at present an extensive opening of the bed. The land belongs to Mr. Thomas Doyle, and the ore to the heirs of the Messrs. Ross. The following is an analysis of the ore:

Black oxide of iron,................................	87.64
Silex and alumina, ...	9.80
Lime and magnesia, ...	2.56
	100.00

Nigger Hill Bed. This mine was discovered between the years 1825 and 1830, and slightly opened by Frederick Hoag. It is about five miles south of the Court House in Elizabethtown, and was long known as the Hoag bed. The ore was used at the Kingdom forge, by Mr. H. R. Noble, in a considerable amount for several years, and was esteemed a good furnace ore. Mixed with the old Sanford bed of Moriah, it worked successfully in a forge. Portions of this ore work admirably alone. This ore bed was sold in 1864, by the heirs of Mr. Noble, for $100,000, to the present owners, the Lake Champlain Ore and Iron Company. The property was assessed in 1868 on the grand list at $12,000. This mine is described as an immense mass of magnetic ore, so rich that it does not require separating, but so hard that it has to be roasted.[1] The following is an analysis of this ore:

Black oxide of iron,................................	89.36
Silex and alumina, ...	6.96
Lime and magnesia, ...	3.68
	100.00

Wakefield Bed was discovered about 1845, and opened by Col. E. F. Williams. The title of the land is in Stephen Pitkin. The ore is owned by the heirs of the Messrs. Ross.

[1] *W. G. Neilson's report.*

Little Pond Bed. This remarkable deposit was found about 1840. It is situated on lot No. 199, Iron Ore tract, and a half mile from the village of Elizabethtown. It was opened by E. F. Williams. A correspondent remarks, "this is a wonderful mass — a mountain of ore." The title to this property has been repeatedly changed, and is now held by W. J. Averill, of Ogdensburg. In a report on the survey of Essex county in 1852, I advanced these views in reference to this deposit: The Little Pond bed is among the most remarkable formations of ore in this county, and from the quality of the ore, the apparent magnitude of the deposit, and its favorable position, may be classed among the most valuable mines of the region. This bed is situated about six miles from the lake, and near a plank road. It apparently forms the mass of an eminence, probably covering at the base an area of forty acres, and elevated nearly two hundred feet. The examinations already made, which are corroborated by the general appearance and indications of the mound, seem to authorize the opinion, that this entire eminence is a mass of ore, covered only by an incrustation of rock and earth of a few feet in depth.

If further developments shall establish this fact, the quantity of the ore in this deposit may be pronounced illimitable, and in value and importance almost beyond computation. The subjoined is an analysis of this ore made by Dr. Chilton:

Protoxide of iron with a little peroxide of iron,	40.27
Silica,	4.11
Alumina,	.22
Lime,	.83
Magnesia,	3.43
Water, etc.,	1.14
	100.00

Judd Bed was discovered in 1845, and was opened to some extent between that year and 1855, by David Judd. The present proprietors are the Kingdom Company of Lake Champlain.

Finney Bed was discovered in 1854 on lot 139, Iron Ore tract, and was opened by O. Abel, Jr., W. W. Root, J. E. McVine and J. H. Sanders. Several hundred tons have been raised and sold from this bed. It melts readily and produces superior iron. In 1865, the bed was sold for five thousand dollars to the present owners, the Vulcan Furnace Company.

Gates Bed was found about the same time as the Finney bed, and upon an adjoining lot. It is supposed to be a continuation of the same vein, which may be distinctly traced for the distance of more than half a mile. It has been partly opened by Willis Gates, who has been offered and refused ten thousand dollars for his interest.

Burt Bed was discovered in 1840. It is located in the extreme south-east corner of Elizabethtown, and near the Fisher Hill mine. The ore is very similar to that taken from that mine, and was formerly pronounced by an experienced manufacturer to be the best forge ore in the county. The vein of the Burt ore dips at an angle of forty-five degrees, and is opened by a slope over three hundred feet long. The area excavated at the bottom was in 1867 about eighty-five feet, with a breast of ore of about fourteen feet. The ore is hoisted, in boxes, which slide on beams laid along the slope, or by horse power. There are several other openings on the same lot, which exhibit strong indications of the presence of valuable veins. The Burt ore has been successfully used both at the Valley and Kingdom forges. This property was purchased by the present owners, the Essex and Lake Champlain Ore and Iron Company, in 1864, at thirty-five thousand dollars. It is assessed on the grand list at fifteen thousand dollars.

Steel Bed is situated about a half mile south-east of the village of Elizabethtown on lot No. 189, Iron Ore tract. The bed was discovered in 1810, and the ore worked in local forges in combination with other ore to some extent.

After the destruction of these forges by the freshet of 1830, the bed was not worked for many years. The ore was originally considered sulphurous, but Messrs. Whallon & Judd in 1850, successfully consumed a considerable quantity, which had been raised for some time and exposed to the action of the elements. Mr. R. Remington in 1866, sunk a shaft, and obtained ore of a superior quality, and apparently free from the infusion of sulphur. The present proprietors of this bed are the Kingdom Iron Ore Company and Mr. Remington. This property is assessed at one thousand dollars.

Odell Bed. Two openings in the eastern part of Elizabethtown have received this name. Neither have been worked to any extent, but they are esteemed good deposits of ore. Mitchell bed is on lot No. 116, Iron Ore tract, and was discovered about 1830. It was partially opened by Eliab Mitchell. The ore is very similar in its qualities to the ore of the Burt bed. The property is owned by the Essex and Lake Champlain Ore and Iron Company.

Buck and Noble Beds. These beds are situated upon lots Nos. 109 and 110 Iron Ore tract, and near the boundary line between Elizabethtown and Moriah. Lot No. 109 is owned by the heirs of Hiram Buck, and No. 110 by the heirs of Henry R. Noble. The deposit was discovered in 1865. It has been sufficiently worked to disclose the existence of a great body of ore, with the most promising evidences of superior qualities. The ore does not require separating, but pounding in the machine prepares it for the forge. The bed on 109 is opened about forty feet in length with an average depth of about twenty feet.

Thompson Shaft. On lot No. 48, Iron Ore tract, and about eight rods from the M. T. Smith shaft on lot No. 47 in Moriah. This mine has been recently opened. A shaft has been sunk one hundred and thirty feet, and about twenty-five tons of ore are raised daily by horse power. The ore is similar to that of the adjoining Smith shaft. The bed is owned by W. Thompson, M. T. Smith and others.

On lot No. 127, North River Head tract, a vein was discovered in 1854. Partially developed it presents a view of about ten feet in thickness of ore suitable for the furnace.

WESTPORT.

The Campbell Bed, now more generally designated the Norway Bed, was opened between the years 1845 and 1850, and lies on lots Nos. 166 and 168, Iron Ore tract. It was worked by Mr. Henry J. Campbell and Whallon & Judd, in 1852 and 1853. Several hundred tons of the ore during that period were manufactured by Whallon & Judd. It has established a reputation as a first class forge ore, very similar in its qualities to the Burt and Fisher hill ores. The ore is lean. The strongest indications exist, that this mine embraces a vast deposit of superior ore. The proprietors of the property are Hon. A. C. Hand, R. Remington and the Kingdom Iron Company of Lake Champlain. A road is now in process of construction to connect the Norway Bed with Lake Champlain at the village of Westport.

The Merriam Bed is situated on lot No. 165, in the Iron Ore tract, about five miles from Westport. It was opened by Messrs. W. P. & P. D. Merriam in 1867. Two other distinct veins are disclosed on the same lot, which have not been developed to any extent. The opening which has been partially worked, exhibits a vein of five feet of very pure ore, from eighteen to twenty feet in width. One shaft has been sunk to the depth of twenty-five feet. This ore, it is claimed, yields more than sixty per cent of separated ore. It is neutral in its qualities, and produces in a forge good iron. It has been successfully used in the forge of the owners, since the bed was opened. The train road of the Norway Company, will, when completed, approach to within forty rods of this bed.

Jackson's Bed. Some years since a bed was opened in Westport, by Mr. F. H. Jackson and slightly worked. He used the ore to some extent in the Sisco furnace but recently it has not been operated.

ESSEX AND WILLSBORO'.

The evidences of iron ore existing in both of these towns are copious, but no large beds have been distinctly revealed. A deposit is now being opened by Messrs. Nichols, Lynde & Ross, about four miles south of the village of Essex and near Split rock, and another, about a mile distant from this, known as the Hill bed, by an Albany company.

Numerous veins of iron ore have been found in Chesterfield, Keene, Jay, St. Armands and Wilmington. The appearance of most of these indicate, that when fully developed, they will prove extensive and valuable. I examined in North Elba, several large deposits, apparently of a high grade of ore. These were strangely overlooked, when the original beds owned by the Elba Company were abandoned, and it was judged necessary to export the raw material from the Arnold bed. Beds of hematite iron ore are found in the various sections of the county. Deposits of iron ore pervade almost every section of the county, and to such a degree, as to often embarrass the operations of the surveyor, in the use of ordinary instruments. I have been able to exhibit a mere outline of the incomputable wealth embraced in the iron mines of the region. The past history and progress of these mines sustain the conviction, that deposits of ore remain unrevealed of equal magnitude and of as high properties as those already discovered. Those known to exist can only be regarded as the types and harbingers of the infinite treasures still hidden in the mountains, and beneath the soil of northern New York. These vast storehouses of private and national wealth will be unlocked when the demands of business and facilities of intercourse shall stimulate the application of enterprise and capital.

The Palmer Bed. This mine, remarkable even in this region for its magnitude and the quality of the ore, lies in the town of Black Brook, Clinton county, on Lot No. 15, in the eighth division of Livingstone's patent, and within a short distance of the Essex county line. It is situated nearly equidistant between the works of Messrs. J. & J. Rogers, at Black Brook, and those at Au Sable Forks, and about three miles from the depot of the Whitehall and Plattsburgh rail road. Its site is upon a bleak and rocky eminence, that reveals no evidence of the vast wealth it embraces. This bed was discovered by Zephaniah Palmer, near the year 1820, both from indications on the surface, and the attraction of the magnet, but was not efficiently worked until 1833. For a period, the title was disturbed by a severe legal controversy; but these have long since been adjusted, and the unquestioned ownership of the property is now held by the Messrs. Rogers, and the Peru Steel and Iron Company; five-eighths belonging to the former, and the balance to the latter. The average yield of this mine, during the last six years, has exceeded twenty thousand tons of raw ore to the Messrs. Rogers, and from twelve thousand to fourteen thousand tons to the other proprietors. Nearly the whole of this large aggregate is consumed by the owners of the bed in their own works, leaving at present none for exportation. This ore has been used principally in forges. It is a lean and magnetic ore, and almost uniformly requires separating.

The long term of years in which the Palmer bed has been worked, has produced excavations that form a large area, but without exhibiting the slightest appearance of exhaustion in the affluent material. The working breasts of ore are reached by a number of distinct shafts or pits; the lowest of which has descended to a depth of eight hundred feet. A map of the premises, which has been obligingly furnished me by Mr. Graves, exhibits the hill as literally honeycombed by these various openings. The ore is raised from these pits by steam power. About one hundred and fifty laborers are employed on the Rogers section of the bed alone. I refer in other places to this interesting locality, its labor and system of operations.

PEAT.

I may here appropriately notice a material which I confidently believe will become intimately associated with the mineral interest of the district. Amid all the exuberant bounties of nature with which providence has endowed this region, one has been withheld, in the want of coal, that causes a serious impediment to its industrial progress and prosperity. It is believed that an article which prevails in every section in great profusion may measurably supply this deficiency, and it is gratifying to know that the attention of prominent manufacturers is directed to the subject of using it for fuel, in their workshops as well as for domestic consumption. The supply of peat is particularly copious in northern New York, and is everywhere accessible. I have examined numerous deposits in the county of Essex, and the amount may be pronounced literally inexhaustible. I can only refer to one bed in Elizabethtown, on the premises of Hon. A. C. Hand, as a type of the whole. This deposit spreads over several acres. A pole was thrust through the peat a length of more than twenty feet below the surface, without reaching the hard pan beneath. By an analysis I caused to be made of peat from the county, it was found to contain more than ninety-three per cent of organic matter, composed of resinous substances, vegetable fibres and other combustible material. If art and science can devise any process, by which this substance, with the requisite economy, may be prepared for practical use, an infinite boon will be presented to the country. In Austria, and various departments of Germany, and in Sweden, peat is used in the manufacture of iron. Even in Great Britain, and in competition with the rich coal mines of that country it is being introduced for that purpose. It is used in Belgium, I am informed by a most intelligent authority, in the manufacture of the more delicate iron fabrics.[1] In some classes

---

[1] *Hon. T. G. Alvord.*

of puddling furnaces peat has been consumed for a fourth of a century. On the Grand Trunk rail road in Canada, which traverses vast forest tracts belonging to the company, where wood may be procured at merely the cost of chopping by cheap labor, peat for the last year has been appropriated for fuel in their engines. It is asserted by an authentic source, that it has been thus exclusively used and by its utilization has effected a saving of ten thousand pounds to the road.[1]

Graphites.

This mineral, more generally known as plumbago, or black lead, seems to pervade Essex county by almost as universal a presence as iron ore. I found pure and choice specimens in Chesterfield, Jay, Newcomb and other towns. A correspondent states, that "Plumbago exists in large quantities in Minerva."[2] I am also informed, that a mine is about being opened on Willsboro' mountain.[3] I examined a deposit of graphite, in which considerable excavation had recently been made, on the furnace property at Port Henry. The mineral here occurs in neither a mass nor vein, but is incorporated by minute particles in the soil, and is easily detected by its glittering appearance. The earth yields on separating about one-seventh part of the mineral. I also noticed large leaves of very pure asbestos cleaving to the fragments of rock, thrown out in this excavation. Ticonderoga, however, is the scene of an extraordinary development of the graphite. Much romantic legend invests the discovery of this deposit. Whether the slipping of an animal on the wet moss revealed the lustrous treasure; or the uncertain sound, returned from the blow of an axe, or accident, or careful research, as is asserted by different traditions, is less important than the fact, that about the year 1815, this immense mass of graphite became known. The circumstance that an Indian arrow was found in an old opening in the vein,

---

[1] *T. B. Hyde's letter.* [2] *E. P. Williams.* [3] *John Ross.*

which was several feet in length, renders the supposition probable, that it was known and worked by the aborigines, at an early period. The graphite mine appears to constitute the principal formation of an eminence, now known as Lead mountain, in the north-west part of Ticonderoga. It is disclosed in seams throughout the vicinity, and is probably injected into the whole ridge that extends into Schroon. I examined two openings, near the works of Messrs. Treadway in that town, which afforded very decided indications of the graphite in large deposits and of an excellent quality. Immediately after the discovery, the different veins which had been disclosed were worked in a rude manner by several claimants, but were subsequently opened with more system by William A. G. Arthur and C. P. Ives. The whole interest has been purchased and is now worked with great energy and success, by the American Graphite Company. In site, this mineral, gleaming like an infinitude of diamonds, is exquisitely beautiful. At Ticonderoga it is found in veins, usually from eight inches to a foot in thickness. Some of the chambers have been opened between one hundred and two hundred feet in length, and from seventy to eighty feet in depth. Three hundred pounds of pure ore have been raised in one hour from a single vein. The Graphite Company employ about forty laborers in their mines and raise and manufacture five hundred tons of the mineral annually. The walls of this mine are quartz or trap rock. Enormous specimens of the graphite of great beauty and purity are excavated. Nearly a total freeness from lime, supposed to exist in a portion of the mineral in these veins, render it of the greatest value in the construction of crucibles.

Galena.

I have most assiduously searched for traces of galena, with a strong impression of its existence within the limits of the county. The coincidence of several circumstances has formed this conviction. It is found in light veins in the fissures of the rocks of several localities. A map procured in London in 1784, which exhibited an exact and minute designation of the headlands and islands, of the soundings and the position of each rock and reef of Lake Champlain, derived from the accurate surveys of the French and English engineers, strengthens this opinion.[1] Upon this map thus maturely and carefully arranged, a point is designated in the mountain range between Chesterfield and Willsboro', as the *Lead ore bed.* A tradition of this ore bed is known to exist among the savage tribes north of the great lakes. A little flotilla of canoes, bearing Indians from that region, as they represent, appear yearly about the middle of autumn, lying on the beach in the vicinity of those mountains. Lingering here for several days, with no ostensible pursuit, they as suddenly disappear. I cannot resist the popular opinion that these periodical visits have some connection with the legend and the existence of this ore bed. Other circumstances tend to fortify this impression. Accounts which have been retained in several families, descended from the early settlers of the county, ancestors of which were carried prisoners into Canada during the revolution, combine to corroborate the following facts. The Indians, who usually were their conductors, were in the habit of uniformly landing near these mountains (which are the last northern spurs of the Adirondacs, and here fall precipitately into the lake), and while a part remained to guard the prisoners, others proceeded into the interior, and after an absence of a few hours, returned to the canoes laded with lead ore of the richest quality. These traditions are all harmonious as to the incident, the locality, and the time employed by the Indians procuring their lead. Several barrels of crude

[1] This map was brought from England by Elkanah Watson, and was loaned by him to a state department at Albany. All trace has since been lost of it. It was a most important and interesting document, and believed to contain the only minute chart of Lake Champlain extant. The steamer Francis Saltus was wrecked in 1852, upon a slight needle rock laid down on this chart, but unknown to many of the navigators of the lake.

lead ore, which had been collected in the same locality, we dispatched from Willsboro' last autumn, for the purpose of being examined and assayed.[1]

Copper.

This metal has been found many feet below the surface in the Phosphate mine and at another locality in Crown Point. Specimens which I have analyzed exhibit the following very favorable results. No. 86 was from the Phosphate mine and 68 from the other site.

	No. 68.	No. 86.
Copper	44.50	46.70
Iron,	31.30	10.45
Sulphur,	30.20	......
Carbonic Acid,	......	23.10
Silica,	3.70	19.85
	99.70	99.85

No. 68 is copper pyrites containing iron as it usually does. This is sufficiently rich in copper to make it valuable if found in any considerable quantity. The greater part of the copper of commerce comes from this kind of ore. No. 86 is a carbonate of copper, and will be very valuable if found in adequate quantities. In reference to the deposit in Crown Point, one of the enterprising proprietors wrote me some years since, "our company expended about three hundred dollars last season in sinking a shaft upon the copper locality, and found more or less all the way, as far as they descended, but no regular lode. Some of the specimens we procured were very rich and beautiful, and I have no doubt but a rich lode of copper would be found by sinking deep. The iron business, however, now pays too well to run much risk on copper." The subject still slumbers in the same position.[2]

---

[1] *A. D. Barber.* [2] *C. F. Hammond, Esq.*

Silver.

An intelligent resident of North Elba in communicating a valuable description of that town, refers to a singular and apparently well authenticated account of the accidental discovery of a vein of silver ore among the Adirondacs and the loss of its trace. He adduces strong evidence of the fact, and that pure silver was produced from the ore.

The geological formation along the shore of Lake Champlain presents an unique and remarkable alternation of the primitive with the higher structures. The former in a general inclination recedes from the lake, but incidentally dislocates the formation of the latter by projecting between them, veins and ledges in lateral spurs. At Ticonderoga, a range of sandstone and limestone rock supervenes. Proceeding northward, we meet at Crown Point, a ledge of regular granite and veins of gneiss succeeded by limestone containing fossil remains and mingled with the black marble. At Port Henry is exhibited a remarkable and scarcely defined and promiscuous mingling of various strata of rocks and minerals. Serpentine, mica in large and beautiful masses, gneissoid granite, primitive limestone, are conspicuous. The pure white of the granular limestone, spotted by the sparkling black specks of plumbago, form most beautiful cabinet specimens. In Keene, I found specimens more rare and exquisitely beautiful of this limestone, dotted by bright green crystals of sahlite. Verd antique occurs in large veins at Port Henry, and is an exceeding rich and brilliant material. An observant gentleman of that place affirmed that a fossiliferous lime stone rock, presenting a perfect stratification, might be seen at low water on the margin of the lake, forming a substratum to these primitive rocks.

The granular limestone which crops out at Port Henry, appears in Ticonderoga, near Lake George, and prevails extensively in Schroon and Minerva. I found but one manifestation of the rock in North Elba, upon the farm of

Mr. Hinckley, where it develops in a ledge, upon a side hill. It appears usually combined with sulphates, phosphates, or other foreign substances. The hyperstene rock projects from the mountains in Westport, and, incidentally traversed by limestone, predominates. The primitive rocks prevail in the southern section of the town of Essex. Here occurs that very extraordinary exhibition of porphyry so elaborately discussed in the report of Professor Emmons. This rock, extending over the surface upon several acres, is peculiarly beautiful in its color, structure, and singular dentritic formation. It affords perfect demonstration of an igneous agency, most potent and terrific, that rent asunder the earth, fused and ejected this vast rock. The extreme hardness of the porphyry is a marked characteristic. Struck with the steel hammer, it evolves a brilliant corruscation of light and sparks. My attention was directed to another remarkable exhibition of porphyry, upon the premises of Mr. Clark, on Willsboro' point. This vein, about a foot wide, is interjected in a seam of blue limestone, and the rock has been evidently dismembered in the process. Scarcely a fragment of the disrupted limestone remains, near the porphyry vein. Various fossils occur in this rock, and also in the slate or shale which lies contiguous. Many of these remains are of great size, and in unusual preservation. A few years since, a single fossil of a reptile was exhumed by Mr. Clark, measuring two feet in length, and so perfect in its preservation, that the form of the minute scales could be distinguished. At Mount Trembleau, as in Willsboro', Westport and Moriah, the hyperstene rock plunges into the lake in a bold, ragged, and perpendicular wall. A very peculiar and large deposit of stalagmite lies upon the north bank of the Boquet, near, but not subjacent apparently, to a mass of limestone. Several veins of kaolin develop at Mount Trembleau, upon the lake shore, beneath the hyperstene. A large deposit exists near Auger pond in Chesterfield. Similar masses occur in other sections of the county. A specimen from Putnam's pond, in Schroon, was subjected to analysis, many years since, by Professor Eaton,[1] and pronounced by him eminently pure and exempt from injurious combinations. Limestone, and very clear quartz rock, supposed to be adapted to the glass manufacture, and beds of clay, of great purity, occur in St. Armands.[2] A bed of feldspar is also situated on lot No. 31, Pliny Moore patent, in Crown Point, is owned by Messrs. S. S. & A. V. Spalding. I am informed that it has been tested in pottery works at Bennington and at Troy, and more recently in New York with success, and that it produces a beautiful ware. The deposit is represented to be inexhaustible.

A long and attractive list of rare and beautiful minerals might be exhibited, which are incorporated with the rocks of Essex county, or imbedded in its earth. Particular localities are peculiarly rich in these deposits. The crest of a hill upon the premises of Col. Calkins, near Lake George, affords a choice field for the researches of the scientific explorer. The avalanches, at Long pond, in Keene, present a site still more lavishly supplied with brilliant gems and minerals.[3] Augite, garnet, zircon, sahlite, sphene, coccolite, adularia, rose colored quartz spar, epidote, clorite, jasper, cornelian, are among the minerals yielded by these remarkable deposits. Veins of colophonite occur in Lewis, Chesterfield and Willsboro'. This exceedingly splendid and beautiful mineral is found in vast conglomerates, refulgent in the colors and lustre of innumerable gems.

---

[1] *Mr. Treadway.* [2] *Elias Goodspeed, Esq.*

[3] I have been favored by the Rev. Mr. Pattee with a more particular and highly interesting description of the latter locality. It is situated near Edmond's pond, at a precipice laid bare by an avalanche in 1830. In the bed of a little brook, which leaps down the slide, innumerable minerals sparkle, and are strewn about the vicinity in every direction. High up the precipice, a series of caves occur, which are the peculiar deposits of the gems and minerals, and almost rival in beauty and variety, the caverns of eastern story. "Here are found large boulders, and even ledges of calcareous spar, blue, white, and sometimes beautifully variegated by crystals of epidote, coccolite, and hornblende. They are occasionally found in stalactitic and crystaline forms, but more generally in amorphous masses." The basalt is chiefly found in veins and dykes."

Native Copperas.

A singular formation of natural copperas exists immediately below the Wilmington Notch, on the bank of the Au Sable river. The impregnated water, oozing from the earth, forms a thick concretion upon the rock, which may be removed in large quantities. It is adapted, in its crude state, to all the usual purposes of the artificial sulphate of iron.

The Beaches.

The naked and barren beaches along the shores of the lake occasionally furnish elements of business, which are profitably used. The detritus of iron formed by the attrition of the water and fragments of rock from the ore, which is known by the circumstance to exist on the bottom of the lake, is thrown up in several localities, in thick deposits. This substance is nearly pure iron, and gathered with care formerly supplied a large demand by the stationers. Subsequently it has been employed in the manufacture of malt and for other purposes. In some seasons it has been a heavy article of exportation. A New York company has recently secured extensive rights, with the view of erecting works, designed to adapt this "iron sand" for use in some mechanical arts.

Gravel thrown up by the waters of the lake and collected on the beaches, is exported in large quantities to Montreal, by the Sorel, the Chambly canal and St. Lawrence, and is extensively consumed in that city, for both useful and ornamental purposes.

Water Cement.

A vein of water cement in the town of Willsboro', of a very superior quality, has been used for practical purposes for many years, and is apparently of great extent. Other deposits of this material occur in various parts of the county. I noticed one of particular promise on the farm of Harris Page in Chesterfield.

A large ledge of limestone believed to be a water cement, occurs in Crown Point.

Paints.

Paint exists in different sections of the county, in numerous deposits and various colors. It is generally disintegrated and pulverized, and is used in its crude state for ordinary painting. When prepared by artificial refinement, it is believed these minerals will be made useful for practical purposes. An ore occurs in Ticonderoga, of a rocky consistence, which presents a bright rich vermillion surface, and is supposed will yield an important paint.

Drift and Diluvial Formation.

Whilst strong and indubitable evidences prevail throughout the county of Essex that an igneous power constituted the stupendous agency that impressed upon this region its peculiar features and characteristics, it is equally manifest that an aqueous action exerted an influence in moulding its existing formation. Without designing to vindicate any opinion or to educe any theory, it seems appropriate that I should present summarily a few prominent facts which may possibly convey to other minds elucidations and arguments on this subject.

Lake Champlain is only ninety-three feet above tide water, and a plummet descending in it six hundred feet has not reached bottom. These facts may be suggestive of important considerations. Marine shells, forming large deposits of marl, occur in the vicinity of the lake, in a state of such preservation that the species may be readily defined, and which induces the belief of their being a comparatively recent deposit. The tenacious blue clay, surmounted by the yellowish clay peculiar to marine formations, may be traced widely disseminated in the county. Numerous deposits are disclosed along the sides of hills and mountains, of large gravel, rounded by attrition and decay, and presenting every assimilation in appearance to the line of a beach that has been washed by the surges. The sand drifts are uniformly, or nearly so, exposed in long and narrow expanses, occupying the tracts of valleys or ravines. The recent formation is perfectly illustrated near the village of Pleasant Valley, where a slide exposes the stratification of the earth to a depth of some twenty feet. The lower stratum revealed is the yellow clay, succeeded by a coarse and rough gravel; this is surmounted by a smaller gravel, clear and abraded; the latter is covered by a stratum of sand, light and washed, and beneath the entire mass projects logs and roots. The lovely valley that borders the Schroon river, and spreads over an area of several miles between Paradox and Schroon lakes, presents equally decisive evidences of a recent formation. This plain is fertile, and now generally under high cultivation. In sinking pits for wells and other purposes, logs nearly entire and prostrate trees are constantly found from twelve to seventeen feet below the surface.[1] I have before referred to the appearance of ripple marks near the base of the walled banks of the Au Sable, and in another connection have mentioned the remarkable fossiliferous rock on Willsboro' point.

In Elizabethtown, on the brow of an eminence, many feet above the valley, a formation in the solid rock, smooth and rounded, may be seen, not unlike in size and general appearance to a common caldron kettle. I examined two others on the premises of Colonel Calkins, and similarly situated upon the crest of a precipice. I also inspected another formation of this kind on the lands of Messrs. Treadway, in Schroon. The half circle of this remains entire; the residue has been apparently destroyed by fragments of rocks, fallen from the cliffs above. The entire circle was probably twenty feet in diameter. This also stands upon the verge of a high and abrupt precipice of probably two hundred feet in depth. The appearance, the form, the position, the smooth and worn surface of

---

[1] *Clark Rawson, Esq.*

these extraordinary structures, all indicate that they have been formed by the abrasions of a rapid and powerful current of water.

The existence of boulders formed of every rock, and disseminated through the county, equally upon the hills and mountains as in the valleys, presents a broad and attractive field for scientific researches and philosophical speculations. Boulder rock, dissimilar in character and belonging to other formations, worn and rounded, are scattered over the county in utter confusion and dislocation. Granite intermingled with sand, sandstone resting upon hyperstene, and gneiss upon limestone, perpetually occur. A gentleman of intelligence assured me, that he had examined a fragment of red sandstone near the summit of a hyperstene mountain, in the centre of the county, and remote from every rock of that description. I saw in Moriah, a Potsdam sandstone block lying upon the surface of a rock of gneiss, many miles from the former in site. Among the Adirondacs, at an elevation of one thousand seven hundred feet, and more than one thousand feet above any known locality of Potsdam sandstone, pebbles of that rock are found, bearing all the close crystaline appearance of that stone at Keeseville.[1] They are found in gravel pits, sand beds, and along the banks of the river. The presence of these boulders, varying in size from the mere pebbles to masses of many tons, occurs in every section of the county. These are among the facts and circumstances existing in this region calculated to illustrate theories and speculations on the subject of the drift formation of the country. A highly corroborative fact has within a few years been revealed to the scientific world by the zeal of the eminent Professor Zadock Thompson, of the Vermont University. It should be understood that a perfect geological analogy exists between the opposite shores of Lake Champlain, in the vicinity of the discovery referred to. While laborers were engaged in the town of Charlotte,

---

[1] *R. Clark.*

Vermont, in forming an excavation for the Rütland and Burlington rail road. They exhumed a quantity of bones embedded in the clay about eight feet below the natural surface of the soil. They were partially broken before their peculiar appearance attracted attention. A portion of the bones was transmitted to Mr. Thompson, who immediately repaired to the place, and after much labor succeeded in collecting sufficient of the remains to enable him to determine, after further inspection, that they were the almost perfect skeleton of a member of the whale family. Aided by the great science of Professor Agassiz, he succeeded in arranging and collecting the bones, and decided the animal to be the *beluga leucas* or small northern white whale of Cuvier. This remarkable fossil, so significant of the theory to which I have adverted, is preserved in the department of natural history at Montpelier.

FERTILIZERS.

Phosphate of Lime. The extraordinary deposit of this rare and valuable mineral in Crown Point, has elicited much interest and attention from both the scientific and agricultural community of England.

The public owe the discovery of the mine in Crown Point to the discriminating observation and sagacious enterprise of C. F. Hammond, Esq. His attention was originally attracted to the locality by an appearance of iron ore, and the presence upon and near the surface of large numbers of quartz crystals. These indications, and the peculiar and unusual formation and texture of the rocks, suggested a minute examination of the place, which revealed a substance, the name and character of which Mr. Hammond was ignorant. In the year 1838, he directed the attention of a naturalist to it, who decided, upon a casual inspection, that it was a new and rare mineral, and designated its name, but pronounced it of no value except for cabinet specimens.[1] The zeal of Mr. Ham-

[1] *C. F. Hammond.*

mond was unabated, and in a subsequent examination urged by him and made in 1850, the mineral was ascertained to be a great desideratum in agriculture — a natural phosphate of lime. In the autumn of the same year ground was broken at the mine, and excavation commenced. The opening is directly upon a public highway, and one mile and a half from the shore of Lake Champlain. A shaft eight to ten feet wide has been sunk one hundred and fifteen feet. Lateral galleries have been projected north and west from the bottom of the shaft. The copper ore already noticed, was discovered in one gallery, and the phosphate was raised from the other. About one hundred and seventy tons of the first quality of the phosphate was exported to New York several years ago, and a large accumulation of an inferior quality remained at the mouth of the shaft. No recent progress has been made in the development of this mine. Phosphates have been disclosed incorporated with the ores of Moriah and other places, taken from near the surface in inconvenient profusion.

Marl. Specimens of marl from the farm of Mr. Tafft, of Crown Point, and the estate of the late Col. Watson, of Port Kent, have been examined and analyzed by Professor Salisbury, with the following results:

	No. 3. Marl Marine Shells.	No. 4. Marl Fresh Water Shells.
Silicic acid,	59.20	22.60
Phosphoric acid,	1.15	2.35
Carbonic acid,	9.92	28.15
Sulphuric acid,	0.15	0.09
Lime,	12.78	36 26
Iron,	3.40	1.15
Magnesia,	0.55	0.35
Potassa,	0.45	0.36
Soda,	0.40	0.07
Chlorine,	0.11	0.12
Organic matter,	11.61	8.44
	99.72	99.94

"The marine marl (No. 3, from Port Kent), is a deposit of great value as a manure; aside from its being rich in phosphoric acid and lime, it contains most of the other inorganic matter which enters into the food of plants. No. 4 will also prove valuable to those in its vicinity."

Limestone. The limestones in every variety so extensively diffused in the county, incorporated as they are almost universally with other fertilizing elements, will prove, I think, of the highest value in the agricultural economy of the county. I procured a specimen of rock in Schroon which has been practically tested as a fertilizer, with a highly favorable result.[1] A careful experiment, comparing it with other agents, exhibits very satisfactory effects. The Nova Scotia plaster proved the most efficacious. In the effect of the Schroon rock and the western plaster, no perceptible difference was manifest. The influence of each was marked and decisive, indicated by the superiority of the crop to which they were applied, over that part which had received no application of either of these materials. A similar stone is found in Elizabethtown.

Muck and *Peat.* These materials exist in boundless quantities in every section of the county. I caused analyses to be carefully made of specimens taken from different localities, which were pronounced peculiarly rich and of great value. The material prevails in sufficient quantities to fertilize every acre of arable land in the district.

Quarries.

I have adverted elsewhere to the hyperstene rock of the Adirondacs, as peculiarly adapted, by its durability and exceeding beauty, for building purposes and ornamental work. If art can succeed in subduing the hard and intractable properties of this stone, and we have seen that experiments have been highly successful in approaching that result, few materials exist more beautiful than portions of the hyperstene, by its rich and glowing texture,

[1] *Letter of Abijah Smith, Esq.*

and by the exquisite coloring, so deeply variegated and singularly blended in its appearance and formation. The hyperstene, after appearing in a wide range, through various sections of the county, abruptly terminates on the lower Au Sable, in contact with the Potsdam sandstone. The latter, for several miles, formed the walled banks of the Au Sable, and expands widely through the valley.

Keeseville Quarries. The Postdam sandstone is largely quarried in the vicinity of Keeseville, and is exported to a considerable amount. Lying in a perfect lamination, it may be excavated in large slabs or blocks. Those sixty feet square are easily obtained. The strata are so clearly defined and separated, that the only power requisite in raising the stone, is the wedge and lever. Mr. S. E. Keeler, the occupant of one of the most extensive deposits, informs me, that in the experience of many years, he has never had occasion to use a blast, in excavations on his quarry. The stone presents, on the horizontal side, a smooth and plane surface. The stone at Keeseville has usually a yellow-gray coloring, and is found admirably adapted to flagging and building purposes. It may be procured in slabs or blocks, from an inch to nearly a foot in thickness. It is asserted that this sandstone is impressed in different sites by very dissimilar qualities, and I am assured, that in some instances, where the Potsdam sandstone has been procured in other localities, and has proved defective, the deficiency has been supplied by stone taken from the Keeseville quarries. In a recent official paper addressed to the commissioners of the new Capitol, it is stated that "the Potsdam sandstone, in many parts of Clinton county, is too friable for any economical use, beyond furnishing sand for glass making." I am not prepared to dissent from these strictures in reference to the stone taken from some quarries, but they are not just, if intended to apply to the Keeseville stone. When first raised, it is slightly soft, not friable, but after exposure to the atmosphere becomes exceedingly hard. Edifices are now standing, which furnish proof of the firmness and durability of this stone, after an exposure of more than half a century, to storms and the action of the elements. The material which forms these buildings, does not exhibit the most remote appearance of decay or disintegration. In another passage of the same report, which may be constructed as a general application to the Potsdam sandstone, it is remarked: "Its commonly striped or variegated color offers an objectionable feature for a general use in building." A solitary specimen of the Keeseville stone occasionally shows a stain from iron, but it is never striped or variegated. It forms, when care and judgment are exercised in a selection, a soft, warm and beautiful building material in its coloring, that is at once ornamental and enduring.

A quarry of marble is situated upon the premises of Mr. J. N. Macomber in Chesterfield, near Keeseville, and apparently of large extent. Its coloring is light brown, variegated by white, with a shelly combination, and receives a brilliant polish. The uncommon appearance and coloring of this marble will probably render it a valuable deposit.

Clark's Quarry, in Willsboro', is on the margin of Willsboro' bay and is worked by S. W. Clark & Co. The rock is the Trenton limestone, and embraces two varieties, the Black river and the Birdseye. The dip of the strata is so slight, that the stone is raised with great facility.[1] A commodious wharf has been erected on the premises, which enables the stone to be shipped at the quarry. The operations of this concern are very extensive, and usually give employment to from forty to sixty laborers. The stones frequently excavated at this quarry are of enormous size. They are exported to various points for material in the construction of public edifices, and for ornamental works, including door steps, columns, sills and monuments. In the spring of 1869, the proprietors of this quarry effected a heavy contract with the commissioners for sup-

[1] *Rev. A. D. Barber.*

plying stone to the new Capitol. They now (autumn, 1869) employ nearly three hundred laborers, and load a canal boat daily from their wharf. A massive rock from this quarry forms the first foundation stone of the new edifice. Near the scene of these operations, another quarry of similar stone is worked by the Messrs. Frisbie, for the manufacture of lime. A large amount of this material is annually burnt at these kilns and exported. In the town of Essex, another primitive limestone kiln is owned and worked by Messrs. William Hoskin & Co. Another large and productive quarry of limestone has for many years been worked in Westport. A quarry of black clouded marble of rare beauty and softness occurs upon the old garrison grounds at Crown Point. Although nearly a century and a half ago the entrenchments of Fort St. Frederic penetrated a section of this quarry, it has excited no interest, until the attention of the Messrs. Hammond a few years since, was directed to it. The texture of the stone is firm and consolidated, but so soft and free from grit, that it may be easily carved by a pocket knife. It opens in large slabs and blocks, receives a high polish, and is adapted for the most delicate fabrics. This quarry has not been worked. Another deposit of dark stone, near the river, in Ticonderoga, is extensive and probably valuable. Harder and less delicate than the marble at Crown Point, it is darker, and appears to be susceptible of a very high finish. Near the marble deposit in Crown Point, an excellent quarry of limestone is successfully worked.

Many quarries of various kinds of rock not embraced in the above description are worked in the county for local convenience, and the production of lime and others are known to exist, but at present are undeveloped.

PART IV.

INDUSTRIAL PROGRESS AND RESOURCES.

The earliest business associations of northern New York were connected with the markets of the St. Lawrence. The illimitable forests of Essex county presented the first field to the settler for the efforts of industry, and has continued to their successors an inexhaustible source of enterprise and wealth. The lumber trade with Canada commenced soon after the permanent occupation of the country subsequent to the revolution. It enlisted for many years almost the whole energies of the population.

The public lands yielded a rich and free harvest to those who entered upon them, while the rights of private owners of wild lands were regarded with exceeding laxity. Norway pine and oak were at that time principally esteemed for the Canadian trade. White pine had little comparative value. The oak sticks, prepared for the northern market, were hewn. The pines were designed for the navy of England, and were transported to Quebec, round, and of any length exceeding twenty feet. Spars of vast dimensions were exported from the shores of Lake Champlain, and sold to the agents of the British government, probably to form

The mast of some tall admiral.

The winter season was chiefly devoted to preparing and collecting these materials, and the whole force of the teams and labor of the country was put in requisition for the object. The timber was gathered in coves or low marshes, protected from the winds and floods of early spring, and there formed into immense rafts. Deals or thick planks of pine, and oak staves were ultimately manufactured, and exported to the same market. These articles were arranged in cribs, and transported with the rafts or piled upon its surface. The rafts were often of great size. They were propelled through the lake by sails and oars, and were borne by the current and tide down the Sorel and St. Lawrence river. In passing the rapids of the former, the rafts were partially taken asunder. The strong currents of the St. Lawrence impelled them rapidly down that stream, but the turbulent tides near Quebec often swept them beyond the havens of that city, with great danger, and at times a total loss. These catastrophes were not unfrequent. The average price at Quebec, of oak timber, was forty cents per cubic foot, and that of pine, about twenty cents. The timber cost, delivered upon the shores of Lake Champlain, from six to eight cents, and the transportation from thence to Quebec, was about two and a half cents in addition, per cubic foot. The profit of this traffic seems to have been exorbitant, yet singularly, it proved to most who engaged in it, unfortunate and disastrous. The magnitude and activity of this business rapidly exhausted the masses of timber contiguous to the lake, and spars and timber were eventually transported from forests fifteen miles in the interior, to the place of rafting. Small rafts of spars and dock stick, formed of the scattered relics of the original forests, are still annually collected and carried to the southern market.

No decked vessel, it is stated, navigated Lake Champlain seventy years ago. The insignificant commerce which at that period existed upon its waters, was conducted in cutters, piraguas, and bateaux. Few wharves had then been constructed.

The emigrants desiring to land their stock, were often compelled to approach some favorable position, and throwing the animals overboard, swim them to the shore. In the more sparsely settled districts, vessels freighted with salt would anchor in same adjacent cove, and announce its presence to the inhabitants, who were often compelled to haul their grain on sleds through the woods, to barter for the salt. In this interchange, a bushel of wheat usually purchased a bushel of salt.[1] The merchant visiting the southern market for goods, before the introduction of steamers upon the lake, which occurred in 1809, consumed generally a month on the journey. The return of the merchandise was still more protracted. This journey was often performed on horseback, and occasionally by a chance vessel. The goods were transported in winter by sleighs, and at other seasons by water, from Whitehall. The village of Essex, for a series of years, was the important business mart of this entire region.

The construction of the Champlain canal gave a different direction, and imparted a new character to the lumbering operations of northern New York. Norway pine became subordinate in value to the white pine. The Quebec trade yielded to the new avenues opened to our own marts. Finer articles of lumber were prepared for the southern markets. The lumber business in its changed aspect again became the paramount occupation of the country. Innumerable saw-mills were erected, and the forests of white pine were demolished with as much rapidity as the Norway pine had been at an earlier day, to supply the Quebec market.

The amount and value of the various fabrics, the produce of the forest, which have been transported by the Champlain canal from Essex county, are almost inappreciable.

The exhaustion of the forests accessible from Lake Champlain, has constrained the lumber manufacturer to seek his resources in the wilds of the interior. Logs are now floated from the most remote districts of Franklin county down the Saranac river and through a portion of Essex county, to supply the mills on that stream. State bounty has been extended with munificence to aid in opening that wilderness to this policy, by important im-

[1] *Norman Page, Esq.*

provements in the navigation of the Saranac, Raquette, and other rivers, which penetrate that territory.

A large and valuable tract of timber land lying in the confines of Wilmington and North Elba, spreads along the acclivities and for many miles around the base of the Whiteface mountain. This is the only district of extent or value occupied by the primitive forest of pine, spruce, and hemlock, now remaining of Essex county and accessible. Environed by lofty mountain barriers, it is impracticable to export manufactured lumber from this region. It is estimated that this tract may yield one million of saw logs.

The numerous and widely diffused branches of the Hudson have annually appropriated for the transit of a very large amount of logs. Insignificant mountain rivulets swollen by the spring freshets, are converted into valuable mediums for this purpose, by the adroit management of the experienced lumberman.

Whiskey.

In the early part of the century numerous distilleries existed in the county, but the business was the most active in the town of Wilmington. The tillage of the town was almost wholly devoted to the production of rye, to supply these works. During the war of 1812, the manufacture of whiskey was an extensive and highly lucrative occupation. I am not aware that a single distillery now exists in the county of Essex.

Potashes.

While the county was passing through its transition from a primitive state to cultivation, the forest yielded a highly lucrative and available resource, in the manufacture of potash. Prohibited exportation by the non-intercourse policy of our own government, this traffic was illicit; but, stimulated by the exorbitant prices which the exigencies of the British affairs attached to the article in the Canadian market, an immense quantity found its way from northern New York into Montreal. This manufacture occupied a large portion of the population in its various connections, while the excitement existed, which was alone terminated by the final declaration of war in 1812. As a distinct business it is now nearly abandoned.

A conflagration of the woods presents a scene in the highest degree imposing and terrific, and often inflicts destructive ravages upon the pursuits of the manufacturer, as well as the products of agriculture. In certain periods of the year, the dried leaves and other combustible materials of the forest form an inflammable mass, which spreads a flame with inconceivable celerity. Impelled by the wind, which constantly accumulates in vehemence, its progress is so rapid that neither man nor beast is secure of safety in flight. It spreads widely its column of flame as it advances. It seizes upon tops of the loftiest trees, and leaping from object to object, it laps up every combustible substance, far in advance of the body of the conflagration. Sparks borne by the whirlwind for furlongs, start new fires. Immense amounts of property, comprising timber, lumber, wood, dwellings, fences, crops of grain and grass are often in a few hours consumed by these inflictions. The intense heat of these fires, by consuming all the organic elements of the soil, frequently destroys for many years the fertility of the earth.

Iron Manufactories.

The progress of the iron manufacturing interests of Essex has not been commensurate with the resources indicated by its immense mineral wealth. In the comparative infancy of a country, this advance could not be expected. Specific causes, however, have exerted an influence which has largely tended to arrest the general manufacturing prosperity of northern New York. The great absence formerly of capital, which is the essential basis of extended manufacturing operations, the remoteness of the district from the centre of business, and the want of all artificial channels of intercourse, were very obvious reasons for this depression. Lake Champlain has furnished the only medium for transportation to markets, and the closing of that navigation for nearly six months of the year suspended all transit, and left the productions of the manufactories for that long term upon the hands of the producers. In all these aspects the changes are most auspicious. Capital is more abundant, and the rail roads now in progress of rapid construction will soon open this sequestered region to a certain and ready intercourse with the world, and animate its slumbering resources.

In pursuing my contemplated plan, I propose, in the succeeding pages to present a brief outline of the origin, progress and existing condition of the iron manufactories of Essex county with an incidental view of all its industrial interests. While the magnitude and prominence of the iron interest will demand particular consideration, I design in noticing the more prominent localities, to embrace an account of other important manufactories connected with them, either in business or by territorial affinities. The numerous affluents of the Au Sable, descending impetuously from high and often mountainous sources, form in their course an infinitude of water privileges. The river itself, for a considerable extent, is the boundary line between the counties of Clinton and Essex. In treating of the valuable manufacturing works situated in the Au Sable valley, I find it impracticable to separate those essentially located on the north side of the river, from those standing specifically on the soil of Essex county. The dams usually rest upon the territory of each county; the interests of these establishments directly affect, and are intimately associated with both counties, and their immense business movements extend their operations widely through all the adjacent territory on either side of the stream. In describing, therefore, the manufacturing interests of Essex county, I am compelled, in this view, to include all that belongs to the Au Sable valley.

Early in the century, the fires of small forges illuminated numerous sequestered spots in almost every section of the county. These works exerted a beneficent local influence. They stimulated the industry of remote districts; they created a market for all the products of husbandry; by a demand for wood and coal, they imparted a value to unprofitable forests, and thus enhanced the price of lands, and promoted the cultivation of the earth. Little hamlets clustered around these sites, and some exhibited the impress of civilization by their varied arts, their schools, and religious movements. While some of these enterprises remain and are prosperous, many have disappeared in the mutation of affairs. With some, the supply of wood has failed; the proprietors of others did not possess the requisite strength to resist the adverse waves that so often roll across the manufacturing interests, and others have been overshadowed or absorbed by more powerful institutions. When we view, amid the ruins of these scenes, the water rushing over decaying dams; the earth strewn with the vestiges of former industry, and the humble dwellings shattered and falling, the heart will be saddened, and we almost accept the spectacle as an evidence of a fallen business and impoverished land. But in reality, new changes have generally proved more favorable to the general interests and expansion of a large district.

William Gilliland appears to have contemplated in 1783 the idea of erecting iron works upon the shores of Lake Champlain, and engaged in an actual negotiation in reference to that design.[1] The iron manufacturing business of Essex county, destined to become an interest of national consideration, was initiated in a feeble establishment at Willsboro' Falls. These works were erected in 1801, by Levi Highbey and George Throop, sustained by the capital of Charles Kane of Schenectady, and primarily designed for the fabrication of anchors. The partners held an unlimited contract for the sale of all that article they might make for a term of ten years. The anchors varying from three hundred to fifteen hundred pounds were to be delivered at

[1] *Champlain Valley*, 190.

Troy. They were transported by water to Whitehall, thence carted to Fort Edward, and there shipped on bateaux. One or two unfavorable experiments were made in exporting them to Quebec. It is a remarkable circumstance that the ore used in these works for ten years, was principally obtained in Vermont, with a few loads from Canada. "A bed at Basin Harbor, owned by Platt Rogers, was the only deposit of iron ore, which at that period had been developed in the whole region. Soon after the close of the ten years contract, the Arnold ore bed in Clinton county was discovered.[1] The foundery, at Willsboro', in addition to anchors, cast mill cranks, grist mill machinery, and ultimately steam boat irons. This property fell into other hands, and was finally converted into a forge. The same year in which this enterprise was commenced at Willsboro', Liberty Newman of Shoreham, Vermont, erected iron works at the upper falls in Ticonderoga.[2] I have not been able to trace the history or results of this movement. At an early period in the century, William D. Ross of Essex, erected a rolling mill on the Boquet, for making nail plates. These plates were manufactured in large quantities, and sold at $8 per cwt., to the nail factory in New Haven, Vermont.

Elba Iron Works. About the year 1809, Archibald McIntire and his associates erected iron works upon a small stream among the head waters of the Au Sable river, and in a remote section of the county, comprised within the limits of the present town of North Elba. It was a forge of four to six fires, and designated the Elba Iron works. The ore used at the commencement was found in that region, but proving impracticable, was abandoned, and the works were afterwards supplied by ore transported from the Arnold bed in Clinton county, a distance of many miles, over roads only passable on snow. The products of the forge were exported both to the St. Lawrence and Lake Champlain, but by routes laborious and expensive.

---

[1] *Letter of late Levi Highbey.* [2] *Goodhue's Shoreham.*

The business for a series of years was eminently prosperous. The works, however, proved too remote from market, and ineligibly situated for enduring success, and in the year 1815 were abandoned. A decayed dam, and fragments of broken wheels and shafts, and similar vestiges, are the only memorials of their former existence. In the meanwhile other forges were gradually appearing in the region, and when, in 1820, the Champlain canal had been constructed, the iron interest rapidly expanded, and at once exhibited in the increase of its varied works, an earnest of its approaching prosperity and importance. The valley of the Au Sable river was early distinguished as the prominent seat of the iron manufactories, and it still maintains that preeminence.

Au Sable Valley.

Wilmington. Some years after the Elba works had been abandoned, the Hon. Reuben Sanford, who occupied several political positions of prominence in the state, created an extensive manufacturing establishment in Wilmington, on the west branch of the Au Sable river and about twelve miles from Au Sable Forks. Severe changes in the fluctuations of business and serious calamities inflicted by the elements impaired his affairs, and the property passed into the proprietorship of others. It has since experienced many vicissitudes. The site is now occupied by a grist mill and starch factory; a saw-mill with three gates and running about forty saws, and a forge owned by Weston & Nye, with two fires but adapted to four. In 1868, about two hundred tons of iron were made at this forge. It consumes charcoal and produces bloom iron. At present it uses the Palmer Hill ore, drawn about thirteen miles, but a bed is now in process of opening, it is represented, with favorable indications in the extent and quantity of the ore. At the village of Bloomingdale, in the adjacent town of St. Armands, and upon a tributary of the Saranac there is at present in operation, a starch factory, and a grist and saw-mill.

Lower Jay Village. Upon the south branch of the Au Sable several mills and factories are in operating, but all of subordinate importance except upon this site. At this place extensive works were erected in 1809. While in the possession of Messrs. G. A. Purmort & Co., they included a grist and saw mill and forge with other minor workshops. These gentlemen suffered severe reverses, and in 1864, the property was purchased by Messrs. J. & J. Rogers. It is at this time embraced within their vast manufacturing domain. The establishment conspires a forge which has recently been rebuilt with six fires, one hammer of five tons, and four horizontal cylinders with various other mechanical works. All are impelled by water power. A brick yard is connected with the property that produced the past year four hundred thousand bricks, which were exclusively used in the business of the firm. The forge consumes charcoal burnt in close kilns, and is supplied with ore from the Palmer Hill mine. Since its construction, the forge is considered a work of the first class.

Au Sable Forks. The West and South Branch unite at this place and form distinctively, the Au Sable river. Each stream presents at this point a valuable water power of nearly equal volume. The premises which include these sites were originally owned by Zephaniah Palmer. Messrs. Burts & Vanderwarker became owners of the property in 1825 and erected a saw-mill with two gates. About the year 1828, this company in connection with Keese, Lapham & Co., with which Caleb & Barton was associated, built a forge of four fires. The forge was chiefly supplied with ore from the Arnold bed, and in part from Palmer hill. Nearly at this time, another saw-mill was erected; and soon after, the association sold out to a stock company, which was organized in 1834 under the name of the Sable Iron Company, and represented by Reuben Sanford, Arden Barker, James Rogers, John Fitzgerald, Richard H. Peabody, Robert B. Hazard, and Calvin Cook, as trustees. The ensuing year, the works were carried on for the company under the agency of John Woodman. In 1836, operations were suspended, and in 1837, the entire property was purchased by Messrs. J. & J. Rogers. The corporate name, for many purposes, is still retained, although the title and exclusive interest is now owned by the Messrs. Rogers. Immediately after these gentlemen had acquired the property, they pursued the most efficient measures to enlarge and improve the works. On the West Branch, a short distance above the confluence of the two streams, a heavy dam has been built. which is thoroughly protected from freshets and ice by strong bulwarks. A forge was erected on this dam in 1848 upon the site of one which had been consumed, and is the only important structure at this place situated on the West Branch. This forge contains four fires, one hammer of five tons and three horizontal oscillating cylinders, thirty-one inches diameter and forty inches stroke. On the south bank of the South Branch and on a peninsula formed by it and the main stream most of the prominent works are located. The rolling mill was built in 1834. It has two trains, three heating furnaces, two engines, and one water wheel. The nail factory contains forty-eight machines, with a capacity of producing eighty thousand kegs of nails and spikes annually. The motive power of the rolling mill is created by water taken from the forge pond on the West Branch, and conducted to the mill by a wooden tube or aqueduct five and a half feet in diameter and ninety rods in length. This aqueduct is carried over the South Branch upon a bridge one hundred and fifty feet long, and eleven feet above the water. A carpenter shop, and stave machinery, are driven by escape water from the forge wheels. These works include all the necessary machinery for preparing the material for making nail kegs. The timber is sawed the appropriate length, the staves as perfectly formed and grooved; the heading is cut out and adjusted in form, and nothing remains for the exercise of manual labor, but to put the different parts together. A wheelwright shop is also attached to this range of buildings. A circular saw forty-eight inches, with a carriage fifty feet long and capable of greater expansion is driven by an overshot wheel. The boilers attached to the engines are chiefly heated by breese (the screenings of the coal), shavings and chips. In the connection may be noticed, an improved and most effective method of economizing fuel. Between the fires and boilers, iron bars, not unlike a grid-iron in form, are arranged, and upon these are placed nail plates, and thus the same fires heat both the boilers and the plates. The rolling mill is now in the most perfect and efficient condition. The cupola furnace and foundery which stands in immediate proximity to the rolling mill are mainly if not exclusively employed in fabricating castings, constantly required by the various departments of the business of the concern. It consumes scrap iron and pigs brought from distant furnaces, and possesses a capacity equal to the casting of articles of five tons weight in a single process.

Another division of this immense business is located on Black brook, a tributary of the Au Sable, and is situated in Clinton county about four miles from Au Sable Forks, and a mile and a half north of the Essex county line. Although separated in location from the works at the Forks, by motives of expediency and convenience, those at Lower Jay and Black Brook are in effect a part of the same establishment, as much as if connected with it by contiguous position. The interests are identical; all their operations are inspired by the same intelligent spirit and guided by the same enlarged business capacities. Each branch and all their varied departments, move in their respective orbits in perfect system and undisturbed harmony. Mr. James Rogers is the resident partner and manager at Au Sable Forks, while Mr. John Rogers, residing at Black Brook, exercises the immediate supervision of the division located at that place. Messrs. Henry D. Graves and Halsey Rogers are the efficient assistant managers at the Forks, and E. Fairbank at Jay.

The works at Black Brook are situated on two sites, about one-fourth mile apart, and designated, the Upper and

Lower village. At the former, the Hon. Halsey Rogers of Saratoga, John McIntire and William McDonald in 1830, erected a saw mill and other structures. In 1832, Messrs. McIntire built a forge of two fires which they run until 1835. Messrs. J. & J. Rogers, in company with the Hon. Halsey Rogers and Mr. Thomas Rogers, now of Dubuque, Iowa, as part owners, in 1832 commenced business at the Lower village. In the year 1835, Messrs. J. & J. Rogers became sole proprietors of both the forges at Black Brook, and soon after one-third owners of the saw-mill and the lands connected with it. Nearly at this time John McGregor purchased the one-third interest of Mr. McDonald in the saw-mill property, and resided on the premises about twenty years. John McIntire soon after sold his one-third of the property to Caleb D. Barton, who after holding it a few years conveyed his interest to Henry Martin. He, after occupying it a short term, sold to Messrs J. & J. Rogers, who subsequently bought the part owned by Mr. McGregor. These transactions occurred between the years 1853 and 1846 and invested Messrs. Rogers with the title of the whole property. In 1832, the six forge fires operating at Black Brook produced six tons of blooms per week; at present ten fires at the same place yield seventy-five tons in the same period. Such has been the amazing progress of manufacturing skill and science. The Messrs. Rogers estimate that one thousand bushels of good coal will now make three tons of iron. Two saw mills are running at Black Brook; one containing two gangs, and the other a single gang, with a circular saw in each mill. These mills cut from one hundred thousand to two hundred thousand pieces of boards annually. These are partly consumed in the various operations of the concern, and the residue, formerly transperted by plank road to Port Kent for exportation. A shingle mill is now completed at Black Brook village.

The forge fires embraced in the different works of the Messrs. Rogers amount in the aggregate to twenty-two fires, and yield an average of one ton each per day. The concern owns forty-three covered kilns for making charcoal, and burn in them every variety of wood. They use charcoal exclusively in their works, except in the process of heating blooms for rolling mills in which they employ Pennsylvania coal. The iron business of the Messrs. Rogers embraces such proportions, and is arranged with so much system and efficiency, that they are prepared for almost every exigency of the market. When nails and bars are the most desirable fabrics, a large proportion of their blooms are rolled, but if blooms occupy a higher place in market, nails and bars become with them a subordinate production. The end chunks, cut from the blooms, are rolled into bars and nail plates. Their nail factory when in full operation presents a spectacle of the greatest animation and interest.

The bloomeries of the Messrs. Rogers are known in trade as Peru iron. Their blooms are chiefly sent to Pittsburg, Penn., and there made into cast steel, which it is asserted, is equal to any made on this continent or in Europe. It is confidently believed by its manufacturers, that American cast steel may soon become an important article of exportation. The ore used in the works of the Messrs. Rogers is derived wholly from the Palmer mine, and they calculate that four tons of this ore in a native condition, or from two to two and a quarter tons of separated ore, will produce a ton of iron. It is considered that the Palmer ore possesses qualities which peculiarly adapt it to the fabrication of steel. The company have two separators on Palmer brook, and another building near the ore bed, and one also at the Forks. The operations of this concern in their diversified forms and singular ramifications transcend in magnitude most business transactions in northern New York, and in all their proportions can scarcely be excelled by any private interest in the state. The Messrs. Rogers possess a landed estate exceeding fifty thousand acres, and this enormous territory is maintained principally to secure an inexhaustible supply of fuel for their works. This domain furnishes nearly every raw material they require in their varied operations. Their interest in the Palmer hill mine secures all the ore they consume; their boundless forests afford wood for the kilns and timber for the saw mills. They own a limestone quarry near the works at Black Brook, of the choicest quality, at which for their own use they burn annually about five thousand bushels of lime. They possess clay beds, where all the brick they need is produced. The immense amount of agricultural commodities they yearly consume, alone exceeds their capacity for producing. The moulding sand used in the foundery they procure from the bed of Mr. Mace, on the bank of the river above Keeseville, although they own a large deposit of the material.

A single fact will illustrate the great and diversified resources of this company. They have recently erected a large and elegant edifice, appropriated to their own use, for a store, warerooms and offices. They have also an extensive store at Black Brook and another at Jay. The building at the Forks is constructed chiefly of brick and iron, and is one hundred and eight feet in height, and fifty-eight feet wide, and stands three stories high — two of thirteen feet and the other of fifteen feet in height, above the basement. The latter is sufficiently high and capacious to allow teams to drive in and unload. The edifice is situated at the Au Sable Forks, and placed in a locality so secluded, is an object that excites alike surprise and admiration. But we are impressed by greater astonishment, when we learn that nearly every article, which entered into its construction, was produced from the premises of the proprietors. The glass, the paints and oil and trimmings were purchased. The felt and cement for the roof were not embraced in their resources, but the gravel to cover it was procured within a mile of the building. The brick was burnt from clay found on their own soil; the nails were made from ore taken from their own mines, and the massive castings which adorn and strengthen the building were fabricated in their workshops; the lumber was felled in their forests and cut at their own mills. In their ardor for the realization of the idea, that this work should be accomplished from their own resources, the Messrs. Rogers utilized the black ash, a denizen of the of swamps, usually deemed of no consideration, and even little value for fuel. This wood has been discovered to be a beautiful building material, and it now decorates their rooms in exquisite panel work and columns. Its dark grain presents richly variegated shades in strong, deep coloring, with a peculiarly soft and rich surface. Is there any other business institution in the country capable of achieving a triumph like this?

That so much energy and enterprise has met with adequate success, seems to be attested by the fact, that the aggregate revenue returns of the different partners, has amounted to more than $200,000 in a single year. The gross sales at Au Sable Forks and Jay, in the year 1867, amounted to $748,837.59. The company has paid internal revenue tax from 1863 to Dec. 1, 1868, $82,541.97.

The course of these gentlemen have not been uniformly prosperous, or exempt from the vicissitudes of human affairs. In 1856 a freshet of unexampled severity occurred in the South Branch, and in the ensuing year another with almost equal violence devastated the West Branch. By each of these the Messrs. Rogers lost about $25,000. They have also suffered severely from fires, particularly in 1864, when their loss, including insurance, amounted to $90,000.

In noticing the affairs of Messrs. Rogers, it is necessary to state that the ore used in their various works annually, is estimated at 23,210 tons delivered at the separating machine, and 9,716 tons drawn from it, and the charcoal consumed at 1,440,000 bushels. Au Sable Forks and Black Brook are connected with Lake Champlain at Port Kent, by a plank road. The former is situated seventeen miles, and the latter four miles farther from the lake. Jay is six miles from the Forks by an earth road. The Plattsburg and Whitehall rail road, which is now in running order from Plattsburg to the Point of Rocks on the Au Sable, a distance of twenty miles, has a depot within three miles of Au Sable Forks.

Clintonville. The great water power formed by the Au Sable river at Clintonville, and situated about six miles above Keeseville, was occupied by forges early in the first quarter of the century. The property passed into the possession of a company of southern capitalists, incorporated under the name of the Peru Iron Company, with a capital of two hundred thousand dollars. Joshua Aiken was the first agent of this company. They established, at an early period, one of the most extended and successful iron works in the state. Nearly fifty years ago their establishment consisted of a forge of eighteen fires, which manufactured from two to three thousand tons of iron annually; a rolling mill, from which was produced yearly, eighteen hundred tons of marked iron and nail plates. A nail factory which fabricated twelve hundred tons of cut nails; a chain cable factory, a pocket furnace, machine shop, and grist mill, all of which belong to the company. The fabrics of these works established a high reputation, and were quoted specifically in the prices current of that period. Their peculiar and superior qualities were essentially imparted by the remarkable properties of the ores from which these fabrics were produced. The ore was derived partially, and at an early day, from two small beds in the vicinity, known as the Winter and Finch veins; but subsequently, the works used exclusively, ore taken from the Palmer bed and Arnold Hill mine, but particularly from the latter. This extraordinary deposit of ore was at that time, esteemed superior to any known to exist in the country, alike in its magnitude and the excellence of its qualities. It is situated on lots Nos. 199 and 200. Maule's patent was discovered in the year 1805, and purchased from Elisha Winter in 1806, for eight hundred dollars, by Elisha Arnold and associates. The mine was occupied by four main veins, from three to eight feet in width, running parallel to each other, but varying decidedly in the character and ingredients of the ore. The most extensive and valuable of these veins was designated the Old blue vein, and has been worked to a depth of more than three hundred feet. The ore from this vein first imparted to the Peru iron the high reputation it has always maintained. The blue ore vein preserves an average width of four to five feet, sometimes compressed to two feet, and again expanding to eight. The properties of these ores, the great abundance of the deposits, and the unlimited demand for their consumption, have rendered this mine a source of great affluence, and several fortunes have been realized from it. It has been abandoned for many years for practical operation. The shaft became filled with water, and the machinery deranged and decaying. These circumstances may, to some extent, be attributed to special causes, but directly to the vast expenditure incident to excavating and raising the ore from the great depth to which the operations had penetrated; the depression and fluctuations of the iron business, and the enhanced cost and difficulty of transporting the crude material to market. The mine has now passed into the hands of iron manufacturers of Pennsylvania, and is approached to the base of the eminence it occupies, by a rail road. The reasonable hope may be cherished that this immense fountain of public and private wealth will be returned to its former importance, where business shall resume its secure and defined channel.

The property at Clintonville has been subjected to many vicissitudes and numerous changes in interests. At one period it was owned by Francis Saltus and subsequently by his son, but the works are now in extensive and successful operation, controlled by proprietors of wealth and enterprise who in April, 1865, were chartered under the name of the Peru Steel and Iron Company, with a capital of eight hundred thousand dollars. Charles Bliven, Esquire, of New York, is president of the corporation, and John L. M. Taylor, vice president, and the efficient and judicious general manager of its affairs at Clintonville. The products manufactured have been modified under the present name and management of the company, and are now essentially restricted to one branch; the fabrication of rolled and billot iron calculated for making cast steel. The ore used now is exclusively excavated from the Palmer hill bed, in which property this company holds a title to three-eighths interest. The elements of this ore, it is considered, peculiarly adapt the iron made from it for the production of steel. The motive power of these works, which occupy more than a mile in length along the northern bank of the river, is created by two dams. The works consisting of forges were originally situated on the opposite side of the river. The upper of these dams rests upon a rocky foundation, and is a firm and ponderous structure nearly vertical in form and crescent-shaped, and designed to resist all freshets. The lower dam exhibits an unusual formation. It is built upon a sandy bottom, and to render it secure from the frequent floods which are peculiar to the stream and from the pressure of the ice often borne down by the current with immense force, a broad base is required. The dam is therefore constructed with two faces, presenting a front in each direction and at a small angle. By this arrangement a broad and effective foundation is attained, and a perpendicular pressure of the water secured which combine to support and strengthen the structure. The plan has proved eminently successful.

At the upper dam there is erected a saw mill, grist mill, rolling mill and a forge of four fires; also a nail factory which formerly contained forty nail machines. The nail manufacture was abandoned by the Peru Iron Company, one of the former proprietors of these works in 1856–57, from the fact, that the superior quality of their iron rendered it more profitable to be sold in market as iron, than when wrought into nails. The forge and rolling mill are under the same roof. The four fires yield at the rate of twenty-four tons of bloomery iron per week, and with the escape heat from these fires, from fourteen to sixteen tons of iron are heated for rolling every twenty-four hours. The furnaces which are heated by the escape heat are called gas furnaces. Each one of these is attached to two of the forge fires. There are also two coal furnaces, for heating iron for rolling, in which bituminous coal is used. Experience has proved that the gas furnaces are the most economical, and for several years the coal furnaces have been almost abandoned. The rolling mill has three trains for rolling iron. The largest is a sixteen inch train, capable of rolling iron $1\frac{1}{2} \times \frac{1}{8}$ to 4×1 inch iron. Rounds and squares from $1\frac{1}{4}$ to 3 inch, and also wide band iron. The next in size is a ten-inch train, from which are rolled H. S. Strapes. Rounds and squares from $\frac{3}{4}$ to $1\frac{3}{4}$, small bands and small tires. The smallest of those trains is used exclusively for rolling rounds and squares from $\frac{1}{4}$ to $\frac{11}{16}$ of an inch.

In connection with the lower dam, an immense forge is constructed, which is believed to be the most extensive upon the continent, and pronounced equally superior in its capacity; and in the completeness of its arrangements and power. This forge embraces sixteen fires, with the appropriate number of hammers. Its motive power is created by water conveyed in a canal nearly half a mile in length, twenty-five feet wide and ten feet high, to the summit of the embankment formed by the material excavated. This stupendous work, which as the creation of private enterprise has few parallels, was constructed in 1834 by the Peru Iron Company. It is securely guarded by sluice ways and waste gates, and presents along its course a scene of great activity and prosperous industry. These works produce per annum from three thousand to three thousand five hundred tons of iron fabrics, and consume in their production twelve to fourteen thousand tons of ore and from one million to one million two hundred thousand bushels of charcoal. This is the principal fuel used, and doubtless influences the character and quality of the iron produced. The charcoal is made in twenty-three kilns owned by the company. Two hundred persons are usually engaged about the works, and three hundred others receive employment in the varied external operations of the company connected with the establishment, and used mainly for its convenience there as a foundery; an extensive wheelwright and blacksmith shop. The company own a wide domain of woodland territory.

Keeseville. The immense hydraulic power afforded by the Au Sable river, at Keeseville and in its immediate vicinity has only been partially occupied. The use of its full capacity would create one of the most extensive manufacturing localities in the state. Commencing at the Upper Falls in the village of Keeseville, and extending to Birmingham, a distance by the stream of more than two miles, four heavy dams are already constructed, creating a vast power on both sides of the river, and in addition to these, several other sites may be made available, and by artificial structures nearly the whole distance is susceptible of conversion into a continuous power, where the water from one wheel might almost literally be discharged upon another.

The enormous amount of choice pines which half a century ago abounded in the region, stimulated the early erection of saw mills on this site. These forests have been long exhausted and more extensive mills now exist. Modern enterprise, which has been developed with magnificent success upon the Saranac, has determined that it is far more easy and economical to transport logs by the agency of streams from the wilderness to the mills and towards market, than to convey the sawed lumber from the interior, may restore to Keeseville its lumber manufacturing preeminence, with vastly enhanced importance and profit. While the inland territory penetrated by the Saranac has been to a large extent denuded of its forests, the timber lands at the head waters of the Au Sable, which spread over a great area, remain as I have remarked already, nearly in their primeval condition. By the creation of artificial facilities, which may be constructed at a trifling cost in comparison with the infinitely valuable results which would be accomplished, this timber, principally spruce and hemlock, but with an important proportion of pines, might be rendered accessible. We have seen, that the aggregate waters of a wide mountain region, accumulate in the channel of the Au Sable and are discharged, with rare intervals of slackened current, by a rapid and often precipitous course. These peculiarities subject this stream to frequent and severe freshets, which although perilous to the structures along its banks, singularly adapt it to the conveyance of logs by floating. No booms now exist on the Main river which would interpose obstacles to this transportation of the raw material to Keeseville, where the construction of gang saw-mills on an extended scale is now in contemplation. No mill site occurs below Birmingham upon the river, but the project exists of erecting large mills at the mouth of the Au Sable to be propelled by steam. What influence the operation of the rail road in progress of construction, and which has already reached the Au Sable, may exert upon these views and calculations can alone be determined by the issue. It is conceded, I think, that the weight and bulk of lumber adapts it to transportation by water rather than rail road. If the theory is just, the fact will to some extent effect the division of this question. Whatever may be the course of business, as it impresses the interests of localities, we may safely calculate, that the incomputable wealth, which now slumbers in the forests upon the upper waters of the Au Sable, will at an early period reward the efforts of industry and capital, and that the volume of the Au Sable will in some form be instrumental in the realization of this desirable result.

The enterprise of the pioneers of Keeseville was directed to the occupation of its hydraulic powers by other manufacturing pursuits. Forges, a woolen factory, flouring mills, a plaster mill, foundery and various other minor establishments were erected. The forges were soon succeeded by more extensive and important iron works. Two rolling mills were built with works on a large scale for the production of cut nails and other fabrics. Each of these for a term of years were eminently prosperous; but in the changes of circumstances, and the revolutions incident to all business pursuits, were ultimately suspended, and the large property passed into different hands. A period of severe depression in the progress and prosperity of Keeseville ensued, but new and more valuable interests, which promise to be far more stimulating to the general success of the region, have at length arisen from the ruins of the former occupation.

A company was formed in the year 1863 with a capital of forty thousand dollars, which was subsequently increased to eighty thousand, for the manufacture of horse shoe nails by a machine invented and patented by Mr. Daniel Dodge of Keeseville. The success of the experiment has been ample, and not more in a financial aspect, than by establishing the superior character of an engine, which exhibits a remarkable triumph of mechanical ingenuity and science. It transcends, it is asserted, any agency of the kind for the execution of its peculiar process, by the magnitude and uniformity of its work, and the perfect quality of the article it produces. The immense and complicated power, combined with extreme simplicity; the beauty and precision of the principle, and the exactness and rapidity of its execution, impart to this machine its marked superiority. Nails formed by other mechanism often present equal external beauty of appearance, but it is assumed, that the force which produces the compression of iron by the Dodge machine communicates to the nail it forms, solidity, a tenacity and toughness that characterizes no other article of the kind. The pressure to which these nails are subject in their fabrication, so consolidates and amalgamates the metallic fibres, that splitting or roughness in the article is deemed almost impossible, while the extreme care and caution exercised in preparing the nails for market are calculated to prevent any poor or defective fabrics reaching the consumer.

A walk through the workshops, and an examination of the various processes connected with the manufacture, sorting and preparing these nails, affords a highly interesting study. Fifty of the machines are in operation at Keeseville, and are increased as rapidly as the demands of the business require. They are all constructed at that place under the immediate supervision of the inventor, and at an expense of $500 for each machine. One person, usually a boy, attends and feeds every machine. At its side is placed a small furnace, supplied by mineral coal, in which eight or ten thin iron rods or strips are heating. A large conductor, through which the air is forced from a reservoir by mechanism, conveys it to each furnace by a small tube, which the workman controls by a valve. These rods, heated to the proper degree, are successively applied to the machine, and when they become too cool, are returned to the furnace and another taken from it, with a celerity that scarcely interrupts the revolutions of the machine. The nails are discharged almost uniformly perfect on an average of forty-five per minute. The article falls from the machine, impressed with the precise form and appearance of the blacksmith's nail formed by the most expert hand. The nails collected from the machine are carried to another room, where they are singly inspected and pass through a process that determines their perfect finish. This duty employs a large number of hands, chiefly boys. When this operation is completed, the nails descend by a funnel into a lower apartment, where they are carefully inspected and assorted, and every nail in the slightest degree imperfect is rejected. Thus, each fabric is handled twice separately, to secure and ascertain its exact perfection. The assorted nails are then placed in small square boxes, holding each twenty-five pounds. The contents of each box is accurately weighed and the top placed upon it, to avoid mistakes or depredations.

A very small fraction of the nails is discharged by the machine in an imperfect form, either from a deficient pointing or other cause. When a point requires adjusting, the nail is transferred to another shop, where it is perfected by hand. Such nails are never sent into market, but are sold at the works for home consumption.

A blacksmith's shop is connected with the establishment, in which the fragments of the rods are welded together and again used in the machine. All the varied refuse is carefully gathered up, cleansed by a separator, and, until the introduction of a new process, returned to market. Another and adjacent room is appropriated to the sharpening of tools and repairing and adjusting the machines. The company own a saw-mill near the works, at which, besides custom and other work, the lumber for constructing the nail boxes is cut. From the mill the boards are conveyed to a planing and cutting machine, where the materials for the boxes are prepared. These materials are conveyed to another apartment, in which the boxes are put together and arranged for use. The conveyance of the iron and nails, and the transportation of all the materials used in the works are performed by the teams and employees of the company. Thus by a wise and efficient arrangement, every department of labor in the concern is executed by the company itself. An extensive coal house is connected with the works. The fuel annually consumed amounts to about five hundred tons.

Each machine produces an average of one hundred and fifty pounds of nails per diem, and runs only during daylight. A boy examines and kegs from one hundred to one hundred and fifty pounds daily. The works yield about five hundred tons of nails per annum, worth not less than $250,000. The best brands of Norway iron are exclusively used in the manufacture of these nails. No American iron has yet been produced adapted to the purpose. Intelligent iron manufacturers do not accept the theory, that this impediment is produced by the quality of our ores, but ascribe it rather to the peculiar processes observed in the production of the iron. The iron is imported from Norway in bars, rolled into rods or slits in New England, and in that shape is conveyed to the works. The company has recently reorganized a rolling mill, situated between Keeseville and Birmingham, and propose soon to prepare their own rods from the imported Norway bars.

The boys employed in these works earn from fifty cents to a dollar and a half per diem, and receive with all the workmen of the company payment in money on every Saturday afternoon. It is pleasant on this occasion to observe their cheerful and contented countenances, when they approach the table of the agent, and as their names are called from the pay roll receive the reward of their industry and steadiness. This scene is an infinite improvement upon the system, which formerly existed in many of the manufacturing institutions of the country, by which the laborers were paid in orders upon a store; or when the merchant's clerk stood ledger in hand at the pay desk to claim and receive his account from the wages of labor. Here the workman is independent and uncontrolled in using the fruits of his toil.

This company is incorporated under the style of the Au Sable Horse Nail Company, of which Silas Arnold, Esquire, is the president, and Edmund Kingsland, Esquire, is the active agent and manager. Mr. Dodge, the ingenious inventor of this valuable machine, has favored me with the following account of the labors and trials incurred in the progress of the invention, which resulted in his signal triumph. It will be read, I think, with great interest. "My first experiments with the view of producing a machine for making horse shoe nails were made in 1848, with a model or miniature machine, on a very small scale. In 1849 I built a complete machine of working proportions. It proved but a partial success, producing nails with great rapidity, but not of sufficient uniformity to satisfy consumers. A series of machines were built on the principle of the first, and each was an improvement on its predecessor. Several of them were so far successful as to produce nails of uniform and satisfactory quality and with great rapidity; but they were found unprofitable for use, as the expense of the repairs consumed the profits. At length in 1854, I abandoned the leading principle on which they had been constructed and adopted a new one, admitting greater simplicity of construction and greater ease in the movement of the parts. On this principle I also built a series of machines, with successive improvements, resulting about the close of 1862, in the perfected machine now used by the Au Sable Horse Nail Company."

A large economy has been attained in the preparation of the refuse crops referred to for their reproduction into bars by the introduction early in 1869 into the works of a powerful hydraulic press.

The foundery at Keeseville formerly transacted a heavy business. It frequently executed orders from California, New Orleans, and various sections of the west. This extended demand for its fabrics was created by the superior quality of the iron used in their manufacture, but especially the unusual excellence of the work. The foundery for a period, in common with the other iron establishments of the place, experienced a great depression; but at present under the energetic management of Nelson Kingland, Esquire, is again in a prosperous condition. Its production the last year amounted to about two hundred and fifty tons of castings. The foundery and machine shop connected with it in the same period did a business of about thirty-five thousand dollars, and possess a capacity for performing work to the amount of seventy-five thousand dollars per annum.

A company has been organized at Keeseville, and recently commenced business for the manufacture from cotton of twine, carpet warp and wicking, and has already in operation a number of machines competent to consume twelve thousand pounds monthly of the raw material. It is starting with the designation of Kingsland, Houghton & Co., under the most favorable auspices, with means and facilities, and the purpose of largely extending its operations if the measure is warranted by adequate success.

The Messrs. Boynton have also just erected several machines for the fabrication of cotton hosiery. The movement is experimental, but if attended with success, the business will become an important feature in the industrial pursuits of the place. Two flouring mills are located on separated sites at Keeseville, a plaster mill, planing mill, furniture and tin factories, and various other subordinate manufacturing establishments are also in prosperous operation. At the village of Birmingham a small part of its vast water power is occupied by a paper mill, two starch factories, and a grist mill.

Works are in progress of construction by Messrs. Pollard & Pease in the vicinity of Keeseville, and near the vast kaolin deposits noticed in a former page for the separating and preparing that article for market.

Boquet Valley.

New Russia Forge. In the southern extremity of Elizabethtown, and upon one of the highest branches of the Boquet, where it almost mingles with the head waters of the Hudson, stands the New Russia Forge. This is one of the oldest iron works of the county, it having been erected about the year 1802. It has been repeatedly rebuilt and in 1860 received a thorough reconstruction. The existing forge, owned by Messrs. E. H. & H. A. Putnam contains four fires, and a wooden hammer of about one thousand eight hundred pounds weight. It possesses both steam and water power. The ore used, is principally taken from the New Russia mine, owned by the company and situated half a mile from the works. The forge is about six miles from the Fisher hill ore bed, from which it has obtained a part of the ore worked. Charcoal, chiefly made in closed kilns, is exclusively consumed in the works. The company own in the vicinity about ten thousand acres of woodland. The products of the forge are slabs for boiler plates, and blooms adapted to the fabrication of wire and steel. These are transported by land carriage to Westport, a distance of twelve miles for shipping. A grist and saw-mill are also in operation on the same site. In 1866, the forge consumed 300,000 bushels of charcoal and 2,400 tons of ore, producing six hundred and seventy-five tons of iron.[1]

[1] For these returns I am indebted to the valuable work of Mr. Wm. G. Neilson, to which I shall frequently refer, when I am unable to procure statistics of a later date.

Kingdom Forge is situated about six miles south-east from the Court House, upon Black creek, a branch of the Boquet. It was erected in 1825, and was formerly owned by Mr. Henry R. Noble. It has been enlarged within a few years by the present proprietors, the Essex and Lake Champlain Ore and Iron Company, from two fires, its original capacity, to six fires. Its supply of ore is chiefly derived from the Burt mine, a distance of five miles. It consumes charcoal. This property was owned by the same interest as the Valley Forge. The company are proprietors of about eleven thousand acres of woodland. Two closed kilns are appropriated toward the supply of the Kingdom forge. These works consume 30,000 bushels of coal and produced seven hundred and fifty tons of iron in 1866.

Valley Forge was erected in 1846, and was several years conducted by Messrs. Whallon & Judd. It stands upon the Boquet, a half mile from the village of Elizabethtown, and has a land carriage eight miles and a half to Westport. The premises have passed through various transitions of proprietorship, and for the term the business has been suspended, but has been recently resumed. It came into the possession of the Essex and Lake Champlain Ore and Iron Company in the year 1864. The forge contains six fires and one hammer, weighing about eleven thousand pounds. The blast is driven by a horizontal engine, with a cylinder of about ten inches diameter and thirty inch thick. There are two blowing cylinders. Steam is supplied by two boilers, heated by escape heat from a part of the forges. Its ore is obtained chiefly from the Burt mine, a distance of about ten miles. This company are the proprietors of numerous ore beds in the district. The forge consumes charcoal burnt in six kilns and the remainder in pits, principally belonging to the company and from its own woodlands. The works annually consume one hundred and twenty thousand bushels of coal and yielded in 1866, ten hundred and fifty tons of iron. They produce bloom iron, which is shipped at Westport to various points south and west. William G. Neilson, Esq., is the resident agent and manager of this company.

Westport Forge stands upon the Boquet, four miles from Westport, was built about 1845. It has been for many years in the occupation of Messrs. W. P. & P. D. Merriam. It contains three fires, one hammer and two wheels. It formerly worked Moriah ore transported by land, from Westport. A mine has been opened on the premises of the company from which the forge is largely supplied. Charcoal is consumed, and is principally burnt in the kilns of the company. In 1866 this forge used eighty thousand bushels of charcoal, and six hundred and thirty tons of ore, producing four hundred and fifty tons of iron. Its products are carried to Westport for shipping.

The *Stower Forge* is situated in Lewis, upon a small branch of the Boquet, and was erected about 1837. It was owned and worked several years by General William E. Merriam, and subsequently by his son, John L. Merriam, and still later by W. H. Roberts. Mr. W. H. Stower purchased the property in the year 1864. The forge stands upon an excellent water power, and contains three fires, three water wheels and a wooden helve hammer, weighing about eighteen hundred pounds. The ore used is chiefly procured from Moriah, which in summer is shipped to Essex or Westport, and thence carried by teams a distance of about eight miles. In winter it is transported directly from the mines, a distance of about twenty miles. Ore beds have been discovered in the town of Lewis, from which a supply to a greater or less extent will be derived. The forge consumes charcoal burnt both in kilns, and several of which are open pits, and uses about eighty thousand bushels with about eight hundred tons of ore. It fabricates blooms and slabs, which are transported to Essex for shipping. Its estimated production annually is seven hundred tons.

Willsboro' Forge is located at Willsboro' falls upon the Boquet, and very near the site occupied by William Gilliland for a saw-mill in 1765, which was supplied for the creation of its motive power by a wing dam. The same site was occupied by Higby & Troop for the forge erected in 1801. The property has been held by a succession of owners. For a period it suspended operations. The forge was rebuilt in 1862, and with other improvements received an iron roof. It is owned by General Belden Noble, and is in the charge of J. M. Ferris, as manager. A large body of woodland owned by the proprietors is appropriated for the supply of charcoal, which is usually burnt in closed kilns. The forge consumes annually about three hundred thousand bushels, and yields twelve hundred tons of iron.[1] These works enjoy peculiar and far greater facilities than any other upon the waters of the Boquet, in the vast economy it effects in the transportation of ore and the shipping of its fabrics. The Boquet is navigable within a short distance of the forge, and canal boats laded with ore from Moriah can in good water approach within a fourth of a mile, and having discharged their cargoes are loaded with iron, which without being reshipped is exported usually to Troy. The forge contains four fires, one iron hammer of about five tons weight, and two wheels, one each for the hammer and bellows. It manufactures blooms and slabs.

A forge of two fires situated on a branch of the Boquet in Lewis, and owned by A. H. Wilder, was built in 1844, and abandoned in 1862. Another containing four fires, standing on the Boquet at Whallonsburg, and owned by Hon. J. S. Whallon, suspended operations in 1856. A grist and saw-mill, clothier works and a plaster mill have been also erected at this place.

Boquet Works. Extensive and important works embracing a rolling mill for the fabrication of bars and iron plates from blooms, were erected about 1827 on the Boquet falls, two miles and a half west of Essex village. Gould, Ross & Low, for a period after they assumed the occupation, carried on a large and prosperous business, but the works

---

[1] *Rev. A. D. Barber.*

were suspended in the year 1856. A grist mill and woolen factory are in operation on this site.

Brainard's Forges, containing two or three fires each, were erected in 1830 and stood on Black river, a few miles from the Court House. They have been long abandoned. A saw mill now alone occupies this very fine water power, which may be used several times successively, on contiguous wheels.[1]

Highland Forge was located on Howard's brook, near Willsboro' bay, and seven miles from Keeseville. It was owned and worked by A. G. Forbes; built in 1837 and suspended operations in 1857.

West Port Furnace stands upon the margin of North West bay and about one mile from Westport village. It was erected about the year 1848 by Mr. Francis H. Jackson, and called by him Sisco furnace. The cost of its original construction exceeded one hundred thousand dollars. For a term of years it was in the possession of Hon. G. W. Goff. The premises are now owned by the Champlain Ore and Furnace Company, but the works have been suspended for a long period. The motive power of this furnace was steam, and its products pig iron. The ore used was chiefly from the Cheever bed, and in part from a bed two or three miles west of the village of Westport, and owned by the proprietors of the furnace, who are also owners of the Goff ore bed in Moriah. Mr. Lewis H. Roe is superintendent of this company.

MORIAH.

The enterprise of Moriah has been diverted from the manufacturing pursuits, which its magnificent capabilities were calculated to cherish, by the more tangible and certain remuneration afforded by the raising and sale of its ores. The works which do exist, however, are on a scale of great magnitude and perfection.

---

[1] *R. W. Livingstone.*

Port Henry Furnace. Major James Dalliba, formerly of the army, in connection with Hon. John D. Dickenson of Troy, erected the first furnace at this place, about the year 1822. A notice of the work produced by the earlier furnaces will strikingly exhibit the vast progress which a quarter of a century has accomplished in both the practical and scientific operations of these works. The furnace of Major Dalliba yielded a product of only fifteen to eighteen tons of iron a week, about one-half of the yield of the present furnace per day. The former run from three to six months for a blast. The ore used was obtained from a vein near the furnace, from another about three-fourths of a mile distant and from Vermont. The iron made was exported to Troy until 1827, when the production of pig metal was abandoned and the works were appropriated to the manufacture of stoves and hollow ware. On the decease of Major Dalliba, the property passed into the hands of Stephen S. Keyes, who sold in 1844 to Cole, Olcott & Tarbell, and they transferred it the succeeding year to Powell & Lansing. These proprietors erected a second furnace on the lake shore. In 1838, the title became vested in Horace Grey, Jr., of Boston, and was transferred by him in 1840, to the Port Henry Iron Company. Mr. Grey was the principal stock holder in this company. He leased individually the furnace property and the Cheever ore bed, in 1846, at a nominal rent. The original furnace was demolished and a new one built, which commenced operations in 1847. On the reverses which occurred to Mr. Grey in the fall of this year, the works were temporarily suspended. Improved intelligence and the application of the hot blast has gradually augmented the yield of the furnace, from two and three tons per day to ten and twelve tons for the same period.

In 1852, Mr. Benjamin T. Reed, of Boston, purchased all the property of the Port Henry Iron Company, and in the following year, the Cheever ore bed was transferred to the Cheever Ore Bed Company, and the furnaces to the Port Henry Furnaces. These were distinct corporations organized under the laws of this state. The Port Henry Furnaces company conveyed its property in 1867 to the Bay State Iron Company, a corporation formed under the laws of Massachusetts, and doing business at South Boston. The stockholders of both incorporations were the same individuals. Under the latter title the business of the furnace property is at this time conducted. The officers of the company are: Samuel Hooper, president; John H. Reed, treasurer; and Wallace T. Foot, superintendent of the works at Port Henry. In 1853, the old charcoal furnaces were repaired and a blast anthracite coal substituted, with water as the motive power. The year after a new furnace was erected on the margin of the lake near the former structure of Powell & Lansing. "This furnace was constructed on a new plan, having an outer casing or shell of boiler iron rivetted together and standing upon plates, supported by cast iron columns. This was the first erection of the kind built in the country, and so far as I am aware in the world; although some have been constructed in Europe, with a boiler iron shell supported by brick arches.[1] The furnace is forty-six feet high, sixteen feet diameter at the top of the boshes, eight feet at the top of the furnace, and is blown through five tuyeres, by a vertical steam engine having a steam cylinder thirty inches in diameter, six feet stroke, and a wind cylinder eighty-four inches diameter, six feet stroke. In 1860 another furnace was commenced, but not completed until 1862. This furnace is propelled by machinery similar to the other, but somewhat enlarged in its proportions and power. The furnace built by Powell & Lansing was taken down in 1855, and that erected by Gray was demolished in 1865.

During the last five years, these furnaces have produced 58,100 tons of pig iron, consuming 107,700 tons of coal

---

[1] Mr. W. T. Foot, the accomplished manager of the works, to whose courtesy I am indebted for most of the facts on this subject incorporated in the text.

and 100,800 tons of ore. The ore used is chiefly from the Cheever and Barton beds. The English method of working a high furnace with a closed top has been recently adopted, and each of the furnaces has been raised twenty feet, giving them an elevation of sixty-six feet. One of them, after an operation of three months under this charge shows a very satisfactory result by an increased production of iron, with a less comsumption of coal per ton of iron made. The company obtains lime from a quarry upon its own property a short distance from the furnaces. The anthracite coal is exclusively used, and is principally transported in return boats from Rondout. The fabrics of the furnaces are chiefly exports to the mill of the company at South Boston. A foundery and repairing shop is attached to the works for the convenience of the establishment. The former is a large edifice one hundred and sixty feet. The last year the foundery has made about two hundred tons of castings. A carpenter's shop contiguous, is worked by the same motive power as the cupola and in it are formed all the patterns required in the works. About one hundred and thirty-five men are usually employed at the furnaces. The coal and cinders are transported in hand carts upon a small rail road to and from the works. The latter are used for filling in the wharf property of the company.

Fletcherville Furnace. This furnace is situated seven and a half miles north-west of Port Henry. It is owned by Messrs. S. H. & J. G. Weatherbee & F. P. Fletcher; its erection was commenced in 1864, and it was blown in, in August, 1865. The stack is of stone, and the boiler house of brick. The height of the furnace is forty-two feet, and width of the boshes eleven feet. The construction and mechanism of this furnace is somewhat peculiar and complicated. As it is not my purpose to present any scientific or technical views, I shall refrain from an attempt to describe it. The ore used in the establishment is obtained mainly from a number of beds owned by the company, but not at present fully developed, which are contiguous to the furnace. Steam is the motive power of the works, and charcoal the only fuel consumed. This is burnt in ten large kilns, capable of containing sixty-five cords of wood. Nearly fifty bushels of charcoal is yielded in these kilns by every cord of seasoned wood The company own extensive ranges of timber land, which supplies the material for the kilns. The average product per week of this furnace has been at some periods seventy-six and a half tons per week.[1] A large proportion of the iron produced here is manufactured in the Bessemer works at Troy. Mr. Thomas F. Weatherbee is the resident agent and manager at this furnace.

Crown Point Iron Company's Furnace. This work is situated ten miles west of Crown Point landing, and is owned by that company, consisting of J. & T. Hammond & E. S. Bogue. A furnace was built on this site in 1845, was burnt down in 1865, and immediately erected anew. It is forty-two feet high, and nine feet across the boshes. It is a charcoal blast furnace, the escape heat being used for generating steam, for power for blast, stamping, sawing coal brands and grinding feed. The furnace consumes 6,500 tons of ore and 650,000 bushels of charcoal, which yield 3,500 tons of pig metal. In the last eight years the furnace has not run more than three-fourths of the time, owing to the insufficient supply of fuel. The charcoal is chiefly burnt in kilns. The ore used is taken from the bed owned by the company, situated about one mile from the works, and the lime is procured from their own quarry about the same distance. This furnace has been peculiarly successful, both in the manner of its operation and the quality of iron it produces. Since the establishment of the Bessemer steel works at Troy, a large portion of the iron from this furnace has been purchased by that institution. The harder and higher qualities of this iron secure a constant market from the manufacturers of malleable

---

[1] *Mr. Neilson's report.*

iron. For their use it is esteemed an eminently desirable material.

In approaching this furnace, then owned by Hammond & Co., in 1852, I observed the road formed for some distance by a very beautiful material, exhibiting a surface soft and lustrous, and glowing in every shade and tint. This substance was the concretion of the slag or cinders of the furnace. When gushing from the stack in fusion, it will form and draw out, by a wire thrust into the boiling mass, an attenuated glass thread the entire length of the furnace, a distance of sixty feet. The glass presents the most delicate and diversified coloring; although combined in the eruption from the furnace with extraneous properties. Thus beautiful in its crude and adulterated condition, may not this substance, purified and refined by science, be rendered subservient to the arts?

Irondale Iron Works are situated six miles west of the lake, and upon Putman's creek, which affords the motive power. The forge which now contains four fires, one wooden twelve hammer, weighing one thousand eight hundred pounds, and two wheels, was erected in 1828. It is at present owned by Penfield, Harwood & Co. The forge consumes charcoal, which is principally burnt in covered kilns, about four miles from the works in the west part of Ticonderoga. Ore from the bed of the company located about five miles from the works, is used in the forge. It manufactures blooms and bars. The iron made in this forge has established the highest reputation. This statement is sustained by the fact that in 1829, the company received an order from the government for a large quantity of their iron to be fabricated into chain cables. It is extensively used for the fabrication of fine ware, and at Pittsburg it is used for making cast steel. The company have a separator near their works, in which the ore is prepared for the forge. It is stated that two tons of separated ore will yield a ton of iron. The annual amount manufactured at this forge is about five hundred tons. There are a saw mill and grist mill standing a few rods below the iron works, and owned by the proprietors.[1]

The other minor industrial pursuits of Crown Point embrace, at the centre village, three miles from the lake, a tannery, woolen factory, grist mill, saw mill, tub and barrel factory, and wheelwright shop; one mile below are a sash and door factory, and a pail and tub factory; still nearer the lake are a grist and saw mill, and wheelwright shop. All these works stand upon Putnam's creek, a small stream I have already described.

TICONDEROGA.

Horicon Iron Company. This forge was erected by the Ticonderoga Iron Company, in 1864, under the direction of Col. W. E. Calkins. It is a very superior forge, and is esteemed equal to any in northern New York. It is built of wood and roofed with slate, and contains six fires with a capability of working twelve. It has two wooden helve hammers weighing about twenty-seven hundred pounds. "The blowing is performed by water power. A forty-eight inch Chapman wheel is used. There are two blast cylinders of five feet in diameter with five feet stroke." This forge, which is supplied by the water that forms its motive power, by a tube four hundred feet long, and about six feet in diameter stands at the Lower Falls about two miles from the steam boat landing, and at the head of the navigation accessible to canal boats from Lake Champlain. These boats may moor directly alongside of the works for discharging and loading. The company own large tracts of woodland on the shores of Lake George. The wood is transported on barges, which are towed by a small tug, to the foot of the lake, where it is burnt into charcoal in five extensive kilns, capable of burning sixty-five cords each. The charcoal is carted a distance of about two miles to the forge. The ore now used, although the company owns extensive mineral property, is principally shipped from Port Henry

[1] *C. Fenton.*

and landed at the works. A separator is erected near the forge. The product of the works, which was bloom iron, in 1865, was about four hundred and fifty tons; in 1866, about three hundred; but at present the forge is not in operation.[1]

A cupola furnace was erected on the lower falls in 1832 by John Porter & Son, and continued until recently, in the occupation of the same family. It is now owned by Clark, Strain & Hooper. The furnace and machine shop connected with it fabricates about eight thousand dollars worth of agricultural implements, stoves, mill irons and general work adapted to home consumption.

The census returns of 1865 report three woolen factories in the county. The most important of these is the works of Messrs. Treadway, situated on the lower falls in Ticonderoga. This factory embraces all the modern improvements, and produces work of the highest quality. It is at this time performing an extensive and prosperous business, but possessing an unemployed capacity of executing very large operations.

American Graphite Company. The business conducted by this company is rare and of peculiar interest. The vast deposits of plumbago or black lead, in this vicinity attracted early attention to its manufactures. In 1832, William Stuart and Nathan Delano commenced mining and preparing the article for market. The former in connection with his sons maintained the business to a late period. Appollos Skinner engaged in it in 1833. He was succeeded by Messrs. Ives & Arthur. They soon after constructed separate works. The business in Ticonderoga is now in the exclusive control of the American Graphite Company. They have erected a large and expensive mill, which is worked night and day, and produces about five hundred tons of black lead annually. The native impurities of the ore are separated by an ingenious process possessed by the company. About sixty men are employed

---

[1] *W. G. Neilson. A. Weed, and H. G. Burleigh & Bro.*

in the mines and works of this concern. The article produced is of very superior quality, and is largely used in the manufacture of crucibles. Mr. William Hooper is superintendent of the company at Ticonderoga.[1] About the year 1818, Guy C. Baldwin introduced the process of grinding the plumbago in millstone with iron ore. Mr. Baldwin subsequently invented a method of manufacturing crayons and pencil points, from this material. He erected a factory for the purpose of fabricating these articles, which was worked many years. This manufacture at Ticonderoga is now discontinued.[2] The amount of lumber at present cut in this town, is computed at about five hundred thousand feet annually.

The Valley of the Hudson.

The head waters of the Hudson pervade every section of the south-western towns of Essex county, and furnish an immense water power. The mountains bear a limitless supply of fuel, and throughout the territory the presence of iron ore is manifested by the clearest indications which research constantly corroborates. All these advantages should tend to the creation of much more extended manufacturing occupations than now exist, but a remoteness from market, and the absence of appropriate artificial communication have impeded the development of the vast natural resources of the district. A new era is dawning upon this seclusion, and very soon enterprise and improvement will awaken the dormant energies of these valleys and mountains. The expense of transportation to Crown Point, a distance from the nearest point of about nineteen miles, over a difficult route, is highly onerous, but at present, the fabrics of the Schroon have no shorter or more direct route to market. The rail road already constructed to Warrensburgh, will soon, it is claimed, reach the confines of Essex county.

---

[1] *Alfred Weed. Messrs. Burleigh.* [2] *Cook, Weed and Burleigh,*

Schroon River Forge stands upon a branch of the Hudson twenty-four miles south-west from the village of Elizabethtown. It was built in 1857 by Mr. Jacob Parmerter, and was operated by E. B. Walker & Co., with which firm he was for a term associated. It became the property of Mr. John Roth in 1861. It has two fires, a hammer of about eighteen hundred pounds weight, and two wheels. One grist and one saw mill occupy the same dam. A little village, marked by the usual appliances of manufacturing hamlets, has sprung up around these works. The ore used is obtained from the Norway bed near Paradox lake, and some portions from the Moriah beds. Three closed kilns are situated near the forge and in the midst of an inexhaustible supply of wood. The works produce blooms, billots and slabs.

Head of Paradox Forge is located near Paradox lake; was built in 1864, and is owned by John Roth, the proprietor of the above. This forge has contained only two fires, but a third is now being introduced. It has one hammer and one wheel, and is principally supplied with ore from the Roth or Norway vein. The charcoal consumed in these works is made in pits at the forge. Three hundred bushels of this coal is required to produce one ton of iron. The two forges of which Mr. Roth is the proprietor, are embraced in the same general system of operations. He esteems the iron produced in these works from the Norway ore of unsurpassed excellence, possessing in its qualities an assimilation to the fabrics of Russia and Norway. Its rare properties, it is pronounced, are recognized in market and control maximum prices. He now manufactures finished billots, which are sent to Pittsburg for the fabrication of steel and other purposes. These forges, with their increased facilities and power, it is anticipated, will possess a capacity of yielding a thousand tons of iron annually, produced in 1866 five hundred and fifty tons. Two forges, the Dead Water Iron Works and the North Hudson Iron Works situated in the town of North Hudson, were formerly owned by the Hon. James S. Whallon, but have long been abandoned.

The Minerva Iron Company have commenced measures for the establishment of a first class forge in that town, and have already expended a large amount in the scheme. The works are incomplete, being not more than half finished. Castings and other materials for the construction of the forge, are already upon the ground. The forge is designed to contain eight fires, with steam as a motive power. It is located about two and a half miles from Olmstead hill, and a little more than six miles from the projected rail road track at Birds Pond Falls. These measures are guided by a powerful and energetic company, and must exert a most auspicious influence upon the development and prosperity of that section of the county.

TANNERIES.

A number of works devoted to the manufacturing of the different descriptions of leather exist in various sections of Essex county. These are chiefly supplied with the raw material by the hides of animals furnished from the district. In the year 1864, two thousand one hundred and forty-three neat cattle, and two thousand one hundred and fifty-four sheep were slaughtered in the county, besides the skins of other animals and those dying from disease or accident. In the towns of Schroon, Minerva and North Hudson, this business is now the predominant and a highly important industrial pursuit. The vast hemlock forests, which spread over that region, afford an abundant and accessible material for these works. It is rare, in manufacturing economics, that a raw material so valuable as the hemlock bark, can be procured not only without detriment to another substance, with which it is connected, but that the process essentially enhances the value of the latter. Such, in these forests, is literally the fact in reference to this bark. The logs, when cut for market, are stripped of their bark and relieved of its heavy weight, they are more easily transported, the floating is facilitated, and the timber preserved from decay and the depredations of insects. By a judicious management, the hemlock of these forests will be adequate to the supply of bark to all the tanneries of the district through a series of years.

The *Burhan's Tannery* is situated upon a small branch of the Schroon river, and in the town of North Hudson. The original works were erected by Erastus B. Potter, and purchased about the year 1859 by the present proprietor, Edgar W. Burhans, who has through large additions and improvements, rendered it one of the most complete tanneries in northern New York. It has the capacity of tanning from twenty-five to thirty thousand sides of sole leather annually. It is chiefly propelled by a steam engine of forty horse power for grinding bark, for pumping and heating the liquor, and with steam for steeping the bark. Spent tan supplies the fuel for running the engine. The works yield a sufficient material for the purpose, and thus secures great economy in the saving of wood. The rolling machine is moved by water power. The hides manufactured in the works are principally South American. They are purchased in New York, and from thence shipped to Crown Point. The leather produced is transported to Crown Point, a distance of nineteen miles from the tannery. The hides are conveyed from the landing to the works by the same route. From twenty to thirty men are occupied about the works and a large additional number are employed both summer and winter, in lumbering, in peeling and transporting bark, and drawing logs by sleighing to the Schroon river, an important tributary of the Hudson, by which they are floated to Glen's Falls and Sandy Hill to be manufactured into lumber for the southern market. All the tanneries pursue the same system. In the efficient management of Mr. Burhans, the business of this establishment is very extensive and equally prosperous.[1] Schroon Lake tannery, was erected in 1852, by Lorenzo Hall, and

---

[1] *John Roth.*

is now owned by Milton Sawyer of Glen's Falls. It is situated on a small brook about one mile west of Schroon lake, and twenty-five miles west of Lake Champlain. The capital employed in these works is about ten thousand dollars. This tannery is capable of producing about sixteen thousand sides per year, and consumes about one thousand five hundred cords of bark.

Schroon Tannery stands on Schroon lake, at the mouth of the stream just mentioned, and was erected in 1861 by William C. Potter and Daniel Wyman. After several transfers the title of the property is now invested in Mr. Gridley T. Thayer. This tannery manufactures about one hundred tons of leather per annum.

Wickham Tannery is a small establishment occupying a site at the mouth of the same stream, and opposite to the Schroon tannery. It is owned by Mr. Benjamin Wickham, and is used exclusively for the manufacture of upper leather.

Hoffman Tannery was erected by Bracket & Boyle, in 1856, but is now owned by Mr. Milton Sawyer. It is situated about six miles west of his Schroon lake tannery, and about thirty miles from Lake Champlain. It possesses the capacity of tanning about one thousand sides, and consumes nine hundred cords of bark yearly. Mr. Sawyer is engaged in erecting a new and extensive tannery on the branch in the north part of Schroon. Sawyer & Mead are now building a first class tannery on the west branch of the Schroon river, about three miles from the state road. It is two hundred and sixty-three by forty feet; will be capable of tanning from two hundred and fifty to three hundred tons of leather per annum, and will consume yearly about three thousand cords of bark.

I am only able to refer, among the industrial pursuits of this district, to a large work situated on Mill creek, east of Schroon lake, and owned by Messrs. Frazier, Major & Co., of New York, which is reported to consume fifteen hundred cords of bark yearly. Numerous and very extensive tanneries are located in the northern sections of Warren county, which are largely supplied with bark from Essex county.

The *Olmsteadville Tannery*, in the town of Minerva, large and valuable works, was destroyed by fire in the year 1867. A part of the structures are still standing, and now owned by Messrs. Frazier, Major & Co. Its correspondent estimates the bark formerly consumed by this tannery, at five thousand cords per annum. The materials intended for the Olmsteadville works, is now transported to the works of the same proprietors at Pottersville, Warren county. The same authority states that the various tanneries owned by this company, requires the bark afforded by twenty thousand logs yearly.

A competent authority computes the bark used in other tanneries at from ten thousand to fifteen thousand cords annually, and that the process of peeling, prepares from one hundred thousand to one hundred and fifty thousand logs for the mills at Glen's Falls, Sandy Hill and Fort Edward.[1]

Ship yards. The large number of vessels of various descriptions employed in the navigation of Lake Champlain, requires the labors of numerous ship yards, for their construction and repairing. Of these, Essex county has its proportion. This business at one time was carried on at Willsboro' to a considerable extent, the estuary of the Boquet presenting a favorable location for the purpose. In the village of Essex, Hoskins, Ross & Co., have established a commodious yard for boat building and repairing, with which is connected a steam saw mill, and shingle planing mill, with a grinding attachment and carriage factory.[2] Since the first occupation by France, Ticonderoga has been a conspicuous point at which boats and vessels navigating the lake have been built and equipped. To provide materials for this purpose, was a prominent motive, for the erection by the French, of the saw mills at the falls. The numerous flotillas which traversed the lakes at different periods, bearing hostile armies, were largely

---

[1] *Mr. John Roth.* [2] *Mr. John Ross.*

constructed at Ticonderoga. Amherst paused here, while awaiting the building and preparation of a fleet for the invasion of Canada. The fleet of Arnold, with which he combated Carleton, was chiefly constructed at this point. Since the opening of the Champlain canal, boat building has been the prominent business occupation of Ticonderoga. Mr. Henry Cassey owns a ship yard at the Lower falls, where a large number of first class canal boats are built yearly. Two other yards in the town are carrying on a regular business, in this industry. During the last ten years an average of ten boats, of one hundred tons burthen each, have been built in these yards annually.[1] Another large ship yard is in operation at Crown Point.

AGRICULTURE.

In describing the topographical features and arrangement of this county, in the preceding pages, I have sufficiently noticed its agricultural capabilities, and the soil and climate of its various districts. The same transitions in its agricultural progress have marked every section of this county. The natural fertility of the soil, when first opened to cultivation, yielded abundant harvests; injudicious tillage gradually exhausted its productive elements; the cause which tended to these results ceased; new interests in the management of the land were excited, and a general improvement in the farms was produced by an ameliorated system of husbandry. The county still exhibits these various phases of its agriculture. Some farms are just emerging from the primeval wilderness; some are impoverished and exhausted; others are commencing the process of renovation; while many others have attained a degree of improved culture and fertility, scarcely exceeded by any portion of the state.

---

[1] *Alfred Reed. H. G. Burleigh & Bro.*

The lumber business in this as in every region, appropriate to its pursuit, captivated the mind of the pioneer, and allures him from other occupations. The winter was devoted to this employment. Every product of the farm calculated to return fertilizing elements to sustain and promote its productiveness, was borne into the forests and there consumed. At the approach of spring, the settler returned to his farm, himself and his team, prostrated by the severe labors of the winter, and illy prepared to perform the recurring duties which pressed upon him. He conducts his farming operations imperfectly and without skill. He has no deposits of manure to apply to his wasting soil. The earth, by constant tillage, without renovation, becomes impoverished. Each succeeding year witnesses a decrease in the harvest. The land, exhausted by this improvident management, is denounced worthless in its soil, and without fertility, and abandoned to briers and desolation, or is sacrificed to some shrewd purchaser, and its owner emigrates to new scenes, to pass through the same alterations. In this stage of society, agriculture is the secondary and subordinate occupation.

The lumbering business closed, the farmer resumes his first duties, and yields to the land the labor and care required for its successful cultivation. In a manufacturing district, and such is preeminently Essex county, the teaming upon the road, which abstracts so much of the time of the farmer, and the fertilizing riches of the farm, from this land, exercises a similar, although far less disastrous effect, upon its agricultural prosperity. Other causes of the slow progress in the agricultural improvement of this county are suggested by an intelligent correspondent,[1] in reference to a single town but applicable to all. "Conflicting titles have cast a shade over some large tracts," and in others "much of the land has been occupied under contracts, in their terms liable to constant forfeiture." Tenures of pro-

---

[1] *C. Fenton, Esq.*

perty so frail and contingent in every region, paralyze the efforts of industry and enterprise.

The early settlers relied chiefly for pasturage and winter fodder upon the wild grasses and herbage, bountifully supplied by the beaver meadows, the marshes and glades of the forests. The indigenous grasses of this region are very numerous, and many of them highly nutritious and valuable. Several varieties of the ferns, brakes and rushes afford excellent hay, particularly for sheep. The instincts of the deer indicate to the pioneer the most useful of these resources.

I hesitate to decide, whether I am authorized in classing the white clover, *trifolium repens*, with the indigenous plants of this region. It is certain that it soon appears, by a spontaneous growth in every opening of the forest, and upon soils of sand and gravel formation. Where gypsum has been applied, or sheep have ranged, it is immediately introduced, forming a massive sward, which constitutes a most important basis for future tillage. The presence of a white clover turf uniformly secures on sandy soils an excellent corn crop with an application of plaster.

Wheat. For a series of years succeeding the first occupation of the county, wheat was the predominant crop, particularly in that section of it which lies upon Lake Champlain. The average yield on new land was about twenty-five bushels to the acre. This culture gradually declined, under the effects of a change of seasons, the exhaustion of the quality of the soil adapted to the production of wheat, and the ultimate infliction of the wevil and rust. It was virtually abandoned, until the introduction of the Black Sea wheat, which gave it a new and successful impulse. The tea wheat and various other spring varieties have been the successive favorites, while the general culture of wheat has been largely extended. Winter wheat is now largely cultivated.

Rye, in several towns of Essex county, was formerly the predominant crop. It is now very generally abandoned as a prominent cereal except upon light and gravelly soils.

Rye is seldom used as an article of human aliment, and in the absence of distilleries, is chiefly cultivated for animal food. The straw is esteemed valuable for that purpose, and when cut is peculiarly esteemed for horse fodder combined with heavy grain.

Oats. The aggregate produced in Essex county is very large. It is cultivated in every description of soil and in every section of the county. The heaviest crops I have examined were raised in the new openings of the forests, upon the slopes of the Adirondacs. The cultivation of oats, in the elevated town of Newcomb has been singularly successful.

Peas are cultivated to some extent, and are highly esteemed as a renovating and subduing crop, and are especially efficient and useful, in the extirpation of weeds and bushes upon new lands. Peas are regarded as a valuable substitute for corn in making pork.

Barley. The culture of this grain has largely increased in the county and with favorable results.

Beans were formerly raised only in connection with corn, but recently the great demand for the article, at enhanced prices, has largely stimulated its more extended cultivation.

Buckwheat and *Indian wheat*, especially the former, are largely cultivated in the county, although many farmers deprecate the husbandry as injudicious and improvident. Both are used extensively for hog feeding, ground or boiled. Buckwheat, floured at the local mills, is exported in a large amount, to the eastern and southern markets.

Potato. This crop has attained great prominence in the agriculture of the county. The prevalence of the disease, which impaired and often nearly suspended the cultivation of the potato, produced an entire change in the tillage connected with it. Heavy, damp and highly manured lands, which once were deemed indispensable to the successful cultivation of the potato, have been abandoned, and light gravelly sandy soils have been substituted. Green unfermented manures are considered unsafe, and charcoal, lime, ashes, plaster and special fertilizers, are now generally in use. The potatoes produced in this district are of the choicest quality. Of late they have been less exported than some years ago, when from a single wharf ten thousand bushels were shipped in a season. In the interior of the county, the numerous starch factories create a certain and generally remunerative market for all this crop the industry of the farmer can produce.

Corn. This crop may be pronounced the agricultural staple of Essex county and the basis of the rotation and renovating system of its husbandry. The stalks of corn are highly valued as a fodder for neat cattle, and when fed to milch cows, from their succulent qualities if carefully preserved, are considered by most farmers superior to hay.

Carrots, *Beets* and *Turnips* are largely cultivated and extensively used in feeding horses, neat cattle and swine.

Flax is seldom cultivated in the county. Only four acres are returned in the census of 1865, as appropriated to the crop, and not a single acre of hemp.

Hay. This crop is of the first importance, and always commands the highest prices. The production of hay, however, in the country, falls immensely below the consumption. Large quantities of pressed hay is annually imported from Washington county, Vermont and Canada.

Stock.

Numerous *dairies* exist in the county, and some of them of a superior character, and embracing excellent cows; most of these possess an infusion of pure blood; but few animals are found in the district exclusively of thorough-bred stock.

It is apparent, from the table of census returns, that the wool growing interest of Essex county has attained very considerable importance. The climate, the physical formation, the soil and position of this region will combine to render this territory one of the most eligible and prosperous wool growing districts of the state.

In no department of its husbandry has this county exhibited more decided progress, than in the quality and character of its stock. I cannot ascertain that a thorough bred animal was owned in the country, until about the year 1847. Grades of Teeswater and Durham had been introdnced probably before that period. It now contains individuals of nearly every breed, that may almost maintain an equal competition with the stock of any section of the state. A race of horses, almost indigenous to its soil, is disseminated through the county, which combine properties of rare excellence. The high reputation of the Black Hawk horses has become widely diffused, and each year adds to their consideration. In no district have they been more extensively bred, or attained greater perfection than in this region.

Fruit.

The Champlain valley is preeminently adapted, in soil and climate, to the production of most varieties of the apple. The list of apples cultivated in this district is very numerous, and the quality generally of the highest excellence.

Many old orchards still exist, which were planted at the first settlement of the country. The pioneer, usually, brought with his household goods, the bag of apple seeds from his New England home, and the young orchard was among the earliest evidences of improvement and civilizátion. The perversion of this rich bounty of providence, for a period, created a prejudice, which led to the neglect of its culture.

A few years ago, five thousand engrafted apple trees were planted in a single season in the town of Crown Point.

Other towns have been equally conspicuous in this enterprise. Large fields are devoted to the apple culture, and in all the eastern towns, young trees not yet in bearing occupy extensive areas and impart to the territory a pleasant aspect of thrift and improvement. In Willsboro' and Essex, it seems as if the whole region would soon be converted into one vast orchard. The former town alone, it is estimated, exported in the autumn of '68, between four and five thousand barrels of apples, of which fourteen or fifteen hundred barrels were selected grafts.[1] Engrafted trees are now chiefly cultivated. The inferior apples not adapted to market, are dried, or used for the feed of animals, and a very small portion is manufactured into cider. A large quantity of this kind of fruit are purchased and transported by bateau loads into Canada.

Plums are cultivated in numerous varieties and of great excellence, and are largely exported. The crop is frequently impaired and often destroyed by the ravages of the circulio. This pestilent insect infests, also, the cherry. Many varieties of the pear are now cultivated successfully and exported to considerable extent.

Much attention is given to the grape culture, and embracing the more hardy variety, with favorable results. The original vine of the Adirondac grape was discovered beneath a cliff of the mountain, at Port Henry upon the grounds of Mr. J. G. Weatherbee. Whether a native growth or a seedling of the Isabella, is, I think, undetermined, but propagated by the skill and enterprise of Mr. J. W. Bailey of Plattsburg, it has attained celebrity as a fruit and proved a source of large income to the proprietors. Other varieties of the native grape might by care and skill be successfully cultivated. The blue or huckleberry appears in great profusion upon new clearings on light soils, and particularly those which have been burnt over. The product of fruit is often immense, and its picking, boxing and transportation, furnish employment to crowds of laborers of every age and sex, through a long term in the summer and autumn. This humble occupation diffuses through the interior of the county, no inconsiderable sums of money.

Public Improvements.

Several projects of public improvement which have been contemplated or now in agitation, demand a brief notice.

---

[1] *Rev. A. D. Barber.*

The *Internal Navigation*. Almost a quarter of a century ago, the plan was agitated of uniting the lakes and rivers of the interior wilderness, and by artificial agency, to form an extended inland navigation. The progress of rail roads, and their approach to that region — circumstances which did not enter into the imaginings of the projectors of this improvement — may render it neither expedient nor practicable, but the facts are of interest, and worthy of historical commemoration.

The prominent idea in this scheme, originally contemplated an artificial communication between Port Kent, on Lake Champlain, and Booneville, on the Black river canal. The system of lakes in the interior, which are united by a series of rivers, indicate the course, and were designed to form the route of this improvement. It appears from the report of Professor F. N. Benedict, that nature has formed a practicable route for this improvement, in the direct line from Purmort's rapids, a point on the Saranac river, on the line between Essex and Clinton counties, to the Moose river, twenty-one miles from Booneville, with which the contemplated navigation must be connected by a canal or rail road. This route, starting from Purmort's rapids, passes through the county of Essex, by the Saranac; along the lower and upper Saranac lakes; the Raquette river, Long, Forked and Raquette lakes, and the intervening streams, to the series of Moose river lakes, and thence down that stream to the western termination. This track may readily be traced on the very accurate maps of this region recently published.

The following impressive facts are established by these investigations. There exists, Professor Benedict states, in this direct course, a navigation competent to steamers, of fifty-six miles, and by small boats of fifty-five miles further. A distance only of seven and one-fourth miles occurs along this route, partially or entirely interrupted by obstructions which will require removing, to complete the navigation the whole line of one hundred and eighteen miles. The lateral navigation, branching from this main trunk, formed by the rivers and lakes, which are mingled with those above enumerated, affords an additional communication, navigable by steamers, of thirty-three miles, and by small boats of ten tons burthen, of thirty-eight miles more, with an intervening obstruction of only one-half mile. The result shows the existence, in that sequestered wilderness, of a navigation adapted to steam boats of eighty-nine miles, and to small boats, of ninety-three miles, which is obstructed by natural impediments interposing in different localities, and embracing in the aggregate, the trifling distance of seven and three-quarters miles. The total length of the proposed improvement is one hundred and ninety miles. The obstacles which exist chiefly occur in low and marshy ground, and may be readily surmounted. Mr. Benedict exhibits minute calculations, in which he estimates the expense of improving the whole one hundred and ninety miles, which embraces the lateral branches, at $312,950; with an average cost per mile of $1,611. The cost of opening the direct route, $292,950; at an average expense per mile of $2,482.

This estimate contemplates merely an improvement of the existing navigation, and surmounting the impediments which occur along the seven and three-quarters miles.

The lateral branches of this navigation, included in the survey of Prof. Benedict, would penetrate deeply towards the west into the forest of St. Lawrence, Hamilton and Franklin counties, and on the eastward along the western limits of Essex, almost touching the vast iron masses of the Adirondacs, and opening their resources to the wants and enterprise of the coal mines of the west. In reference to this navigation, he says: "Extensive lines of small boat navigation, with very few and short interruptions, traverse all considerable sections of the surface. The aggregate extent of these lines is probably no less than three hundred miles, all of which could be rendered navigable for boats of fifty tons burthen at comparatively trifling expense.

Rail Roads.

I elsewhere speak of the infinite importance to the utilizing of the vast undeveloped wealth of Essex county that rail roads should penetrate this secluded section of the state. I have also adverted to the road now in progress, which was intended to traverse the south-western part of the county, and to local train ways in the towns of Moriah and Westport. The former of these roads, which is now believed to be in vigorous prosecution, or a branch has been authorized by special statutes to pass up the valley of the Schroon and to unite with some other road, by which it may form a connection with the St. Lawrence. Partial surveys, in accordance with this privilege, have been already made.

Several organizations at different periods have been formed, with the purpose of accomplishing the great public and commercial necessity I have mentioned, but with results wholly unsatisfactory. A more recent project, conducted by the White Hall and Plattsburg Rail Road Company, and aided to a small extent by a state donative, promises a more certain and practical issue. A space of twenty miles from Plattsburg to a locality on the Au Sable known as the Point of Rocks, within three miles of Au Sable Forks, has been completed upon which trains are now running. Another section of this road south of Port Henry and about nine miles in length is nearly finished. In the intermediate distance it is understood the route is surveyed and located. The Hon. John Hammond is president of this company. Another company has been organized under the name of Northern Air Line Rail Road Company, with Silas Arnold, Esq., president, which proposes to construct a line, that shall connect with the former in Peru or Plattsburg at the north, and in Westport or Moriah at the south.

Plank Roads.

A number of these works were constructed some years ago in various parts of the county. Although they have been immensely valuable and productive to the transporting business of the region, these roads have not, from their perishable nature, under the abrasion of heavy teams, proved remunerative financial investments by the direct returns of dividends. Many of the roads have been abandoned, and none, I think, yields more than sufficient to sustain the necessary repairs.

Commerce.

The commerce of Lake Champlain is now large and every year augments. The lumber, the ore, and iron fabrics of the north, combined with the grain and flour of the west, and the coal and merchandise from the south constitute a vast trade. To their domestic resources may be added the productions of Canada, which seek a market by this avenue, and the goods chiefly bonded that pass into the dominion from American ports, and much of which is returned under fresh entries, all swelling this immense internal commerce. Numerous Canadian vessels, designed for the navigation of the St. Lawrence, and readily distinguishable from American craft by their peculiar structure and appearance, reach the waters of Champlain by the Chamblee canal. Vessels from the upper lakes are occasionally observed in our harbors. A large class of the population contiguous to the lake is connected with its navigation. This occupation forms an admirable school for the acquisition of nautical skill and experience, and creates a bold and expert body of mariners. If the public exigencies shall again demand a national fleet upon Champlain, her own marine would promptly supply daring and efficient crews. The following tabular statement presents a view of this commerce and the sailors engaged in it:

Statement of the Number, Tonnage and Crews of Vessels navigating Lake Champlain on the 20th of June, 1868.

	Number.	Tonnage.	Crews.
Steamers, ships, and canal boats, District of Champlain,	672	43,512	1,800
Vermont,	34	4,847	300
Canadian vessels,	165	13,656	753
American vessels from other districts (estimated),	150	12,350	450
Total,	1,021	73,865 [1]	

[1] I have received the above from the kindness of Hon. Jacob Parmerter, collector of the Champlain district.

APPENDIXES.

APPENDIX A.

LETTER FROM GENERAL WEBB TO COLONEL MUNROE.

Fort Edward, August 4th, 12 at noon.

SIR: I am directed by General Webb to acknowledge the receipt of three of your letters bearing date nine o'clock yesterday morning and one about six in the evening by the rangers which are the only men that have got in here, except two yesterday morning with your first, acquainting him that the enemy were in sight. He has ordered me to acquaint you that he does not think it prudent (as you know his strength at this place) to attempt a junction or to assist you, till reinforced by the militia of the colonies, for the immediate march, of which, repeated expresses have been sent. One of our scouts brought in a Canadian prisoner last night from the investing party, which is very large, and have possessed all the grounds five miles on this side of Fort William Henry. The number of the enemy is very considerable the prisoners say, eleven thousand, and have a large train of artillery with mortars, and were to open their batteries this day.

The general thought proper to send you this intelligence, that in case he should be so unfortunate, from the delays of the militia, not to have it in his power to give you timely assistance, you might be able to make the best terms left in your power.

The bearer is a sergeant of the Connecticut forces, and if he is happy enough to get in, will bring advices from you. We keep continual scouts going to endeavor to bring intelligence from you. I am, sir, with the heartiest and most anxious wishes for your welfare, your most obedient, humble servant,

E. BARTRAM, Aid-de-camp.

To Col. Monroe, or officer commanding at Fort William Henry.

APPENDIX B.

Montcalm.

M. Jean Pierre de Bougainville addressed the subjoined letter to William Pitt:

To the Right Hon. Wm. Pitt.

Sir: The honor paid during your ministry to the memory of Mr. Wolfe gives me room to hope that you will not disapprove of the grateful efforts made by the French troops to perpetuate the memory of the Marquis de Montcalm. The corpse of that general who was honored with the regret of your nation, is buried at Quebec. I have the honor to send you an epitaph, which the Academy of Inscriptions and Belles-Lettres have wrote for him, and I would beg the favor of you, sir, to read it over, and if there be nothing improper in it, to procure me a permission to send it to Quebec, engraved in marble to be put over the Marquis Montcalm's tomb. If the permission should be granted, may I presume, sir, to entreat the honor of a line to acquaint me with it, and at the same time to send me a passport that engraved marble may be received on board an English vessel, and that Mr. Murray, governor of Quebec, may give leave to have it put up in the Ursuline Church. I ask pardon, sir, for taking off your attention, even for a moment, from your important concerns, but to endeavor to immortalize great men and illustrious citizens, is to do honor to you. I am, etc.,

Bougainville.

Paris, March 26th, 1761.

Reply of Mr. Pitt.

Sir: It is a real satisfaction to me to send you the king's consent on such an interesting subject, as the very handsome epitaph drawn by the Academy of Inscriptions at Paris, for the Marquis de Montcalm, which is desired to be sent to Quebec, engraved on marble, to be set up on the tomb of that illustrious warrior. The whole sentiments expressed in the desire to pay this tribute to the memory of their general, by the French troops who served in Canada, and who saw him fall at their head, in a manner worthy of him and worthy of them, cannot be too much applauded.

I shall take pleasure, sir, in facilitating a design so full of respect to the deceased, and as soon as I am informed of the measures taken for embarking the marble, I shall immediately give the passport you desire, and send orders to the governor of Canada for its reception. As to the rest, be assured, sir, that I have a just sense of the obliging things said to me in the letter with which you honored me, and that I think it a singular happiness to have an opportunity to express those sentiments of distinguished esteem and consideration with which I have the honor to be, etc.,

W. PITT.

April 10th, 1761.

This correspondence, so graceful and dignified, and worthy the exalted subject, resulted in the engraving of the magnificent epitaph annexed by the Academy of Inscriptions and Belles Lettres of Paris:

GENERAL MONTCALM'S EPITAPH.

HIC JACET.

Utroque in orbe æternûm Victurus
LUDOVICUS JOSEPHUS DE MONTCALM GOZON,
Marchio Sancti Verani, Baro Gabriaci,
Ordinis Sancti Ludovici, Commendator,
Legatus Generalis Exercituum Gallicorum.
Egregius et Cives et Miles,
Nullius Rei appetens, præterquam veræ laudis,
Ingenio felici et litteris exculto,
Omnes Militiæ gradus per continua decora emensus,
Omnium belli Artium, temporum, discriminum gnarus
In Italiâ, in Bohemiâ, in Germaniâ,
Dux Industrius;
Mandata sibi, ita semper gerens, ut majoribus par haberetur.
Jam claris periculis,
Ad tutandum Canadensem Provinciam missus
Parvâ Militûm manu, Hostium copias, non semel repulit:
Propugnacula cepit viris armisque, instructissima.
Algoris, Inediæ, vigilarum, laboris patiens,
Suis unicè prospiciens, immemor sui,
Hostis acer, Victor Mansuetus.
Fortunam virtute, virium inopiam, peritiâ
Et celeritate, compensavit.
Imminens Coloniæ Fatum et consilio et manu per quadriennium sustinuit.
Tandem ingentem exercitum Duce strenuo et audaci,
Classemque omni bellorum mole gravem,
Multiplici prudentiâ, diû ludificatus,
Vi pertractus ad dimicandum,
In primâ acie, in primo conflictu, vulneratus,
Religioni, quam semper coluerat, innitens,
Magno suorum desiderio, nec sine hostium mœrore extinctus est.
Die XIV Septem. A. D. M.DCC.LIX.
Ætat. XLVIII.
Mortales optimi Ducis exuvias, in excavatâ humo,
Quâm Globus bellicus decidens, disiliensque defoderat,
Galli lugentes deposuerunt
Et generosæ Hostium fidei commendârunt.[1]

---

[1] *Hough's Pouchot.*

The letter of Montcalm from which extracts are introduced in the text is copied by Carlyle in his *Frederick the Great* (vol. v, pages 149–51) from a work by Beatson entitled *Plains of Abraham* which embraces a correspondence ranging from 1757 to 1759 between M. M. Berryer and De La Molè and Montcalm. The genuineness of these letters has been questioned, but Carlyle uses them without dissent, and in my view they are impressed by inherent evidences of authenticity. My limits only permit me to reproduce in addition to the extracts in the text, the closing paragraphs copied by Carlyle:

"So confident am I of what I write that I will allow but ten years after the conquest of Canada to see its fulfillment.

"Thus as a Frenchman do I to-day console myself for the danger so imminent and pressing of seeing this colony lost to my country."

The courtesy of an eminent scholar and jurist of Canada (the Honorable Charles Mondelét of the court of appeals) has enabled me to subjoin some valuable particulars connected with these events.

M. Jean Pierre de Bougainville, the elegant correspondent of Pitt, was brother to Colonel Bougainville, the protegé and aide of Montcalm, and the great circumnavigator. In accordance with the wishes of the French troops, animated by their ardent sentiments, in which the memory of Montcalm was cherished, Bougainville caused the inscription to be prepared by the Academy and engraved it is supposed upon a marble slab designed for a mural monument to be placed in the church of the Ursulines at Quebec. It is believed that in pursuance of the assent of the British government, the slab was sent to Canada, but no traces or vestige of it now exist.

APPENDIX C.

Civil List of Essex County.

Supreme Court.—Fourth District.

Augustus C. Hand,......... 1847

County Judges.

Daniel Ross,................. 1800
Dean Edson, ... 1823
Reuben Whallon, ... 1831
Wolcott Tyrill, ... 1838
Henry H. Ross, ... 1847
John E. McVine,.... 1848
Robert S. Hale,.............. 1856
Byron Pond, ... 1864

Representatives in Congress, residents of Essex County.

Benjamin Pond,..1811 and 1813
Asa Adgate, ...1815 and 1817
Ezra C. Gross, ...1819 and 1821
Henry H. Ross, ...1825
Isaac Finch,................... 1829
Reuben Whallon, ... 1833
Augustus C. Hand,......... 1839
Thomas A. Tomlinson,..... 1841
Orlando Kellogg,......... 1847, 1862, 1864

George R. Andrews,........ 1849
Geo A. Simmons, 1853 and 1855
Robt. S. Hale to fill vacancy, 1865

State Senators.

Reuben Sanford, ... 1828
Augustus C. Hand,......... 1844
James S. Whallon,..... ... 1847
Eli W. Rogers,.............. 1852
Ralph A. Loveland, ... 1857
Palmer E. Havens,......... 1863
Matthew Hale, ... 1867

Members of Asembly.

Wm. Gilliland (Clinton and Essex,)................. ... 1800
William Bailey,.............. 1802
Thomas Stower (Essex,) .. 1803
Theodoross Ross,........... 1804, 1805, 1806
Stephen Cuyler, ... 1807
Benjamin Pond, ... 1808, 1809, 1810
Delavan DeLance, Jr., ... 1811, 1812
Manoah Miller, ... 1813
Levi Thompson,............. 1814
Reuben Sanford,........... 1815, 1816, 1817
John Hoffnagle,..... ...... 1818, 1819, 1820, 1827
Ebenezer Douglass,........ 1821
Isaac Finch, ...1822 and 1824
Asa Adgate,................. 1823
William Smith,...1825 and 1826
Ezra C. Gross,.....1828 and 1829
William Kirby, ... 1830
Joseph S. Reed, ... 1831
Isaac Vanderwarker,....... 1832
Almerin Smith,............. 1833
Barnabus Myrick,.......... 1834
Thomas A. Tomlinson,..... 1835
Thomas A. Tomlinson,..... 1836
Gideon Hammond,......... 1837, 1838, 1839, 1844
George A. Simmons,...... 1840, 1841, 1842
Samuel Shumway,........... 1843
John C. Hammond,......... 1845
Caleb D. Barton,............ 1846
William H. Butrick,...... 1847, 1848
George W. Goff, 1849 and 1850
AbrahamWeldon, ... 1851, 1852
Jonathan Burnett,......... 1853, 1854
Nathaniel C. Boynton, ... 1855
John A. Lee, ... 1856
Ralph A. Loveland, ... 1857
Monroe Hall,............... 1858, 1859
Martin Finch, ... 1850, 1851
Palmer E. Havens, ... 1862, 1863, 1867
William H. Richardson, 1864, 1865, 1866
Samuel Root,.............. 1868, 1869

Sheriffs.

Thomas Stower,.. 1799
Jonathan Lynde,... 1802
John Hoffnagle, Jr.,........ 1806
William Kirby, ... 1808, 1821, 1822
Delavan De Lance, ... 1812
George Throop, ... 1813
Luther Adgate,.............. 1819
Coughton Lobdell,........... 1815
Samuel Murdock, ... 1825, 1831

Leander J. Lockwood,...... 1828
Solomon Everest,............ 1831
John Harris,................... 1837
Alanson Wilder,............ 1840
Chilion A. Tremble,........ 1843
Norman Page,............... 1846
Aaron B. March,........... 1849
Charles W. Ensign,........ 1852
Jacob Parmerter,............ 1855
Elisha A. Adams,........... 1858
William W. Tabor,......... 1861
Ransom L. Locke,......... 1864
Abijah Perry,............... 1867

County Clerks.

Stephen Cuyler,............ 1799
Simeon Frisbee,............ 1808
William Kirbey,........... 1813
Thomas Stower,.............. 1815
Ashley Pond,.................. 1821
Leonard Stow,................ 1827
Edward S. Cuyler,......... 1833
Edmund F. Williams,...... 1839
George S. Nicholson,...... 1848
Elisha A. Adams,.......... 1851
Robert W. Livingstone,... 1857
William E. Calkins,........ 1860

County Treasurers under constitution of 1846.

Safford E. Hale, Nov... 1848
John L. Merriam, " ... 1857
Charles N. Williams, "..... 1860

Surrogates.

William Gilliland, Mar. 24, 1800
James McCrea, Oct. 29, 1801
Thomas Treadwell, Mar. 14, 1807
Ezra C. Gross, Feb. 13, 1815
Ashley Pond, Mar. 2, 1819
John Calkins, Mar. 3, 1821
Augustus C. Hand, Apr. 15, 1831
Orlando Kellogg, Jan. 24, 1840
Robert W. Livingstone, Jan. 24, 1844

In 1846 *duties assigned to County Judge. Special Judge and Surrogate.*

Martin F. Nicholson, Nov. 1857
Office abolished, Jan. 1860

District Attorney.

Ralph Hascall, Jun. 13, 1818
Dean Edson, Mar. 3, 1821
David B. McNeil, Oct. 2, 1828
Gardner Stone, Apr. 11, 1833
Moses T. Clough, Sept. 24, 1844
Edward S. Shumway, resigned, Nov. 1850
James P. Butler, Apr. 12, 1852
Hiram M. Chace, Nov. 1855
Byron Pond, Nov. 1858
Martin Finch, 1864
Arod K. Dudley, 1867

Delegates to Constitutional Convention.

Thomas Treadwell (Clinton and Essex), convention of, 1801
Reuben Sanford, Essex, convention of, 1821
George A. Simmons, 1846
Mathew Hale, 1867

Regent of University.

Robert S. Hale, Mar. 29, 1859

APPENDIX D.

The census returns of Essex for 1865 embrace the following statistics :

	Acres.
Land improved,	246,824
Lands unimproved,	442,186
	No.
Sheep shorn,	62,201
Milch cows,	9,219
	Pounds.
Wool,	252,226
Butter,	654,174
	Tons.
Tons of hay,	48,712
	Bushels.
Spring wheat,	26,388
Oats,	913,912
Winter rye,	63,68
Buckwheat,	38,110
Indian corn,	101,324
Potatoes,	400,574
	Pounds.
Maple sugar,	92,940
	Bushels.
Beans,	13,943

My limits will not permit the reproducing the elaborate statistical tables, which will be found by reference to census returns.

Table showing the Aspect of Population in Essex County.

Town.	1810.	1825.	1830.	1835.	1840.	1845.	1850.	1860.
Chesterfield, taken from Willsboro', 1821,	631	1,151	1,671	2,083	2,697	3,022	4,171	3,179
Crown point,	1,082	1,728	2,041	2,189	2,212	2,261	2,378	3,552
Elizabethtown, taken from Crown Point, 1798,	1,362	1,029	1,015	856	1,061	1,194	1,635	1,343
Essex, taken from Willsboro,' 1805,	1,186	1,288	1,543	1,529	1,681	1,720	2,351	1,633
Jay, taken from Willsboro', 1792,	1,164	1,216	1,729	1,732	2,260	2,431	2,688	2,514
Keene, taken from Elizabethtown and Jay, 1808,	642	707	287	700	730	809	798	734
Lewis, taken from Willsboro', 1805,	537	1,101	1,305	1,358	1,500	1,681	2,058	1,807
Minerva, taken from Schroon, 1817,	....	371	358	335	455	496	586	903
Moriah, taken from Crown Point and Elizabethtown, 1808,	584	1,251	2,742	2,293	2,595	2,807	3,065	3,406
Newcomb, taken from Moriah and Minerva, 1828,	....	....	62	46	74	126	277	157
North Elba, taken from Keene, 1849,	....	....	....	....	....	....	210	366
North Hudson, taken from Moriah, 1848,	....	....	....	....	....	....	561	297
St. Armands, taken from Wilmington, 1844,	....	....	....	....	...	129	210	131
Schroon, taken from Crown Point, 1804,	689	1,290	1,614	1,723	1,660	1,705	2,031	2,550
Ticonderoga, taken from Crown Point, 1804,	985	1,833	1,996	2,080	2,168	2,309	2,669	2,271
Westport, taken from Elizabethtown, 1815,	....	1,322	1,513	1,724	1,932	2,094	2,352	1,981
Willsboro',	663	1,166	1,316	1,253	1,667	1,424	1,932	1,519
Wilmington, taken from Jay, 1821,	...	637	895	798	928	894	1,176	861
Total,	9,525	15,993	19,386	20,699	23,620	25,102	31,148	28,214

INDEX.

Abercrombie, his antecedents, 84; expedition against Ticonderoga, 85; conduct at Ticonderoga, 92; retreats to Lake George, 95.
Abraham, Plains of, 114.
Adams, H. J., 275, 280, 287.
Aerial currents, 370.
Agassiz, Prof., 351, 426.
Agriculture, 477; how affected by lumbering, 478; by teaming, 478; by conflicting titles, 11; products of, 479; stock, 481; statistics of, 495.
Aiken, C. H., 238.
Albany, convention at, 39.
Allen, Ebenezer, takes Mt. Defiance, 187; captures English near Essex, 188.
Allen, Ethan, captures Ticonderoga, 134; at St. John, 139; notice of, 140; defeated and captured at Montreal, 145; his treatment, 145.
Allen, W., 238.
American army, its condition, 147, 152; sickness of, 153; sufferings at Crown Point, 162.
Amherst repairs to Lake George, 102; character, 102; delay, 104; occupies Ticonderoga and Crown Point, 104; constructs road to Charlestown, 105; expedition of returns to Crown Point, 109; relics of, 109; works of at Crown Point and Ticonderoga, 112; advances against Montreal, 114, and captures it, 116.
Archer, Lester, 253, 256.
Armstrong, Thomas, 292.
Arnold, Benedict, holds commission from Massachusetts, 133; at Ticonderoga, 133; seizes vessels at St Johns, 139; constructs fleet, 163; attacked at Valcour, 168; defeated and burns his vessels, 171; expedition to Quebec,
Arnold, continued—149; fails to surprise it, 151; leads a column at Quebec, wounded and repulsed, 155; superseded by Thomas, 159; governor of Montreal, 160; retreats from Montreal, 160.
Arnold, R. W., 244.
Arnold, Silas, 484.
Asbestos, 415.
Assembly, members of, 493.
Attorneys, district, 494.
Au Sable pond, 325; valley, 437; walled banks of, 331; saw mills at the mouth of, 453, horse nail company, officers of, 457.
Aurora borealis, 370.

Bacon, Major, 262.
Baker, G. J., 238.
Baker, J. L., 238.
Baker, Remember, 134.
Barker, A., 262.
Barker, E. J., 258, 263, 264, 272.
Bartlett, L. A., 238.
Bates, H. J., 238.
Beaches, the, iron sand and gravel on, 422.
Beaman, Nathan, 120.
Beaumont, C. D., 231, 236.
Beaver meadows, 125.
Beaver, the, 388.
Bees, wild, 360.
Belding, J. W., 245, 248.
Bellamy, C. F., 238.
Benedict, Joel, 257.
Benedict, Professor F. N., 484.
Benzel, Adolphus, 120.
Bissell, E. L., 238.
Boice, Colonel, 273.
Boquet valley, 459.
Boudrye, L. N., 261, 273.
Bougainville, 490, 492; at Quebec, 111.
Boulamarque in command at Ticonderoga, 104; burns bridges near Lake George, and retreats, 86.

Boynton, J. H., 275.
Bradstreet, at Ticonderoga, 94; at Frontenac, 95.
Brown, Colonel John, 133; at Quebec, 154; attacks Ticonderoga, 187.
Brown, John, notice of, 220; his career, 222; at Harper's Ferry, 224; capture and execution, 227; remarks on, 227; Mr. Vallingdigham's opinion of, 227; Governor Wise's opinion of, 228.
Bryant, L. S., 274, 289.
Brydon, J., 274, 288, 290.
Buck, Hiram, 231, 233.
Burgey, Daniel, 231, 237, 238.
Burgoyne succeeds Carleton, 174; his army, 174; his subordinates, 175; treaty at Boquet, 175; proclamation, 176; attacks Ticonderoga, 180; erects battery on Mt. Defiance, 180; pursues Long to Skeensboro', and defeats him, 183.
Butrick, G. M., 274.

Cadwell, M. P. S., 231, 237.
Calkins, A. F., 238.
Cameron, D., 238.
Campbell, G. F., 274, 286.
Campbell, G. W., 252.
Canada, exhaustion of, 98; corruption in, 99; feelings towards the French in, 99; suffering, 79; population of, 79; corruption in, 79.
Canadians favorable to Americans, 142, 145; zeal of, 81; friendly receive lands from New York, 162; their bravery, 100.
Carillon, 50, 51.
Carleton, escapes to Quebec, 147; pursues, 163; builds a fleet at Valcour, 168; takes Crown Point, 173; returns to Canada, 173; humanity of, 162.
Carleton, Major, takes Forts George and Ann, 190.
Carter, J. M., 282.
Cartier, discovers the St. Lawrence, 3; sees mountains of New York and Vermont, 3; kidnaps Indians, 4.
Caughnawaga Indians, claim of, 204.
Cedars, the, disaster at, 161.
Cement water, 422.
Champlain, 5; early life, 6; voyages of, 9, 10; founds Quebec, 10; discovers Lake Champlain, 12;
Champlain, continued —
battle with Iroquois, 15; returns from France, 19; battle at the Richelieu, 19; on the Ottawa, 20, 21; at Nipissing, 21; sees Lake Huron, 21; attacks Indian fort, 22; wounded, 23; builds castle St. Louis, 24; defends Quebec, 24; death and character, 24.
Champlain canal, 434.
Champlain, Lake, 1; names of, 3; opening and closing navigation, 371; former trade on, 434.
Charlotte county organized, 129.
Chasm at Port Kendall, 332; at Split Rock, 333.
Chastes, Aymer de, 5.
Chauvin, 5.
Chesterfield, account of, 211.
Chipman, Nathaniel, 197.
Choiseuls, predicts injury to England from cession to Canada, 116.
Civil list, 39, 482.
Clark, Robert, 374.
Clerks, county, 494.
Climate, 370; and winds, 368.
Clinton county organized, 203.
Coates, G. B., 239, 293, 294.
Cochrane, Mrs., letter on Lord Howe, 88.
Colonies dissatisfied and alarmed, 45, 48.
Colonies, English, conditions of, 80; inferiority of British officials in, 82.
Colonies, French, 81; feudal system in, 81; character of French officials, 82.
Colvin, Alvin, 109, 371.
Commerce, 487.
Compact, written, of 5th Cavalry, 257.
Congress, action of, on capture of Ticonderoga, 137; decides to attack Canada, 137; representatives in, 492.
Constitution formed at Chatham, Canada, 224.
Conventions, delegates to, 494.
Cook, H., 238.
Copper, 418.
Copperas, 422.
Corlear, Arent, 29.
Corlear's lake, 37.
Courcelles attacks Mohawks, and suffering of, 28.
Crown Point described, 41; army for reduction of, 49; ruins at, 112; early importance of, 117;

Crown Point, continued — description of, 118; attention of English government to, 120; siege of, 203; account of, 211; supplies troops, 231, 265.
Cullen, Colonel, 253.
Cunningham, J. L., 275, 276.

D'Avignon, F. J., 250, 254.
Davis, C. H., 245.
Dean, Silas, 132.
Deer, 247.
DeForest, O., 258.
Delany, P. H., 275.
Dellius Grant, 38.
DeMonts, 8; colony of, 8; explores New England, 9.
DePontbriand, Bishop, he defends Montcalm, 111.
DeTracy, expedition against Mohawks, 31.
DeTrèpesée, fight at Ticonderoga and death, 86.
Dickerson, M. J., 289.
Dieskau, 51; advances to attack Johnson, 56; defeated and captured, 60; danger of assassination, 61; death and character, 61.
Dobie, D. F., 288.
Dodge, Daniel, horse nail machine, 454; account of, 455.
Dominy, L. S., 280, 284, 289.
Donohoe, Col., 287.
Doolittle, L. L., 231, 239.
Douglass, W., 244.
Drift and diluvial formation, 423.
Dunder Rock, 37.
Dwyer, S. C., 232, 241, 242.

Easterbrooks, A. L., 238.
Edgerly, E. F., 231, 236, 237, 238.
Elizabethtown, 211, 334.
Elmore, Mrs., anecdote of, 172.
English boats repulsed at Ticonderoga, 65.
English colonies, exactions on, 102.
English policy, 36, 44.
Essex and Clinton, population of, 208; account of, 211.
Essex and Vermont, comparison of, 215.
Essex county organized, 207; original county shire, 208; in war of 1812, 208; origin and habits of the people, 209; in season of 1816, 210; volunteers, 294; disbursements of, 295.

Fairman, J., 250.
Farnsworth, J. H., 244.
Feldspar bed, Spalding's, 421.
Fertilizers, 426; phosphate of lime, 426; marl, 427; muck and peat, 428.
Fifth New York Cavalry, history of, 256.
Fire on Whiteface mountain, 320.
First settlers, George and William Trimble, 203.
Fish of interior lakes, trout, 357; small, 358; white or frost, 358.
Fish of Lake Champlain, 351; chaousarou, 351; salmon, 351; shad, 352; pickerel, 353; sturgeon, 354; smaller, 355; ling, 355; smelt, 356.
Fishing by torchlight, 356.
Folsom, Capt., at Lake George, 61.
Foot, W. T., 465.
Forest trees, 364; changes in growth, 366; diseases of, 367.
Forty-fourth Regiment, 243.
Francis, Col., killed, 185.
French claims, 39; names, their beauty, 47; policy, 26, 42; settlements on Lake Champlain, 117.
Frisbie, Col., 236.
Frontenac, Count, attacks Mohawks, 35.
Fruit, 482; apples, plums, 486; Adirondac grapes, 486; pears, 486; huckleberry, 486.

Galena, 416; Indian's visit to bed of, 417.
Gall, Adjutant, 264.
Game, 125.
Garden Island, account of, 170.
Gas, inflammable, 135.
Gates at Ticonderoga, 173.
Geology, notice of rocks at Port Henry, 419.
Gibbs, N. J., 275, 287, 289.
Gilliland, James, 128.
Gilliland the younger, 130.
Gilliland, William, locates lands, 122; colonized the Boquet, 124; narrative of, 127; account of, 154; collision with Arnold, 165; Hartley prefers charges against, 165; denunciation of Arnold, 166; misfortunes, 202; death, 203.
Glass, 468.
Glen's Falls Republican, 290.

Goodhue, Rev. J. T., 134.
Grace, C. A., 275.
Grants and patents, account of, 296; Abeel, 299; Benzel, 300; Benson, 300; Bruyn, 301; Campbell, Allen, 301; Campbell, D., 301; Connelly, 301; Deal, 302; Field, 302; Friswell, 303; Frelegh, 303; Gilliland, 303; Gilliland & Watson, 303; Grant, 303; Guise, 304; Hicks, 304; Judd, 305; Kellett, 305; Kelly, 305; Kennedy, 305; Legge, 306; Miller, 307; Mallory's, 308; Mathews, 308; Maule, 308; McIntosh, 308; McBride, 308; McDonald, 309; McKensie, 309; Montressor, 309; Old Military Tract, 309; Ord, 310; Porter, 310; Potts, 310; Ross, 310; Ryerse, 310; Stoughton, 311; Skene, 311; Small, 311; Sutherland, 311; Springer, 311; soldiers rights, 312; Stevenson, 313; Stewart, 313; Summervale, 313; Totten & Crossfield, 313; Tomlin, 316; Wharton, 316; Wriesburgh, 316.
Grants, French, 121.
Graphite, 380, 415, 416.
Graphite Company, American, 470.
Gray, C. O., 250, 251.

Hagar, C. L., 275.
Haldimand documents, 201.
Hale, Colonel Nathan, notice of, 184.
Hale, F. C., 299.
Hall, Hiland, 201.
Hammond, C. F., 426; supplies horses to cavalry, 258.
Hammond, John, 257, 258, 259, 260, 261, 262, 264, 266, 267, 268, 484.
Hand, A. C., 134.
Hasbrook, Captain, 263.
Haviland advances from Crown Point against Montreal, 115.
Hayward, E. B., 258.
Hayward, J. F., 245, 249.
Henderson, J. A., 244.
Hendrik, 56; killed, 58.
Hendrik's speech at Albany, 49.
Herrick, Captain, seizes Skeensboro', 135.
Hessians, the, 174.
Hetzil, S., 244.
Hinds, G. W., 250.
Hinman, Colonel Benjamin, takes command at Ticonderoga, 141.
Hochelaga named Mont Royal, 3.
Holbrook, A. H., 238.
Holden, A. W., 238.
Horicon, 50.
Horicon, corporal, 249.
Howe, Lord, his zeal, 84; Howe & Stark, 86; killed, 87; effect of his death, 87; his burial, 89.
Hoystradt, W. H., 238.
Hubbardton, battle of, 183.
Hudson, 19.
Huff, William, 281.
Hunter's Pass, 333.
Huntley, C. W., 231, 237, 238.
Hyperstene, 379, 420.

Indian Pass, 329.
Indian wars, 27; fraternity, 57; battle at Elizabethtown, 216; land purchasers prohibited, 313.
Indians at Boquet, 175; at Valcour, 169; valuable aid of, 68; at Lake George, 72; contract small pox from the dead, 77; unreliable to the French, 101.
Industrial pursuits, 432.
Inland navigation, state aid, 434.
Iron manufactories, 436, 437; Willsboro', 438; Boquet, 439; Ticonderoga, 439; Elba works, 439; Au Sable Valley, 440; Wilmington, 440; J. &. J. Rogers, 441; Lower Jay, 444; Clintonville, 448; at Keeseville, 453, 454, 458; at Elizabethtown, 459, 463; in Westport, 461, 463; in Willsboro', 461, 463; In Lewis, 461, 462; Essex, 462; Moriah, 463; Port Henry Furnace, 464; Fletcherville, 466; Hammond, 467; Irondale, 468; Ticonderoga, 469; Schroon, 472, Minerva, 473; rolling mills, 453, 456, 462.
Iron ore beds, 372; Adirondac district, 372; remarks on, 377; in Minerva, 380; Schroon, 382; Crown Point, 383; Arnold, 439, 441, 448; Finch & Winter, 448; New Russia, 459; in Lewis, 461.
Iroquois, their eloquence and progress, 2; armor, 16; engaged in the royal cause, 143; confederacy, 57.

Jay, 213.
Johnson, William, at Lake George, 53; at battle Lake George, 62; want of magnanimity, 63; at

Johnson, continued — Ticonderoga, 90; appointed to command army, 44; desires to relieve William Henry, 73.
Johnson, Col., joins Brown at Ticonderoga, 187.
Johnson, Sir John, expedition against Mohawk valley, 189.
Judges, Supreme Court, 492; county and Special, 494.

Kaolin, 420; factory, 459.
Keene, 212.
Keese, Oliver, Jr., 274, 284.
Keeseville, horse nail works, 452; Twine factory at, 458; hosiery factory, flouring mills, and minor works, 459.
Kelley, J. E., 250, 251.
Kellogg, R. C. 275, 284.
Kingsley, G. C., 238.
Knox, Gen. Henry, moves cannon to Boston, 138.
Knox, M. V. B., 274.
Krom, Capt., 266, 272.

Labradorite, 370.
La Caron, 20, 23.
La Due, W., 239.
Laffin, B., 239.
Lake Champlain, 321.
Lakes, interior, 323; Paradox, 324; Placid, 324, George, 327; Avalanche, 381.
Lansing, W., 245, 249.
Lennon, M., 245, 248.
Lewis, 211.
Limestone, 419, 428.
Livingstone, A. C. H., 232, 241.
Livingstone and Brown 155; take Chambly, 144.
Livingstone, R. W., 274, 281, 282, 290, 295.
Logs, stripped of bark, 473; floating, 434, 435, 452, 474; Warren co., 476; Minerva, 476.
Long, Colonel, at battle of Lake George, 58.
Longueil, Carleton defeated by Warner at, 146.
Loring, Captain, constructs fleet, 108; destroys French vessels at Valcour, 109.
Louisburg, fall of, 101.
Lumber trade, 433, 434.
Lyman, General, at battle of Lake George, 62.
Lyon, W., 244, 246.

McCall, P., 238.
McCormick, J., 239, 293, 294.
McCoy, J. W., 258.
McGinnis, Captain, killed at Lake George, 61.
McGuire, J. G., 292, 293.
McIntire, S. P., 239.
McKenzie, Col., 252.
McKie, John, Jr., 232, 237.
McLean, Col., returns to Quebec, 149; and defends at, 151.
McLean, J. B., 244.
McLean, P. V. N., 275, 289, 290.
McMullen, Lt., sent back to Crown Point by Rogers, 106.
McWilliams, M., 249.
Manufacturing works at Birmingham, 459; at New Russia, 459; Crown Point, 469; at Ticonderoga, 470; Keeseville, 452, 458; at Clintonville, 450; in Schroon, 472; in Essex, 476; Wilmington, 440; Bloomingdale, 440; J. & J. Rogers, 441, 442, 444.
Marin, 68; exploits, 69; at Fort Ann, 96.
Marsh hay, 125.
Merrill, W. E., 245, 249.
Miller, George, 281.
Mineral springs, 343.
Mineralogy and geology, 372.
Minerals and rock of the Adirondac district, 379.
Minerals, list of, 421.
Minerva, 212.
Moffitt, S., 254, 289.
Mohawks on St. Lawrence, 2; conquest of, 2; their hatred of the French, 2; defeat De Courcelles, 29; capture Montreal, 31; hereditary boundaries, 37; at battle of Lake George, 58; wish to pursue French, 62; at Ticonderoga, 90.
Molang, 68.
Mondelet, Charles, 492.
Montcalm, early history of, 66; arrives at Quebec, 69; takes Oswego, 69; holds Indian council, 70; takes William Henry, 71; receives order St. Louis, 73; connection with massacre at William Henry, 75; his subsequent measures, 77; his opinion of Vaudreuil, 80; interference with, 80; thinks of evacuating Ticonderoga, 90; victory of, 94; activity of, 96; quotes

Montcalm, continued—
Mirabeau, 99; despondency of, 103; his letter, 103, 109; death of, 110; strictures on, 111; opinion of Canadians, 100; disgusts the Indians, 101; repairs to Quebec, 104; letter on cession of Canada, 116; Bougainville and Pitt, correspondence on, 490; epitaph of, 491; letters of, 492.
Montgomery, Richard, 115; appointed brigadier-general under Schuyler, 142; seizes Isle aux Noix, 142; assumes the command, 144; his early life, 144; attacks St. John's, 144; seizes Sorel, and takes St. John's, 145; his trials, 147; his influence, 148; appears before Quebec, 152; his policy, 153; attacks the city, 154; killed, 155; burial of, 158.
Montreal, 20.
Montreuil at Lake George, 60.
Mooers, J. H., 275.
Moose, the, 349.
Morgan at the attack of Quebec, 155.
Moriah, account of, 211.
Mould, H. M., 275.
Moulding sand, 446.
Mount Defiance, 178.
Mount Hope, 180, 181; recaptured by Brown, 187.
Mount Independence, 178.
Mountains, 318; Pharaoh, Dix, Bald, 318; Marcy, 319; McIntire, Dial, Seward, McMartin, Colden, Keene, Whiteface, 320.
Munroe, Colonel, capitulates at William Henry, 73.
Murray, J., 249.
Myers, Corporal, 249.

Nail works, 442, 444, 445, 448.
Nails, at Keeseville, 453.
Natural curiosities, 329.
Natural History, 346.
Nelson, W. G., 459.
Newcomb, 213.
Newman, T. W., 250, 251.
New Netherland, cession of, 27.
Nichols, G. F., 274, 276, 280, 281, 282, 287, 288, 290.
Ninety-sixth regiment, history of, 250; officers of, mustered out, 255.
Norris, Capt., 276.
North Elba, description of, 214; Indian remains in, 216; Iron works, 216; progress of, 216; negro settlement in, 217.
North Hudson, 212.
Northern New York, account of, 336.
Northrup, H. J., 275.
Norton, F., 245.

O'Callaghan, E. B., 30, 110.
O'Connor, D. A., 275, 289.
One Hundred and Eighteenth Regiment, history of, 273; officers of mustered out, 290.
Onontio, 73.
Ormsby, L., 231, 237, 238.
Orr, G. S., 244, 248.

Paints, 423.
Paris, treaty of, 116.
Parker, Col., defeated at Sabbath Day Point, 69.
Parkman, 25.
Parmerter, Jacob, 274, 283.
Partisans, French, 67.
Patent, Field's, 123.
Patents, 296.
Pattee, Rev. Mr., 421.
Peabody, O. D., 231, 237, 238.
Pean, Madam, 79.
Pease, C. M., 258.
Penfield, J. A., 257, 260, 265.
Peru Steel and Iron Company, 449.
Phelps, Walter, Jr., 232, 238.
Phillips occupies Lake George, 186.
Physical geography, 317.
Pierce, E., 250, 254.
Pierce, J. H., 274, 282.
Pierson, C. B., 256.
Pioneer population, changes of, 129.
Place, Sergeant, 278.
Plattsburg Republican, 169.
Plumbago, see Graphite.
Poke O' Moonshine, 330.
Pontgrave, 11.
Popular organization formed, 129.
Porphyry, 420.
Port Royal founded, 9.
Porteous, J. G., 275, 287.
Potashes, 435.
Potter, J. F., 335.
Potter, Lieut., 289.
Pouchot, 106.
Pourtraincourt, 9.
Prescott, General, capitulates Montreal, 147.
Pringle, Capt., attacks Arnold, 168.

Proclamation, king of Great Britain, Oct., 1763, 121.
Province, a new, contemplated, 130.
Pruyn, C. E., 275, 283, 284.
Public improvements, 484; inland navigation, 484; Rail Roads, 484; Plank Roads, 487.
Putnam, battle of, near Whitehall, 83.
Putnam's capture and perils, 97.

Quarries, 428; Keeseville, 429; McOmbers, 430; Clark's, 430; Essex, 431; Frisbie, 431; Westport, 431; Crown Point, 431; Ticonderoga, 431.
Quebec, 10; battle of, 110; trade with, 432.

Rail Roads, 486; Moriah and Westport, 486; Whitehall and Plattsburgh, 486; Northern Air line, 486.
Rainbow Falls, 333.
Ralph, Alexander, 374.
Rangers, American, 67.
Ransom, Capt., 279, 282.
Rebellion, the, 219.
Refugees burn Boquet settlement, 189.
Regent of University, 495.
Reggio, Great rock Regione or Rogeo, 37.
Renner, L. F., 258.
Reptiles, 360.
Reynolds, M., 282.
Richards, S. F., 274.
Riggs, Capt., 276.
Rivers, 326; Hudson, 327; outlet Lake George, 327; Putnam creek, 327; Boquet, 327; Au Sable, 328.
Roads, public, 205.
Roberval, 5.
Roche, De La, 5.
Rogers, a royalist, 98; expedition against St. Francis Indians, 105; incursions into Canada, 114.
Rogers & Putnam, battle with Marin near Fort Ann, 96.
Rogers, exploits of, 63; note to Montcalm, 64; defeat of, 82; slide, 82.
Rogers, J. & J., their business, 445, 446.
Rogers, Platt, ferry and bridges, 205.
Rowe, C. W., 245, 247, 249.
Royal Savage raised, 169.
Ryswick, treaty of, 40.

Sabbath Day point, 69.
Sable Iron Company, 441.
St. Armands, 214.
St. Clair, Arthur, in charge of Ticonderoga, 177; evacuates it, 182; suspended, 186.
St. Frederick built by French, 42.
St. Pierce, killed, 61.
St. Sacrament, Lake, 50.
Salisbury, Prof., 344.
Salt traffic, 433.
Sanborn, J. H., 250.
Sanger, W. H., 293, 294.
Saunders, Lt., 289.
Scalps borne to Montcalm, 83.
Schenck, J. W., 238.
Schenectady, relieves French army, 29; burning of, 31.
Schroon, name of, 212.
Schuyler, Gen. P., 142; commands northern department, 177; his forces, 177; superseded, 186; appointed to command Canadian army, 142.
Schuyler, John, attacks La Prairie, 33.
Schuyler, Peter, attacks La Prairie, 34, 35.
Seaman, J. R., 231, 238, 274, 289.
Second Cavalry, 293.
Senators, state, 493.
Seventy-seventh Regiment, 244; history of, 244; officers mustered out, 249.
Sheldon, O. F., 130.
Sheriffs, 493.
Sherman, Sam, 275, 282.
Sherman, S. D., 238.
Ship yards, 475.
Sillery, Murray, defeated at, 114.
Silver, 419.
Smith, Gerrit, 217–219.
Smith, W. H., 232, 241.
Snow shoes, battle on, 83.
Spalding, Henry, 260.
Split Rock, 332.
Squirrels, 350.
Stannard, Gen., 252; report, 288.
Stark, exploits of, 64.
Statistics, agriculture and political, 495, 496.
Stephens, Lt., abandons Rogers, 107
Stetson, M. V. B., 254, 289.
Stevens, C. E., 244, 245, 248, 249.
Stevenson, W. H., 275, 276, 277, 281, 282.
Stone, Dennis, 282.
Stone, J. S., 275, 282.
Strong, T. M., 237, 238.
Subterranean passages, 334.

Sullivan, Gen., assumes command of American army, 160; burns vessels at St. Johns and retreats to Crown Point, 161.
Surrogates, 494.
Suitor, J. A., 239.

Tanneries, 473; in North Hudson, 474; Minerva, 475.
Tar, made for Amherst & McDonough, 109.
Teller, M. L., 238.
Thirty-eighth regiment, 241; privates in, killed and wounded at Bull run, 242.
Thirty-fourth regiment, 329.
Thomas, Gen., takes command at Quebec, 159; retreats and dies at Sorel, 160.
Thomas, G. T., 231, 232, 236, 238.
Thompson, Prof. Zadock, 215, 251, 425, 426.
Thompson's Vermont, 178.
Thoreau, 25.
Three Rivers, repulse at, 160.
Ticonderoga, account of French works at, 89, 211; De Levis arrives at, 90; battle of, 91; incident at, 95; notice of the captors of, 138; taken, 104; ruins at, 112; works at, 178; bridge at, 178; effect of capture of, 185.
Town meetings, how conducted, 204.
Townsend, Adjt. General, killed, 104.
Treadway, W., 274, 282, 288.
Treasurers, county, 494.
Twenty-second regiment, 232.

Utrecht, treaty of, 28.

Valleau, J., 238.
Valley of the Hudson, 471.
Vaudrueil, attack on William Henry, 65; at Quebec, 111; persecuted in France, 112; charges against Montcalm, 80; his controversies with Montcalm, 100; surrenders Montreal, 116.
Vaudrueil the younger arrives at Ticonderoga, 95.
Vermont, negotiations of leaders with British, 190; remarks on negotiations, 199; supplies Gates, 174.
Viall, J. G., 257.
Volunteers, call for, 210, 231.

Waldron, A. P., 250.
Walker, T., 242.
War declared between France and England, 63.
Wardner, N., 250, 253.
Warner, Seth, covers retreat from Canada, 161; takes Crown Point, 136.
Warren, W., 242.
Washburn, M. L., 274.
Washington county formed, 203.
Watson, Elkanah, 417; on the burial of Howe, 88.
Webb, General, letter to Monroe, 489; his pusillanimity, 72.
Weed, Alfred, 250, 251.
Weidman, M., 238.
Wells, C. W., 275.
Weston, Clifford, 246.
Westport, account of, 211.
Wetmore, G., 238.
Whale, skeleton of, 426.
Whiskey, 435.
White, Major, 262, 264, 266, 268.
Whiting, Col., rallied fortunes at Lake George, 58.
Wickham, B. F., 237, 238.
Wild land near Whiteface Mt., 435.
Wilderness, northern, 335; vestiges of roads and bridges in, 32; navigation in, 484.
William Henry, fort, attacked and taken by Montcalm, 74; massacre at, 75.
Williams, Ephraim, 56; killed, 58.
Willsboro', account of, 211; size of, 204; Melchior Hoffnagle first supervisor, and Daniel Sheldon first town clerk, 204.
Wilmington, 214.
Wilmington notch, 330.
Wilson, L. E., 238.
Wing, E. A., 282.
Wolfe at Quebec, 110.
Woods, conflagration of, 436.
Wooster, David, 132; brigadier-general under Schuyler, 132
Wright, J. B., 231.

www.ingramcontent.com/pod-product-compliance
Lightning Source LLC
LaVergne TN
LVHW021310110826
845150LV00003B/539

* 9 7 8 1 4 2 5 5 5 8 4 1 3 *